What People Are Saying Abou

"Shelley Case is one of the foremost experts on the gluten-
information out there about the diet, but Shelley's book can be trusted to be current, accurate, and thoroughly researched."

Danna Korn, Founder of R.O.C.K. (Raising Our Celiac Kids) and Author of *Kids with Celiac Disease: A Family Guide to Raising Happy, Healthy, Gluten-Free Children* and *Wheat-Free, Worry-Free: The Art of Happy, Healthy Gluten-Free Living*

"Each edition of Shelley Case's *Gluten-Free Diet: A Comprehensive Resource Guide* gets better and better with more practical information for all people with wheat and gluten sensitivities. A 'must have' resource for the newly diagnosed person with celiac disease."

Janet Y. Rinehart, Former President, Celiac Sprue Association/USA, Inc.

"Having been diagnosed with celiac disease and practicing as a Registered Dietitian for over 20 years, I know the importance of professional-looking, detailed, and accurate information. Shelley's book accomplishes this and much more! I highly recommend this book to people with celiac disease, as well as dietitians, physicians and other health professionals."

Mark A. Dinga, MEd, RD, LD, Pittsburgh, Pennsylvania

"This book is a wonderful guide to navigating the sometimes frustrating, often overwhelming, journey to a healthy gluten-free lifestyle."

Peggy Wagener, Publisher, *Living Without* magazine, Illinois

"This is a phenomenal book. Shelley has managed to research, compile and organize volumes of valuable information and present it in a logical manner that is easy to understand. It is the most thorough gluten-free reference book on the market today."

Connie Sarros, Author of *Wheat-Free, Gluten-Free Cookbooks*

"Shelley has produced a thoughtful, well-researched book. As a leading nutrition expert in celiac disease, she has given the celiac community the foundation for a long, healthy gluten-free lifestyle."

Elaine Monarch, Founder/Executive Director, Celiac Disease Foundation, California

"This comprehensive book provides a wealth of critically important information for anyone who lives gluten-free. Get your copy right away!"

Carol Fenster, PhD, Author of *Gluten-Free 101* and *Cooking Free*

"This guide is full of information on what's safe and healthy for people with celiac disease, and is presented in a practical, clearly organized, 'no-nonsense' format. It is a must for the celiac bookshelf."

Bev Ruffo, Honorary Life Member, Canadian Celiac Association

"Shelley Case's book is a must for everyone's library. I use it in my cooking classes and for grocery shopping. It is an excellent gift for the newly diagnosed, as well as family and friends who are looking for gluten-free sources."

LynnRae Ries, Author of *What? No Wheat? A Lighthearted Primer to Living the Gluten-Free, Wheat-Free Life* and *Waiter, Is there Wheat in My Soup?*

"Shelley's book is stuffed with practical information and helpful hints. I consult it frequently and have learned more about the gluten-free diet from it than from any other single resource."

Lani K. Thompson, Publisher, *Clan Thompson Gluten-Free Databases*, Bridgton, Maine

"I've recommended Shelley Case's book to my patients with celiac disease since its very first edition. I trust the research and respect the dedication that she put into writing this educational book. The material is equally useful for those newly diagnosed learning about hidden gluten to those seeking ways to increase variety in their diets with new products, grains, recipes and meal plans."

Melinda Dennis, MS, RD, LDN, Nutrition Coordinator, Celiac Center at Beth Israel Deaconess Medical Center

"Shelley Case should be congratulated for her efforts in contributing such a valuable reference tool to the field of celiac disease."

Mavis Molloy, RDN, Dietitian, Member of the Professional Advisory Board, Canadian Celiac Association

"I needed this book before I accumulated the mountain of computer printouts and handouts that adorn my office. Buy it or spend the next 20 years of your life unnecessarily duplicating this research."

Jacqueline Maxwell, Jackson, Tennessee and Area Celiac Support Group

"I am so impressed by this book. This is exactly the concise compilation of facts and sources of information that I have been looking for. I will be enthusiastically sharing information about this book with our members and local stores."

Sallie Smith, Gluten-Free Support Group of Northwestern Pennsylvania

"Shelley's book is a wonderful well-researched resource and an indispensable tool for people with celiac disease and for any health professional who is working with the celiac community."

Mary K. Sharrett, MS, RD, LD, CNSD, Nutrition Support Dietitian, Children's Hospital and Founder/Dietitian Advisor of the Gluten-Free Gang, Columbus, Ohio

"I heard about this book at a Celiac Support Group meeting, immediately ordered it and read it cover to cover. Even though my son was diagnosed 2 years ago with celiac disease, and I read everything I can find, I learned a great deal from this book. Thank you for writing such an excellent reference book for people with celiac disease."

Susan Garramone, Hopedale, Massachusetts

"A concise resource with all the key information clinicians AND patients frequently need to get started. We recommend this book to all patients referred to us in our GI nutrition clinic with celiac disease."

Carol Rees Parrish, RD, MS, Nutrition Support Specialist, University of Virginia Health System, Digestive Health Center of Excellence, Charlottesville, Virginia

"Shelley certainly does her research! She goes beyond merely listing ingredients as safe or unsafe. Her book describes the background as to why ingredients are categorized as such. I recommend this comprehensive resource to everyone requiring a gluten-free diet."

Trisha B. Lyons, RD, LD, Dietitian, MetroHealth Medical Center, Cleveland, Ohio

"I've really enjoyed this reference book. It's a good 'common sense' approach to gluten-free living."

Becky Warlick, RN, MSN, Duke University Medical Center, Durham, North Carolina

"This is a must-have book for dietitians, doctors and patients. It is a critical component to the nutrition education sessions I provide and is an excellent resource for products and recipes."

Jacquelyn Stern, RD, LD, Digestive Disorders Associates, Annapolis, Maryland

"People who purchase our cookbooks often ask us where to purchase gluten-free ingredients. We feel comfortable recommending Shelley's book as we know it is complete and accurate."

Donna Washburn, P.HEc. *and* **Heather Butt, P.HEc.**, Authors of *125 Best Gluten-Free Recipes* and *The Best Gluten-Free Family Cookbook.*

Shelley Case
BSc (Nutrition & Dietetics), RD
Registered Dietitian

Gluten-Free Diet – A Comprehensive Resource Guide

by
Shelley Case, BSc (Nutrition & Dietetics), RD (Registered Dietitian)

First Edition – May 2001
Revised Edition – April 2002
Third Printing – July 2003
Fourth Printing – May 2004
Fifth Printing – January 2005
Expanded Edition – April 2006

Published by:
Case Nutrition Consulting
1940 Angley Court
Regina, Saskatchewan
Canada S4V 2V2
www.glutenfreediet.ca
Email: info@glutenfreediet.ca
Phone/FAX: 306-751-1000

Canadian Cataloguing in Publication Data

Case, Shelley

Gluten-free diet – a comprehensive resource guide

Includes index.
ISBN 1-897010-28-1

1. Gluten-free diet – Handbooks, manuals, etc. 2. Gluten-free diet – Recipes. I. Title.

RM237.86.C37 2002 613.2'6 C2002-910464-5

Cover Design by:
Brian Danchuk, Brian Danchuk Design, Regina, Saskatchewan

Page design and formatting by Iona Glabus, Centax Books

Designed, Printed and Produced in Canada by:
Centax Books, A Division of PrintWest Communications Ltd.
Publishing Director – Margo Embury
1150 Eighth Avenue, Regina, Saskatchewan, Canada S4R 1C9
(306) 525-2304 Fax: (306) 757-2439
centax@printwest.com www.centaxbooks.com

DEDICATION

To GOD

✦ who gives meaning and purpose to my life

✦ for His amazing love, wisdom, strength and answers to prayer

✦ for His countless blessings, especially my family

To my husband, Blair

✦ the love of my life for almost 30 years

✦ for your incredible devotion, patience and support

To my daughters, Erin and Jennifer

✦ for your encouragement and unconditional love

To my mother, Helen

✦ for your wonderful support, generosity and encouragement

To my late father, Gord

✦ whose entrepreneurial spirit taught me that anything was possible

ACKNOWLEDGMENTS

When I contemplate the African proverb, "It takes a whole village to raise a child," I think of the amazing group of people involved in creating this book. I would like to acknowledge all of them and also the spirit of their contributions. From family and friends, to dietitians, physicians, authors, government departments in Canada and the USA, the food industry and others in the gluten-free community, their generosity in providing information and help was truly amazing. I am very blessed to have received such assistance and kindness. I would especially like to thank all those who purchased my first books because, frankly, without you this expanded edition would not have been possible. The writing of this acknowledgment is a daunting task because there are so many to whom I owe so much.

First and foremost, a huge debt of gratitude goes to my mom for all of her incredible support in the production and distribution of every edition of the *Gluten-Free Diet* over the past six years. The countless hours of editing and proofing, often into the wee hours of the night, and all the other "behind the scenes" work is deeply appreciated. Her dedication, even in spite of a two-week hospital stay, was amazing. Thanks, mom, for everything!

To my husband, Blair, words cannot express my sincere appreciation for his wonderful encouragement, patience, understanding, continued support and love. Throughout my career, especially during the last seven years of researching and writing each edition and frequently being away from home on speaking engagements, he kept the home-front running smoothly while successfully managing his thriving business. His selfless devotion to our family and to others is one of the many character qualities I have always admired.

To my precious daughters Erin and Jennifer a big thanks for their awesome support, and to Jennifer, thank you for always being there to encourage me and for those great back rubs!

To Wolf Rinke for inspiring me to "dream big" and change career paths.

I'm forever grateful to Enid Young, past president of the Regina chapter of the Canadian Celiac Association, who believed in my idea for this book from the very beginning and encouraged and supported me in so many ways, including reviewing the numerous manuscripts.

To my dear friend, mentor and dietitian colleague, Marion Zarkadas, heartfelt thanks for her excellent advice and editorial assistance with the manuscript. Her amazing attention to detail and specific suggestions were incredibly helpful.

Carol Fenster, a wonderful friend and colleague, deserves an enormous thank you for her expert advice, encouragement and generosity.

Thank you to the many dietitians who provided further information, constructive feedback and/or support, especially – Alexandra Anca, Beth Armour, Amy Barr, Pam Cureton, Jenny Dean, Melinda Dennis, Mark Dinga, Nancy Patin Falini, Kelly Fitzpatrick, Jacquelin Gates, Cindy Heroux, Cynthia Kupper, Anne Lee, Mavis Molloy, Carol Rees Parrish, Jackie See, Mary K Sharrett, Lauren Swann, Tricia Thompson and Jeannie Zibrida.

To the many physicians and scientists for their technical advice and support – Dr. Scott Bean, Dr. Vern Burrows, Dr. Decker Butzner, Dr. Pekka Collin, Dr. Carlo Catassi, Dr. Jeff Dahlberg, Dr. Alessio Fasano, Dr. Peter Green, Dr. Ciaran Kelly, Dr. Joseph Murray, Dr. Michelle Pietzak, Dr. Mohsin Rashid, Dr. Lloyd Rooney, Dr. Cynthia Rudert, Dr. Connie Switzer, Dr. Fred Townley-Smith and Dr. Ralph Warren.

Dina Aronson from NutraWiz, thank you for the nutritional analysis of the recipes and for providing valuable data. You really are a "wiz."

To all the gluten-free culinary experts for their sage advice and practical suggestions, especially Heather Butt, Carol Fenster, Connie Sarros and Donna Washburn.

To all those individuals who contributed recipes – Dina Aronson, Heather Butt, Michael and Bev Calihan, Leslie Cerier, Carol Fenster, Bruce Gross, Bette Hagman, Laurel Hutton, Barbara Kliment, Jane Reinhardt-Martin, Vesanto Melina, Amy Perry, Rebecca Reilly, LynnRae Ries, Karen Robertson, Sheri Sanderson, Connie Sarros, Rosie Schwartz, Girma and Ethiopia Sahlu, Jo Stepaniak, Donna Washburn and Merdith Wiking. And to those companies – Amazing Grains Growers Cooperative, Bob's Red Mill, The Birkett Mills, El Peto, The Flax Council of Canada, Northern Quinoa Corporation, Nu World Amaranth, Riese's Canadian Lake Wild Rice, San Pedro Mesquite, Saskatchewan Flax Development Commission, Saskatchewan Pulse Growers and The Teff Company.

I'm grateful to all those in the gluten-free community for their valuable contributions, especially Hertha Deutsch, Association of European Coeliac Societies; Cynthia Kupper, Gluten Intolerance Group; Andrea Levario, American Celiac Disease Alliance; Norma McGough, Coeliac UK; Elaine Monarch, Celiac Disease Foundation; Graham Price, Coeliac Society of Australia; Lani Thompson, Clan Thompson Resources; Peggy Wagener, *Living Without* and Ann Whelan, *Gluten-Free Living*.

To the many staff from various government departments in Canada and the USA, a special thank you for the assistance and information about food standards and labeling regulations.

Thank you to all the food companies that provided detailed information, with special appreciation to Cassidy Berliner, Matt Cox and Yvonne Fayan (Bob's Red Mill), Elisabeth Carlson (The Teff Company), Peter Felker (Casa deFruta), Bob Hansen (Briess Malt and Ingredient Company), Cindy Kaplan and Scott Mandell (Enjoy Life Foods), Peggy McKeon (Kingsmill Foods), Steve Rice (Authentic Foods), Raj Sukul (Maplegrove Foods) and Larry and Diane Walters, Susan Walters-Flood (Nu World Amaranth) for their additional support and for digging up hard-to-find information.

To my good friend Glenda Francis for your support and prayers!

Thanks Aunt Carolyn for the many ways in which you helped in the research and reviewing of the book over the years.

Librarians Martina Hahnefeld and Doris Hein, thanks a million for tracking down all those reference articles from around the world.

To Mark Humphreys and Mike Warnecke, big thanks for coming to the rescue to solve my on-going computer malfunctions. You were lifesavers!

To Carie Romanuik who deciphered and typed my first hand-written manuscripts.

I am deeply indebted to the team at Centax Books, especially Margo, Iona, Kathryn, Tracy and Cheryl, for all their hard work and incredible dedication to making every edition a continuing success.

And for the many people whose names I have not mentioned but who also contributed to this book, I say a heartfelt thank you.

TABLE OF CONTENTS

MEET SHELLEY CASE, BSc, RD

A registered dietitian, Shelley Case is a leading North American nutrition expert on celiac disease and the gluten-free diet. She is a member of the Medical Advisory Boards of the Celiac Disease Foundation and Gluten Intolerance Group in the United States and the Professional Advisory Board of the Canadian Celiac Association.

Shelley is a frequent guest on television and radio, including the *NBC Today Show*. A popular speaker, she has delivered numerous lectures and workshops at national and regional medical, dietetic, celiac and food industry conferences throughout the USA and Canada, including the National Institutes of Health Consensus Development Conference on Celiac Disease, American Dietetic Association annual conference and Natural Products Food Expo conferences.

She is the author of many articles on celiac disease and the gluten-free diet in leading publications such as *Gastroenterology, Pediatrics, Journal of Human Nutrition and Dietetics* and *Today's Dietitian*. In addition, she co-authored the celiac section in the *Manual of Clinical Dietetics (6th edition)* by the American Dietetic Association and Dietitians of Canada, and has contributed to a variety of other resources.

In recognition of Shelley's major contributions to the celiac community and dedication to educating health professionals and individuals with celiac disease in Canada and the United States, she was awarded the Queen Elizabeth Golden Jubilee Medal.

Shelley earned a Bachelor of Science Degree in Nutrition and Dietetics from the University of Saskatchewan and completed her Dietetic Internship at the Health Sciences Center in Winnipeg, Manitoba. Over the past 25 years, Shelley has helped thousands of people improve their eating habits and manage a variety of disease conditions through good nutrition. Currently, she has her own nutrition consulting company that offers a variety of services to individuals, health organizations and businesses.

Professionally, Shelley is a member of the Dietitians of Canada, Saskatchewan Dietitians Association and American Dietetic Association, as well as the Nutrition Entrepreneurs, Dietitians in Business and Communications and the Medical Nutrition Practice Groups of the American Dietetic Association. She also serves on the Advisory Board of *Living Without* magazine.

Very active in her community and church, she has chaired many conferences and special events. Shelley is an accomplished musician who enjoys playing piano and electric keyboard. She lives with her husband and two children in Regina, Saskatchewan, Canada.

PREFACE

In the Beginning

As a new graduate dietitian in 1981, I was excited to finally enter the workforce after five challenging years of university and internship. My passion, which continues to this day, was to be able to help people eat nutritiously and improve their overall health and well-being. In my first job at a large outpatient diabetes and diet education center I was responsible for counseling children and adults with various conditions such as diabetes, heart disease, high blood pressure, obesity, cystic fibrosis, food allergies and gastrointestinal disorders, including celiac disease. I was well prepared to counsel individuals with many different problems, however celiac disease was definitely not one of them! Never having seen anyone with celiac disease during internship, and receiving only minimal information in one nutrition class at university, left me ill-prepared. The day I was to counsel my first patient with celiac disease, I remember scrambling to find any relevant information about the disease itself and especially about the gluten-free diet. The little information I did find was out of date and of little use. Realizing I needed help, I contacted the local celiac support group in Regina, Saskatchewan, which welcomed me and taught me so much about the disease and diet, and provided me with some basic materials for counseling future patients. After attending several meetings, I was asked to be their dietitian advisor. I accepted the position and, over time, my knowledge of the disease and diet grew. Ten years later I was invited to become a member of the Canadian Celiac Association Professional Advisory Board, a position I have held ever since.

The Birth of an Idea

Every patient that I saw with celiac disease always wanted very specific and practical information on food labeling and ingredients; names of gluten-free companies/products and where to find them; recipes; meal planning suggestions; tips for eating out; how to prevent cross-contamination and other gluten-free diet resources. However, such information was usually only available from many different pamphlets, books, manuals and other sources, which meant that the patient had a pile of loose papers to take home after the counseling sessions! In addition to educating patients, I often got calls from other dietitians in the city, and from around the province, seeking information, as they too felt their knowledge of the disease and diet was inadequate. It soon became apparent that there was a real need for a more comprehensive resource, for both health professionals and patients, on celiac disease. This was the birth of the idea for the *Gluten-Free Diet: A Comprehensive Resource Guide*.

Dreams Become a Reality

In 1997 I left a very rewarding career at a hospital to pursue a dream of starting a nutrition consulting business. In 1999 I decided to get serious about turning this gluten-free resource idea into a reality and dedicated the next two years to researching and writing my first book – *Gluten-Free Diet: A Comprehensive Resource Guide*. It was self-published in May 2001. The next big hurdle was letting health professionals and individuals with celiac disease know about the resource. Without the backing of a large publishing house, it required creative promotional strategies on a shoestring budget. As the book became better known, positive feedback from individuals with celiac disease and from dietitians was very encouraging. News about the book continued to spread and more of my consulting time was being devoted to celiac disease. Being the marketing representative, shipper and accountant, as well as author and speaker has given me a new appreciation for the role of authors and publishers, and even more for the importance of accurate up-to-date resources for those with celiac disease.

The Continuing Saga

The gluten-free world continues to grow in both the number of individuals being diagnosed and the products and resources available in the marketplace. These changes have necessitated several revisions to the *Gluten-Free Diet* to include more information to meet this huge demand. I'm thrilled to finally release this expanded edition, packed full of new information, products and resources that I hope will make your gluten-free life easier and healthier.

An Amazing Journey

Twenty-five years ago I never would have dreamed that I would be a dietitian specializing in celiac disease and the gluten-free diet, let alone be the author of a national best-seller or being interviewed by Matt Lauer on the *NBC Today Show*. Rather ironic for a dietitian from Saskatchewan, the province known as the "bread basket of the world." So, for everyone out there with an idea or dream – pursue it, work hard and never give up. Who knows where you may end up! I'm amazed and truly blessed to have had the opportunity to become involved in such an incredible field, meeting so many wonderful individuals with the disease, along with health professionals and those in industry and government, from the USA and Canada and around the world, who are working so hard to improve the lives of people with celiac disease. The Canadian Celiac Association's motto "Together We're Better" is a worthy ideal. I look forward to working together with you and continuing on this challenging gluten-free journey.

Shelley M. Case, BSc, RD

FOREWORD

The day you were diagnosed with celiac disease and started on a gluten-free diet, your life changed for the better. With a gluten-free diet the damage to the lining of the small bowel begins to heal and intestinal function starts to return to normal. With this healing process comes a renewed sense of health and well-being and an improved quality of life. Strict adherence to a gluten-free diet reduces the risks of developing other illnesses that occur with increased frequency in individuals with untreated celiac disease. The gluten-free diet is the only treatment for celiac disease.

Shelley's book is a valuable resource to help you conquer the challenges of managing and living with a gluten-free diet for life.

Connie M. Switzer, MD, FRCPC, Clinical Professor of Medicine, University of Alberta, Edmonton, Alberta and Chair of the Canadian Celiac Association Professional Advisory Board.

INTRODUCTION TO THE GLUTEN-FREE DIET A COMPREHENSIVE RESOURCE GUIDE

Gluten-Free Diet – A Comprehensive Resource Guide was written for those with celiac disease or its skin form, dermatitis herpetiformis, who must follow a strict gluten-free diet for life. This book provides practical information, in an easy-to-read format, about celiac disease and the gluten-free diet. It is also a valuable resource for:

- ✦ Family members and caregivers of those with celiac disease or dermatitis herpetiformis
- ✦ Dietitians, nutritionists, physicians, nurses and other health practitioners
- ✦ Educators in health science, food service and culinary programs
- ✦ Food manufacturers – research and development staff and consumer representatives
- ✦ Chefs, cooks, servers and other food-service staff
- ✦ Managers of grocery, health food and specialty food stores

Celiac Disease

The first section of this Guide provides a brief overview of celiac disease and dermatitis herpetiformis, including the prevalence, signs and symptoms, other associated conditions, complications and diagnosis. Recommended references are listed for those needing more detailed information about these conditions.

Foods Allowed

In order to successfully follow a gluten-free diet, it is essential to have a good understanding of which foods and ingredients contain gluten. Unfortunately, there is considerable misinformation published about what constitutes a gluten-free diet. As a result, many individuals are often confused and needlessly avoid certain foods and ingredients, thus limiting the variety in their diet which may lead to nutritional imbalances. The gluten-free diet section contains background information and references on the gluten-free status and safety of numerous foods and ingredients, including the acceptability of oats. The Gluten-Free Diet By Food Groups table is a handy tool that organizes foods and ingredients into three categories – foods allowed, foods to question and foods to avoid. Food labeling regulations in the USA and Canada are reviewed along with a detailed discussion of specific gluten-free labeling regulations and standards in North America, Europe, Australia/New Zealand and the international Codex Alimentarius Commission.

Nutritional Concerns

Specific nutritional concerns such as anemia, bone disease and lactose intolerance are addressed. Recommended amounts of key nutrients (iron, folate, vitamin B_{12}, calcium, vitamin D and fiber) and gluten-free food sources for these nutrients are found in tables throughout this section. Information about nutritious gluten-free grains and seeds and how to incorporate them into the diet is included. Healthy Gluten-Free Dietary Guidelines have been developed which incorporate key components of the new MyPyramid food guidance system in the USA and Canada's Food Guide to Healthy Eating. Comprehensive nutritional composition tables of various gluten-free foods and ingredients are provided at the end of the section.

Meal Planning

This section provides suggestions for meals and snacks along with a number of recipes. Specific tips for improving the nutritional quality of meal plans and a Sample Seven-Day Gluten-Free Menu are also featured.

Gluten-Free Cooking

Information about many different gluten-free flours and starches, substitutions, baking hints and recipes are included in this section. Each recipe includes a nutritional analysis for calories, carbohydrate, dietary fiber, fat, protein, iron, calcium and sodium, which is particularly helpful for individuals who have both celiac disease and type 1 diabetes.

Shopping

Gluten-free shopping tips, a sample shopping list, and how to prevent cross-contamination of gluten-free foods with gluten-containing foods are highlighted in this section. The need for careful reading of ingredients on food labels on a regular basis and contacting the company when in doubt about the gluten-free status of a food is stressed.

The growing demand for gluten-free foods has resulted in an increased number and wide variety of items in many different food and beverage categories. This Guide provides the company name, product name and package size in both grams and ounces for over 2,600 foods in the following categories: cereals, breads and other baked products, desserts, cookies, crackers, baking mixes, flours, grains and legumes, pastas, entrées and side dishes, soups, snacks, miscellaneous items and dairy and non-dairy substitutes. The company directory section contains an extensive listing of gluten-free specialty and natural product food companies and distributors in North America and Europe, and whether their products are made in a dedicated gluten-free facility.

Other Resources

A variety of recommended books, cookbooks, magazines, newsletters and other materials are featured in the gluten-free resource section. In addition, celiac research and education centers in the USA and a directory of celiac organizations in the USA, Canada and other countries around the world are listed.

Closing Remarks

The information in this book has been exhaustively researched from a wide variety of sources believed to be reliable and representative of the best current scientific research and opinions on the subject at the time of printing. These sources include health professionals; food scientists; agricultural specialists; culinary experts; medical, dietetic and food science/technology organizations; governmental departments; food manufacturers and associations; and celiac organizations. Information from these sources was obtained through personal communication (telephone, email and/or mail), the internet, and libraries. Textbooks, manuals, books, position papers, journal articles, professional and trade magazines, newsletters and product labels were used as references. The author does not endorse any products or resources in this Guide. Inclusion of brand-name products and resources is strictly for information purposes. Please notify the author if you learn that information in this Guide has changed, so that the changes can be included in future revisions.

CELIAC DISEASE AND DERMATITIS HERPETIFORMIS

Celiac Disease

Celiac disease, also known as gluten-sensitive enteropathy or celiac sprue, is a chronic autoimmune intestinal disorder. When genetically susceptible individuals consume specific proteins in the grains wheat, rye and barley, which are collectively known as "gluten," the absorptive surface of the small intestine is damaged. This surface contains tiny finger-like projections called villi that become inflamed and flattened (known as villous atrophy) due to the immunologic reaction to gluten, causing malabsorption of nutrients needed for good health. Iron, calcium and folate are key nutrients often affected since they are absorbed in the first part of the small intestine. If the damage progresses further down the small intestinal tract, malabsorption of carbohydrates (especially lactose), fat and fat-soluble vitamins (A, D, E, K), protein and other nutrients may also occur. The development of celiac disease involves a combination of genetic, environmental and immunological factors. Celiac disease can occur at any age, including the elderly, and may be triggered by a gastrointestinal or viral infection, severe stress, surgery or pregnancy.

Continued exposure to gluten can result in vitamin and mineral deficiencies causing conditions such as anemia and osteoporosis; neurological disorders (e.g., ataxia, seizures and neuropathy); and an increased risk for developing other autoimmune disorders (e.g., thyroid disease, type 1 diabetes, connective tissue diseases, Addison's disease) and certain types of cancer, especially gastrointestinal malignancies. Also, there is an increased risk of miscarriage or having a low-birth-weight baby, and infertility in both women and men. For more information about celiac disease, see the references listed on page 18, nutritional concerns on pages 73-75, 91, 92, 97, 101-103, celiac organizations on pages 311-312 and other resources on pages 313-322.

Prevalence

Originally thought to be rare disorder, celiac disease is now recognized as one of the most common inherited diseases, with a world prevalence estimated at 1:266 people. Recent studies have revealed that celiac disease affects approximately 1% of the U.S. population (1:100 individuals) which is similar to data from European countries.

Symptoms

Celiac disease not only affects the gastrointestinal system but many other systems in the body, resulting in a wide range and severity of symptoms that can vary greatly from one person to another (see page 16). These symptoms may occur singly or in combination in children and adults. Many individuals have "silent celiac disease" (i.e., have no or very subtle symptoms) in spite of gluten sensitivity.

Symptoms of Celiac Disease

- Iron, folate and/or vitamin B_{12} deficiency
- Other vitamin and mineral deficiencies (A, D, E, K, calcium)
- Chronic fatigue and weakness
- Abdominal pain, bloating and gas
- Indigestion/reflux ("heartburn")
- Nausea and vomiting
- Diarrhea, constipation or intermittent diarrhea and/or constipation
- Lactose intolerance
- Weight loss (note that CD can also occur in obese individuals)
- Bone/joint pain
- Easy bruising of the skin
- Edema (swelling) of hands and feet
- Migraine headaches
- Depression
- Mouth ulcers (canker sores)
- Menstrual irregularities
- Infertility (in both women and men)
- Recurrent miscarriages
- Elevated liver enzymes

Additional symptoms in children

- Irritability and behavioral changes
- Concentration and learning difficulties
- Failure to thrive (delayed growth and short stature)
- Delayed puberty
- Dental enamel abnormalities

Associated Conditions

Celiac disease can also occur more frequently in a variety of other disorders. Individuals with any of the following conditions and symptoms of celiac disease should be screened for celiac disease:

- Type 1 diabetes
- Other autoimmune disorders (e.g., autoimmune thyroid disease, autoimmune liver disease, Sjögren's syndrome, Addison's disease, alopecia areata)
- Osteoporosis
- Down syndrome
- Turner Syndrome
- Selective IgA deficiency

Diagnosis

The diagnosis of celiac disease is often very difficult because of the broad range of symptoms that can vary from mild to severe or none at all. Individuals are often misdiagnosed with irritable bowel syndrome, lactose intolerance, fibromyalgia, chronic fatigue syndrome or ulcers. Recent studies by Columbia University in New York and the Canadian Celiac Association have reported that many people have suffered with symptoms for more than 10 years and have seen numerous physicians before a correct diagnosis of celiac disease was made.

There are specific blood tests, including IgA endomysial (EMA) and IgA tissue transglutaminase (tTG) antibody tests, to detect celiac disease. Unfortunately these tests are not 100% accurate and some individuals test negative in spite of having celiac disease. Therefore, the only definitive test for diagnosing celiac disease is the small intestinal biopsy. **A gluten-free diet should never be started before the blood tests and biopsy are completed as this can interfere with making an accurate diagnosis.**

Treatment

Once a diagnosis for celiac disease is confirmed, it is essential to follow a strict gluten-free diet for life. Additional vitamin and mineral supplements may be necessary to correct the malnutrition. Some individuals may also need to eliminate lactose until the damaged bowel is healed (see pages 101-102).

Dermatitis Herpetiformis

Dermatitis herpetiformis (DH) is another form of celiac disease. This chronic skin condition is characterized by an intense burning, itchy and blistering rash. The rash is symmetrically distributed and commonly found on the elbows, knees and the buttocks, but can also occur on the back of the neck, upper back, scalp and hairline. Initially, groups of small blisters are formed that soon erupt into small erosions. Most people with DH will also have varying degrees of small intestinal villous atrophy although many will have no bowel complaints. A small percentage may present with bloating, abdominal pain and diarrhea, especially if the bowel involvement is severe, and some individuals may show evidence of malabsorption and malnutrition.

Prevalence

Approximately 10% of individuals with celiac disease have DH with a male to female ratio of 2:1. The age of onset is typically between 25-45 but can also occur in children and older adults.

Diagnosis

Individuals with DH are frequently misdiagnosed with other skin conditions such as eczema, contact dermatitis, allergies, hives, herpes or psoriasis and treated with a variety of topical creams. The only way to correctly diagnose DH is a skin biopsy from unaffected skin adjacent to blisters or erosions. A small intestinal biopsy is not essential if the skin biopsy is positive for DH.

Treatment

Treatment for DH is a **strict gluten-free diet for life**. For some individuals, Dapsone, a drug from the "sulphone family," may be prescribed to reduce the itching. Response to the medication can be dramatic (usually 48-72 hours). However, Dapsone has no effect on the ongoing immune response or intestinal atrophy. Following a strict gluten-free diet will result in:

- ✦ Improvement in the skin lesions.
- ✦ Major reduction in drug dosage for those people initially started on Dapsone. After a time, it is often possible to discontinue the drug to control the skin rash. Flare-ups due to inadvertent or intentional gluten consumption may require temporary use of Dapsone.
- ✦ The gut function will return to normal.

NOTE: Once a diagnosis of celiac disease or dermatitis herpetiformis is confirmed, it is essential to consult with a registered dietitian with expertise in celiac disease and the gluten-free diet for nutritional assessment, diet education, meal planning and assistance with social and emotional adaptation to the new gluten-free lifestyle. Also, joining a celiac support organization for further information and ongoing support is highly recommended.

References

- NIH Consensus Development Conference on Celiac Disease http://consensus.nih.gov/2004/2004celiacdisease118html.htm
- Celiac Disease: Proceedings of the NIH Consensus Conference on Celiac Disease. *Gastroenterology* 2005; 128(4): S1-S141. http://www2.us.elsevierhealth.com/inst/serve?action=searchDB&searchDBfor=iss&id=jgast051284b&target=
- Green PHR, Jabri B. Celiac disease. *Lancet* 2003; 362 (9381):383-391.
- Zarkadas M, Case S. Celiac disease and the gluten-free diet: An overview. *Top Clin Nutr* 2005; 20:127-138.
- Alaedini A, Green P. Narrative review: celiac disease. Understanding a complex autoimmune disorder. *Ann Intern Med* 2005; 142:289-298.
- Lee AR. Celiac disease: Detection and treatment. *Top Clin Nutr* 2005; 20:139-145.
- Fasano A, Berti I, Gerdarduzzi T, et al. Prevalence of celiac disease in at-risk and not-at-risk groups in the United States: A large multicenter study. *Arch Intern Med* 2003; 163:286-292.
- Cranney A, Zarkadas M, Graham I, et al. The Canadian Celiac Health Survey. *Dig Dis Sci* In press 2006.
- Rashid M, Cranney A, Zarkadas M, et al. Celiac disease: Evaluation of the diagnosis and dietary compliance in Canadian children. *Pediatrics* 2005; 116: e754-759. http://pediatrics.aappublications.org/cgi/content/full/116/6/e754?
- Zarkadas M, Cranney A, Case S, et al. The impact of a gluten-free diet on adults with coeliac disease: results of a national survey. *J Hum Nutr Dietet* 2006; 19:41-49.
- Green PHR, Stavropoulos S, Panagi SG, et al. Characteristics of adult celiac disease in the USA: Results of a National Survey. *Am J Gastroenterol* 2001; 120: 636-651.
- Lee AR, Newman J. Celiac disease: Impact on quality of life. *J Am Diet Assoc* 2003; 103:1533-1535.
- Guidelines for the diagnosis and treatment of celiac disease in children: Recommendations of the North American Society for Pediatric Gastroenterology, Hepatology and Nutrition. JPGN 2005; 40:1-19, 2005 http://www.naspghan.org/PDF/PositionPapers/celiac_guideline_2004_jpgn.pdf
- Collin P and Reunala. Recognition and management of the cutaneous manifestations of celiac disease: A guide for dermatologists. *Am J Clin Derm* 2003;4: 13-20.

THE GLUTEN-FREE DIET

Gluten Defined

Gluten is the general name for the storage proteins (prolamins) found in wheat, rye and barley. These specific prolamins damage the small intestine in people with celiac disease and dermatitis herpetiformis. The actual names of the toxic prolamins are gliadin in wheat, secalin in rye and hordein in barley. All forms of wheat, rye and barley must be avoided and are outlined in the table on page 20. Although rice contains the prolamin called orzenin and corn contains zein, these prolamins are not toxic to persons with celiac disease. The corn prolamin is sometimes erroneously referred to as "corn gluten" by the food industry, however, it does not need to be restricted on a gluten-free diet.

Oats

Historically, the avenin prolamin in oats was also thought to be toxic based on the early work of Dr. W.K. Dicke and his colleagues in 1953, however, the safety of oats has been widely debated since then. Many studies in Europe and the USA over the past 10 years in both children and adults with celiac disease have revealed that consumption of moderate amounts of oats is safe for most people. It is important to note that the majority of these studies used pure, uncontaminated oats. Unfortunately, the majority of commercial oat products on the market are contaminated with wheat, barley and/or rye during harvesting, transportation, storage, milling and processing. An American study by dietitian Tricia Thompson tested three brands of commercially available oats (12 samples) and found varying levels of gluten contamination. Another study by Størsrud also tested commercially available oat products (88 samples) in Sweden and found gluten contamination at various levels. Cross-contamination has been the major reason why most health professionals and celiac groups have not allowed oats on a gluten-free diet. Fortunately, a number of companies in Europe and North America are currently or in the process of offering pure, uncontaminated oat products (see page 275 for information about purchasing these oat products).

It has been reported that a very small number of individuals with celiac disease may not tolerate even pure, uncontaminated oats. The mechanism causing this intolerance has not been established but may be due to an avenin-reactive T cell reaction. Further research on the incidence of oat intolerance in people with celiac disease is needed due to the limited information available at this time.

Based on the existing research on oats in celiac disease, a growing number of health professionals, celiac organizations, celiac research centers and other associations around the world allow consumption of moderate amounts of pure, uncontaminated oat products in a gluten-free diet. Some groups do not recommend oats or restrict oats under certain conditions.

See pages 21-27 for Position Statements/Guidelines on the Use of Oats in Celiac Disease from various organizations.

Gluten-Containing Foods & Ingredients To Avoid

Wheat

Atta*
Bulgur
Couscous
Dinkel (also known as spelt)**
Durum**
Einkorn**
Emmer**
Farina
Farro or Faro (also known as spelt)**
Fu***
Graham Flour
Hydrolyzed Wheat Protein
Kamut**
Matzoh, Matzoh Meal
Modified Wheat Starch
Seitan****
Semolina
Spelt (also known as farro or faro; dinkel)**
Triticale
Wheat Bran
Wheat Flour
Wheat Germ
Wheat Starch

* A fine whole-meal flour made from low-gluten, soft-textured wheat used to make Indian flatbread (also known as chapatti flour)

** Types of wheat

*** A dried gluten product derived from wheat that is sold as thin sheets or thick round cakes. Used as a protein supplement in Asian dishes such as soups and vegetables.

**** A meat-like food derived from wheat gluten used in many vegetarian dishes. Sometimes called "wheat meat."

Barley

Ale*
Barley (Flakes, Flour, Pearl)
Beer*
Brewer's Yeast
Lager*
Malt**
Malt Extract/Malt Syrup/Malt Flavoring***
Malt Vinegar
Malted Milk

* Most regular ale, beer and lager are derived from barley which is not gluten-free. However, there are several new varieties of gluten-free beer derived from buckwheat, sorghum and/or rice which are gluten-free. See page 266.

** Malt is an enzyme preparation usually derived from sprouted barley which is not gluten-free. Other cereal grains can also be malted and may or may not be gluten-free depending on the additional ingredients used in the malting process.

*** These terms are used interchangeably to denote a concentrated liquid solution of barley malt that is used as a flavoring agent.

Rye

Rye Bread
Rye Flour

Oats*

Oatmeal
Oat Bran
Oat Flour
Oats

* Celiac organizations in Canada and the USA do not recommend consumption of commercially available oat products as they are often cross-contaminated with wheat and/or barley. However, pure, uncontaminated specialty oat products from North America are now available and many organizations allow consumption of moderate amounts of these oats for persons with celiac disease. For more information about the use of oats in celiac disease and where to purchase these specialty oat products see pages 19, 21-29, 275.

Position Statements/Guidelines on the Use of Oats in Celiac Disease from Various Organizations

The position statements and/or guidelines on the use of oats from various celiac, dietetic, medical and other health related organizations are highlighted below. It should be noted that this is not an all-inclusive list. The information was current at the time of printing, however, the various organizations' positions on the use of oats in celiac disease may change based on new research findings.

North American Organizations

Canadian Celiac Association

Professional Advisory Board Position Statement on Oats, March 13, 2006

The safety of oats in individuals with celiac disease has been extensively investigated. Clinical evidence confirms that consumption of pure, uncontaminated oats is safe in the amount of 50 to 70 grams per day (1/2 - 3/4 cup dry rolled oats) by adults and 20 to 25 grams per day (1/4 cup dry rolled oats) by children with celiac disease. Studies looking at the consumption of oats over five years have confirmed their safety. However, the studies looking at safety of oats in celiac disease have involved a small number of subjects, the oats used were pure, free of gluten contamination and the amount allowed per day was also limited.

In Canada, **pure and uncontaminated*** oats are now being produced. Individuals with celiac disease who wish to add oats or oat products to their diet must ensure that the oats they are eating are free from gluten contamination.

A small number of individuals with celiac disease may not tolerate even pure, uncontaminated oats. To ensure that persons with celiac disease are not intolerant to pure and uncontaminated oats, proper clinical follow-up with the physician is advised when introducing oats to a gluten-free diet.

The Canadian Celiac Association will continue to monitor the scientific developments in the area of oats in celiac disease and will keep its members updated.

**These oats will meet or exceed the purity standards of Foundation #1 as defined by the* Canada Seeds Act.

Reference:
www.celiac.ca
Accessed March 16, 2006.

Celiac Disease Foundation

Medical Advisory Board Position Statement, January 18, 2006

"The addition of oats to the diet of individuals with celiac disease has been the subject of research studies which indicate that the prolamin avenin (protein fraction) in oats is not toxic. However, it has been shown that commercial oat products can be contaminated with wheat if they are grown, stored, transported or processed in a facility that also processes wheat. For these reasons, the source and processing methods of oats should be thoroughly researched so that the individual can make an informed decision before eating oats.

"Clinical studies suggest that **pure, uncontaminated oats** consumed daily in moderation (1 cup cooked) can be tolerated by most people with celiac disease. Oats add soluble fiber and added nutrients to the gluten-free diet that may have limited amounts of whole grains.

"The CDF Medical Advisory Board suggests that the celiac individual and their healthcare team discuss the options and consequences together before deciding to introduce oats into their gluten-free diet. If the individual chooses to consume oats, they should have their antibody (IgA and tTGA) levels reviewed annually."

This position has been approved by the Celiac Disease Foundation Medical Advisory Board.

Reference:
Personal communication with Elaine Monarch, Executive Director, Celiac Disease Foundation February 24, 2006.

Celiac Sprue Association (CSA)

"The appropriateness of oats in the gluten-free diet has been pondered for over 20 years. Studies continue with mixed conclusions on this subject of whether the consumption of oats evokes an immune response in those with celiac disease and dermatitis herpetiformis. Until it can be determined if the responses that occur are due to cross-contamination in commercially processed oats, to the protein structure of the grain or to other individual differences, CSA recommends that excluding oats is the only risk-free choice for those on a gluten-free diet. As always, the individual is responsible to make decisions that he or she deems best for optimum health and well-being."

Reference:
www.csaceliacs.org/InfoonOats.php
Accessed on December 16, 2005.

Gluten Intolerance Group (GIG)

Medical Advisory Board Position Statement, October 2005

"Research suggests that pure, uncontaminated oats in moderation (1 cup cooked) daily are safe for most persons with celiac disease. There is concern by health professionals that most oats are cross-contaminated with glutenous grains. Oats add soluble fiber and added nutrients to the GFD that are otherwise lacking or have limited availability. Some studies indicate that compliance with the GFD is increased when oats are included. Some persons using oats may notice increased abdominal discomfort, gas and stool changes. This may be due to the increased fiber from oats. Introducing oats slowly may decrease this discomfort. Rarely, some persons with celiac disease may have a hypersensitivity to oats. There is insufficient research to suggest this is related to a gluten-like reaction, or an allergic reaction. The GIG Medical Advisory Board suggests you work closely with your health care team before deciding to introduce oats in your diet, and that you have your antibody levels reviewed periodically."

Reference:
GIG Quarterly Newsletter, Fall 2005, Volume 28, pages 4, 5.

Celiac Center at Beth Israel Deaconess Medical Centre (BIDMC), Harvard Medical School

"The role of oats in celiac disease and the gluten-free diet remains controversial. Based on numerous studies conducted with adults and children in Europe and the United States, it appears that the majority of individuals with CD can tolerate oats[1-4].

"In practice, however, oats are often grown or processed with other cereals leading to cross-contamination by wheat, barley or rye. Currently there are also very few known producers of pure gluten-free oats in North America. The American Dietetic Association recommends that those with newly diagnosed celiac disease avoid oats, and that the addition of oats be discussed with the individual's clinician only after the intestine has healed as documented by normalization of blood work and small intestinal biopsy appearance.

"Although oats appear to be safe in the vast majority of individuals with celiac disease, there is evidence that, in some individuals, avenins in oats can trigger an immune response similar to gluten[5-6]. In addition, some people may need to avoid oats due to sensitivities or allergies, similar to other foods, such as nuts or shellfish. For these reasons, close monitoring by a healthcare professional experienced in celiac disease is recommended during introduction of oats into a gluten-free diet.

"Currently, avoiding consumption of oats is recommended by the clinicians of the Celiac Center at BIDMC for newly diagnosed patients until it can be clearly demonstrated that celiac disease is well-controlled. Good control is demonstrated by the complete resolution of symptoms (diarrhea, other symptoms of malabsorption or DH skin rash) and a normal tissue transglutaminase level (IgA tTG). At that point, under physician guidance, the gradual addition of pure oats up to 50 grams/day (a little more than ½ cup rolled oats or ¼ cup steel-cut oats) from a dedicated gluten-free facility may be attempted. Routine follow-up with the patient's gastroenterologist is expected three to six months after the addition of oats into the gluten-free diet.

"We remain optimistic that uncontaminated sources of oats will become more widely available and affordable in this country and can be a safe and useful addition to the gluten-free diet."

Referenced Articles:

1. Storsrud S, Olsson M, Arvidsson Lenner R, Nilsson LA, Nilsson O, Kilander A. Adult coeliac patients do tolerate large amounts of oats. *Eur J Clin Nutr* 2003 Jan;57(1):163-9.

2. Janatuinen EK, Pikkarainen PH, Kemppainen TA, et al. A comparison of diets with and without oats in adults with celiac disease. *N Engl J Med*1995;333:1033-1037.

3. Hogberg L, Laurin P, Flath-Magnusson K, et al. Oats to children with newly diagnosed coeliac disease: a randomized double blind study. *Gut* 2004; 53:649-654.

4. Janatuinen EK, Pikkarainen PH, Kemppainen TA, et al. Lack of cellular and humoral immunological responses to oats in adults with coeliac disease. *Gut* 2000;46:327-331.

5. Peraaho M, Kaukinen K, Mustalahti K, Vuolteenaho N, Maki M, Laippala P, et al. Effect of an oats-containing gluten-free diet on symptoms and quality of life in coeliac disease. A randomized study. *Scand J Gastroenterol* 2004, Jan;39(1):27-31.

6. Arentz-Hansen H, Fleckenstein B, Molberg O, Scott H, Koning F, Jung G, Roepstorff P, Lundin KE, Sollid LM. The molecular basis for oat intolerance in patients with celiac disease. *PLoS Med* 2004 Oct;1(1):e1. Epub 2004. Oct 19.

Reference:

Email and telephone correspondence with Dr. Ciaran Kelly, Medical Director and Melinda Dennis, MS, RD, LDN, Nutrition Coordinator, Celiac Center on December 9, 2005.

Celiac Disease Center at Columbia University, New York City

"We recommend the use of oats (from companies that claim them to be gluten-free) for people with celiac disease because most (99%) tolerate them fine. Oats add fiber, needed nutrients and diversity to the diet. Advise to gradually introduce oats in small amounts due to the increased fiber intake which may not be tolerated by all patients. Limit consumption to 50 grams per day."

Reference:

1. Email correspondence with Dr. Peter Green, Medical Director and Anne Lee, RD, Nutritionist, Celiac Disease Center, Columbia University on December 5, 2005.

2. Celiac Disease Center at Columbia University, May/June 2005 Newsletter www.celiacdiseasecenter.columbia.edu

Celiac Clinic, Mayo Clinic

"At Mayo Clinic Rochester, Celiac Clinic, the clinicians discourage ingestion of oats by our patients unless verified gluten-free in their production and free of contamination (by testing) from wheat, rye or barley. Recent studies have demonstrated that most oats, including McCanns, Country Choice and organic oats, are contaminated with gluten. We do not want to expose our patients to this risk (versus we must warn our patients of this risk). Although the majority of people with celiac disease can tolerate oats, patients who try oats should be monitored closely for reactions. People who do not react to the ingestion of gluten with outward symptoms should be especially wary of trying oats.

Patients whose celiac disease is not well controlled are discouraged from trying oats. We will continue to monitor new information as it pertains to this important issue."

Reference:
Email correspondence with Jackie See, MS, RD, Nutritionist, and Dr. Joe Murray on behalf of the clinicians in the Celiac Disease Clinic, Mayo Clinic Rochester on February 6, 2006

University of Maryland Center for Celiac Research

"Several studies have been performed showing that oats did not cause any harm to celiac patients. However, concerns still remain, mainly due to two issues: 1) The possibility of cross-contamination of the oats with wheat or barley during processing of the grains and 2) A subgroup of celiac patients has been found to react to the oat prolamin avenin and may suffer intestinal damage. We continue to review the literature and current studies and will revisit our policy as a source of pure oats becomes available and those patients that do not tolerate oats can be identified."

Reference:
Email and telephone correspondence with Dr. Alessio Fasano, Medical Director, and Pam Cureton, RD, LDN, Dietitian, Center for Celiac Research on December 9, 2005.

American Dietetic Association

Gluten Intolerance/Celiac Disease Evidence Analysis Project Introduction Section: Excerpt on Oats

"Inclusion of oats in the gluten-free diet remains an area of controversy. The study group decided to include the question of oats in the project even though research is still evolving on the topic. According to Don Kasarda of the USDA and his work on plant taxonomy, oats are not as closely related to wheat as rye and barley[6]. Although oats have been eliminated on a gluten-free diet in this country they have been recently included as a safe grain in many parts of Europe. There have been numerous studies in which research-grade oats were included on the gluten-free diet and found to be safe[7]. Arentz-Hansen and others have found oats to cause villous changes in some individuals while causing no immunologic changes in others[8]. This raises the question of whether the oat protein avenin may cause its own specific intestinal reaction in sensitive individuals. Oats therefore present two distinct issues. There is the issue of cross-contamination with gluten-containing grains during the growing, harvesting and processing of the oats. The second issue is that of a separate intolerance to the protein avenin in certain individuals. At this time there is not sufficient evidence to draw specific conclusions. Therefore oats should be neither excluded nor included universally. Rather the inclusion of oats must be based on individual tolerance and the selection of research-grade (clean) oats. If included, the individual tolerance should be closely monitored for potential intolerance."

Reference Articles:

6. Kasarda D. Defining cereals toxicity in celiac disease. In: Feighert C, O'Farrelly F. eds. *Gastrointestinal Immunology and Gluten Sensitive Disease* Dublin, Ireland: Oak Tree Press 1994: 203-220.

7. Janatuinen EK, KemppainenTA, Julkunen RJ, et al. No harm from five year ingestion of oats in celiac disease. *Gut* 2002; 50: 332-335.

8. Arentz-Hansen H, Fleckenstein B, Molberg Ø, et al. The molecular basis for oat intolerance in patients with celiac disease. *PloS Med* 2004;1:84-89.

Evidence Analysis Question:

"How does the inclusion of oats in a dietary pattern for people with celiac disease impact effectiveness and acceptability of the dietary pattern?

"Studies have shown that incorporating oats uncontaminated with wheat, barley or rye, into a gluten-free dietary pattern for people with celiac disease, at intake levels of approximately 50 g dry oats per day, is generally safe and improves compliance. However, many studies report that the introduction of oats may result in gastrointestinal symptoms such as diarrhea and abdominal discomfort. These symptoms tend to be the primary reason for study subject withdrawal. Additional adverse effects that have been reported include dermatitis herpetiformis, villous atrophy and an increased density of intraepithelial lymphocytes, indicating that some persons with celiac disease may be unable to tolerate oats. Since limited research has been conducted on the similarities among those with adverse reactions to oats, further research is needed in this area. Further research is also needed regarding the contamination of oats by wheat, barley and rye". Grade III rating.

See the web links below for the entire statement including all the references that discuss the evidence analysis question.

Reference:
www.adaevidencelibrary.com
www.adaevidencelibrary.com/topic.cfm?cat = 2826
Accessed: March 10, 2006.

American Dietetic Association

Nutrition Care Manual 2006
Celiac Disease Section: Oats

"Whether a patient consumes oats is a decision that should be made in consultation with his or her physician and/or dietitian. Patients consuming oats should be advised to limit consumption to amounts found safe in several studies (i.e., approximately 50 g dry oats) (Thompson, 2003) and ideally, only consume oats that have been tested and found to be free of gluten contamination."

Reference:
www.nutritioncaremanual.org
Accessed March 10, 2006.

Dietitians of Canada

Practice-based Evidence in Nutrition (PEN)
Celiac Disease Knowledge Pathway

Question 7: "Is consumption of moderate amounts of uncontaminated oats by adults (50-70 gm/day) and children (20-25 gm/day) safe for people with celiac disease?

1. Moderate amounts of pure, uncontaminatd oats (50-70 gm/day) can be included in a gluten-free diet for most adults with stable celiac disease. Moderate amounts of pure, uncontaminated oats (20-25 gm/day) can be included for most children with stable celiac disease without apparent adverse effects.
2. It is recommended that the person consult with their physician or dietitian before trying pure, uncontaminated oats."

Reference:
http://www.dieteticsatwork.com/PEN/index.asp?msg
Accessed November 30, 2005.

National Institutes of Health (NIH)

Consensus Development Conference on Celiac Disease, June 28-30, 2004.

"A gluten-free diet is defined as one that excludes wheat, rye and barley. These dietary grains contain the peptides or glutens known to cause celiac disease. Even small quantities of gluten may be harmful. Oats appear to be safe for use by most individuals with celiac disease, but their practical inclusion in a gluten-free diet is limited by potential contamination with gluten during processing."

Reference:
http://consensus.nih.gov/2004/2004CeliacDisease118html.htm
Accessed January 4, 2006.

North American Society for Pediatric Gastroenterology Hepatology and Nutrition (NASPGHAN)

Guideline for the Diagnosis and Treatment of Celiac Disease in Children: Recommendations of the North American Society for Pediatric Gastroenterology, Hepatalogy and Nutrition

"Previously, oats were implicated in the development of villous damage in CD. More recently this has been questioned as both in vivo and in vitro immunologic studies suggest oats are safe (193-199). Despite the accumulating evidence that oats are safe for individuals with CD, there remains some concern about recommending consumption of this grain to CD patients. Contamination of oats with gluten during the harvesting and milling process is known to occur, so unless the purity of the oats can be guaranteed, their safety remains questionable."

Note: To read references 193-199 in the above statement see the full article at the website below.

Reference:
Journal of Pediatric Gastroenterology and Nutrition 40:1-19, 2005 (Quote from page 11). http://www.naspghan.org/PDF/PositionPapers/celiac_guideline_2004_jpgn.pdf
Accessed December 4, 2005.

International Organizations

Association of European Coeliac Societies (AOECS)

"AOECS is the umbrella organization of coeliac societies from 25 European countries. In September 2005 the AOECS General Assembly adopted that the square brackets around oats in the Codex Draft Revised Standard for Gluten-free Foods should be removed and oats should be kept as a gluten-containing cereal (ALINORM 04/27/26 page 42, Appendix III of the world-wide Draft Revised Standard for Gluten-free Foods, 2.1 a).

A world-wide Standard must also protect very sensitive coeliacs. A review of the literature reveals that, although the chemical structure of avenin is slightly different from gliadin, secalin and hordein, not all coeliacs can tolerate oats. When comparing oats/avenin with wheat/gliadin, oats contain less protein than wheat and the avenin is less toxic than gliadin. Therefore, in summary, attention should be paid to whether the recommended "small/moderate" amounts of oats should be considered in the light of the individual sensitivity to trace amounts of gluten, which can be consumed from several sources, not only from oats. It could be the same as the wheat-starch issue: Some coeliacs are tolerating the gluten-trace-residues in the "gluten-free wheat starch," some not. However it must be mentioned, that there are different wheat-starch types available with considerably different gluten-residues and some are definitely not recommended for the gluten-free diet.

If oats would be adopted as a "gluten-free cereal" in Codex and also in the food-legislation, we are facing two major health risks:

(a) the advice to consume only "small/moderate amounts of oats" would no longer be possible (as oats would be called a gluten-free cereal) and as a consequence some coeliacs could consume very large amounts of oats.

(b) the contamination problem cannot be excluded and would pose a major health risk: the contamination with wheat can be up to 20% because of using shared equipment for the transport, milling, processing and packing."

Reference:
Email and telephone correspondence with Hertha Deutsch, Chair of the AOECS Working Group Codex, Labelling and Symbol and President of the Austrian Celiac Society on March 13 and 14, 2006.

The Coeliac Society of Australia

"The inclusion of oats (even if pure and uncontaminated) is not recommended. It has been shown that approximately 1:5 people with coeliac disease react to oat protein. If there is a compelling reason to consume oats, it may be that a systematic challenge with oats and endoscopic biopsy before and during is the only definitive test for oats sensitivity."

Reference:
Email and telephone correspondence with Graham Price, Technical Officer, The Coeliac Society of Australia on December 5-7, 2005.

Coeliac UK

General Guidelines:

1. Moderate amounts of pure, uncontaminated oats (50 g/day) may be consumed by most people with coeliac disease.
2. Introduction of oats can occur once the person is well established on the gluten-free diet and the disease is well controlled.
3. The decision to add oats to the gluten-free diet should be done in consultation with their local health care team.
4. Careful follow-up is necessary to assess tolerance to oat products.

Reference:
Email and telephone correspondence with Norma McGough, BSc., SRD, Dietetic Services Manager, Coeliac UK on November 9, 2005.

Danish Coeliac Society (Dansk Coliaki Forening)

"Research has shown that most people with celiac disease can tolerate oats. It is important to use specially processed clean oats as regular oats are contaminated with gluten-containing grains in the field and/or at the mill. Children and adults should not consume clean oats until their disease is well controlled and the blood tests have normalized. Children should limit oat consumption to 25-50 grams/day, however, there are no restrictions for adults on the amounts of oats per day that can be consumed. It should be noted that if symptoms develop while consuming oats, they should be discontinued."

Reference:
1. Email correspondence with Milena Hasdorf, Secretary, November 10, 2005 and January 17, 2006.
2. "Coeliaki og mad uden gluten" at: www.foedevarestyrelsen.dk/Fdir/Publications/2005214/Rapport.htm

Finnish Coeliac Society (Suomen Keliakialiitto ry)

"In 1998, the scientific advisory board issued a statement whereby oat-containing gluten-free products were permissible for adults with celiac disease. The statement was extended in 1998 to concern patients with dermatitis herpetiformis and to children in 2000."

Reference:
Quote from the article: Oats can diversify a gluten-free diet in celiac disease and dermatitis herpetiformis by Peraaho, M., et al. *J Am Diet Assoc* 2004; 104:1148-1150.

Oats References

- Arentz-Hansen H, Fleckenstein B, Molberg Ø, Scott H, Konding F, Jung G, Roepstorff P, Lundin K, Sollid L. The Molecular basis for oat intolerance in patients with celiac disease. *PLoS Med* 2004;1(1):84-92
- Hardman C, Fry L, Tatham A, Thomas HJ. Absence of toxicity of avenin in patients with dermatitis herpetiformis. *N Engl J Med* 1999;340(4):321.
- Högberg L, Laurin P, Fälth-Magnusson K, Grant C, Grodzinsky E, Jansson G, Ascher H, Browaldh L, Hammersjö JA, Lindberg E, Myrdal U, Stenhammar L. Oats to children with newly diagnosed coeliac disease: a randomised double blind study. *Gut* 2004;53(5):649-54.
- Hoffenberg EJ, Haas J, Drescher A, Barnhurst R, Osberg I, Bao F, Eisenbarth G. A trial of oats in children with newly diagnosed celiac disease. *J Pediatr* 2000;137(3):361-6.
- Hollén E, Högberg L, Stenhammar L, Fälth-Magnusson K, Magnusson KE. Antibodies to oat prolamines (avenins) in children with coeliac disease. *Scand J Gastroenterol* 2003;38(7):742-6.
- Hollén E, Holmgren Peterson K, Sundqvist T, et al. Coeliac children on a gluten-free diet with or without oats display equal anti-avenin antibody titres.. *Scand J Gastroenterol* 2006; 41(1):42-47.
- Janatuinen EK, Kemppainen TA, Julkunen RJ, Kosma VM, Mäki M, Heikkinen M, Uusitupa MI. No harm from five year ingestion of oats in coeliac disease. *Gut* 2002;50(3):332-5.
- Janatuinen EK, Kemppainen TA, Pikkarainen PH, Holm KH, Kosma VM, Uusitupa MIJ, Mäki M, Julkunen RJK. Lack of cellular and humoral immunological responses to oats in adults with coeliac disease. *Gut* 2000;46:327-331.
- Janatuinen EK, Pikkarainen PH, Kemppainen TA, Kosma VM, Järvinen RM, Uusitupa MI, Julkunen RJ. A comparison of diets with and without oats in adults with celiac disease. *N Engl J Med* 1995;333(16):1033-7.
- Kilmartin C, Lynch S, Abuzakouk M, Wieser H, Feighery C. Avenin fails to induce a Th1 response in coeliac tissue following *in vitro* culture. *Gut* 2003;52(1):47-52.
- Lundin KE, Nilsen EM, Scott HG, Loberg EM, Gjøen A, Bratlie J, Skar V, Mendez E, Løvik A, Kett K. Oats induced villous atrophy in coeliac disease. *Gut* 2003;52(11):1649-52.
- Peräaho M, Collin P, Kaukinen K, Kekkonen L, Miettinen S, Maki M. Oats can diversify a gluten-free diet in celiac disease and dermatitis herpetiformis. *J Am Diet Assoc* 2004;104(7):1148-50.
- Peräaho M, Kaukinen K, Mustalahti K, Vuolteenaho N, Mäki M, Laippala P, Collin P. Effect of an oats-containing gluten-free diet on symptoms and quality of life in coeliac disease. A randomized study. *Scand J Gastroenterol* 2004;39(1):27-31.
- Picarelli A, Di Tola M, Sabbatella L, Gabrielli F, Di Cello T, Anania MC, Mastracchio A, Silano M, De Vincenzi M. Immunologic evidence of no harmful effect of oats in celiac disease. *Am J Clin Nutr* 2001;74(1):137-40.
- Reunala T, Collin P, Holm K, Pikkarainen P, Miettinen A, Vuolteenaho N, Mäki M. Tolerance to oats in dermatitis herpetiformis. *Gut* 1998;43(4):490-3.
- Schmitz J. Lack of oats toxicity in coeliac disease. *BMJ* 1997;314(7075):159-60.

- Srinivasan U, Leonard N, Jones E, Kasarda DD, Weir DG, O'Farrelly C, Feighery C. Absence of oats toxicity in adult coeliac disease. *BMJ* 1996;313(7068):1300-1.
- Størsrud S, Hulthén LR, Lenner RA. Beneficial effects of oats in the gluten-free diet of adults with special reference to nutrient status, symptoms and subjective experiences. *Br J Nutr* 2003;90(1):101-7.
- Storsrud S, Olsson M, Arvidsson Lenner R, Nilsson LA, Nilsson O, Kilander A. Adult coeliac patients do tolerate large amounts of oats. *Eur J Clin Nutr* 2003;57(1):163-9.
- Størsrud S, Yman IM, Lenner RA. Gluten contamination in oat products and products naturally free from gluten. *Eur Food Res Technol* 2003;217:481-485.
- Thompson T. Do oats belong in a gluten-free diet? *J Am Diet Assoc* 1997;97(12):1413-6.
- Thompson T. Oats and the gluten-free diet. *J Am Diet Assoc* 2003;103(3):376-9.
- Thompson T. Gluten contamination of commercial oat products in the United States. *N Engl J Med* 2004;351(19):2021-2.
- Thompson T. Contaminated oats and other gluten-free foods in the United States. *J Am Diet Assoc* 2005;105(3):348. Letter in response to: Peräaho et al. Oats can diversify a gluten-free diet in celiac disease and dermatitis herpetiformis. *J Am Diet Assoc.* 2004;104(7):1148-50. Author reply 348-9.

Hidden Gluten

Gluten is the substance in flour responsible for forming the structure of dough, holding products together and leavening. While the presence of gluten is evident in baked goods (e.g., breads, cookies, cakes, crackers) and pasta, it is often a "hidden ingredient" in many other items such as sauces, marinades, gravies, salad dressings, soups, prepared meats (hamburger patties, deli meats, hot dogs), candy, flavored coffees and teas, as well as some medications and nutritional supplements. For a more comprehensive listing of foods allowed, foods to question, and foods to avoid, see the chart entitled **Gluten-Free Diet By Food Groups** on pages 30-34.

Other Ingredients

It is not uncommon to find a lot of misinformation written about the gluten-free status and safety of a number of ingredients on the internet, in pamphlets, books, magazines, and from other sources. A list of frequently questioned ingredients, their gluten-free status, additional background information and reputable references, including specific sections of the U.S. *Code of Federal Regulations* (CFR) and *Canadian Food and Drug Regulations* (FDR) for certain ingredients where applicable is found on pages 45-58. Background information and the web links for these regulations are on pages 59-60. Additional information on ingredients is also found in the **Gluten-Free Diet By Food Groups** Table on pages 30-34 and **Gluten-Free Additives and Ingredients** Table on page 44. The Canadian Celiac Association's *Acceptability of Foods and Food Ingredients for the Gluten-Free Diet Pocket Dictionary* and *Gluten-Free Living* magazine are two excellent resources on the status of ingredients (see page 314).

Gluten-Free Diet By Food Groups[1]

Food Category	Foods Allowed[a]	Foods to Question[b]	Foods to Avoid[c]
Milk & Dairy	Milk, cream, most ice cream, buttermilk, plain yogurt, cheese, cream cheese, processed cheese, processed cheese foods, cottage cheese	Flavored yogurt, frozen yogurt, cheese sauces, cheese spreads, seasoned (flavored) shredded cheese	Malted milk, ice cream made with ingredients not allowed
Grains & Starches	**Breads, Baked Products and Other Items:** Made with amaranth, arrowroot, buckwheat, corn bran, corn flour, cornmeal, cornstarch, flax, legume flours (bean, garbanzo or chickpea, garfava, lentil, pea), mesquite flour, millet, Montina flour (Indian ricegrass), nut flours (almond, chestnut, hazelnut), potato flour, potato starch, pure uncontaminated oat products (oat flour, oat groat, oatmeal)*, quinoa, rice bran, rice flours (brown, glutinous, sweet, white), rice polish, sago, sorghum flour, soy flour, sweet potato flour, tapioca (cassava, manioc), taro, teff * See pages 19-27, 275 for discussion about oats and where to purchase pure, uncontaminated oat products.	Items made with buckwheat flour	Items made with wheat bran, wheat farina, wheat flour, wheat germ, wheat-based semolina, wheat starch**, durum flour, gluten flour, graham flour, atta, bulgur, einkorn, emmer, farro, kamut, spelt, barley, rye, triticale, commercial oat products (oat bran, oat flour, oat groats, oatmeal)*** **Imported foods labeled "gluten-free" made with wheat starch ***See pages 19-27 for discussion about oats.

1 Table adapted and revised October 2000 by S. Case, M. Molloy and M. Zarakadas from *Celiac Disease Needs a Diet for Life Handbook*, Canadian Celiac Association. Further revisions made by S. Case for *Gluten-Free Diet: A Comprehensive Resource Guide*, May 2001, April 2002, July 2003, May 2004, January 2005 and March 2006.

(a), (b), (c) See pages 35-43 for further background information on foods allowed, foods to question and foods to avoid.

Food Category	Foods Allowed[a]	Foods to Question[b]	Foods to Avoid[c]
Grains & Starches	**Cereals: Hot** Puffed amaranth, cornmeal, cream of buckwheat, cream of rice (brown, white), hominy grits, pure, uncontaminated oatmeal*, quinoa, rice flakes, soy flakes, soy grits *See pages 19-27, 275 for discussion about oats and where to purchase pure, uncontaminated oatmeal.	Rice and corn cereals, rice and soy pablum	Cereals made from wheat, rye, triticale, barley and commercial oats*** ***See pages 19-27 for discussion about oats.
	Cold: Puffed (amaranth, buckwheat, corn, millet, rice), rice crisps or corn flakes (with no barley malt extract or barley malt flavoring), rice flakes, soy cereals		Cereals made with added barley malt extract or barley malt flavoring
	Pastas: Macaroni, spaghetti and noodles made from beans, corn, lentils, peas, potato, quinoa, rice, soy, wild rice	Buckwheat pasta	Pastas made from wheat, wheat starch and other ingredients not allowed (e.g., orzo)
	Rice: Plain (e.g., basmati, brown, jasmine, white, wild)	Seasoned or flavored rice mixes	
	Miscellaneous: Corn tacos, corn tortillas, rice tortillas		Wheat flour tacos and tortillas Matzoh, matzoh meal, matzoh balls, couscous, tabouli
	Plain rice crackers, rice cakes & corn cakes	Multi-grain or flavored rice crackers, rice cakes & corn cakes	
	Gluten-free communion wafers	Low gluten communion wafers* *See page 38.	Regular communion wafers

Food Category	Foods Allowed[a]	Foods to Question[b]	Foods to Avoid[c]
Meats & Alternatives	**Meat, Fish, Poultry:** Plain (fresh or frozen)	Deli or luncheon meats (e.g., bologna, salami), wieners, frankfurters, sausages, pâte, meat and sandwich spread, frozen burgers (meat, fish, chicken), meatloaf, ham (ready to cook), seasoned/flavored fish in pouches, imitation fish products (e.g., surimi), meat substitutes, meat product extenders	Canned fish in vegetable broth containing hydrolyzed wheat protein Frozen turkey basted or injected with hydrolyzed wheat protein. Frozen or fresh turkey with bread stuffing Frozen chicken breasts containing chicken broth (made with ingredients not allowed) Meat, poultry or fish breaded in ingredients not allowed
	Eggs: Fresh, liquid, dried or powdered	Flavored egg products (liquid or frozen)	
	Others: Dried beans (e.g., black, garbanzo [also known as chickpea, besan, channa, gram], kidney, navy, pinto, soy, white), dried peas, lentils.	Baked beans	
	Plain nuts and seeds (flax, sesame, pumpkin, Salba, sunflower)	Seasoned or dry roasted nuts, seasoned pumpkin or sunflower seeds	
	Plain tofu	Flavored tofu Tempeh, miso	Fu, Seitan
Fruits & Vegetables	**Fruits:** Fresh, frozen and canned fruits & juices	Dates, fruits with sauces	
	Vegetables: Fresh, frozen and canned vegetables & juices	Vegetables with sauces, French-fried potatoes cooked in oil also used for gluten-containing products	Scalloped potatoes (containing wheat flour), battered deep-fried vegetables
Soups	Homemade broth, gluten-free bouillon cubes, cream soups and stocks made from ingredients allowed	Canned soups, dried soup mixes, soup bases and bouillon cubes	Soups made with ingredients not allowed, bouillon cubes containing hydrolyzed wheat protein

Food Category	Foods Allowed[a]	Foods to Question[b]	Foods to Avoid[c]
Fats	Butter, margarine, lard, shortening, vegetable oils, salad dressings with allowed ingredients	Salad dressings, suet	Salad dressing made with ingredients not allowed.
Desserts	Ice cream, sherbet, whipped toppings, whipping cream, milk puddings, custard, gelatin desserts, cakes, cookies, pies and pastries made with allowed ingredients	Cake icings and frostings	Bread pudding, ice cream made with ingredients not allowed (e.g., cookie crumbs), cakes, cookies, muffins, pies and pastries made with ingredients not allowed
	Gluten-free ice cream cones, wafers and waffles		Ice cream cones, wafers and waffles made with ingredients not allowed
Others	**Sweets:** Honey, jam, jelly, marmalade, corn syrup, maple syrup, molasses, sugar (brown and white), icing sugar (confectioner's)	Honey powder	
	Gluten-free licorice	Hard candies, Smarties®, chocolates, chocolate bars	Licorice and other candies made with ingredients not allowed
	Snack Foods: Plain popcorn, nuts, soy nuts, potato chips, taco (corn) chips	Seasoned (flavored) potato chips, taco (corn) chips, nuts, soy nuts	Potato chips with ingredients not allowed
	Gluten-free pizza		Pizza made with ingredients not allowed
	Beverages: Tea, instant or ground coffee (regular or decaffeinated), cocoa, soft drinks	Flavored and herbal teas, flavored coffees, coffee substitutes	Cereal and malt-based beverages (e.g., Ovaltine [chocolate malt and malt flavor], Postum)
	Distilled alcoholic beverages (e.g., bourbon, gin, rum, rye whiskey, scotch whiskey, vodka and liqueurs), wine	Flavored alcoholic beverages (e.g., coolers, ciders, Caesar vodka beverage)	
	Gluten-free beer, ale and lager		Beer, ale and lager derived from barley
	Most non-dairy beverages made from nut, potato, rice & soy		Non-dairy beverages (nut, potato, rice, soy) made with barley malt extract, barley malt flavoring or oats

Food Category	Foods Allowed[a]	Foods to Question[b]	Foods to Avoid[c]
Others	**Condiments/Sauces:** Ketchup, relish, plain prepared mustard, pure mustard flour, herbs, spices, salt, pepper, olives, plain pickles, tomato paste, vinegars (apple or cider, balsamic, distilled white, grape or wine, rice, spirit), gluten-free soy sauce, gluten-free teriyaki sauce, other sauces and gravies made with allowed ingredients	Specialty prepared mustards, prepared mustard flour, mustard pickles, worcestershire sauce, curry paste	Malt vinegar, soy sauce (made from wheat), teriyaki sauce (made with soy sauce containing wheat), other sauces and gravies made with wheat flour and/or hydrolyzed wheat protein
	Miscellaneous: Plain cocoa, pure baking chocolate, carob chips and powder, chocolate chips, baking soda, cream of tartar, coconut, monosodium glutamate (MSG), vanilla, pure vanilla extract, artificial (synthetic, imitation) vanilla extract, vanillin, yeast (active dry, autolyzed, baker's, nutritional, torula), xanthan gum, guar gum	Baking powder	Brewer's yeast

Notes on Foods Allowed

Food Category	Food Products	Notes
Grains	Garfava™ Flour	A specialty flour from garbanzo beans (chickpeas) and fava beans developed by Authentic Foods.
	Mesquite Flour	Made from the ground pods of the mesquite tree.
	Montina™ Flour	Made from Indian ricegrass.
	Quinoa	A small seed of a South American plant that can be cooked and eaten whole or ground into flour or flakes.
	Glutinous Rice Flour	Also known as sweet, sticky or sushi rice flour. Made from a sticky short-grain rice that is higher in starch than brown or white rice. Does not contain any gluten.
	Sago	An edible starch derived from the pith of the stems of a certain variety of palm trees. Usually ground into a powder and used as a thickener or dense flour.
	Tapioca (Cassava, Manioc, Yucca)	A tropical plant that produces a starchy edible root that is peeled and can be boiled, baked or fried. The peeled root can also be dried and washed with water to extract the starch (known as tapioca starch) which can be used to make baked products and tapioca pearls.
	Taro (Dasheen, Eddo)	A tropical plant harvested for its large, starchy tubers which are consumed as a cooked vegetable or made into breads, puddings or Poi (a Polynesian dish).
	Teff	A tiny seed of a grass native to Ethiopia that can be cooked and eaten whole or ground into flour.
	Hominy Grits (Corn Grits)	Corn kernels that are coarsely or finely ground that are cooked and eaten as a hot breakfast cereal or side dish.
	GF Communion Wafers	No-gluten host made from soy and rice flour by Ener-G Foods. These hosts are allowed by most major denominations except the Catholic Church.

Notes on Foods Allowed

Food Category	Food Products	Notes
Meats & Alternatives	Salba	This is the trademark name for an oilseed of the ancient plant species belonging to the mint family called Chia which is grown in Central and South America. It is high in omega-3 fatty acids and fiber. The seed should be ground in order to get the maximum benefit of all the nutritional components.
Other	Distilled Alcoholic Beverages	Rye whiskey, scotch whiskey, gin, vodka and bourbon are distilled from a mash of fermented grains. Even though they are derived from a gluten-containing grain, the distillation process removes the gluten from the purified final product. Rum (distilled from sugar cane) and brandy (distilled from wine) are also gluten-free. Liqueurs (also known as cordials) are made from an infusion of a distilled alcoholic beverage and flavoring agents such as nuts, fruits, seeds or cream.
	Gluten-Free Beer, Ale and Lager	Can be made from fermented rice, buckwheat and/or sorghum.
	Plain Prepared Mustard	Made from distilled vinegar, water, mustard seed, salt, spices and flavors.
	Pure Mustard Flour	A powder made from pure ground mustard seed.
	Vinegars	Produced from various ingredients: Balsamic (grapes), cider (apples), rice (rice wine), white distilled (corn, wheat or both), wine (red wine). All these vinegars are gluten-free (including distilled white derived from wheat as the distillation process removes the gluten from the final purified product). Except for malt vinegar (see page 43).
	Vanilla	Pure vanilla and pure vanilla extract are derived from the vanilla bean pods of a climbing orchid grown in tropical locations. The vanilla beans are chopped and soaked in alcohol and water; aged and then filtered. It must contain at least 35% ethyl alcohol by volume. The pure vanilla is bottled or the pure extract can be mixed with sugar and a stabilizer and then bottled.
	Natural Vanilla Flavor	Derived from vanilla beans but contains less than 35% ethyl alcohol. May also contain sugar and a stabilizer.
	Artificial (Imitation, Synthetic) Vanilla-Vanillin Extract/ Flavoring	Made from a by-product of the pulp and paper industry or a coal-tar derivative that is chemically treated to mimic the flavor of vanilla. Also contains alcohol, water, color and a stabilizer.
	Baker's Yeast	A type of yeast grown on sugar beet molasses. It is available as active dry yeast granules (sold in packets or jars) or compressed yeast (also known as wet yeast, cake yeast or fresh yeast) which must be refrigerated.

Notes on Foods Allowed

Food Category	Food Products	Notes
Other	Autolyzed Yeast/Autolyzed Yeast Extract	A special process that causes yeast to be broken down by its own enzymes resulting in the production of various compounds that can be used as flavoring agents. Autolyzed yeast is almost always derived from baker's yeast.
	Torula Yeast	A yeast grown on wood sugars (a by-product of waste products from the pulp and paper industry). Used as a flavoring agent that has a hickory smoke characteristic.
	Nutritional Yeast	A specific strain of an inactive form of baker's yeast that is grown on a mixture of sugar beet molasses which is fermented, washed, pasteurized and dried at high temperatures. Used as a dietary supplement as it contains protein, fiber, vitamins and minerals. Available in pills, flakes or powder.
	Xanthan Gum	It is produced from the fermentation of corn sugar. This powder is used to thicken sauces and salad dressings, Also used in gluten-free baked products to improve the structure and texture.
	Guar Gum	A gum extracted from the seed of an East Indian plant. Available as a powder that is used as a thickener and stabilizer. Can be substituted for xanthan gum in gluten-free baked products. It is high in fiber and may have a laxative effect if consumed in large amounts.

Notes on Foods to Question

Food Category	Food Products	Notes
Milk & Dairy	Cheese Spreads, Cheese Sauces (e.g., Nacho), Seasoned (flavored) Shredded Cheese	May be thickened with wheat flour or wheat starch. Seasonings may contain hydrolyzed wheat protein, wheat flour or wheat starch.
	Flavored Yogurt, Frozen Yogurt	May contain granola, cookie crumbs or wheat bran.
Grains & Starches	Buckwheat Flour	Pure buckwheat flour is gluten-free, however, some buckwheat flour may be mixed with wheat flour.
	Rice & Corn Cereals	May contain barley malt, barley malt extract, barley malt flavoring.
	Buckwheat Pasta	Also called Japanese Soba noodles. Some Soba pasta contains pure buckwheat flour which is gluten-free but others may also contain wheat flour.
	Seasoned or Flavored Rice Mixes	Seasonings may contain hydrolyzed wheat protein, wheat flour or wheat starch or have added soy sauce that contains wheat.
	Multi-grain or Flavored Rice Crackers, Rice Cakes & Corn Cakes	Multi-grain products may contain barley and/or oats. Some contain soy sauce (made from wheat), seasonings containing hydrolyzed wheat protein, wheat flour or wheat starch.
	Low-Gluten Communion Wafers	The Catholic Canon Law, code 924.2, requires the presence of some wheat in communion wafers and will not accept the gluten-free hosts made with other grains. A very low-gluten host made with a small amount of specially processed wheat starch is available from the Benedictine Sisters of Perpetual Hope. The level of gluten in these hosts is extremely small (less than 37 micrograms or 0.037 milligrams per wafer). The Italian Celiac Association's scientific committee approved the use of the low gluten host. Many health professionals allow the use of this host. Some recommend consuming only 1/4 of a wafer per week. The decision of whether to use this host should be discussed with your health professional. The hosts can be purchased by contacting 1-800-223-2772 or email: altarbreads@benedictinesisters.org or write to Benedictine Sisters Altar Bread Department, 31970 State Highway P, Cyde, MO, 64432, USA. More information for Catholics with celiac disease can be found at www.catholicceliacs.org

Notes on Foods to Question

Food Category	Food Products	Notes
Meats & Alternatives	Deli/Luncheon Meats, Hot Dogs & Sausages	May contain fillers made from wheat. Seasonings may contain hydrolyzed wheat protein, wheat flour or wheat starch.
	Meat & Sandwich Spreads	Products such as pâte may contain wheat flour or seasonings containing hydrolyzed wheat protein, wheat flour or wheat starch.
	Frozen Burgers (Meat, Poultry and Fish) and Meatloaf	May contain fillers (wheat flour, wheat starch, bread crumbs). Seasonings may contain hydrolyzed wheat protein, wheat flour or wheat starch.
	Ham (ready to cook)	Glaze may contain hydrolyzed wheat protein, wheat flour or wheat starch.
	Seasoned/Flavored Fish in Pouches	May contain wheat or barley.
	Imitation Fish Products (e.g., Surimi)	Imitation crab/seafood sticks may contain fillers such as wheat starch.
	Meat Substitutes (e.g., vegetarian burgers, sausages, roasts, nuggets, textured vegetable protein)	Often contain hydrolyzed wheat protein, wheat gluten, wheat starch or barley malt.
	Flavored Egg Products (frozen or liquid)	May contain hydrolyzed wheat protein.
	Baked Beans	Some are thickened with wheat flour.
	Seasoned or Dry Roasted Nuts, Pumpkin or Sunflower Seeds	May contain hydrolyzed wheat protein, wheat flour or wheat starch.
	Flavored Tofu	May contain soy sauce (made from wheat) or other seasonings that contain hydrolyzed wheat protein, wheat flour or wheat starch.
	Tempeh	A meat substitute made from fermented soybeans and millet or rice. Often seasoned with soy sauce (made from wheat).
	Miso	A condiment used in Oriental cooking made from fermented soybeans and/or barley, wheat or rice. Wheat or barley are the most common grains used.

Notes on Foods to Question

Food Category	Food Products	Notes
Fruits & Vegetables	Dates	Chopped, diced or extruded dates are packaged with oat flour, dextrose or rice flour. Oat flour or dextrose are the most common sources used.
	French-Fried Potatoes	Often cooked in the same oil as gluten-containing foods (e.g., breaded fish and chicken fingers) resulting in cross-contamination.
Soups	Canned Soups, Dried Soup Mixes, Soup Bases & Bouillon Cubes	May contain noodles or barley. Cream soups are often thickened with wheat flour. Seasonings may contain hydrolyzed wheat protein, wheat flour or wheat starch.
Fats	Salad Dressings	May contain wheat flour, malt vinegar or soy sauce (made from wheat). Seasonings may contain hydrolyzed wheat protein, wheat flour or wheat starch.
	Suet	The hard fat around the loins and kidneys of beef and sheep. Flour may be added to packaged suet. Suet can be used to make mincemeat, steamed Christmas pudding and Haggis (a traditional Scottish dish).
Desserts	Cake Icing & Frostings	May contain wheat flour or wheat starch.
Sweets	Honey Powder	This commercial powder is used in glazes, seasoning mixes, dry mixes and sauces. May contain wheat flour or wheat starch.
	Hard Candies & Chocolates	May contain barley malt flavoring and/or wheat flour.
	Smarties®	Canadian product contains wheat flour.
	Chocolate Bars	May contain wheat flour or barley malt flavoring.
Snack Foods	Seasoned Potato Chips, Taco (corn) Chips, Nuts, Soy Nuts	Some potato chips contain wheat starch. Seasoning mixes may contain hydrolyzed wheat protein, wheat flour or wheat starch.
Beverages	Flavored or Herbal Teas Flavored Coffees	May contain barley malt flavoring. Some specialty coffees may be prepared with a chocolate chip-like product that contains cookie crumbs.
	Coffee Substitutes	Roasted chicory is the most common coffee substitute and is gluten-free. Other coffee substitutes are derived from wheat, rye, barley and/or malted barley.
	Flavored Alcoholic Cooler Beverages	May contain barley malt.
	Caesar Vodka Beverage Mix	May contain hydrolyzed wheat protein.

Notes on Foods to Question

Food Category	Food Products	Notes
Condiments/ Sauces	Specialty Prepared Mustards	Some brands contain wheat flour.
	Prepared Mustard Flour	Made from ground mustard seed, sugar, salt and spices which are gluten-free. However, some brands also contain wheat flour.
	Mustard Pickles	May contain wheat flour and/or malt vinegar.
	Worcestershire Sauce	May contain malt vinegar.
	Curry Paste	Made from the pulp of the tamarind pod and a variety of spices. Some curry pastes may also contain wheat flour or wheat starch.
	Baking Powder	Most brands contain cornstarch which is gluten-free. However, some brands contain wheat starch.

Notes on Foods to Avoid

Food Category	Food Products	Notes
Milk Products	Malted Milk	Contains malt powder derived from malted barley.
Grains	Semolina	A coarsely ground grain (usually made from the refined portion of durum wheat) that can be used to make porridge or pasta.
	Atta	A fine whole-meal flour made from low-gluten, soft texturized wheat used to make Indian flat bread. Also known as chapatti flour.
	Bulgur (Burghul)	Quick-cooking form of whole wheat. Wheat kernels that are parboiled (partially cooked), dried and then cracked. Used in soups, pilafs, stuffing or salad (e.g., Tabouli).
	Einkorn, Emmer, Farro, Kamut, Spelt	Types of wheat. Many "wheat-free" foods are made from these varieties of wheat, especially kamut and spelt. Remeber that "wheat-free" does not always mean "gluten-free."
	Triticale	A cereal grain that is a cross between wheat and rye.
	Orzo	A type of pasta that is the size and shape of rice. Used in soups and as a substitute for rice.
	Matzoh	Unleavened bread made with wheat flour and water that comes in thin sheets. Used primarily during Passover.
	Matzoh Meal	Ground matzoh.
	Matzoh Balls	Dumplings made of matzoh meal which is not gluten-free. However, can be made with potato flour which is gluten-free.
	Couscous	Granules of semolina (made from durum wheat) that are precooked and dried. Cooked couscous is served hot or cold as a dish or salad.
	Tabouli	A salad usually made with bulgur wheat or couscous which are not gluten-free. Can also be made with quinoa which is gluten-free.

Notes on Foods to Avoid

Food Category	Food Products	Notes
Meats & Alternatives	Fu	A dried gluten product derived from wheat that is sold as thin sheets or thick round cakes. Used as a protein supplement in Asian dishes such as soups and vegetables.
	Seitan	A meat-like food derived from wheat gluten used in many vegetarian dishes. Sometimes called "wheat meat."
Other	Licorice	Regular licorice contains wheat flour.
	Cereal & Malted Beverages	Contain malted barley or other grains such as wheat or rye (e.g., Postum, Ovaltine).
	Beer, Ale & Lager	Basic ingredients include malted barley, hops (a type of flower), yeast and water. As this mixture is only fermented and not distilled, it contains varying levels of gluten.
	Potato Chips	Some brands of plain potato chips contain added wheat flour and/or wheat starch.
	Soy Sauce	Many brands are a combination of soy and wheat.
	Malt Vinegar	Made from malted barley. As this vinegar is only fermented and not distilled, it contains varying levels of gluten.
	Brewer's Yeast	A dried inactive yeast that is a bitter by-product of the brewing industry. It is not commonly used as a flavoring agent in foods. ELISA tests are unable to accurately confirm the amount of residual gluten in this type of yeast.

Gluten-Free Additives and Ingredients

Additives

- Acetic Acid
- Adipic Acid
- Benzoic Acid
- BHA
- BHT
- Calcium Disodium EDTA
- Fumaric Acid
- Glucono-delta-lactone
- Lactic Acid
- Lecithin
- Malic Acid
- Mono and diglycerides
- Polysorbate 60; 80
- Propionic Acid
- Propylene Glycol
- Rennet
- Silicon Dioxide
- Sodium Benzoate
- Sodium Metabisulphite
- Sodium Nitrate
- Sodium Nitrite
- Sodium Sulphite
- Sorbate
- Sorbic Acid
- Stearic Acid
- Tartaric Acid
- Titanium Dioxide

Coloring Agents

- Natural Colors [e.g. annatto, caramel color: pg. 57, carotene, beta carotene, paprika]
- Artificial Colors [e.g., tartrazine*, sunset yellow FCF, erythrosine, citrus red No. 2, brilliant blue FCF, fast green FCF, titanium dioxide]

Flavoring Agents**

- Ethyl Maltol
- Maltol
- Monosodium Glutamate (MSG)
- Vanilla
- Vanilla Extract
- Vanilla Flavoring
- Vanillin

Sugars/Sweeteners

- Acesulfame-potassium
- Agave
- Aspartame
- Brown Sugar
- Corn Syrup/Solids
- Dextrose
- Fructose
- Glucose
- Glucose Syrup: pg. 53
- Honey
- Invert Sugar
- Isomalt
- Lactose
- Maltitol
- Maltitol Syrup
- Maltose
- Mannitol
- Molasses
- Saccharin
- Sorbitol
- Stevia
- Sucralose
- Sucrose
- White Sugar
- Xylitol

Vegetable Gums

- Acacia Gum (Gum Arabic)
- Agar (Agar-Agar)
- Algin (Alginic Acid)
- Carageenan
- Carboxymethylcellulose (Cellulose Gum)
- Carob Bean (Locust Bean)
- Guaiac Gum
- Guar Gum
- Karaya Gum
- Methylcellulose
- Tragacanth Gum
- Xanthan Gum

Miscellaneous

- Ascorbic Acid
- Autolyzed Yeast
- Baker's Yeast
- Beta Carotene
- Cream of Tartar
- Gelatin
- Lecithin
- Maltodextrin: pg. 52
- Modified Food Starches (except wheat starch) pg. 51-52
- Nutritional Yeast
- Papain
- Pectin
- Psyllium
- Starches (except wheat starch) pg. 51
- Torula Yeast

* A very small number of individuals may experience an allergic-type reaction to the yellow food color tartrazine, however this is unrelated to gluten.

** For more information on natural and artificial flavorings see pags 45-47.

Note: This is not an all-inclusive listing. For a more comprehensive listing of ingredients see the Canadian Celiac Association's *Pocket Dictionary: Acceptability of Foods and Food Ingredients for the Gluten-Free Diet* on page 314.

Hydrolyzed Plant Protein or Hydrolyzed Vegetable Protein (HPP or HVP)

- Hydrolyzed plant/vegetable proteins are used as flavoring agents in a wide variety of foods such as soups, sauces, gravies and seasoning mixtures.
- Most hydrolyzed plant proteins are made from corn, soy or wheat (or a combination of 2 or 3 plant proteins) but can be made from other protein sources such as peanut.
- Hydrolysis involves breaking down the protein by acids or enzymes. Depending on the type of hydrolysis and degree of hydrolysis, the protein is not always completely broken down, resulting in residual protein levels in the final product. It is for this reason that hydrolyzed wheat protein should be avoided.

<table>
<tr><td>USA
(Code of Federal Regulations)</td><td>Sec.102.22 Protein Hydrolysates
The common or usual name of a protein hydrolysate shall be specific to the ingredient and shall include the identity of the food source from which the protein was derived (e.g., "Hydrolyzed wheat gluten," "hydrolyzed soy protein"). The names "hydrolyzed protein" and "hydrolyzed vegetable protein" are not acceptable because they do not identify the food source of the protein.</td></tr>
<tr><td rowspan="2">CANADA
(Food & Drug Regulations)</td><td>B.01.009 (1) #30
Components of ingredients or of classes of ingredients are not required to be shown on a label of foods identified in this section of the Regulations. In this case "Hydrolyzed plant protein" is acceptable and the plant source does not have to be identified.
Note: This refers to plant proteins hydrolyzed by methods other than enzymatic (e.g., acid hydrolysis).</td></tr>
<tr><td>B.01.010 (3) (a) #8
The ingredient or component of an item shall be shown in the list of ingredients by the common name. Hydrolyzed plant protein produced by the enzymatic process must be listed "hydrolyzed" plus the "name of the plant" plus "protein" (e.g., "hydrolyzed soy protein").
Note: At the time of printing this book, recommendations for identifying the plant source of all types of hydrolyzed plant proteins and including it in the common name of the list of ingredients are being considered under the Enhanced Labelling of Priority Allergens, Gluten Sources and Sulphites in Foods.</td></tr>
</table>

Flavorings

- There are several thousand substances that can be used to flavor foods, including those derived from natural sources (e.g., fruits, vegetables, plant materials, spices, meats, fish, poultry, eggs, dairy products and yeast) and artificial sources (e.g., those obtained by chemical synthesis).
- Canadian and American food labelling regulations differ in how they define the term flavorings (see pages 46-47).
- According to flavor experts from industry and government in Canada and the USA, gluten-containing grains are not commonly used as flavoring agents. However, there are two exceptions:

1. Hydrolyzed wheat, corn and/or soy proteins can be used as "flavors" or "flavor enhancers" in a variety of foods. In Canada and the USA, they must be declared as "hydrolyzed proteins" and not hidden on the label as "flavor" or "natural flavor" [*Food and Drug Regulations* B.01.009 (3) in *Canada and Code of Federal Regulations* Sec. 101.22 (h) (7) in the USA].
2. Barley malt extract/syrup can be used as a flavoring agent and is almost always listed on the label as "barley malt," "barley malt extract" or "barley malt flavoring." Some companies may list it as "flavor (contains barley malt)" and very rarely is it listed as only "flavor" or "natural flavor." See pages 55-56 for more information on barley malt extract/syrup/flavoring.

✦ It would be rare to find a "natural or artificial flavoring" containing gluten because: (a) hydrolyzed wheat protein cannot be hidden under the term "flavor," and (b) barley malt extract or barley malt flavoring is almost always declared as "barley malt extract" or "barley malt flavoring." For this reason, most experts do not restrict natural and artificial flavorings in the gluten-free diet.

USA *(Code of Federal Regulations)*	**Sec.101.22 Foods; labeling of spices, flavorings, colorings and chemical preservatives** **(a) (1) Artificial Flavor or Artificial Flavoring:** Any substance, the function of which is to impart flavor, which is not derived from a spice, fruit or fruit juice, vegetable or vegetable juice, edible yeast, herb, bark, bud, root, leaf or similar plant material, meat, fish, poultry, eggs, dairy products, or fermentation products thereof. Artificial flavor includes the substances listed in Sec. 172.515 (b) and 182.60 [Synthetic flavoring substances and adjuvants] except where these are derived from natural sources. **(a) (3) Natural Flavor or Natural Flavoring:** The essential oil, oleoresin, essence or extractive, protein hydrolysate, distillate, or any product of roasting, heating or enzymolysis, which contains the flavoring constituents derived from a spice, fruit or fruit juice, vegetable or vegetable juice, edible yeast, herb, bark, bud, root, leaf or similar plant material, meat, seafood, poultry, eggs, dairy products, or fermentation products thereof, whose significant function in food is flavoring rather than nutritional. Natural flavors include the natural essence or extractives obtained from plants listed in Sec. 182.10, 182.20, 182.40 and 182.50 and substances listed in 172.510 [natural flavoring substances and natural substances, e.g., include flowers, roots, herbs, leaves.]
	Sec.101.22 Foods; labeling of spices, flavorings, colorings and chemical preservatives **(h) Labeling of a food to which Flavor is added:** (1) Spice, natural flavor and artificial flavor may be declared as "spice", "natural flavor" or "artificial flavor" or any combination thereof. (7) Because protein hydrolysates function in foods as both flavorings and flavor enhancers, no protein hydrolysate used in food for its effects on flavor may be declared simply as "flavor," "natural flavor" or "flavoring." The ingredients shall be declared by its specific common or usual name as provided in Sec. 102.22.

	Sec. 403 (i) (2) Spices, flavorings and colors, when used as ingredients in other foods, are exempt from a declaration of their components, except for "hypoallergenic foods " Sec. 105.62 (see page 66). **Note:** Effective January 1, 2006, the new *Food Allergen Labeling and Consumer Protection Act* requires the components of flavorings to be declared on the label if they contain any of the top eight allergens which includes wheat but not barley or rye. See pages 66-67.
CANADA *(Food & Drug Regulations)*	**B.01.010 (3) (b)** The ingredients or components may be shown in the list of ingredients by the common name. **#4 "Flavour"** One or more substances prepared for their flavouring properties and produced from animal or vegetable raw materials or from food constituents derived solely from animal or vegetable raw materials. **#5 "Artificial Flavour," "Imitation Flavour" or "Simulated Flavour"** One or more substances prepared for their flavouring properties and derived in whole or in part from components obtained by chemical synthesis. **#13 "Name of Plant or Animal Source Plus Flavour"** One or more substances the function of which is to impart flavour and that are obtained solely from the plant or animal source after which the flavour is named.
	B.01.009 (2) #2, #3 and #10 Flavouring preparations, artificial flavouring preparations and food flavour-enhancer preparations, when used as ingredients in other foods, are exempt from a declaration of their ingredients or components, except for the ingredients or components listed in B.01.009 (3) and (4).
	B.01.009 (3) Salt, glutamic acid, or its salts, including MSG, hydrolysed plant protein, aspartame, potassium chloride and any ingredient or component that performs a function in, or has any effect on, that food when present in the preparations or mixture listed in B.01.009 (2) must always be shown by their common names in the list of ingredients to which the preparation or mixture is added, as if they were ingredients of that food.
	B.01.009 (4) Peanut oil, hydrogenated peanut oil and modified peanut oil when present in the foods listed in B.01.009 (1) and the preparations and mixtures listed in B.01.009 (2) must always be listed by name in the list of ingredients. **Note:** At the time of printing this book, recommendations for identifying all cereal grains containing gluten when they are present in foods as ingredients or components in the list of ingredients are currently being considered under the *Enhanced Labelling of Priority Allergens, Gluten Sources and Sulphites in Foods*.

SPICES, HERBS AND SEASONINGS

- A wide variety of spices and herbs are used in foods for flavoring purposes.
- Canadian and American regulations have some differences in how they define the terms spices, seasonings and herbs (see pages 49-50).
- **Spices, herbs and seeds do not contain gluten.** Although an anti-caking agent may sometimes be added to spices, it is often silicon dioxide, calcium silicate or sodium aluminum silica and NOT wheat flour or wheat starch. Some imitation black peppers contain other ingredients such as buckwheat hulls and ground rice in addition to black pepper. The author has not been able to find any companies using wheat as a filler in imitation pepper or spices.
- In general terms "seasonings" are a blend of flavoring agents (e.g., spices, herbs) and an anti-caking agent (e.g., calcium silicate) which are often combined with a carrier agent (e.g., salt, sugar, lactose, whey powder, starches or flours). **The carrier agent in seasoning mixtures in gravy mixes, sauces and snack foods often contain wheat flour or wheat starch.** Seasonings are usually combined with the other dry ingredients in sauces or gravy mixes, however, snack foods are coated with the seasoning mixture, which requires a larger quantity of the carrier agent.
- If a seasoning mixture/blend is sold separately as a bottled or packaged seasoning such as Cajun Seasoning, Taco Seasoning Mix, etc., the components of ingredients must be declared. For example:

  Cajun Seasoning: Spice (including red pepper), salt, dehydrated vegetables (onion, green bell pepper, celery, garlic, parsley), sugar, hydrogenated soybean and cottonseed oil, calcium silicate, disodium inosinate and guanylate, ascorbic acid, modified cornstarch, extractives of lemon.

  Taco Seasoning: Spice (including red pepper), dehydrated onion, salt, garlic powder, hydrolyzed wheat protein, citric acid, yeast extract.
- It should be noted that, in Canada, seasoning, spice or herb mixtures, when used as ingredients in other foods are exempt from a declaration of their components (see page 50). Although it is not currently required by regulation, Health Canada strongly urges manufacturers to declare components of ingredients such as seasonings if they contain allergens or gluten sources. Fortunately many companies are voluntarily labeling the components of seasonings when used in other foods. Also, Health Canada has proposed new labeling regulations entitled *Schedule No. 1220- Enhanced Labelling of Priority Allergens, Gluten Sources and Sulphites in Foods* that would make it mandatory to declare allergen and gluten sources if used as components of ingredients (see pages 70-71).
- In the USA, effective January 1, 2006, the new *Food Allergen Labeling and Consumer Protection Act* requires that all components of ingredients when used in other foods be declared if they contain any of the top eight allergens. Also, whenever the term "seasoning" is used in the ingredient statement of a meat or poultry product, its components must be identified as a sublist. (Note: meat and poultry product labeling is under the jurisdiction of the USDA {United States Department of Agriculture}. However, if a meat or poultry product is used as an ingredient in relatively small amounts in another food product, it falls under the jurisdiction of FDA {Food and Drug Administration} in the USA).

USA *(Code of Federal Regulations)*	**Sec.101.22 (2) (a) Spices** The term spice means any aromatic vegetable substance in the whole, broken or ground form, except for those substances which have traditionally been regarded as foods, such as onions, garlic and celery; whose significant function in food is seasoning rather than nutritional; that is true to name; and from which no portion of any volatile oil or other flavoring principle has been removed. Spices include the spices listed in sec.182.10 (such as the following: allspice, anise, basil, bay leaves . . .). Paprika, turmeric and saffron or other spices which are also colors, shall be declared as "spice and coloring" unless declared by their common name.
	Sec. 170. Food Additives **Sec. 170.3 (26) Definitions** Herbs, seeds, spices, seasonings, blends, extracts and flavorings, including all natural and artificial spices, blends and flavors.
	Sec. 182.10 Spices and Other Natural Seasonings and Flavorings Spices and other natural seasonings and flavorings that are generally recognized as safe for their intended use, within the meaning of section 409 of the act, are as follows (83 items are listed by their common name and botanical name). **Sec. 403 (i) (2)** Spices, flavorings and colors, when used as ingredients in other foods are exempt from a declaration of their components (except for "hypoallergenic foods" Sec. 105.62 – see page 66). **Note:** There is no specific definition of the term "seasoning". However, sections 101.22, 170.3 and 182.10 refer to spices that act as a "seasoning agent."

CANADA *(Food & Drug Regulations)*	**B.01.010 (3) (b) #6** The ingredients or components may be shown in the list of ingredients by the common name. One or more spices, seasonings or herbs (except salt) can also be called "spices," "seasonings" or "herbs."
	B.01.009 (2) #4 & #5 Spice mixtures or seasoning or herb mixtures, when used as ingredients in other foods are exempt from a declaration of their components except for those ingredients or components listed in B.01.009 (3) and (4).
	B.01.009 (3) Salt, glutamic acid, or its salts, including MSG, hydrolyzed plant protein, aspartame, potassium chloride and any ingredient or component that performs a function in, or has any effect on, that food when present in the preparations or mixture listed in B.01.009 (2) must always be shown by their common names in the list of ingredients to which the preparation or mixture is added, as if they were ingredients of that food.
	B.01.009 (4) Peanut oil, hydrogenated peanut oil and modified peanut oil when present in the foods listed in B.01.009 (1) and the preparations and mixtures listed in B.01.009 (2) must always be listed by name in the list of ingredients. **Note:** 1. There is no specific definition of the term seasoning. 2. The class name "seasoning" is permitted if a seasoning mixture is added to a food at 2% or less of weight of the final product. 3. At the time of printing this book, recommendations for identifying all cereal grains containing gluten when they are present in foods as ingredients or components in the list of ingredients are currently being considered under the *Enhanced Labelling of Priority Allergens, Gluten Sources and Sulphites in Foods*.

References

- Author's personal communication with the Canadian Flavour Manufacturers Association (CFMA), United States Flavor and Extract Manufacturers Association (FEMA), various manufacturers in Canada and the USA, Canadian Food Inspection Agency (CFIA), Health Canada (HC) and the Food and Drug Administration (FDA).
- Tainter D, Grenis A. *Spices and Seasonings in Food Technology Handbook*, John Wiley and Sons, New York, 2001; pages 198-232.
- *Gluten Free Living* magazine. November/December 2000; Vol. 5, No. 6.

STARCHES

- Starches are used as a thickening agent; binding agent; and carrier agent (especially in seasonings).
- A variety of starches can be used in foods such as corn, waxy maize, potato, milo (sorghum), waxy milo, potato, tapioca, arrowroot, rice, wheat, etc.
- The single word "starch" on a food label in Canada and the USA refers to "cornstarch."
- When other starches such as potato, tapioca or wheat are used in food products, the source of the starch must be declared.
- **Wheat starch must be avoided due to residual gluten levels.**

USA *(Compliance Policy Guideline)*	**CPG Sec. 578.100** There is no standard identity for food starches in the *Code of Federal Regulations*. However the CPG Sec. 578.100 provides guidelines for the labeling of starches. **Sec. 578.100 Starches** The single word "starch" on a food label is considered the common or usual name for starch made from corn; alternatively, the name "cornstarch" may be used. Starches from other sources should be designated by some non-misleading term that indicates the source of such starch, for example, "potato starch", "wheat starch", or "tapioca starch."
CANADA *(Food & Drug Regulations)*	Starches are presently required to be identified by plant source on the food label except cornstarch, which can be called "cornstarch" or just "starch" made from maize. **B.13.011 [S]** cornstarch shall be starch made from maize.

MODIFIED FOOD STARCHES

- A common ingredient in foods used as a texture stabilizing agent; thickener or binding agent; anti-caking agent.
- A starch that has been chemically modified to alter its physical properties.
- Modified food starches can be made from corn, waxy maize, tapioca, potato, wheat or other starches.
- In North America, modified corn, waxy maize and potato are the most common sources, with tapioca and wheat used occasionally.
- Wheat starch is used more frequently in European countries. A special type of modified wheat starch is used in some European gluten-free products. However, wheat starch is not permitted in food labeled gluten-free in Canada. There is debate within the scientific community as to the safety of gluten-free products using this special type of wheat starch. The concern is that not all traces of protein can be removed during the processing of wheat starch, resulting in various levels of residual gluten. See references on wheat starch on pages 57-58 and background information on pages 62-63. **Further research is necessary to determine what level of gluten is safe for people with celiac disease, including the use of wheat starch.**

USA *(Code of Federal Regulations)*	**Sec. 172.892 Food Starch – Modified** Regulations for how food starches may be modified. However, there is no requirement for the identification of the name of the plant source of the modified food starch. **Note:** Effective January 1, 2006 the new *Food Allergen Labeling and Consumer Protection Act* requires the top eight allergens (which includes wheat) to be declared on all product labels. If wheat is used in modified food starch it must be declared on the label as modified wheat starch or modified food starch (wheat).
CANADA *(Food & Drug Regulations)*	There is no requirement for the identification of the name of the plant source of the modified food starch. **Note:** At the time of printing this book, recommendations for identifying the plant source of all types of starches and modified starches and including them in the list of ingredients are being considered under the *Enhanced Labelling of Priority Allergens, Gluten Sources and Sulphites in Foods.*

MALTODEXTRIN

- It is used as an anti-caking and free-flowing agent, formulation aid, processing aid, carrier agent for flavors, bulking agent, stabilizer and thickener, or surface-finishing agent in a wide variety of foods.
- Maltodextrin is a purified, concentrated, non-sweet nutritive mixture of saccharide polymers obtained by hydrolysis of edible starch.
- Can be derived from different starches such as corn, waxy maize, potato, rice or wheat.
- Corn, waxy maize or potato are the most common sources in North America.
- Wheat-based maltodextrin is used more frequently in Europe and is now being used in a few North American products. **Although maltodextrin may be derived from wheat, it is highly processed and purified (significantly more than modified food starches) and rendered gluten-free.** North American and European scientists using the most sensitive, scientifically validated R5 ELISA Tests have not detected gluten in wheat-based maltodextrin.

USA *(Code of Federal Regulations)*	**Sec. 184.1444 Maltodextrin** CAS Reg. No. 9050-36-6. It is a nonsweet nutritive saccharide polymer that consists of D-glucose units linked primarily by [alpha]-1-4 bonds and has a dextrose equivalent (DE) of less than 20. It is prepared as a white powder or concentrated solution by partial hydrolysis of cornstarch, potato starch or rice starch with safe and suitable acids and enzymes. **Note:** FDA also permits the use of other starches including wheat. For example, if wheat is used it must be labeled "wheat maltodextrin".
CANADA *(Food & Drug Regulations)*	There is no standard for maltodextrin. The Food Chemical Codex is often used as a guide, however, different starches can be used. Food companies are strongly encouraged to indicate the source if it is from the major food allergens such as wheat.

DEXTRIN

- It is used as a thickener; colloidal stabilizer; binder or surface finishing agent in cosmetics, medications and industrial applications. Not commonly used in foods.
- Dextrin is starch partially hydrolyzed by heat alone or by heating in the presence of suitable food-grade acids and buffers from any of several grain or root-based native (unmodified) starches (e.g., corn, waxy maize, milo, waxy milo, potato, arrowroot, wheat, rice, tapioca, sago, etc.).
- Usually made from corn or tapioca, although occasionally it can be derived from wheat.
- As dextrin is only partially hydrolyzed, there is residual protein in the final product. **Wheat-based dextrin when used in foods must be avoided due to residual gluten levels.**

USA *(Code of Federal Regulations)*	**Sec. 184.1277 Dextrin** Definition is based on the Food Chemical Codex CAS Reg. 9004-53-9. **Note:** Effective January 1, 2006 the new *Food Allergen Labeling and Consumer Protection Act* requires the top 8 allergens (which includes wheat) to be declared on all product labels. If wheat is used in dextrin it must be declared as wheat dextrin or dextrin (wheat).
CANADA *(Food & Drug Regulations)*	**Division 18** Although dextrin does not appear in the standards for Sweetening Agents of Division 18, it is considered a food ingredient of this category.

GLUCOSE SYRUP

- Used extensively in foods for sweetening, browning, texture-modification, bulking, moisture control and enhancing shelf-life of various foods.
- Can be derived from a variety of starches such as corn, tapioca, potato, wheat, sorghum or rice.
- Corn is the most common source in North America, whereas wheat starch is more commonly used in Europe.
- Glucose syrups are highly processed and purified in order to separate and remove the protein from the starch mixture. Enzymes (usually fungal or bacterial) are then added to break down the starch to form the glucose syrup. **Although glucose syrup can be made from wheat, the processing renders it gluten-free.** This has been verified by scientists and research centers in Europe, Australia and other countries using the highly sensitive R5 ELISA tests.

USA *(Code of Federal Regulations)*	**Sec. 168.120 Glucose Sirup** a) Glucose sirup is the purified, concentrated, aqueous solution of nutritive saccharides obtained from edible starch. c) The name of the food is "Glucose Sirup". When the food is derived from a specific type of starch, the name may alternatively be "___ sirup", the blank to be filled in with the name of the starch. For example, "corn sirup," "wheat sirup," "tapioca sirup." When the starch is derived from sorghum grain, the alternative name of the food is "sorghum grain sirup." The word "sirup" may also be spelled "syrup."
	Sec. 184.1865 Corn Syrup a) Corn syrup, commonly called "glucose sirup" or "glucose syrup" is obtained by partial hydrolysis of corn starch with safe and suitable acids or enzymes. It may also occur in the dehydrated form (dried glucose sirup). Depending on the degree of hydrolysis, corn syrup may contain, in addition to glucose, maltose and higher saccharides.
CANADA *(Food & Drug Regulations)*	**B.18.016 [S] Glucose or Glucose Syrup** a) shall be the purified concentrated solution of nutritive saccharides obtained from the incomplete hydrolysis by means of acid or enzymes, of starch or a starch-containing substance;
	B.18.017 [S] Glucose Solids or Dried Glucose Syrup a) shall be glucose or glucose syrup from which the water has been partially removed;

RICE SYRUP

✦ Consumers and the food industry use this type of glucose syrup as a substitute for sugar, honey or other refined sweeteners. Like other starch-based syrups, rice syrups are used for other functions in addition to sweetening such as browning, texture modification, bulking, controlling moisture and enhancing shelf-life of various foods.

✦ Used in rice drinks, snack bars, cereals, baked goods and other foods.

✦ There are several different types of rice syrups available.

✦ Can be made from brown or white rice and the addition of laboratory-produced enzymes (bacterial or fungal), Koji enzymes (cultured rice made from rice and koji mold spores) or barley malt enzymes. Rice, water and the enzymes are gently heated which causes the starch, protein and fat to be broken down. This mixture is processed and slowly cooked to produce a thick, sweet syrup. Unlike glucose syrups which are derived only from the starch component of grains and are highly processed, rice syrup is derived from the grain (brown rice syrup is from the whole grain including the fiber) and is less processed. As a result, rice syrup, especially brown rice syrup contains a small amount of protein, vitamins and minerals.

✦ **Most rice syrups in North America are gluten-free as they are made using bacterial or fungal enzymes. Occasionally it is made with barley malt enzymes which may contain very low levels of residual gluten.**

✦ Rice syrup is sometimes referred to as "rice malt." However the rice does not undergo the process of germination/sprouting as in malted barley. Instead, the rice is cooked with an enzyme preparation to break down the starch into a syrup.

BARLEY MALT

- Used in the production of malted beverages (e.g., beer, ale, lager and malted milk), distilled alcoholic beverages and malt vinegar. May also be used in doughs to increase the fermentation rate and improve baking properties.
- Barley malt can be further processed into various extracts/syrups (see below).
- Derived from whole-grain barley that has been soaked, germinated (sprouted) and dried.
- A very wide variety of malts in many different flavors and colors can be produced by altering the length of time and temperature of the drying process. Brewer's malts contain higher amounts of active enzymes, starches and sugars used for the fermentation process. Specialty malts contain lower amounts of enzymes and sugars available for fermentation and are used more for flavoring agents.
- Available as a powder or liquid.
- **Contains varying levels of gluten.**

BARLEY MALT EXTRACT/BARLEY MALT SYRUP

- These terms are often used interchangeably.
- Malt extract/syrup is used by both the brewing and food industries. During the brewing of beer, it is added for specific flavoring and coloring properties. Food companies also use malt extract/syrup in many foods such as cereals and granola, baked products, crackers, cookies and beverages.
- Malt extract/syrup is derived from a mixture of malted barley and water that is steeped, mashed, filtered and then evaporated to remove the excess water, resulting in a sweet, viscous liquid containing approximately 75-80% solids. Because malt extract/syrup is made from the whole-grain malted barley, it contains proteins and free amino acids, nutritive carbohydrates, phytochemicals, vitamins and minerals. These constituents increase the nutritional value of malt extract compared to starch-based glucose syrups (e.g., corn, wheat) that are highly processed and void of these nutritional components. It is these nutritional constituents in barley malt extract that account for its fermentation and browning properties.
- To reduce the cost of barley malt extract/syrup, some companies use a combination of malted barley and malted corn. However, this must be labeled as "extract of malted barley and corn" and not "malt extract/syrup."
- Available as a powder or liquid.
- **Contains varying levels of gluten.**

USA *(Code of Federal Regulations)*	**Sec.184.1443a Malt** (a) Malt is an enzyme preparation obtained from barley which has been softened by a series of steeping operations and germinated under controlled conditions. It is a brown, sweet, and viscous liquid or a white to tan powder. Its characterizing enzyme activities are [alpha]-amylase and [beta]-amylase. (c)(1) The ingredient is used as an enzyme as defined in Sec. 170.3(o)(9) of this chapter to hydrolyze starch or starch-derived polysaccharides.
	Sec. 184.1445 Malt Syrup (malt extract) (a) Malt is the product of barley (Hordeum vulgare L.) germinated under controlled conditions. Malt syrup and malt extract are interchangeable terms for a viscous concentrate of water extract of germinated barley grain, with or without added safe preservative. Malt syrup is usually a brown, sweet and viscous liquid containing varying amounts of amylolytic enzymes and plant constituents. Barley is first softened after cleaning by steeping operations and then allowed to germinate under controlled conditions. The germinated grain then undergoes processing, such as drying, grinding, extracting, filtering and evaporating, to produce malt syrup (malt extract) with 75-80% solids or dried malt syrup with higher solids content. The ingredient is used as a flavoring agent and adjuvant as defined in Sec. 170.3(o) (12) of this chapter.
	Compliance Policy Guide 7105.02 Sec. 515.200 Malt Extract; Malt Syrup; Malted Cereal Syrup; Liquid Malt; Dried Malt Policy: The designation "malt extract" and "malt syrup" should be used only for concentrated water infusions of malt, with or without added safe preservative. The terms "malt extract" and "malt syrup" unqualified should be applied only to products prepared from barley. If any other malted grain is used, the extract or syrup may be designated by a specific name such as "extract of malted barley and corn." The term "liquid malt" is considered false and misleading as applied to mixtures of malt extract or malt syrup with corn syrup or other substances which are not normal constituents of malt extract.

BARLEY MALT FLAVORING

- Malt flavoring can be made from barley malt extract/syrup; a combination of barley malt extract/syrup and corn syrup; or synthetic ingredients not derived from barley.
- Most companies use a combination of barley malt extract/syrup AND corn syrup.
- Contains less gluten than barley malt and barley malt extract/syrup as it is usually mixed with corn syrup and is used in smaller amounts than pure barley malt or barley malt extract/syrup. **Nevertheless, it still must also be avoided as it contains varying levels of gluten.** For example, corn and rice cereals with barley malt flavoring have recently been tested and found to contain over 200 ppm (see pages 63-64, 68 on testing of foods in gluten and measurement levels).

CARAMEL COLOR

- Used extensively in a wide variety of food and beverages such as baked products and mixes, cereals, snack foods, soups, sauces, gravies, spice blends, processed meat products, soft drinks and alcoholic beverages (e.g., beer, whiskey, rum and liqueurs) as a coloring agent. Can also act as a flavor enhancer.
- Produced by carefully controlled heat treatment of food-grade nutritive sweeteners consisting of fructose, dextrose (glucose), invert sugar, sucrose and/or starch hydrolysates and fractions thereof in the presence of food-grade acids, alkalis and/or salts.
- There are many types of caramel color on the market ranging from tannish yellow to reddish brown to nearly black with an odor of burnt sugar and a pleasant but slightly bitter taste.
- Although gluten-containing ingredients (barley malt syrup and starch hydrolysates) can be used in the production of caramel color, North American companies use corn as it has a longer shelf life and makes a superior product. European companies use glucose syrup derived from wheat starch, however **caramel color is highly processed and contains no gluten.**

USA *(Code of Federal Regulations)*	**Sec. 73.85 Caramel** (a) Identity. (1) The color additive caramel is the dark-brown liquid or solid material resulting from the carefully controlled heat treatment of the following food-grade carbohydrates: dextrose, invert sugar, lactose, malt sirup, molasses, starch hydrolysates and fractions thereof, sucrose. (2) The food-grade acids, alkalis, and salts listed in this subparagraph may be employed to assist caramelization, in amounts consistent with good manufacturing practice. (c) Uses and restrictions. Caramel may be safely used for coloring foods generally, in amounts consistent with good manufacturing practice, except that it may not be used to color foods for which standards of identity have been promulgated under section 401 of the act unless added color is authorized by such standards.

References and Information Sources for Starches, Maltodextrin, Dextrin, Glucose Syrup, Rice Syrup, Barley Malt and Caramel Color

- Canadian Celiac Association *Pocket Dictionary: Acceptability of Foods and Food Ingredients for the Gluten-Free Diet* (Second edition) 2005.
- Caballero B., Trugo C.L, Finglas P.M., *Encyclopedia of Food Sciences and Nutrition*, Academic Press, Elsevier Science Ltd., 2003
- Valdes L, García E, Llorente M, Méndez E. Innovative approach to low-level gluten determination in foods using a novel sandwich enzyme-linked immunosorbent assay protocol. *Eur J Gastroenterol Hepatol* 2003; 15:465-474.
- Collin P, Thorell L, Kaukinen K, Mäki M. The safe threshold for gluten contamination in gluten-free products. Can trace amounts be accepted in the treatment of coeliac disease? *Aliment Pharmacol Ther* 2004; 19: 1277-1283.
- Chartrand L, Russo P, Duhaime A, Seidman E. Wheat starch intolerance in patients with celiac disease. *J Am Diet Assoc* 1997; 97: 612-618.

- Thompson T. Wheat starch, gliadin, and the gluten-free diet. *J Am Diet Assoc* 2001; 101:1456-1459.
- Inclusion of wheat starch-based gluten-free foods in a dietary pattern for people with celiac disease. American Dietetic Association Evidence Analysis Library. Accessed November 25, 2005. www.adaevidencelibrary.com
- CAS Reg. No. 9050-36-6 (maltodextrin), CAS Reg. No. 9004-53-8 (dextrin) and CAS Reg. No. 8028-89-5 (caramel color) in the Food Chemical Codex, Fourth Edition, 1996, National Academy Press, Washington, DC, USA
- Association des Amidonneeries de Céréales de l'Union Européene. Industry views. Accessed December 2, 2005. http://www.aac-eu.org/html/industry.html
- Opinion of the Scientific Panel on Dietetic Products, Nutrition and Allergies, European Food Safety Authority. EFSA-Q-2004-091 and 092. Accessed December 2, 2005 http://www.efsa.eu.int/science/nda/nda_opinions/catindex_en.html
- List of food ingredients and substances provisionally excluded from Annex IIIa of Directive 2000/13/EC, Commission Directive 2005/26EC of March 21, 2005. Accessed December 2, 2005.
  http://europa.eu.int/eur-lex/lex/LexUriServ/site/en/oj/2005/l_075/l_07520050322en00330034.pdf
- Email correspondence with Dr. Sue Hefle, Associate Professor and Program Co-Director, Food Allergy Research and Resource Program, University of Nebraska, Lincoln, NE.
- Email correspondence with G. Rizzetto, Assistant Regulatory Affairs Manager, Association des Amidonneeries de Céréales de l'Union Européene.
- Email correspondence with Mr. Philippe Looten, Manager of Quality Assurance, Roquette, Cedex, France.
- Email correspondence with Mr. Graham Price, Technical Officer, The Celiac Society of Australia.
- Is maltodextrin still safe? *Gluten-Free Living* magazine, 2003; Vol. 8, No. 2.
- Glucose syrup "sweet" for celiacs. *Gluten-Free Living* magazine, 2004;Vol, 9, No. 2.
- Telephone and email correspondence with Mr. Bob Hansen, Manager of Technical Services, Briess Malt and Ingredient Company, Chilton, WI. www.briess.com
- Gélinas, P. Analysis of gluten-free products. Report prepared for the Fondation Québécoise de la maladie Coeliaque (FQMC) and the Canadian Celiac Assocation. Presented on October 1, 2005 at the Annual Meeting of the FQMC, Saint-Hyacinthe, Québec, Canada. See www.fqmc.org/content/view/334/70/
- Kamuf W, Nixon A, Parker L, Barnum GC. Overview of Caramel Colors. *Cereal Foods World*. 2003; 48: 64-69.
- Telephone correspondence with D.D. Williamson and Co. Inc. Further information also accessed on website at www.caramel.com on December 5, 2005.
- Molloy M. What is the difference between caramel colour and caramel flavour? Are they gluten-free? *Canadian Celiac Association Newsletter*, 1997. Winter Edition, page 4.
- Round up the usual suspects including caramel color. *Gluten Free Living* magazine. November/December 2000; Vol. 5, No. 6.

Labeling of Foods and Food Ingredients

Most countries have specific regulations and guidelines for the labeling of food products. Development, revision and enforcement of these regulations often falls under different jurisdictions within various government departments. The following is a summary of American and Canadian regulations, including web links for more detailed information.

USA

Together, the Food and Drug Administration (FDA) of the United States (U.S.) Department of Health and Human Services and the Food Safety and Inspection Service (FSIS) of the U.S. Department of Agriculture (USDA) have regulatory authority over most of the food supply. In addition, the Alcohol and Tobacco Tax and Trade Bureau, U.S. Department of Treasury, regulates wines that contain 7% or more alcohol by volume and all distilled spirits and malt beverages, irrespective of their alcohol content.

The *Federal Food, Drug, and Cosmetic Act* is the major law that provides the Secretary of Health and Human Services the authority to regulate the vast majority of foods marketed in the U.S., excluding those under the jurisdiction of other Federal Departments. The *Federal Meat Inspection Act*, the *Poultry Products Inspection Act* and the *Egg Products Inspection Act* collectively provide the Secretary of Agriculture authority to regulate meat, poultry and processed egg products. When meat, poultry and processed egg products are used as ingredients in relatively small amounts in other food products, those other food products fall under the jurisdiction of FDA. To reduce confusion about jurisdiction, the FSIS and FDA are currently examining this issue and seeking input from various stakeholders in order to develop clear and consistent rules about product categorization and agency jurisdiction.

The FSIS meat, poultry and egg product regulations, along with other labeling policies and guidelines can be accessed at these links:

http://www.fsis.usda.gov/Regulations_&_Policies/Acts_&_Authorizing_Statutes/index.asp

http://www.fsis.usda.gov/Regulations_&_Policies/Ingredients_Guidance/index.asp

http://www.fsis.usda.gov/OPPDE/larc/Policies/Labeling_Policy_Book_082005.pdf

http://www.fsis.usda.gov/about/labeling_&_consumer_protection/index.asp

Title 21 of the *Code of Federal Regulations* (CFR) represents the regulations of the FDA. Title 21 CFR Parts 100-199 contain FDA's food-related regulations and Part 101 contains most of the FDA's food labeling regulations that can be accessed at the following link by scrolling down to find Title 21 *Food and Drugs*:

http://www.access.gpo.gov/nara/cfr/cfr-table-search.html#page1

In addition to food labeling regulations in 21 CFR the new *Food Allergen Labeling and Consumer Protection Act of 2004* (FALCPA), enacted on August 2, 2004, requires the eight major food allergens that are used as ingredients to be declared in plain English terms on the label of all prepackaged foods under FDA's purview. See pages 66-67, as well as Section 203 of FALCPA at the following link for further information:

http://www.cfsan.fda.gov/~dms/alrgact.html

A major food allergen is defined by FALCPA to be one of the following eight foods/food groups or an ingredient that contains a protein derived from them: milk, egg, fish, crustacean shellfish, tree nuts, wheat, peanuts and soybeans. FALCPA labeling requirements do not apply to raw agricultural commodities and the law excludes from its definition of a major food allergen: 1) highly refined oils and ingredients defined from them and 2) ingredients exempt under a petition or notification process described in the new law. FDA guidance materials on FALCPA for industry and consumers can also be accessed at FDA's *Information About Food Allergens* website at:

http://www.cfsan.fda.gov/~dms/wh-alrgy.html

Canada

The *Food and Drugs Act* regulates foods, drugs, cosmetics and medical devices. Health Canada (HC) and the Canadian Food Inspection Agency (CFIA) share administration of the *Food and Drugs Act*. HC is responsible for establishing policies and standards relating to safety and nutritional quality of foods sold in Canada. CFIA is involved in the development of regulations and policies related to food labeling and quality and composition standards. The CFIA is also responsible for all food inspection, compliance and enforcement activities of the *Food and Drugs Act, Consumer Packaging and Labelling Act, Agriculture and Agri-Food Administrative Monetary Penalties Act, Canada Agricultural Products Act, Feeds Act, Fertilizers Act, Fish Inspection Act, Health of Animals Act, Meat Inspection Act, Plant Breeders' Rights Act, Plant Protection Act and Seeds Act* and all of their associated regulations.

Further information about the FDR and CFIA can be found at these links:

http://www.hc-sc.gc.ca/fn-an/legislation/acts-lois/index_e.html

http://laws.justice.gc.ca/en/C-16.5/30783.html

http://www.inspection.gc.ca/english/toc/labetie.shtml

Health Canada is proposing to amend the *Food and Drug Regulations* to enhance the labeling of priority allergens, gluten sources and sulphites in foods. For more information see page 70, 71 and the following links:

http://www.hc-sc.gc.ca/fn-an/label-etiquet/allergen/allergy_label_letter-lettre_etiquetage_alergene_e.html

http://www.hc-sc.gc.ca/fn-an/label-etiquet/allergen/allergy_label_letter-lettre_etiquetage_alergene_2004_09_27_e.html

http://www.inspection.gc.ca/english/fssa/invenq/inform/20041018e.shtml

http://www.hc-sc.gc.ca/fn-an/label-etiquet/allergen/index_e.html

http://www.hc-sc.gc.ca/fn-an/securit/allerg/cfia-acia/allergen_paper-evaluation_allergene-03_e.html

Gluten-Free Labeling

There is no single world-wide definition for the term "gluten-free." Some countries have specific gluten-free labeling regulations that identify which foods and ingredients are allowed and not allowed on a gluten-free diet; what terminology and symbols can be used on the product label; and acceptable levels of gluten. Unfortunately these regulations vary considerably from one country to another, resulting in confusion within the celiac community. For example, some European countries and the United Kingdom (U.K.) allow gluten-free foods to be made from gluten-containing ingredients such as wheat starch that has been specially processed to remove significant amounts of gluten (see page 51 on wheat starch). Other countries such as Canada, Australia and Italy do not allow wheat starch to be used in foods labeled gluten-free. Currently in the United States (U.S.) there is no specific definition for the term gluten-free and what ingredients cannot be used in products labeled gluten-free. However, to comply with a directive in the new *Food Allergen Labeling and Consumer Protection Act of 2004* (FALCPA), the Food and Drug Administration (FDA) plans to issue a proposed rule in August 2006 to define the food-labeling term gluten-free. The final rule to establish a regulatory definition for the term gluten-free in the U.S. is not expected until August 2008 (see pages 66-67).

There are two major reasons why it has been very difficult to develop a universal standard for gluten-free. One is the limited scientific data on a safe threshold level of gluten for people with celiac disease. The other has been a lack of an accurate, consistently reproducible analytical method that has undergone a multi-laboratory validation for the detection and quantification of gluten in food products. However, the latter has been recently addressed with the development of the new R5 enzyme-linked immunosorbent assay (ELISA) test (see pages 63-65). In spite of these challenges, a number of organizations and countries have developed standards, regulations and/or guidelines for foods labeled gluten-free.

The following is a summary of some of the gluten-free standards and regulations which have been developed internationally and nationally.

Codex Alimentarius Commission

The World Health Organization (WHO) and the Food and Agriculture Organization (FAO) in 1963 formed an international group called the Codex Alimentarius Commission with a mandate to develop internationally agreed upon food standards to ensure fair trade practices. This organization includes representatives from many countries around the world including the U.S., Canada, most European countries, Africa, Asia and Latin America, however, not all participating countries adopt the standards developed by the Commission and many have their own standards and specific regulations.

The Codex Committee on Nutrition and Foods for Special Dietary Uses (CX/NFSDU) developed a standard for gluten-free foods in 1976 which was adopted in 1981. This standard is referred to as Codex Stan 118-1981. In 1983 amendments to the section on labeling of this standard were adopted. Key components of this standard are found on page 62. There have been further proposed revisions to the Codex Proposed Draft Revised Standard for Gluten-Free Foods which is currently at Step 7 of an 8-step process as of March 2006 (see pages 63-64).

Codex Standard for "Gluten-Free Foods"

Codex Stan 118-1981 (amended 1983)

1. Scope

1.1 This standard applies to those processed foods which have been specially prepared to meet the dietary needs of persons intolerant to gluten.

1.2 The standard refers only to the specific provisions related to the special dietary purpose for which these foods are intended.

1.3 This standard does not apply to foods which in their normal form do not contain gluten.

2. Description

2.1 **Definition**

Gluten-free food is a food so described:

(a) consisting of or containing as ingredients such cereals as wheat, triticale, rye, barley or oats, or their constituents, which have been rendered "gluten-free"; or

(b) in which any ingredients normally present containing "gluten" have been substituted by other ingredients not containing "gluten."

2.2 **Subsidiary Definition**

2.2.1 For the purpose of this standard, gluten is defined as those proteins commonly found in wheat, triticale, rye, barley or oats to which some persons are intolerant.

2.2.2 For the purpose of this standard, gluten-free means that the total nitrogen content of gluten-containing cereal grains used in the product does not exceed 0.05 g per 100 grammes of these grains on a dry matter basis.

3. Essential Composition and Quality Factors

3.1 A ***gluten-free food*** shall be based on or shall contain:

(a) gluten-containing cereals such as wheat, triticale, rye, barley or oats or their constituents, which have been rendered "gluten-free": according to Section 2.2.2; or

(b) ingredients which do not contain gluten in substitution for the ingredients containing gluten which are normally used in food of that kind; or

(c) any mixture of two or more ingredients as in (a) or (b).

To read the entire standard see **www.codexalimentarius.net/web/standard_list.do** Once at the web link click on Codex Stan 118 and then open the pdf.

The Codex Stan 118-1981 applies to products made from **gluten-containing grains** that were specially processed to remove most of the toxic protein fraction from the starch component. The nitrogen content for this earlier definition was based upon analyses that use an indirect method to determine the protein content of cereals and wheat starch. Section 2.2.2 states that the nitrogen content of the grain used in the product must not exceed 0.05 grams per 100 grams of grain on a dry-matter basis. At the time when this Codex definition was established, the newer ELISA-based methods for detecting and estimating the gluten content of foods were not available. Using earlier methodology, it was estimated that specially prepared wheat starch used in gluten-free foods that met this Codex standard could contain approximately 40-60 mg of gluten per 100 grams, which is equivalent to 20-30 mg gliadin or 200 to 300 ppm gliadin.

There are now more sensitive tests available for analyzing the gluten content of foods. One such method is the new highly sensitive and specific R5 ELISA test, developed by Enrique Mendez from Spain, which can detect and quantify the specific prolamins (gliadin in wheat, secalin in rye and hordein in barley) to levels as low as 3.2 ppm gluten. To put this in perspective, 1 slice of white bread (20grams) contains approximately 2.5 grams of gluten which is equivalent to 125,000 ppm gluten (62,500 ppm gliadin). For information on how to calculate these conversions see pages 64, 68.

The Working Group on Prolamin Analysis and Toxicity (WGPAT) of the Codex Committee on Nutrition and Foods For Special Dietary Uses (CX/NFSDU) report of October 2003 recommended that the R5 ELISA test be evaluated by the Codex Committee on Methods of Analysis and Sampling (CCMAS). In 2004 the CCMAS agreed to temporarily endorse the R5 ELISA method test for the determination of gluten as a Type I method. They informed the CX/NFSDU of this decision along with the need to make an amendment to the Proposed Draft Revised Standard for Gluten-Free Foods *at Step 7* to insert the word "gluten" after "10 ppm" in section 6.2 of the Standard (see below). The CX/NFSDU approved this amendment at their November 2004 meeting.

Although the testing issue has been addressed, the limited research on a safe threshold level of gluten for people with celiac disease continues to make it a challenge to establish a specific level of gluten in the standard. As of March 2006, this standard continues to be under consideration for further revisions and discussion by the CX/NFSDU.

Proposed Draft Revised Standard for Gluten-Free Foods *at Step 7*

(Alinorm 03/27/26, Appendix III)

1. **Scope**

    1.1 This standard applies to those foodstuffs and ingredients which have been especially processed or prepared to meet the dietary needs of persons intolerant to gluten.

    1.2 The standard refers only to the special dietary purpose for which these foodstuffs and ingredients are intended.

2. **Description**

    2.1 Definition

    Gluten-free foodstuffs so described:

    a) consisting of or made only from ingredients which do not contain any prolamins from wheat or all *Triticum* species such as spelt (Triticum spelta L.), kamut (Triticum polonicum L.), or durum wheat, rye, barley, [oats], or their crossbred varieties with a gluten level not exceeding [20 ppm] or,

    b) consisting of ingredients from wheat, rye, barley, oats, spelt or their crossbred varieties, which have been rendered "gluten-free"; with a level of gluten not exceeding [200 ppm]; or

    (c) any mixture of ingredients of the two ingredients as in a) and b) with a gluten level not exceeding [200 ppm]

2.2 Subsidiary Definitions:

2.2.1 Gluten

For the purpose of this standard "gluten" is defined as a protein fraction from wheat, rye, barley, [oats] or their crossbred varieties and derivatives thereof, to which some persons are intolerant and that is insoluble in water and 0.5M NaCl.

2.2.2 Prolamins

Prolamins are defined as the fraction from gluten that can be extracted by 40-70% of ethanol. The prolamin from wheat is gliadin, from rye is secalin, from barley hordein and from oats avenin. It is however an established custom to speak of gluten sensitivity. The prolamin content of gluten is generally taken as 50%.

6. General outline of the method of analysis and sampling:

6.1 Determination of gluten

Enzyme-Linked Immunoassay R5 Mendez (ELISA) Method

6.2 Determination of gluten in foodstuffs and ingredients

Methods used for determination should be traceable and calibrated against an internationally accepted standard, if available. The detection limit has to be appropriate according to the state of the art and the technical standard. The quantitative determination of gluten in foodstuffs and ingredients shall be based on an immunologic method. The antibody to be used should react with the cereals that are toxic for persons sensitive to gluten and should not cross-react with other cereals or other constituents of the foodstuffs and ingredients. The qualitative analysis as indicating presence of protein shall be based on DNA-methods or other relevant methods. The detection limit of the method should be at least **10 ppm** gluten in the product on a dry matter basis.

To read the entire standard (including sections 3-5) see **www.codexalimentarius.net** and click on past reports and then choose the 27th session of the Codex Alimentarius and 25th session of the CX/NFSDU. It is found on page 42 and 43 of Alinorm 03/27/26.

The items in the square brackets [ ] pertain to the specified gluten levels and inclusion of oats which are still pending until there is further information and consensus. The two proposed gluten levels of 20 ppm and 200 ppm were developed in order to accommodate different views of Codex member countries on the gluten limit in gluten-free foods that would be adequately protective of sensitive people with celiac disease. It should be noted, however, that there is limited clinical scientific data on safe threshold levels. The current figures of 20 ppm (20 mg/kg) and 200 ppm (200 mg/kg) do not represent values that are supported by a consensus of scientific opinion and do not include any safety factor. As a result, the standard is still under discussion and in the proposed draft format.

Gluten Equivalents*

mg/100 g	mg/kg	ppm
2	20	20
20	200	200
* 2 mg/100 g = 20 mg/kg = 20 ppm		

References

- Codex Alimentarius Reports of CX/NFSDU, CCMAS and WGPAT available at www.codexalimentarius.net
- Joint FAO/WHO Food Standards Program. Codex Alimentarius Commission. Codex Standard for "gluten-free foods". Codex Stan 118-1981. Codex Alimentarius. 1994; 4:100-103.
- Joint FAO/WHO Food Standards Program. Codex Committee on Nutrition and Foods for Special Dietary Uses. Draft revised standard for gluten-free foods. CX/NFSDU 98/4. July, 1998:1- 4.
- Joint FAO/WHO Food Standards Program. Report of the Working Group on Prolamin Analysis and Toxicity (WGPAT) of the Codex Committee on Nutrition and Foods for Special Dietary Uses. CX/NFSDU 03/4. October, 2003.
- Joint FAO/WHO Food Standards Program. Codex Alimentarius. Codex Committee on Nutrition and Foods for Special Dietary Uses. Report of the 25th Session of the CX/NFSDU in Bonn, Germany, 3-7 November, 2003. Alinorm 03/27/26. paras 27-35.
- Joint FAO/WHO Food Standards Program. Codex Alimentarius. Codex Committee on Methods of Analysis and Sampling (CCMAS) Report of the 25th Session of the CX/CCMAS in Budapest, Hungary, 8-12 March, 2004. Alinorm 04/27/23. paras 7,8, 92-101.
- Joint FAO/WHO Food Standards Program. Codex Alimentarius. Codex Committee on Nutrition and Foods for Special Dietary Uses. Report of the 26th Session of the CX/NFSDU in Bonn, Germany, 1-5 November, 2004. Alinorm 05/28/26. paras 6, 7, 148.
- Hekkens, WthJM. The determination of prolamins in gluten-free food. Introductory remarks. *Panminerva Med* 1991; 33;61-64.
- Janssen FW. Codex standard for gluten-free products. In: Lohiniemi S, Collin P, Mäki M, eds. *Changing Features of Coeliac Disease*: Tampere, Finland: The Finnish Coeliac Society; 1998: 31-36.
- Mäki M, Kaukinen K, Holm K, Collin P. Treatment of coeliac patients with oats and wheat starch. In: Lohiniemi S, Collin P, Mäki M, eds, *Changing Features of Coeliac Disease*: Tampere, Finland: The Finnish Coeliac Society; 1998: 93-96.
- Thompson T. Wheat starch, gliadin, and the gluten-free diet. *J Am Diet Assoc* 2001; 101: 1456-1459.
- Valdes, I., Garcia, E., Llorente, M and Mendez, E. Innovative approach to low-level gluten determination in foods using a novel sandwich enzyme-linked immunosorbent assay protocol. *Eur J Gastroenterol Hepatol* 2003, 15:465-474.
- Chartrand LJ, Russo PA, Duhaime AG, Seidman EG. Wheat starch intolerance in patients with celiac disease. *J Am Diet Assoc* 1997; 97:612-618.
- Garcia E, Llorente M, Hernando A, Kieffer R, Wieser H, Mĕndez E. Development of a general procedure for complete extraction of gliadins for heat processed and unheated foods. *Eur J Gastroenterol Hepatol* 2005; 17:529-539.
- Mĕndez E, Vela C, Immer U, Janssen FW. Report of a collaborative trial to investigate the performance of the R5 enzyme linked immunoassay to determine gliadin in gluten- free food. *Eur J Gastroenterol Hepatol* 2005; 17:1053-1063.
- Hischenhuber C, Crevel R, Jarry B, et al. Review article: safe amounts of gluten for patients with wheat allergy or coeliac disease. *Aliment Pharmacol Ther* 2006; 23:559-575.

United States

Currently, there is no specific Federal regulation that defines the term "gluten-free," however, FDA interprets this term to mean "no" gluten. In accordance with FDA policy, when manufacturers label a product "gluten-free" that purports to be or is represented to be for special dietary use, manufacturers should adhere to the provisions for hypoallergenic foods specified in 21 CFR 105.62 Hypoallergenic Foods.

CFR 105.62 Hypoallergenic Foods

If a food purports to be or is represented for special dietary use by reason of the decrease or absence of any allergenic property or by reason of being offered as food suitable as a substitute for another food having an allergenic property, the label shall bear:

(a) The common or usual name and the quantity or proportion of each ingredient (including spices, flavoring and coloring) in case the food is fabricated from two or more ingredients.

(b) A qualification of the name of the food, or the name of each ingredient thereof in case the food is fabricated from two or more ingredients, to reveal clearly the specific plant or animal that is the source of such food or of such ingredient, if such food or such ingredient consists in whole or part of plant or animal matter and such name does not reveal clearly the specific plant or animal that is such a source.

(c) An informative statement of the nature and effect of any treatment or processing of the food or any ingredient thereof, if the changed allergenic property results from such treatment or processing.

Food Allergen Labeling and Consumer Protection Act of 2004 (FALCPA)

On August 2, 2004, the *Food Allergen Labeling and Consumer Protection Act of 2004* (Title II of Pub.L.108-282) became law. This new legislation requires any ingredients that are or contain one of the eight major food allergens (i.e., peanuts, tree nuts, soy, fish, shellfish, milk, eggs and **wheat** or a protein derived from any of these foods)* to be declared in plain English terms on the labels of all packaged foods under FDA's purview that are labeled on or after January 1, 2006. This includes all conventional foods, dietary supplements, infant formulas and medical foods regulated by the FDA, but excludes meat, poultry and certain egg products regulated by the USDA. FALCPA requirements apply to both products manufactured in the U.S. and those manufactured abroad and imported into the U.S. If one of the major food allergens is used in a product, either as a food or component of an ingredient, the product must be labeled appropriately. Major food allergens used as ingredients in flavorings, colorings, seasoning mixtures and incidental additives must be listed in accordance with these requirements. For example, if a snack food included seasonings containing whey powder and wheat flour, the terms "milk" and "wheat" must be declared on the label of the snack food. However, distilled vinegar derived from wheat would not have to declare wheat on its food label, as the distillation process removes the wheat protein and is not in the final product.

* Although wheat is one of the top 8 allergens that must always be declared, the FALCPA labeling requirements do not apply to the other gluten-containing grains (barley and rye). However, many manufacturers are aware of the increasing need for information about the presence of gluten in ingredients and are more frequently declaring the gluten sources on product labels voluntarily.

The FALCPA also mandated the Secretary, in consultation with appropriate experts and stakeholders, to issue a proposed rule to define and permit the use of, the term "gluten-free" on food labels by August 2006, with the final ruling by August 2008.

There are some cases when a food ingredient's "common or usual name" (e.g., "casein") does not identify the presence of major food allergen by its food source name (e.g., "milk"). In such cases and when the same food source name is not already disclosed elsewhere on the product's list of ingredients for another allergenic ingredient, companies have a choice between two alternatives for identifying major food allergens on the product label.

One way is to state the food source name parenthetically immediately after the ingredient's name [e.g., casein (milk)] within the list of ingredients. The other way is to include a separate "Contains" statement immediately following or adjacent to the ingredient list in a type size no smaller than that used for the list of ingredients that declares the food source names of any ingredients that are major food allergens (e.g., "Contains Milk"). This "Contains" statement must declare the food source names of all major food allergens used as ingredients to make that packaged food. If casein and egg whites were the only two major food allergens used as ingredients to make a product, one example of an appropriate "Contains" statement for that product is "Contains milk and egg."

If "semolina" or "durum" is used as an ingredient to make a food, to comply with FALCPA, either the term "wheat" must be declared after those ingredients [e.g., semolina (wheat), durum (wheat), or durum wheat] when "wheat" is not already stated elsewhere in the ingredient list or the term "wheat" must be declared in a separate "Contains" statement.

It is important to note that although all products packaged and labeled on or after January 1, 2006 must comply with the new act, there will be existing products on the shelves that were packaged and labeled before January 1, 2006 that are not required to meet FALCPA requirements. Depending on the shelf life and turnover of the product in the store, some products might be found on the shelves for months and possibly a year or longer. Unfortunately, during this transitional period of time, consumers may not be able to determine whether the food is labeled in accordance with the new law so consumers may want to contact the company directly to confirm the ingredient status of a particular product.

USA Websites on Food Allergen and Gluten-Free Labeling

Food Allergen Labeling and Consumer Protection Act of 2004 (FALCPA)
http://www.cfsan.fda.gov/~dms/alrgact.html

Guidance for Industry: Questions and Answers Regarding Food Allergens and the FALCPA
http://www.cfsan.fda.gov/~dms/alrguid2.html

Advice to Consumers: FALCPA Questions and Answers
http://www.cfsan.fda.gov/~dms/alrgqa.html

FDA Information about Food Allergies (also addresses gluten-free issues)
http://www.cfsan.fda.gov/~dms/wh-alrgy.html

FDA information on Specific Topics and Categories addressing food labeling and nutrition
http://www.cfsan.fda.gov/~dms/lab-cat.html

Update on Gluten-Free Labeling

On behalf of the Secretary of Health and Human Services, the Food and Drug Administration, Center for Food Safety and Applied Nutrition (FDA/CFSAN) consulted with appropriate experts and stakeholders to help the agency develop a proposed regulation to define and permit the voluntary use of the term "gluten-free" on food labels. Two key meetings have been held to date to examine this issue.

FDA/CFSAN Food Advisory Committee on Thresholds for Major Food Allergens & Gluten in Food

The FDA/CFSAN Food Advisory Committee held a meeting July 13-15, 2005 called "Approaches to Establish Thresholds for Major Food Allergens and for Gluten in Food". The meeting on July 14 brought together scientific experts and stakeholders representing Federal government agencies, trade associations, the food industry, consumers and others. A panel of experts listened to presentations on and discussed the characteristics and treatment of celiac disease, the quality of life issues faced by patients and their families, the relationship between gluten proteins in various grains and celiac disease, analytical methods for measuring gluten levels in food, the value and use of prospective and retrospective gluten tolerance studies, and examples of existing national and international definitions of "gluten-free" standards for food labeling.

Two presentations that examined safe gluten threshold levels were given by Dr. Alessio Fasano, Professor of Pediatrics, Medicine & Physiology, and Director of the Mucosal Biology Research Center, affiliated with the Center for Celiac Research at the University of Maryland and Dr. Pekka Collin, Professor from the University of Tampere Medical School in Finland. Dr. Fasano highlighted the preliminary results of the Italian gluten micro-challenge study that examined the consequences of protracted ingestion of minimal gluten intakes of either 10 or 50 mg/day for 3 months in adults with celiac disease. It revealed that there was a trend towards an increase in inflammatory cells in the villi (called intraepithelial lymphocytes) at 50 mg/day. Based upon the results of this study and Italy's experience with allowing up to 20 ppm in foods marketed as gluten-free in that country, Dr. Fasano suggested that 20 ppm of gluten is a safe threshold for most people with celiac disease who did not exceed a maximum intake of 300 grams of gluten-free products/day which would be equivalent to a total of 6 mg gluten/day. Dr. Collin presented retrospective data suggesting a safe threshold level of gluten to be 100 ppm if the daily gluten-free flour intake was less than 300 grams/day. This would be equivalent to a maximum of 30 mg gluten/day. Based on these two presentations, it appears that there are various gluten tolerance levels in people with celiac disease that may be between 6-30 mg gluten/day. Further research is necessary to determine safe gluten threshold levels and the amounts of gluten-free specialty products that can safely be consumed by the celiac population at large.

The entire agenda, speaker presentations and slides and meeting summary can be accessed at:
http://www.fda.gov/ohrms/dockets/ac/cfsan05.html

Daily Gluten Intake Based on Amount of Gluten (in ppm) of Varying Weights of GF Products*

Gluten content in products (expressed as ppm)	**Amount of gluten-free foods (in grams) per day**			
	50 grams	**100 grams**	**200 grams**	**300 grams**
20 ppm	1 mg	2 mg	4 mg	6 mg
50 ppm	2.5 mg	5 mg	10 mg	15 mg
100 ppm	5 mg	10 mg	20 mg	30 mg
200 ppm	10 mg	20 mg	40 mg	60 mg

Calculation Facts:

20 ppm gluten = 2 mg gluten/100 grams of food

$$\frac{\text{2 mg gluten}}{\text{100 grams of food}} = \frac{\text{6 mg gluten}}{\text{300 grams of food}}$$

100 ppm = 10 mg gluten/100 grams of food

$$\frac{\text{10 mg gluten}}{\text{100 grams of food}} = \frac{\text{30 mg gluten}}{\text{300 grams of food}}$$

*Adapted from: Collin P, Thorell L, Kaukinen K, Mäki, M. The safe threshold for gluten contamination in gluten-free products. Can trace amounts be accepted in the treatment of coeliac disease? *Aliment Pharmacol Ther* 2004; 19:1277-83.

FDA/CFSAN Public Meeting on Gluten-Free Food Labeling

The CFSAN held a meeting on August 19, 2005 that included presentations from representatives of Federal government agencies, the food industry, the scientific community and celiac disease groups. The purpose of the meeting was to help FDA gain a better understanding of how manufacturers produce gluten-free foods, the analytical methods used to verify that foods are gluten-free, costs of producing gluten-free foods, and the food-purchasing practices of consumers with celiac disease and their caregivers related to products marketed or labeled "gluten-free" compared to those products without a "gluten-free" designation. In addition to the presentations at the meeting, individuals and groups not able to attend were invited to submit comments to the FDA.

Various links for the Gluten-Free Food Labeling Public Meeting can be found at:

http://www.cfsan.fda.gov/~lrd/vidtel.html

The link to docket #2005N-0279 that lists the public comments FDA has received in response to this public meeting can be found at:
http://www.fda.gov/ohrms/dockets/dockets/05n0279/05n0279.htm

The transcript of the meeting is at:
http://www.cfsan.fda.gov/~dms/glutran.html

Canada

Health Canada's *Food and Drug Regulations* (FDR), Division 24 "Foods for Special Dietary Use" defines the terms for foods that have been specially processed or formulated to meet the particular requirements of individuals for whom a physical or physiological condition exists. Sections B.24.018 and B. 24.019 defines the terms for food labeled "gluten-free" (see below). Canada has not accepted the Codex Standard for gluten-free foods.

The Bureau of Food Safety and Consumer Protection Division of the Canadian Food Inspection Agency (CFIA) has a "Fair Labelling Practices Program" that monitors various labeling claims. This includes random testing of products to determine compliance with various regulations. The "gluten-free" claim in Canada means free of gluten. CFIA monitors this claim using an ELISA test which has an analytical limitation of 20 ppm. This is the level used as guidance for their enforcement action. However, more sensititve methods of analysis are under review.

Food and Drug Regulation B.24.018

No person shall label, package, sell or advertise a food in a manner likely to create an impression that it is gluten-free unless the food does not contain wheat, including spelt and kamut, or oats, barley, rye or triticale or any part thereof.

Food and Drug Regulation B.24.019

The label of a food that is labelled, packaged, sold or advertised as "gluten-free" shall carry the following information, per serving of stated size of the food:

(a) the energy value of the food, expressed in Calories (Calories or Cal) and kilojoules (kilojoules or kJ) and;

(b) the protein, fat and carbohydrate content of the food, expressed in grams.

Health Canada is currently reviewing the use and labeling of pure, uncontaminated oats in the gluten-free diet. At the time of printing this book, no regulatory provision has been made to allow pure, uncontaminated oats in foods labeled "gluten-free." However, Health Canada does not prohibit the sale of pure, uncontaminated oats and the Canadian Celiac Association's position statement on oats does allow the use of pure, uncontaminated oats in moderate amounts in a gluten-free diet (see page 21).

Schedule of Amendments No. 1220 – *Enhanced Labelling of Priority Allergens in Foods, Gluten Sources and Sulphites in Foods*

Health Canada (HC) and the Canadian Food Inspection Agency (CFIA) have developed (after many years of extensive consultation with health professionals, consumer groups and industry) proposed regulatory amendments to the *Food and Drug Regulations* to enhance the labeling of priority allergens, gluten sources and sulphites in foods (see page 71 for the web links). Although these proposed amendments must be published in Canada Gazette Part I with invitation for further comment, HC and CFIA have strongly recommended that manufacturers declare the eight major food allergens, their protein derivatives, gluten-containing cereals and sulphites when present as ingredients or components of ingredients, on the food label. Fortunately, many Canadian manufacturers have made significant changes to the labeling of their food ingredients with respect to allergens, gluten and sulphites, not only in response to HC and CFIA, but due to consumer demand. Identification of the plant source of starches, modified food starches and hydrolyzed proteins are now more commonly declared.

The proposed regulatory amendments affecting the labeling of gluten would include:

1) (a) The label declaration of the following foods, or any protein-containing derivatives of these, in the list of ingredients by their common name if added directly as an ingredient in prepackaged foods:

   - peanuts; naming the tree nuts; sesame; milk; eggs; naming the fish; naming the crustaceans; naming the shellfish; soy; and wheat, including spelt and kamut, or oats, barley, rye or triticale or any protein-containing part thereof and hybridized strains of these grains;

   (b) if the name of the allergenic food is not already identified in the common name of the derivative, then the name of the allergenic food would have to appear in brackets following the ingredient;

2) (a) amendments to section B.01.009, which exempts certain ingredients or classes of ingredients from label declaration, to require the declaration of the foods mentioned above or any protein-containing derivative, when they are added as a component of an ingredient listed in the Table to subsection B.01.009 (1);

   (b) the declaration would be made in the list of ingredients by common name, as if they were an ingredient of that food, followed, in brackets, by the name of the specific allergenic food specified above (e.g., durum (wheat)) if it is not already identified in the common name of the derivative;

   (c) if more than one component of an ingredient contains the same priority allergen or gluten source, the name of the specific allergen or gluten source may be declared only once in the list of ingredients;

3) identification of the plant or animal source in the common name of all hydrolysed proteins;

4) identification of the specific source of the plant in the common name of all forms of starch (including maltodextrin) or modified starch;

7) a requirement for a statement on the principal display panel of standardized vinegars and alcoholic beverages that the product contains one or more priority allergens, protein-containing derivatives of these allergens and sulphites (if the sulphites are present at a level of 10 ppm or more) should they have been added directly or indirectly to the product;

8) consequential amendments to paragraph B. 01.010(3), which lists common names for groups of specific ingredients or components, to reflect the requirements for the declaration of priority allergens and gluten sources.

The proposed amendments can be found at this link:

http://www.hc-sc.gc.ca/fn-an/label-etiquet/allergen/allergy_label_letter-lettre_etiquetage_alergene_e.html

Australia/New Zealand

Food Standards Australia New Zealand (FSANZ) is a bi-national independent authority that develops specific food standards for composition and labeling, done in collaboration with the various government agencies and input from stakeholders including industry, consumers and health professionals in both countries. The *Australia New Zealand Food Standard Code* (known as the *Code*) contains various food labeling regulations including specific gluten-free labeling regulations . Standard 1.2.3 clause 4 pertains to the mandatory declaration of certain substances in food when present as an ingredient, component of an ingredient, food additive or processing aid. These include cereals containing gluten and their products, namely, wheat, rye, barley, oats and spelt and their hybridised strains; egg; fish; milk; peanuts; tree nuts; soybeans; sesame seed; fish; crustacea and sulphites. Clause 1 of Standard 1.2.8 defines gluten as "the main protein in wheat, rye, oats, barley, triticale and spelt relevent to the medical conditions, Coeliac disease and dermatitis herpetiformis". Clause 16 parts 2 and 3 of Standard 1.2.8 was amended on October 14, 2004 and states : "A claim to the effect that a food is **"gluten-free"** must not be made in relation to a food unless the food contains no detectable gluten; and no oats or their products; or cereals containing gluten that have been malted, or their products. A claim to the effect that a food has a **"low-gluten"** content must not be made in relation to a food unless the food contains no more than 20 mg gluten per 100 g of the food" (Note that 20 mg gluten/100 grams is equivalent to 200 ppm). These dual gluten labeling definitions were developed in order to accomodate the opposing views of the Australian and New Zealand Coeliac Societies and health professionals. The Australian Celiac Society does not support the "low-gluten" claim and only recommends the "gluten-free" claim, whereas the New Zealand Coeliac Society does endorse the low gluten claim.

FSANZ and the Code can be found at:

http://www.foodstandards.gov.au/

http://www.foodstandards.gov.au/foodstandardscode/

European Union

The European Union (EU) is a group of 25 European countries committed to working together by setting up common institutions where they delegate some of their sovereignty so that decisions on specific issues of mutual concern can be made democratically at the EU level. The EU consists of a Parliament of 732 members and a Council of the European Union which consists of ministers from national governments of all 25 EU countries. Both groups have the responsibility of passing laws and making policy decisions. The European Commission (EC) has 25 members (one from each country) and represents the interests of Europe as a whole and is independent of national governments. Proposals for new laws come from the EC such as food safety laws. The Health and Consumer Protection Directorate General is responsible for enforcing the EU laws.

Directive 2000/13/EC of March 20, 2000 regarding labeling, presentation and advertising of foodstuffs was amended by Directive 2003/89/EC on November 10, 2003. This new legislation was passed November 2004 and became mandatory effective November 24, 2005. It requires allergens and their derivatives (cereals containing gluten, fish, crustaceans, egg, peanut, soy, nuts, celery, mustard, sesame seed, sulphites and milk and dairy products including lactose) to always be declared on the food label.

The EC had requested the Scientific Panel on Dietetic Products, Nutrition and Allergies of the European Food Safety Authority (EFSA) to review the evidence supporting the identification of foods, food components and food ingredients which cause food allergies and intolerances. The Panel was also asked to determine, if possible, thresholds that exist and/or identify specific elements (including food processing) that would indicate food components/ingredients are no longer responsible for triggering adverse reactions. Their report entitled "Opinion of the Scientific Panel on Dietetic Products, Nutrition and Allergies on a request from the Commission relating to the evaluation of allergenic foods for labeling purposes" was adopted on February 19, 2004. Food companies were permitted to submit scientific data on ingredients that could be provisionally exempt from declaration by August 25, 2004. The EFSA published its opinions on wheat-based maltodextrins and glucose syrups (derived from wheat starch and barley starch) November 19, 2004. They concluded that these ingredients "are unlikely to cause an adverse reaction in individuals with coeliac disease" and "are not very likely to cause severe allergic reactions in the majority of cereal allergic individuals". As a result, Directive 2005/26/EC of March 21, 2005 established a list of food ingredients and substances that were provisionally excluded from Annex IIIa of Directive 2000/13/EC until November 25, 2007. This will allow food manufacturers or their associations to conduct further scientific studies on specific ingredients and their components in order for the EC to determine which substances may be permanently exempted.

Further information about EU food labeling can be found at these links:

http://europa.eu.int/comm/food/food/labellingnutrition/foodlabelling/comm_legisl_en.htm

http://europa.eu.int/eur-lex/pri/en/oj/dat/2000/l_109/l_10920000506en00290042.pdf

http://europa.eu.int/comm/food/food/labellingnutrition/foodlabelling/fl_com2003-89_en.pdf

http://europa.eu.int/comm/food/food/labellingnutrition/foodlabelling/guidelines.pdf

http://europa.eu.int/eur-lex/lex/LexUriServ/site/en/oj/2005/l_075/l_07520050322 en00330034.pdf

http://www.efsa.eu.int/science/nda/nda_opinions/341/opinion_nda_04_en1.pdf

http://www.efsa.eu.int/press_room/press_release/697/pr_nda03_allergens_en1.pdf

http://www.efsa.eu.int/science/nda/nda_opinions/catindex_en.html

http://www.efsa.eu.int/science/nda/nda_opinions/681_en.html

http://www.efsa.eu.int/science/nda/nda_opinions/682_en.html

http://www.efsa.eu.int/science/nda/nda_opinions/683_en.html

http://www.aac-eu.org

NUTRITION AND THE GLUTEN-FREE DIET

Learning how to eliminate gluten from the diet can be very challenging, as outlined in the previous chapter. Although it is essential to know about specific ingredients and foods that must be avoided or questioned, and those which are allowed, emphasis on the nutritional quality of the gluten-free diet is also important but is frequently overlooked. This section addresses specific dietary concerns, how to use nutritious gluten-free alternatives, guidelines for healthy eating, as well as the nutritional composition of a variety of gluten-free ingredients and foods.

Nutritional Quality of Gluten-Free Foods

Several studies have examined the nutritional composition of gluten-free products. American dietitian Tricia Thompson assessed the thiamin, riboflavin and niacin content of 368 gluten-free products (1999) and evaluated the folate, iron and dietary fiber content of 83 products (2000). These North American gluten-free products included flours, mixes, breads, cereals and pastas. As most were not enriched/fortified and many were made from refined flours and starches, they tended to be lower in nutrients and dietary fiber than whole-grain and refined gluten-containing products that they replace.

Fortunately, food and drug regulations in both the USA and Canada allow gluten-free flours, breads, cereals and pasta products to be enriched at the same level as their gluten-containing counterparts. Many companies are now enriching more of their gluten-free products (e.g., breads, buns, bagels, cereals, pasta) with thiamin, riboflavin, niacin, iron, folate and other nutrients. They are also incorporating healthier ingredients such as amaranth, buckwheat, flax, mesquite, millet, Montina™, quinoa, sorghum and teff into many products. For background information, including the nutritional composition of these gluten-free alternatives, see pages 111-122, 126-128.

Nutritional Status of Individuals on a Gluten-Free Diet

No large-scale studies have been done on the nutritional adequacy of gluten-free diets. Most studies that have investigated food consumption patterns and nutrient intakes of children or adults with celiac disease were small in number, ranging from 26-71 individuals, although an Italian study by Annibale et al. (2001) on the efficacy of a gluten-free diet on the recovery from iron deficiency anemia evaluated 190 adults for 2 years (majority recovered within 6-12 months). Hallert et al. (2002) assessed the vitamin B_6, B_{12} and folate levels in 30 Swedish adults with celiac disease who had been following a gluten-free diet for 8-12 years and found poor vitamin status in half of the patients. Another Italian study by Bardella et al. (2000) of 71 adults with well-controlled celiac disease found that the weight, height and body mass index of males and the weight and body mass index of females were significantly lower than 142 control subjects without celiac disease. Also, in females diagnosed in adulthood, bone mineral content was significantly lower. Mariani et al. (1998) examined the diets of 47 Italian adolescents with celiac disease and discovered low levels of iron (especially in girls), calcium and fiber. A study by De Lorenzo et al. (1999) of 43 Italian adolescents who had been diagnosed with celiac disease, for at least one year or more, found that all had significantly lower body weight, height, fat-free mass, body mass index and bone mineral density than the 30 healthy control subjects.

The diets of 47 adults (39 females and 8 males) in the USA were recently analyzed by Thompson et al. (2005). Recommended amounts of calcium, iron and fiber were consumed by only 32, 44 and 46% of women and 63, 100 and 88% of men, respectively. Many adults, particularly women, did not consume adequate amounts of grain products. The authors concluded that persons with celiac disease should be encouraged to: 1) consume 6-11 servings per day (depending on caloric intake) of gluten-free grain products (emphasis on whole grain or enriched); 2) increase intake of non-grain food sources of thiamine, riboflavin, niacin, folate and iron; 3) consume 3 servings/day of low-fat or non-fat dairy products and 4) consider the use of gluten-free calcium and multivitamin and mineral supplements. Also, individuals with lactose intolerance should consume gluten-free, low lactose/lactose-free dairy products and/or non-dairy sources of calcium.

References

- Thompson T. Thiamin, riboflavin, and niacin contents of the gluten-free diet: Is there cause for concern? *J Am Diet Assoc* 1999;99:858-862.
- Thompson T. Folate, iron and dietary fiber contents of the gluten-free diet. *J Am Diet Assoc* 2000;100:1389-1396.
- Annibale B, Severi C, Chistolini A, et al. Efficacy of gluten-free diet alone on recovery from iron deficiency anemia in adult celiac patients. *Am J Gastroenterol* 2001;96:132-137.
- Hallert C, Grant C, Grehn S, et al. Evidence of poor vitamin status in coeliac patients on a gluten-free diet for 10 years. *Aliment Pharmacol Ther* 2002;16:1333-1339.
- Bardella MT, Fredella C, Prampolini L, et al. Body composition and dietary intakes in adult celiac disease patients consuming a strict gluten-free diet. *Am J Clin Nutr* 2000;72:947-939.
- Mariani P, Viti MG, Montuori M, et al. The gluten-free diet: a nutritional risk factor for adolescents with celiac disease? *J Pediatr Gastroenterol Nutr* 1998; 27:519-523.
- De Lorenzo A, Di Campli C, Andreoli A, et al. Assessment of body composition by bioelectrical impedence in adolescent patients with celiac disease. *Am J Gastroenterol* 1999;94:2951-2955.
- Thompson T, Dennis M, Higgins LA, et al. Gluten-free diet survey: are Americans with coeliac disease consuming recommended amounts of fibre, iron, calcium and grain foods? *J Hum Nutr Dietet* 2005;18:163-169.

Specific Nutritional Concerns

ANEMIA

Definition: This condition results from a deficiency in the size or number of red blood cells or the amount of hemoglobin in these cells. There are many causes of anemia, however, the most common is due to iron, folate or vitamin B_{12} deficiency. In celiac disease damage to the intestinal villi in the area where iron and folate are absorbed frequently results in a deficiency of these nutrients. As the disease progresses, villous atrophy in the lower part of the small intestine (terminal ileum), resulting in vitamin B_{12} malabsorption, can also occur in some individuals. Other reasons for inadequate absorption of B_{12} may be due to small intestinal bacterial overgrowth, low stomach acid levels (caused by the long-term use of gastric acid blocking agents for the treatment of reflux or ulcers) or pernicious anemia (an autoimmune disease that produces antibodies that destroy specific cells in the stomach which contain the Intrinsic Factor (IF) that is necessary for the absorption of B_{12} from foods).

Types of Anemia

Nutrient	Role	Deficiency
Iron	Essential for the production of hemoglobin, a component of red blood cells that carries oxygen throughout the body. Oxygen is used to release energy from the food that is eaten.	Develops slowly after the normal stores of iron in the body have become depleted. Results in a microcytic anemia (decreased number and size of red blood cells due to inadequate levels of hemoglobin). Symptoms include major fatigue, weakness, irritability, pale skin, headache, brittle nails, decreased appetite and increased susceptibility to infections. Can also cause a reduced attention span in children resulting in behavioral and developmental problems.
Folate	This B vitamin is necessary for the production of DNA, the building block of cells and for the formation of red blood cells. It is particularly important during infancy and pregnancy, when new cells are rapidly being formed. Women of child-bearing age who may become pregnant need to consume adequate amounts of folate, especially during the first few months of pregnancy to reduce the risk of neural tube defects such as spina bifida and anencephaly.	A deficiency of folate results in macrocytic megaloblastic anemia which is characterized by very large immature red blood cells. Symptoms are similar to iron deficiency but can also include tinnitus (ringing in the ears), cracked lips, sore tongue and an irregular heart beat and chest pain.
Vitamin B_{12}	Essential for the formation and normal growth of red blood cells and synthesis of DNA. Also plays a role in the maintenance of the nervous system. Vitamin B_{12} is involved in the formation of myelin, which is part of the insulating sheath around the nerves.	Develops slowly after the normal stores of vitamin B_{12} in the liver have become depleted (may take up to 3 years). A deficiency of vitamin B_{12} results in macrocytic megaloblastic anemia as above. Symptoms of vitamin B_{12} deficiency are similar to folate deficiency but can also include depression, numbness and tingling of the hands and feet, muscle weakness, lack of coordination and balance problems and confusion. Prolonged vitamin B_{12} deficiency can cause irreversible nerve damage.

Treatment: Once a diagnosis of celiac disease is confirmed and the gluten-free diet is initiated, the villi begin to heal which allows for the absorption of nutrients. Response to the gluten-free diet varies from one individual to another and may take on average from 2-18 months until the nutritional deficiencies are corrected and symptoms resolve. In addition to a strict gluten-free diet, it is important to include foods high in iron, folate and vitamin B_{12}. Nutrition supplements may be required if the deficiency is severe. In the case of pernicious anemia, life-long vitamin B_{12} supplementation (shots, intranasal or oral supplements) are necessary. Discuss with your physician and dietitian about supplementation. More information about iron, folate and vitamin B_{12}, including the dietary reference intakes and sources, can be found on pages 77-91.

IRON

There are two types of iron in foods, heme iron and non-heme iron:

Heme Iron

- ✦ Is more readily absorbed by the body (approximately 23% of heme iron consumed is absorbed).
- ✦ Absorption is not changed by other foods in the diet.
- ✦ Is found only in red meat, fish and poultry.

Non-Heme Iron

- ✦ Is not absorbed as well as heme iron (only 3-8% of non-heme iron consumed is absorbed).
- ✦ Absorption can be increased or decreased by other foods in the diet.
- ✦ Is found in fruits, vegetables, grains and eggs.

How To Maximize Iron Absorption

1. Choose foods with a higher iron content (see pages 78-82).
2. Eat a source of heme iron with non-heme iron at the same meal:
   e.g., • Stir-fried beef, chicken, pork or fish with vegetables (e.g., broccoli) and rice and toasted almonds or sesame seeds.
   • Chili with meat and beans.
3. Vitamin C increases absorption of non-heme iron so combine vitamin C-rich foods with non-heme iron foods at the same meal.
   e.g., • Poached egg and glass of orange juice.
   • Casserole with rice, beans, canned tomatoes or tomato sauce.
   • Spinach salad with strawberries or orange segments.
   * Citrus fruits and juices, kiwi fruit, strawberries, cantaloupe, broccoli, tomatoes, potatoes, green and red peppers and cabbage are good sources of vitamin C:
4. Avoid coffee or tea with meals rich in iron as these beverages contain tannins which interfere with iron absorption. It is better to drink these beverages between meals.
5. If taking iron supplements, consume supplement with vitamin C-rich foods..

Adapted from: ***Iron Essential for Good Health*** *by* **Beef Information Centre, Canada**.

DIETARY REFERENCE INTAKES (DRI'S)

For more than 50 years, nutrition experts have produced a set of nutrient and energy standards known as the Recommended Dietary Allowances (RDA's). A new set of standards has been developed called the Dietary Reference Intakes (DRI's) which reflect collaborative efforts of American and Canadian scientists, through a review process overseen by the National Academy of Science's Food and Nutrition Board, Institute of Medicine, National Academies.

The newly established levels for vitamins, minerals, protein, fats, cholesterol, carbohydrate, fiber, and energy levels can be found at this link:

http://www.iom.edu/cms/3788/4574.aspx

Dietary Reference Intake (DRI) for Iron

	Age	Iron (mg/day)
Infants	0-6 months	0.27*
	7-12 months	11
Children	1-3 years	7
	4-8 years	10
Males	9-13 years	8
	14-18	11
	19-30	8
	31-50	8
	51-70	8
	> 70	8
Females	9-13 years	8
	14-18	15
	19-30	18
	31-50	18
	51-70	8
	> 70	8
Pregnancy	< 18 years	27
	19-30	27
	31-50	27
Lactation	< 18 years	10
	19-30	9
	31-50	9

* Adequate Intake (AI)

Iron Content of Flours & Starches

Flours & Starches	1 cup (weight in grams)	Iron (mg)
Almond Flour (Almond Meal)	112	4.3
Amaranth Flour	135	10.3
Arrowroot Starch (Arrowroot Starch Flour)	128	0.4
Buckwheat Bran (Farinetta™)	137	13.6
Buckwheat Flour (whole groat)	120	4.9
Chestnut Flour	100	2.4
Cornmeal (Yellow, degermed, enriched)	138	5.7
Corn Bran	76	2.1
Corn Flour (Yellow, whole grain)	117	2.8
Corn Flour (Yellow, degermed, enriched)	138	5.7
Cornstarch	128	0.6
Flax Seed Meal (Ground Flax)	130	7.5
Garbanzo Bean (Chickpea) Flour	120	7.5
Garfava™ Flour (Garbanzo and Fava Bean Flours)	157	7.9
Hazelnut Flour	112	5.3
Mesquite Flour	146	5.1
Millet Flour	120	9.2
Montina™ Flour	150	10.8
Pea Flour (Golden)	116	7.3
Potato Flour	160	2.2
Potato Starch	192	2.9
Quinoa Flour	112	10.4
Rice Bran	134	10.3
Rice Flour (Brown)	158	3.1
Rice Flour (Sweet)	120	0.0
Rice Flour (White)	158	0.6
Rice Polish	112	9.0
Sorghum Flour	136	6.0
Soy Flour (defatted)	100	9.2
Soy Flour (full fat)	84	5.4
Tapioca Starch (Tapioca Flour)	120	0.0
Teff Flour	130	8.7

References for the iron values of flours and starches are on page 79.

Iron Content of Grains & Cereals

Grains & Cereals	1 cup (weight in grams)	Iron (mg)
Amaranth	195	14.8
Buckwheat Groats (roasted, dry)	164	4.1
Flax Seed	168	9.6
Millet	200	6.0
Quinoa	170	15.7
Rice (Brown, long grain)	185	2.7
Rice (White, long grain, parboiled, enriched)	187	9.8
Rice (Wild)	160	3.1
Sorghum	192	8.5
Teff	180	12.1

Iron values for flours, starches and grains are from:

- USDA Nutrient Data Base for Standard Reference, Release #18.
  http://www.nal.usda.gov/fnic/foodcomp/Data/SR18/sr18.html
  http://www.nal.usda.gov/fnic/foodcomp/search/
- Almond Flour, Garbanzo Flour, Hazelnut Flour, Potato Starch, Millet Flour, Sorghum Flour, Sweet Rice Flour and Tapioca Starch from Bob's Red Mill, Milwaukie, OR, USA.
  www.bobsredmill.com
- Buckwheat Bran (Farinetta™) from Minn-Dak Growers, Grand Forks, ND, USA.
  www.minndak.com
- Garfava™ Flour from Authentic Foods Company, Gardena, CA, USA.
  www.authenticfoods.com
- Mesquite Flour from research articles. See page 131.
- Montina™ Flour from Amazing Grains Grower Cooperative, Ronan, MT, USA.
  www.amazinggrains.com
- Pea Flour (Golden) from Mountain Meadows Food Processing Ltd., Legal, AB, Canada.
  www.peabutter.ca
- Rice Bran and Rice Polish from Ener-G Foods, Seattle, WA, USA.
  www.ener-g.com
- Teff Flour and Grain analyzed by Silliker Canada Co., Markham, ON, Canada.

Iron Content of Meats & Alternatives

Meat, Fish & Poultry	Serving Size	Iron (mg)
Beef Liver (cooked)	3.5 oz	5.8
Ground Beef (cooked)	3.5 oz.	2.1
Roast Beef (cooked)	3.5 oz.	1.9
Beef Steak (cooked)	3.5 oz.	3.1
Chicken Breast (cooked)	3.5 oz.	1
Clams	9 small or 4 large	3.4
Egg, Whole (cooked)	1 large	0.7
Oysters (canned)	3.5 oz.	6.7
Pork Chop (cooked)	3.5 oz.	1
Pork Tenderloin (cooked)	3.5 oz.	1.4
Salmon (canned, drained, bones)	3.5 oz.	1.1
Sardines (canned in oil)	8 medium	3.5
Shrimp (canned, drained)	3.5 oz.	2.7
Shrimp (fresh, cooked)	3.5 oz.	3.1
Tuna (white, canned, drained)	3.5 oz.	1
Turkey (dark meat, cooked)	3.5 oz.	2.3
Beans, Lentils & Peas		
Cranberry Beans/Romano Beans (cooked)	1 cup	3.7
Garbanzo Beans/Chickpeas (cooked)	1 cup	4.7
Kidney Beans (cooked)	1 cup	5.2
Lentils (cooked)	1 cup	6.6
Navy Beans (cooked)	1 cup	4.5
Pinto Beans (cooked)	1 cup	4.5
Soybeans (cooked)	1 cup	8.8
Split Peas (cooked)	1 cup	2.5
White Beans (cooked)	1 cup	6.6
Nuts & Seeds		
Almonds (whole, blanched)	1 cup	5.4
Brazil Nuts (dried, blanched)	1 cup	4.8
Peanuts	1 cup	6.7
Pecans (halves)	1 cup	2.7
Walnuts, English (shelled, halved)	1 cup	2.9
Pumpkin Seeds (kernels, dried)	1 cup	20.7
Sesame Seeds (kernels, dried, decorticated)	1 cup	11.7
Sunflower Seeds (hulled kernels, dry roasted)	1 cup	4.9

Iron values for meats and alternatives are from:

- USDA Nutrient Data Base for Standard Reference, Release #18.
  http://www.nal.usda.gov/fnic/foodcomp/Data/SR18/sr18.html
  http://www.nal.usda.gov/fnic/foodcomp/search/

Iron Content of Fruits, Vegetables & Miscellaneous

Fruits	Serving Size	Iron (mg)
Apricots (dried)	1 cup	6.1
Prunes (dried)	1 cup	4.2
Prune Juice	1 cup	3
Raisins, seedless	1 cup	3.4
Vegetables		
Acorn Squash (cooked)	1 cup	1.9
Asparagus (cooked)	1 cup	1.3
Broccoli (cooked)	1 cup	1.3
Brussels Sprouts (cooked)	1 cup	1.8
Collards (frozen, cooked)	1 cup	1.9
Green Peas (cooked)	1 cup	2.5
Potato (white, baked with skin)	1 medium	2.7
Spinach (cooked)	1 cup	6.4
Spinach (raw)	1 cup	0.8
Miscellaneous		
Blackstrap Molasses	1 tbsp.	3.3

Iron values for meats and alternatives, fruits, vegetables and miscellaneous are from:

- USDA Nutrient Data Base for Standard Reference, Release #18.
  http://www.nal.usda.gov/fnic/foodcomp/Data/SR18/sr18.html
  http://www.nal.usda.gov/fnic/foodcomp/search/

Iron Content of Specialty Products

Products (enriched with iron)	Serving Size	Iron (mg)
Kinnikinnick Tapioca Rice Sesame Bagel	1 bagel (94 g)	4.9
Perky's O's Cereal (Original Flavor)	¾ cup (33 g)	4.5
Enjoy Life Cranapple Crunch Cereal	¾ cup (52 g)	2.7
Pastariso Fortified Spaghetti	2 oz (56 g) dry	2.2
Pastato Fortified Spaghetti	2 oz (56 g) dry	2.2
Ener-G Foods Seattle Brown Bread	1 slice (52 g)	1.8
Enjoy Life Cinnamon Raisin Bagel	1 bagel (91 g)	1.8
Ener-G Foods White Rice Bread	1 slice (38 g)	1.1
Kinnikinnick Robin's Honey Brown Bread	1 slice (46 g)	1.0
Enjoy Life Foods Sandwich Bread	1 slice (36 g)	0.7

Iron values for gluten-free specialty products are from package labels and/or company websites.

Iron Content of Specialty Products

Products (naturally occurring iron)	Serving Size	Iron (mg)
Bumble Bar Original with Cashew (made with organic sesame seeds, cashews, flax seeds)	1 bar (45 g)	3.6
Altiplano Gold Instant Hot Quinoa Cereal (Oaxacan Chocolate variety)	1 packet	2.7
Sylvan Border Farm Classic Dark Bread Mix (made with brown rice, garbanzo bean, amaranth, white rice and potato starch flours)	1 slice (56 g) prepared	2.7
Perfect 10 Natural Energy Bar Apricot (made with apricots, dates, figs, hazelnuts, pecans, almonds, flax seeds, poppy seeds, sunflower seeds, pumpkin seeds)	1 bar (50 g)	2.2
Nu-World Amaranth O's Cereal Original Flavor	¾ cup (22.5 g)	2.2
Ancient Harvest Quinoa Flakes	⅓ cup (34 g) dry	1.8
Heartland's Finest Linguine (made with navy bean and yellow corn flours)	2 oz (56 g) dry	1.8
Authentic Foods Pancake & Baking Mix (made with brown rice flour and Garfava™ flour)	¼ cup (35 g)	1.4
Larabar Snack Bars (made with dried fruits and nuts)	1 bar (1.8 oz) (51 g)	1.4
Bob's Red Mill GF Mighty Tasty Hot Cereal™ (made with brown rice, corn, sorghum and buckwheat)	¼ cup (42 g) dry	1.4
Bob's Red Mill Organic Creamy Buckwheat Hot Cereal	¼ cup (41 g) dry	1.4
Pamela's Amazing Wheat Free Bread Mix (made with sorghum flour, tapioca flour, sweet rice flour, brown rice flour, white rice flour, millet flour, rice bran)	1/16 loaf (56 g) prepared	1.1
Mary's Gone Crackers Original Flavor (made with organic brown rice, quinoa, flax seeds, sesame seeds)	15 crackers (30 g)	1.1
The Ruby Range Southwest Pancake Mix (made with white rice flour, mesquite meal, potato starch flour, teff flour, tapioca flour)	2 pancakes (prepared)	0.9
Breads from Anna Yeast-Free Bread Mix (made with tapioca flour, arrowroot flour, chickpea flour, navy bean flour, potato starch, millet, Montina™ flour)	43 grams mix	0.7

Iron values for gluten-free specialty products are from package labels and/or company websites.

Folate

The terms folate and folic acid are used interchangeably for this water-soluble B vitamin. Folates are found naturally in a variety of foods, whereas folic acid is the synthetic form used in vitamin and mineral supplements and fortified foods. The FDA announced in March 1996 that the addition of folic acid to enriched flour and other enriched cereal grain products would be permitted and on January 1, 1998 this enrichment policy became mandatory. Following the US decision, Health Canada permitted folic acid fortification of white flour, bread, cereal and pasta in December 1996. It became mandatory November 1998.

It should be noted that in addition to gluten-containing cereal products, a growing number of gluten-free specialty products are now being fortified with vitamins and minerals including folate. The folate content of gluten-free flours, starches and grains, as well as meats/alternatives, fruits, vegetables and gluten-free specialty products are also listed on pages 84-88. The Dietary Reference Intake (DRI) for folate for various age groups is outlined below.

Dietary Reference Intake (DRI) for Folate

	Age	Folate (micrograms)
Infants	0-6 months	65
	7-12 months	80
Children	1-3 years	150
	4-8 years	200
Males	9-13 years	300
	14-18	400
	19-30	400
	31-50	400
	51-70	400
	> 70	400
Females	9-13 years	300
	14-18	400*
	19-30	400*
	31-50	400*
	51-70	400
	> 70	400
Pregnancy	< 18 years	600**
	19-30	600**
	31-50	600**
Lactation	< 18 years	500
	19-30	500
	31-50	500

* In view of evidence linking folate intake with neural tube defects in the fetus, it is recommended that all women capable of becoming pregnant consume 400 micrograms from supplements or fortified foods in addition to intake of food folate from a varied diet.

** It is assumed that women will continue consuming 400 micrograms from supplements or fortified food until their pregnancy is confirmed and they enter prenatal care, which ordinarily occurs after the end of the periconceptional period – the critical time for formation of the neural tube in the fetus.

Folate Content of Flours & Starches

Flours & Starches	1 cup (weight in grams)	Folate (micrograms)
Almond Flour (Almond Meal)	112	42
Amaranth Flour	135	66
Buckwheat Bran (Farinetta™)	137	41
Chestnut Flour	100	110
Corn Bran	76	3
Corn Flour (Yellow, whole grain)	117	29
Corn Flour (Masa, enriched)	114	266
Corn Flour (Yellow, degermed, unenriched)	126	60
Cornmeal (Yellow, degermed, enriched)	138	322
Cornmeal (Yellow, degermed, unenriched)	138	66
Cornmeal (Yellow, whole grain)	122	30
Flax Seed Meal (Ground Flax)	130	113
Garbanzo Bean (Chickpea) Flour	120	668
Hazelnut Flour	112	127
Mesquite Flour	146	26
Potato Flour	160	40
Quinoa Flour	112	55
Rice Bran	134	36
Rice Flour (Brown)	158	25
Rice Flour (White)	158	6
Soy Flour (defatted)	100	305
Soy flour (full fat)	84	290
Teff Flour	130	97

References for the folate values of flours and starches are on page 85.

Folate Content of Grains & Cereals

Grains & Cereals (raw)	1 cup (weight in grams)	Folate (micrograms)
Amaranth	195	96
Buckwheat Groats (roasted, dry)	164	69
Flax Seed	168	146
Millet	200	170
Quinoa	170	83
Rice (Brown, long grain)	185	37
Rice (White, long grain, parboiled, enriched)	187	481
Rice (Wild)	160	152
Teff	180	135

Folate values for flours, starches and grains are from:

- USDA Nutrient Data Base for Standard Reference, Release #18.
  http://www.nal.usda.gov/fnic/foodcomp/Data/SR18/sr18.html
  http://www.nal.usda.gov/fnic/foodcomp/search/
- Almond Flour, Garbanzo Flour, Hazelnut Flour, Potato Starch, Millet Flour, Sorghum Flour, Sweet Rice Flour and Tapioca Starch from Bob's Red Mill, Milwaukie, OR, USA.
  www.bobsredmill.com
- Buckwheat Bran (Farinetta™) from Minn-Dak Growers, Grand Forks, ND, USA.
  www.minndak.com
- Garfava™ Flour from Authentic Foods Company, Gardena, CA, USA.
  www.authenticfoods.com
- Mesquite Flour from research articles. See page 131.
- Montina™ Flour from Amazing Grains Grower Cooperative, Ronan, MT, USA.
  www.amazinggrains.com
- Pea Flour (Golden) from Mountain Meadows Food Processing Ltd., Legal, AB, Canada.
  www.peabutter.ca
- Rice Bran from Ener-G Foods, Seattle, WA, USA.
  www.ener-g.com
- Teff Flour and Grain analyzed by Silliker Canada Co., Markham, ON, Canada.

Folate Content of Meats & Alternatives

Meat, Fish, Poultry & Nuts	Serving Size	Folate (micrograms)
Beef Liver (cooked, braised)	100 grams	2563
Chicken Liver (cooked, simmered)	100 grams	578
Egg (whole, raw)	1 large	47
Almonds (whole, blanched)	1 cup	44
Brazil Nuts (dried, unblanched)	1 cup	31
Hazelnuts (filberts)	1cup	153
Peanuts (dry roasted)	1cup	350
Pecan (halves)	1cup	22
Walnuts (English, shelled, halves)	1cup	98
Beans, Lentils & Peas		
Cranberry (Romano Bean)	1 cup cooked	366
Fava Beans	1 cup cooked	177
Garbanzo Bean (Chickpea)	1 cup cooked	282
Kidney Bean (Red)	1 cup cooked	230
Lentils	1 cup cooked	358
Navy Beans	1 cup cooked	255
Pinto Beans	1 cup cooked	294
Soybeans (Green)	1 cup cooked	200
Soybeans (Mature)	1 cup cooked	93
Split Peas	1 cup cooked	127
White Beans	1 cup cooked	145
Seeds		
Pumpkin Seeds (kernels, dried)	1 cup	80
Sesame Seeds (kernels, dried, decorticated)	1 cup	172
Sunflower Seeds (hulled kernels, dry roasted)	1 cup	303

Folate values for meats and alternatives are from:

- USDA Nutrient Data Base for Standard Reference, Release #18.
  http://www.nal.usda.gov/fnic/foodcomp/Data/SR18/sr18.html
  http://www.nal.usda.gov/fnic/foodcomp/search/

Folate Content of Fruits & Vegetables

Fruits	Serving Size	Folate (micrograms)
Banana	1 medium	242
Cantaloupe Melon	1 cup diced	34
Honeydew Melon	1 cup diced	32
Orange	1 medium	39
Orange Juice (frozen concentrate with 3 parts water)	1 cup	110
Strawberries	1 cup	40
Tomato Juice	1 cup	49
Vegetables		
Asparagus	4 spears cooked	89
Beets	1 cup cooked	136
Broccoli	1 cup cooked	168
Brussels Sprouts	1 cup cooked	157
Chinese Cabbage	1 cup cooked	70
Collards (frozen, chopped)	1 cup cooked	129
Corn (yellow, sweet, cream style, canned)	1 cup cooked	115
Lettuce (romaine)	1 cup cooked	76
Okra (frozen)	1 cup cooked (boiled)	269
Peas (green, frozen)	1 cup cooked	94
Spinach (raw)	1 cup (raw)	58
Spinach	1 cup cooked, (boiled)	26

Folate values for fruits and vegetables are from:

- USDA Nutrient Data Base for Standard Reference, Release #18.
  http://www.nal.usda.gov/fnic/foodcomp/Data/SR18/sr18.html
  http://www.nal.usda.gov/fnic/foodcomp/search/

Folate Content of Specialty Products

Products (enriched with folate)	Serving Size	Folate (micrograms)
Enjoy Life Very Berry Snack Bar	1 bar (28 g)	240
Perky's O's Cereal (Original Flavor)	¾ cup (33 g)	180
Enjoy Life Cranapple Crunch Cereal	¾ cup (52 g)	140
Enjoy Life Cinnamon Raisin Bagel	1 bagel (91 g)	120
Pastariso Fortified Spaghetti	2 oz (56 g) dry	110
Pastato Fortified Spaghetti	2 oz (56 g) dry	110
Enjoy Life Foods Sandwich Bread	1 slice (36 g)	100
Ener-G Foods Seattle Brown Bread	1 slice (52 g)	40
Ener-G Foods White Rice Bread	1 slice (38 g)	32
Kinnikinnick Tapioca Rice Hamburger Bun	1 bun (100 g)	22
Kinnikinnick Tapioca Rice Sesame Bagel	1 bagel (94 g)	15

Folate values are from product labels and/or company websites.

VITAMIN B_{12}

Vitamin B_{12}, also known as cobalamin, is found only in animal foods such as meat, fish, poultry, eggs and dairy products. Vegetarians who do not consume foods of animal origin must rely on a B_{12} supplement or fortified foods. Vitamin B_{12} supplements are available in 50 to 1,000 microgram tablets or in a special type of nutritional yeast (grown on cane and sugar beet molasses) which is gluten-free (e.g., Red Star® Vegetarian Support Formula™ Nutritional Yeast – 1 tbsp. {8 grams} of flakes = 4 micrograms B_{12}, plus other vitamins/minerals including folic acid). Some brands of soy and other non-dairy beverages, veggie "meats" and USA breakfast cereals are fortified with B_{12}, however, most vegetarian meat substitutes and regular breakfast cereals contain wheat and are not gluten-free. The vitamin B_{12} content of various foods are listed on page 90. The Dietary Reference Intake (DRI) for vitamin B_{12} for different age groups is outlined below.

Dietary Reference Intake (DRI) for Vitamin B_{12}

	Age	Vitamin B_{12} (micrograms/day)
Infants	0-6 months 7-12 months	0.4 0.5
Children	1-3 years 4-8 years	0.9 1.2
Males	9-13 years 14-18 19-30 31-50 51-70 > 70	1.8 2.4 2.4 2.4 2.4* 2.4*
Females	9-13 years 14-18 19-30 31-50 51-70 > 70	1.8 2.4 2.4 2.4 2.4* 2.4*
Pregnancy	< 18 years 19-30 31-50	2.6 2.6 2.6
Lactation	< 18 years 19-30 31-50	2.8 2.8 2.8

* Because 10-30% of older people may malabsorb food-bound B_{12}, it is advisable for those older than 50 years to meet their requirement mainly by consuming foods fortified with B_{12} or a supplement containing B_{12}.

Vitamin B_{12} Content of Various Foods

Foods	Serving Size	Vitamin B_{12} (micrograms)
Clams (canned, drained)	3 oz	84.06
Beef Liver (cooked, braised)	100 grams	70.66
Chicken Liver (cooked, simmered)	100 grams	16.85
Salmon (sockeye, cooked)	3 oz	4.93
Salmon (pink, canned with bones)	3 oz	3.70
Tuna (light, canned in water, drained)	3 oz	2.54
Ground Beef (85% lean, cooked, broiled)	3 oz	2.24
Lamb (loin, lean, broiled)	3 oz	2.14
Cottage Cheese (low fat/1%)	1 cup	1.42
Yogurt (plain, skim milk)	8 oz	1.38
Soy Beverage (Pacific Foods Ultra, plain)	1 cup	1.50
Milk (low fat/1%)	1 cup	1.07
Egg (whole, raw)	1 extra large	0.75
Mozzarella Cheese (partially skimmed)	1 oz	0.66
Ham (lean, roasted)	3 oz	0.60
Chicken (dark meat, fried)	3 oz	0.28

Vitamin B_{12} values are from:

- USDA Nutrient Data Base for Standard Reference, Release #18.
  http://www.nal.usda.gov/fnic/foodcomp/Data/SR18/sr18.html
  http://www.nal.usda.gov/fnic/foodcomp/search/

References for iron, folate and vitamin B_{12}

- Haapalahti M, Kulmala P, Karttunen TH, et al. Nutritional status in adolescents and young adults with screen-detected celiac disease. *J Pediatr Gastroenterol Nutr* 2005;40:566-570.
- Ransford RAJ, Hayes M, Palmer M, et al. A controlled prospective screening study of celiac disease presenting as iron deficiency anemia. *J Clin Gastroenterol* 2002;35:228-233.
- Howard MR, Turnbull AJ, Morley P, et al. A prospective study of the prevalence of undiagnosed coeliac disease in laboratory defined iron and folate deficiency. *J Clin Pathol* 2002;55:754-757.
- Murray J. Celiac disease in patients with an affected member, type 1 diabetes, iron-deficiency, or osteoporosis. *Gastroenterol* 2005;128:S52-56.
- Annibale B, Severi C, Chistolini A, et al. Efficacy of gluten-free diet alone on recovery from iron deficiency anemia in adult celiac patients. *Am J Gastroenterol* 2001;96:132-137.
- Dietary Reference Intakes (DRI's) from the Food and Nutrition Board, Institute of Medicine, National Academies. http://www.iom.edu/cms/3788/4574.aspx
- Folic acid to fortify US food products to prevent birth defects. http://www.cfsan.fda.gov/~lrd/hhsfolic.html
- USA Code of Federal Regulations Sec. 172.345 Folic Acid (folacin) http://www.access.gpo.gov/cgi-bin/cfrassemble.cgi?title=200521
- Canadian Food and Drug Regulation Amendment: Folic Acid Fortification. http://canadagazette.gc.ca/partII/1998/19981125/html/sor550-e.html
- Canadian Food and Drug Regulations B.13.001, B.13.022, B.13.051, B.13.060. http://www.hc-sc.gc.ca/fn-an/legislation/acts-lois/fdr-rad/index_e.html
- Dahele A, Ghosh S. Vitamin B_{12} deficiency in untreated celiac disease. *Am J Gastroenterol* 2001;96:745-750.
- Dickey W. Low serum vitamin B_{12} is common in coeliac disease and is not due to autoimmune gastritis. *Eur J Gastroenterol Hepatol* 2002;14:425-427.

BONE DISEASE

A variety of nutrients, especially calcium, vitamin D and phosphorus are necessary for the formation and maintenance of healthy bones and teeth throughout the life-cycle. A deficiency or alteration in the metabolism of these nutrients is common in undiagnosed/untreated celiac disease and can result in conditions such as osteomalacia, osteopenia and osteoporosis (see below). Early diagnosis of celiac disease and treatment with a strict gluten-free diet and/or supplementation with specific nutrients and the use of bone-enhancing medications (for those with osteopenia or osteoporosis) can often reverse the bone disease condition or result in a significant improvement in the condition. However, bone mass may not be completely restored to normal levels in individuals with osteoporosis and celiac disease that was diagnosed later in life. Nevertheless it is essential to prevent further deterioration of the bones by following a life-long, nutritious gluten-free diet and consuming adequate amounts of calcium, vitamin D and other nutrients. For more information about calcium, vitamin D and tips for healthy bones in celiac disease see pages 93-99.

Bone Diseases in Celiac Disease

Condition	Description
Osteomalacia	✦ A failure to deposit calcium into newly formed bones causing them to become soft, flexible, and weak. ✦ Caused by a deficiency of vitamin D, calcium and/or phosphorus due to malabsorption of these nutrients in the small intestine. ✦ Can occur in children and adults. ✦ Osteomalacia in children is called rickets. Symptoms can include bone pain, skeletal deformities (e.g., bowlegs, curved spine), dental deformities (e.g., delayed formation of teeth, holes in the enamel, cavities), bone fractures and short stature. ✦ Symptoms in adults include bone pain, muscle weakness and fractures. ✦ Treatment with vitamin D and calcium can improve the condition of the bones within several weeks, with complete healing in 6 months for most individuals. In children, the skeletal deformities can often be corrected, however, some may not reach their full growth potential and be short as adults.
Osteopenia	✦ Mild thinning of the bone tissue and bone loss but not as severe as osteoporosis. ✦ Bone density is between 1 and 2.5 standard deviations (SD) below the normal. ✦ Increased risk for development of osteoporosis. ✦ Caused by a deficiency of calcium and vitamin D. ✦ Treatment with calcium, vitamin D and/or bone enhancing medications.
Osteoporosis	✦ Significant thinning of the bone tissue and loss of bone mass. ✦ Bone density is 2.5 SD or more below the normal. ✦ Results in porous, weak and brittle bones that can easily break. Common fracture areas are the spine, hip, ribs and wrist. ✦ Caused by a variety of factors such as failure to obtain maximum bone density in childhood and adolescence; malabsorption of calcium and vitamin D; an increased production of cytokines (substances produced from the inflammatory process in the small intestine) and the autoimmune process that not only damages the villi of the small intestine but can also attack the bones directly. ✦ Treatment with calcium, vitamin D and/or bone-enhancing medications.

Tips for Healthy Bones in Celiac Disease

- Follow a strict gluten-free diet for life.
- Get adequate amounts of calcium and vitamin D (see pages 94-96, 98-99).
- Eat a variety of foods to ensure adequate amounts of other nutrients that help build and maintain bone density (see Gluten-Free Dietary Guidelines for Healthy Eating on pages 123-125).
- Limit caffeine intake (2-3 cups of coffee, cola or tea/day) and sodium intake from processed foods and table salt as excessive amounts can cause calcium to be lost in the urine.
- Stay active. Regular weight-bearing activities such as brisk walking, hiking, stair climbing, dancing, tennis, as well as resistance training with weights can help maintain bone mass. Consult your physician before starting a regular exercise program.
- Don't smoke and also limit alcohol intake as these are risk factors for osteoporosis.

CALCIUM

Calcium is the most abundant mineral in the body found in the skeleton, teeth, blood, muscles and the fluid between cells. The majority of calcium (99%) is located in the bones and teeth. Calcium is needed on a daily basis throughout life for many important functions. It is used to build and maintain strong bones and teeth, aids in blood clotting, plays a role in contraction and relaxation of muscles, nerve transmission, regulation of the heartbeat, and secretion of enzymes and hormones. The body has a tightly regulated system to ensure a constant level of calcium within the body fluids and tissues at all times. It does this by absorbing calcium from foods consumed, slowing down the amount of calcium that is lost through the urine and taking calcium from the bones if there are insufficient amounts available from the diet. It is essential that adequate amounts of calcium be consumed and absorbed in order to prevent the loss of calcium from bones.

Milk and milk products are important sources of calcium, as well as phosphorus, magnesium, riboflavin, vitamins A, D, B_{12} and protein. Milk products supply more than 75% of the calcium in the American and Canadian diets. Other foods contain some calcium but most contain smaller amounts or the calcium is in a form that the body absorbs less efficiently. See pages 95-96 for the calcium content of various dairy products and other foods. If an individual is unable to consume enough calcium from dietary sources, a calcium supplement may also be necessary. Discuss with your dietitian or physician about supplementation. The dietary reference intake for calcium for various age groups is outlined below.

Dietary Reference Intake (DRI) for Calcium

	Age	Calcium (mg/day)
Infants	0-6 months	210
	7-12 months	270
Children	1-3 years	500
	4-8 years	800
Males	9-13 years	1300
	14-18	1300
	19-30	1000
	31-50	1000
	51-70	1200
	> 70	1200
Females	9-13 years	1300
	14-18	1300
	19-30	1000
	31-50	1000
	51-70	1200
	> 70	1200
Pregnancy	< 18 years	1300
	19-30	1000
	31-50	1000
Lactation	< 18 years	1300
	19-30	1000
	31-50	1000

Calcium Content of Dairy Products

Dairy Products	Serving	Calcium (mg)	Rating
Brie Cheese	2 oz.	92	★
Buttermilk	1 cup	303	★★★
Camembert Cheese	2 oz.	194	★★
Cheese, firm, such as Brick, Cheddar, Colby, Edam and Gouda	2 oz. 1" x 1" x 3"	350	★★★
Cottage Cheese (creamed, 2%, 1%)	½ cup	76	★
Feta Cheese	2 oz.	255	★★
Ice Cream	½ cup	90	★
Ice Milk	½ cup	138	★
Milk (whole, 2%, 1%, skim)*	1 cup	315	★★★
Milk (chocolate)	1 cup	301	★★★
Milk Powder (dry)	3 tbsp.	308	★★★
Mozzarella Cheese	2 oz.	287	★★★
Mozzarella Cheese (partly skimmed)	2 oz.	366	★★★
Parmesan Cheese (grated)	3 tbsp.	261	★★
Processed Cheese Slices	2 thin	256	★★
Processed Cheese Slices	2 regular	384	★★★
Processed Cheese Spread	3 tbsp.	270	★★
Ricotta Cheese	¼ cup	135	★
Ricotta Cheese (partly skimmed)	¼ cup	177	★★
Swiss Cheese	2 oz.	480	★★★
Yogurt Drink	1 cup	274	★★★
Yogurt (frozen)	½ cup	147	★
Yogurt (fruit-flavored)	¾ cup	240	★★
Yogurt (plain)	¾ cup	296	★★★

From: ***Calcium For Life: Are You on the Right Track*, Dairy Farmers of Canada**

Calcium values from: Health Canada, *Canadian Nutrient File*, 1997.

* Add about 100 mg of calcium for calcium-enriched milk

Code: ★ – Source of calcium
★★ – Good source of calcium
★★★ – Excellent source of calcium

This rating is established according to Canadian *Food and Drugs Regulations*. It is based on the content of calcium in foods and is not based on the amount of calcium actually absorbed by the body.

Calcium Content of Various Foods

Foods	Serving	Calcium (mg)	Rating
Almonds	½ cup	(200)	★★
Baked Beans	1 cup	(163)	★★
Bok Choy (cooked)	½ cup	84	★
Brazil Nuts	½ cup	130	★
Broccoli (cooked)	½ cup	38	
Chickpeas (cooked)	1 cup	85	★
Chili Con Carne	1 cup	(72)	★
Collards (cooked)	½ cup	81	★
Dates	¼ cup	14	
Figs (dried)	3	81	★
Kale (cooked)	½ cup	49	
Lentils (cooked)	1 cup	49	
Nuts (mixed)	½ cup	51	
Orange	1 medium	56	★
Orange Juice (calcium fortified)	1 cup	300-350	★★★
Prunes (dried, uncooked)	3 medium	12	
Raisins	1/4 cup	21	
Red Kidney Beans (cooked)	1 cup	(52)	
Rice (white or brown, cooked)	½ cup	10	
Salmon (pink, canned, with bones)	half a 7.5 oz. can	225	★★
Salmon (sockeye, canned, with bones)	half a 7.5 oz. can	243	★★
Sardines (canned, with bones)	6 medium	275	★★★
Sesame Seeds	½ cup	(89)	★
Soybeans (cooked)	½ cup	93	★
Soy Beverage	1 cup	10	
Soy Beverage (fortified)	1 cup	312	★★★
Tofu (regular, processed with calcium sulfate)*	⅓ cup	150	★
White Beans (cooked)	1 cup	(170)	★★

The numbers between parentheses ( ) indicate the calcium from these sources is known to be absorbed less efficiently by the body.

* The Calcium content for tofu is an approximation based on products available on the market. Calcium content varies greatly from one brand to the other and can be quite low. Tofu processed with magnesium chloride also contains less calcium.

Code: ★ – Source of calcium
★★ – Good source of calcium
★★★ – Excellent source of calcium

VITAMIN D

Vitamin D plays an important role in bone health by maintaining normal blood levels of calcium and phosphorus. This fat-soluble vitamin, known as the "sunshine vitamin" is found in a limited number of foods such as fatty fish, fish oils and egg yolk and is added to milk and margarine. Some yogurt and yogurt-based beverages may also be fortified with vitamin D, however, other dairy products including cheese, ice cream, ice milk and frozen yogurt are not fortified. Most non-dairy beverages (made from soy, potato, rice or nuts) are fortified with vitamin D. In the USA, orange juice and other fruit juices, as well as some breakfast cereals may contain added vitamin D. See page 99 for the vitamin D content of various foods.

In addition to food sources, vitamin D can also be produced naturally by the body when the skin is exposed to sunlight. Although this can be a major source of vitamin D for some people, several factors can decrease or inhibit this process. For example, sunlight exposure during the winter months for those individuals living at northern latitudes is insufficient to produce significant amounts of vitamin D in the skin. And in the summer months, the use of suntan lotion with a sun protection factor (SPF) of 8 or greater blocks the skin's production of vitamin D. It is essential to regularly use sunscreen to help prevent skin cancer, however, limited sun exposure of the hands, face and arms for 10-15 minutes at least two to three times per week without sunscreen can help meet vitamin D requirements. After 10-15 minutes of sun exposure, sunscreen should be applied. Unfortunately, as people age the skin does not produce vitamin D from sunlight exposure as efficiently so older adults need to get their vitamin D from diet and/or supplements.

For those individuals with limited sun exposure (e.g., housebound individuals such as the elderly, people living in northern latitudes, individuals who wear robes and head coverings) it is important to consume adequate amounts of vitamin D from food sources and/or supplements. Multivitamin and mineral supplements contain 400 IU of vitamin D and some calcium supplements have added vitamin D. Vitamin D is also available as a single supplement in doses ranging from 200-1000 IU. The Dietary Reference Intake (DRI) for vitamin D for various age groups is found on page 98. Vitamin D levels may be expressed as International Units (IU) or micrograms. The biological activity of 1 microgram of vitamin D is equivalent to 40 IU.

Dietary Reference Intake (DRI) for Vitamin D

	Age	Vitamin D (micrograms/day)*
Infants	0-6 months 7-12 months	5 5
Children	1-3 years 4-8 years	5 5
Males	9-13 years 14-18 19-30 31-50 51-70 > 70	5 5 5 5 10 15
Females	9-13 years 14-18 19-30 31-50 51-70 > 70	5 5 5 5 10 15
Pregnancy	< 18 years 19-30 31-50	5 5 5
Lactation	< 18 years 19-30 31-50	5 5 5

* Expressed as cholecalciferol. 1 microgram of cholecalciferol = 40 IU vitamin D. Recommended amounts in the absence of adequate exposure to sunlight.

Sources of Vitamin D

Foods	Serving Size	Vitamin D (micrograms)
Cod Liver Oil	1 tbsp.	1360
Salmon (sockeye, canned, drained with bones)	3 oz	649
Salmon (cooked)	3½ oz	360
Mackerel (cooked)	3½ oz	345
Tuna (canned in oil, drained)	3 oz	200
Sardines (canned in oil, drained)	1¾ oz	250
Milk (low fat/1%)	1 cup	100
Soy Beverage (fortified)	1 cup	100
Orange Juice (fortified with vitamin D)	1 cup	100
Margarine	1 tbsp.	60
Pudding (made with fortified milk)	½ cup	50
Yogurt (fortified with vitamin D)	½ cup	40
Egg (whole, raw)	1 large	18

Vitamin D values are from:

- USDA Nutrient Data Base for Standard Reference, Release #18.
  http://www.nal.usda.gov/fnic/foodcomp/Data/SR18/sr18.html
  http://www.nal.usda.gov/fnic/foodcomp/search/
- http://ods.od.nih.gov/factsheets/vitamind.asp
- product labels

References for bone diseases, calcium and vitamin D

- Murray J. Celiac disease in patients with an affected member, type 1 diabetes, iron-deficiency, or osteoporosis. *Gastroenterol* 2005;128:S52-56.
- Barera G, Beccio S, Proverbio MC, Mora S. Longitudinal changes in bone metabolism and bone mineral content in children with celiac disease during consumption of a gluten-free diet. *Am J Clin Nutr* 2004;79:148-154.
- Sategna-Guidetti C, Grosso SB, Grosso S, et al. The effects of 1-year gluten withdrawal on bone mass, bone metabolism and nutritional status in newly diagnosed adult coeliac disease patients. *Aliment Pharmacol Ther* 2000;14:35-43.
- Mora S, Barera G, Beccio S, et al. A prospective, longitudinal study of the long-term effect of treatment on bone density in children with celiac disease. *J Pediatr* 2001;139:473-475.
- Meyer D, Stavropolous S, Diamond B, et al. Osteoporosis in a North American adult population with celiac disease. *Am J Gastroenterol* 2001;96:112-119.
- Kalayci AG, Kansu A, Girgin N, et al. Bone mineral density and importance of a gluten-free diet in patients with celiac disease in childhood. *Pediatrics* 2001;108:E89.
- Dietary Reference Intakes from Food and Nutrition Board, Institute of Medicine, National Academies.
  http://www.iom.edu/cms/3788/4574.aspx
- Office of Dietary Supplements, National Institutes of Health, Fact Sheets on Calcium and Vitamin D.
  http://dietary-supplements.info.nih.gov/factsheets/calcium.asp
  http://ods.od.nih.gov/factsheets/vitamind.asp
- Medlines Plus, National Library of Medicine, National Institutes of Health.
  http://www.nlm.nih.gov/medlineplus/ency/article/000376.htm
  http://www.nlm.nih.gov/medlineplus/ency/article/000360.htm

LACTOSE INTOLERANCE

Definition

Milk and milk products contain a natural sugar called lactose. People who are lactose intolerant or, more precisely, who are lactose mal-digesters, lack enough of the enzyme lactase needed to completely digest the lactose into its simple sugars, glucose and galactose. As a result, undigested lactose passes through the intestinal tract, drawing fluid with it. It is then fermented by bacteria in the large intestine producing short-chain fatty acids and gases. Symptoms of lactose intolerance may include some or all of the following: abdominal cramping, bloating, gas, nausea, headache and diarrhea. These symptoms can occur 15-30 minutes or as long as several hours after consuming lactose.

Causes of Lactose Intolerance

Primary lactase deficiency: The level of lactase enzyme activity in some people may gradually fall with age to the point where they no longer tolerate as much as they used to. This type of intolerance affects as many as 70% of the world's population. It is more prevalent in Asians, Africans, Hispanics and North American aboriginals.

Secondary lactase deficiency: This is usually a temporary condition in which the level of lactase has fallen as a result of injury to the gastrointestinal tract in conditions such as celiac disease, inflammatory bowel disease, surgery, infections and with the use of certain drugs.

Dietary Recommendations for Lactose Intolerance

Tolerance to specific levels of lactose varies considerably among individuals. Those with secondary lactose intolerance, as a result of celiac disease, may need to temporarily eliminate lactose until the villi of the small intestine are healed and the lactase enzyme levels are restored to normal. This may take weeks to months depending on individual response. Most individuals with lactose intolerance can digest small amounts of lactose. In addition, many can become less lactose intolerant over time by **gradually** introducing milk products into their diet. Other factors can affect tolerance besides the total lactose content of foods. The following tips can help improve tolerance:

Milk

- Drink small amounts of milk throughout the day, ¼ - ½ cup; avoid drinking large amounts at once.
- Enjoy milk with meals or snacks; avoid drinking it on an empty stomach.
- Try heating the milk; it may be easier to tolerate.
- The higher the fat content in the milk, the slower it is digested and more easily tolerated. For example, whole milk may be better tolerated than low-fat or non-fat milk.
- Cultured buttermilk and acidophilus milk are usually tolerated to the same degree as plain milk.

Yogurt

Yogurt is often better tolerated than milk. Although yogurt contains lactose, the lactase enzymes in the active cultures digest this lactose. Look for brands that contain "active" or "live" cultures as they are tolerated more easily.

Cheese

- Aged, natural cheeses such as Cheddar, Swiss, Parmesan, and mozzarella, are low in lactose. In these cheeses most of the lactose is removed with the whey and the small amount remaining is broken down during the aging process, therefore, most aged cheeses are well tolerated.
- Fresh cheeses, such as creamed cottage cheese, ricotta and quark contain varying amounts of lactose.
- Dry-curd cottage cheese contains less lactose than creamed cottage cheese.
- Processed cheese has a lactose content similar to that of natural, aged cheeses.
- Processed cheese food and processed cheese spread often contain added modified milk solids, therefore their lactose content may be higher than plain processed cheese.
- Light cheese products also contain modified milk solids that replace milk fat. They tend to be high in lactose.

Special Products

Several products have been specially developed to help in the management of lactose mal-digestion. For more product information see pages 262-265.

- **Lacteeze Milk** is a lactose-reduced milk available in skim, 1% and 2% in the dairy case of grocery stores. The lactase enzyme has been added to the milk and 99% of the naturally occurring lactose has been converted to simple, easily digested sugars. Lactose-reduced milk is slightly sweeter than regular milk but it has the same nutritional value and can be used in cooking and baking.
- **Lactaid Milk** is another brand of lactose-reduced milk available in skim and 2% (in Canada) and fat-free, low-fat, reduced-fat, whole and calcium-fortified (in USA) in the dairy case of grocery stores.
- **Dairy-Ease** is another brand of lactose-reduced milk available in fat-free, reduced-fat and fat-free in the USA in the dairy case of grocery stores.
- **Lacteeze Enzyme Drops*** contain enzymes that can be added to liquid dairy products making them more easily digestible. Approximately 90% of the lactose is broken down based on the number of drops used (8-10 drops) per liter. This product is available in drug stores.
- **Lacteeze 4000 Tablets*** contain extra-strength natural enzymes that a person takes just before meals or snacks that contain lactose. These mint-flavored tablets are available from most drug stores.
- **Lacteeze Children's Tablets*** in strawberry flavor are also available in drug stores.
- **Lactaid Tablets*** is another brand of lactase enzymes available in Original (Regular) and Fast Act Extra-Strength (Ultra) caplets or Fast Act Chewable Tablets (vanilla twist flavor).
- **Non-Dairy Beverages** made from nuts, potatoes, rice or soy do not contain any lactose. Look for brands that are gluten-free (i.e., do not contain any barley malt flavoring) and are enriched with calcium, vitamin D and other nutrients.

* The nutritional value of dairy products is not changed when you use enzyme drops or tablets.

DIETARY FIBER

Dietary fiber is the part of whole grains, fruits, vegetables, legumes (dried beans, peas and lentils), nuts and seeds that cannot be broken down by the human digestive system. Although fiber is not readily digested, it plays an important role in the body, particularly through its effects on the digestive system. Fiber helps to maintain regular bowel movements. A high-fiber diet can also play a role in the prevention of certain chronic diseases such as coronary artery disease, diabetes, colon cancer and diverticular disease.

Consuming adequate amounts of fiber is especially important for people with celiac disease. Newly diagnosed individuals may have symptoms of diarrhea due to malabsorption caused by gluten damaging the absorptive surface of the small intestine. However, once a gluten-free diet is initiated, the intestinal tract begins to heal and the malabsorption and diarrhea eventually resolve. Some people may then have problems with constipation. This is often due to an inadequate fiber intake as they are no longer able to consume high-fiber gluten-containing foods such as wheat bran and whole-wheat breads and cereals. Many gluten-free foods are made with starches and/or refined flours which are lower in fiber. During refining, the outer layer of the grain which contains most of the fiber is removed, leaving only the starchy inner layer which contains very little fiber.

Dietary Reference Intake (DRI) for Fiber

	Age	Fiber (grams/day)
Infants	0-6 months 7-12 months	ND* ND*
Children	1-3 years 4-8 years	19 25
Males	9-13 years 14-18 19-30 31-50 51-70 > 70	31 38 38 38 30 30
Females	9-13 years 14-18 19-30 31-50 51-70 > 70	26 26 25 25 21 21
Pregnancy	< 18 years 19-30 31-50	28 28 28
Lactation	< 18 years 19-30 31-50	29 29 29

* **ND** – Not determinable due to lack of data of adverse effects in this age group and concern with regard to lack of ability to handle excess amounts. Source of intake should be from food only to prevent high levels of intake.

Reference Source:
Dietary Reference Intakes from the Food and Nutrition Board, Institute of Medicine, National Academies.
http://www.iom.edu/cms/3788/4574.aspx

Healthy Tips to Increase Your Fiber Intake

- Gradually increase fiber in the diet (i.e., start with a small amount at a time to prevent major abdominal pain and gas).
- Increase consumption of fluids, especially water. Aim for a minimum of 6-10 glasses a day.
- Choose a variety of high-fiber gluten-free foods on a regular basis. See pages 105-110.
- Choose gluten-free flour mixes or recipes with high-fiber flours and starches (e.g., almond, amaranth, brown rice, buckwheat, hazelnut, legumes [bean and pea flours], mesquite, millet, Montina™, quinoa, sorghum and teff).
- Add corn bran, ground flax, mesquite flour, rice bran or rice polish to pancake batter, in hot cereals or baked products.
- Use brown rice, buckwheat, millet, quinoa, teff or wild rice in salads or pilafs.
- Add chickpeas (garbanzo beans), kidney beans or other bean varieties to salads or casseroles.
- Make soups with lentils or split peas.
- Choose high-fiber snacks such as dried fruits, nuts, seeds, popcorn, gluten-free snack bars (with dried fruits, nuts and seeds), raw fruits and vegetables.
- Add dried fruits, nuts or seeds to hot cereal; in salads or stir-fry dishes; in muffin, cookie or bread recipes.
- Eat whole fruits or vegetables rather than drinking juice.
- Choose higher-fiber pastas such as bean, brown rice, lentil, quinoa, soy or wild rice instead of white rice.
- In addition to fiber sources, your physician or dietitian may also recommend a commercial fiber supplement such as Benefiber®, Metamucil® (powder and capsules are gluten-free but not the wafers), Citrucel®.

Dietary Fiber Content of Flours & Starches

Flours & Starches	1 cup (weight in grams)	Dietary Fiber (grams)
Almond Flour (Almond Meal)	112	14.7
Amaranth Flour	135	12.6
Arrowroot Starch (Arrowroot Starch Flour)	128	4.4
Buckwheat Bran (Farinetta™)	137	22.7
Buckwheat Flour (whole groat)	120	12.0
Cornmeal (Yellow, degermed,enriched)	138	10.2
Corn Bran	76	60.0
Corn Flour (Yellow, whole grain)	117	15.7
Corn Flour (Yellow, degermed, enriched)	138	2.4
Cornstarch	128	1.2
Flax Seed Meal (Ground Flax)	130	35.5
Garbanzo Bean (Chickpea) Flour	120	20.9
Garfava™ Flour (Garbanzo & Fava Bean Flours)	157	12.0
Hazelnut Flour	112	10.9
Mesquite Flour	146	46.1
Millet Flour	120	10.3
Montina™ Flour	150	36.0
Pea Flour (Golden)	116	11.6
Potato Flour	160	9.4
Potato Starch	192	0.0
Quinoa Flour	112	6.6
Rice Bran	118	39.0
Rice Flour (Brown)	158	7.3
Rice Flour (Sweet)	120	1.2
Rice Flour (White)	158	3.8
Rice Polish	112	12.0
Sorghum Flour	136	8.6
Soy Flour (defatted)	100	17.5
Soy Flour (full fat)	84	8.1
Tapioca Starch (Tapioca Flour)	120	0.0
Teff Flour	130	8.1

Dietary fiber value references for flours and starches see page 106.

Dietary Fiber Content of Grains & Cereals

Grains & Cereals (raw)	1 cup (weight in grams)	Dietary Fiber (grams)
Amaranth	195	18.1
Buckwheat Groats (roasted, dry)	164	16.9
Flax Seed	168	45.9
Millet	200	17.0
Quinoa	170	10.0
Rice (Brown, long grain)	185	6.5
Rice (White, long grain, parboiled, enriched)	187	4.1
Rice (Wild)	160	9.9
Sorghum	192	12.1
Teff	180	11.2

Dietary fiber values for flours, starches and grains are from:

- USDA Nutrient Data Base for Standard Reference, Release #18.
  http://www.nal.usda.gov/fnic/foodcomp/Data/SR18/sr18.html
  http://www.nal.usda.gov/fnic/foodcomp/search/
- Almond Flour, Garbanzo Flour, Hazelnut Flour, Potato Starch, Millet Flour, Sweet Rice Flour and Tapioca Starch from Bob's Red Mill, Milwaukie, OR, USA.
  www.bobsredmill.com
- Buckwheat Bran (Farinetta ™) from Minn-Dak Growers, Grand Forks, ND, USA.
  www.minndak.com
- Garfava ™ Flour from Authentic Foods Company, Gardena, CA, USA.
  www.authenticfoods.com
- Mesquite Flour from research articles. See page 131.
- Montina™ Flour from Amazing Grains Grower Cooperative, Ronan, MT, USA.
  www.amazinggrains.com
- Pea Flour (Golden) from Mountain Meadows Food Processing Ltd., Legal, AB, Canada.
  www.peabutter.ca
- Rice Bran and Rice Polish from Ener-G Foods, Seattle, WA, USA.
  www.ener-g.com
- Sorghum Flour from research articles. See page 131.
- Teff Flour and Grain analyzed by Silliker Canada Co., Markham, ON, Canada.

Dietary Fiber Content of Beans, Lentils, Peas, Nuts & Seeds

Beans, Lentils & Peas (cooked)	1 cup (weight in grams)	Dietary Fiber (grams)
Cranberry Beans (Romano)	177	17.7
Fava Beans (Broad Beans)	170	9.2
Garbanzo Beans (Chickpeas)	164	12.5
Kidney Beans	177	13.1
Lentils	198	15.6
Navy Beans	182	11.7
Pinto Beans	171	14.7
Soybeans	172	10.3
Split Peas	196	16.3
White Beans	179	11.3
Nuts & Seeds		
Almonds (whole, blanched)	145	15.1
Brazil Nuts (dried, blanched)	140	7.6
Peanuts	146	12.4
Pecans (halves)	108	10.4
Walnuts (English, shelled halves)	100	6.7
Pumpkin Seeds (kernels, dried)	138	5.4
Sesame Seeds (kernels, dried, decorticated)	150	17.4
Sunflower Seeds (hulled kernels, dry roasted)	128	14.2

Dietary fiber values for beans, lentils, peas, nuts and seeds are from:

- USDA Nutrient Data Base for Standard Reference, Release #18.
  http://www.nal.usda.gov/fnic/foodcomp/Data/SR18/sr18.html
  http://www.nal.usda.gov/fnic/foodcomp/search/

Dietary Fiber Content of Fruits

Fruits	Serving Size	Dietary Fiber (grams)
Apple	1 medium	3.7
Applesauce (unsweetened)	1 cup	2.9
Apricots (dried)	½ cup	5.9
Apricots (fresh)	2	1.7
Banana	1 medium	2.8
Blackberries	1 cup	7.6
Blueberries	1 cup	3.9
Boysenberries (frozen)	1 cup	5.1
Cherries (sweet, raw)	20	3.2
Cranberries (whole)	1 cup	4.0
Figs (dried)	2	4.6
Grapes (seedless)	20	1.0
Kiwi	1 medium	2.6
Mango	1 whole	3.7
Nectarine	1 medium	2.2
Orange	1 medium	3.1
Peach	1 medium	2.0
Pear	1 medium	4.0
Pineapple (diced, raw)	1 cup	1.9
Plums	2 small	2.0
Prunes (dried)	2	1.2
Raisins	1 cup	6.6
Raspberries	1 cup	8.4
Rhubarb (cooked)	1 cup	4.8
Strawberries	1 cup	3.5

Dietary fiber values of fruits are from:

- USDA Nutrient Data Base for Standard Reference, Release #18.
  http://www.nal.usda.gov/fnic/foodcomp/Data/SR18/sr18.html
  http://www.nal.usda.gov/fnic/foodcomp/search/

Dietary Fiber Content of Vegetables

Vegetables	Serving Size	Dietary Fiber (grams)
Asparagus (cooked)	1 cup	2.9
Beans, Green (cooked)	1 cup	8.0
Beets (cooked)	1 cup	3.4
Broccoli (cooked)	1 cup	4.5
Brussels Sprouts (cooked)	1 cup	4.0
Cabbage (cooked)	1 cup	3.5
Carrots (cooked)	1 cup	5.1
Cauliflower (cooked)	1 cup	3.3
Corn (cooked)	1 cup	4.6
Celery	11" stalk	1.1
Eggplant (cooked)	1 cup	2.5
Lettuce, Iceberg (shredded)	1 cup	0.8
Lettuce, Romaine (shredded)	1 cup	1.0
Mushrooms (cooked)	1 cup	3.4
Okra (cooked)	1 cup	4.0
Onions (cooked)	1 cup	2.9
Parsnips (cooked)	1 cup	6.2
Peas, Green (cooked)	1 cup	8.8
Peppers, Sweet, Green (chopped)	1 cup	2.7
Potato (baked with skin)	1 medium	4.8
Pumpkin (canned)	½ cup	3.5
Radish (sliced)	1 cup	1.9
Snow Peas (cooked)	1 cup	4.5
Spinach (cooked)	1 cup	4.3
Sweet Potato (baked with skin)	1 medium	3.4
Squash, Acorn (cooked)	1 cup	9.0
Turnips (cooked)	1 cup	3.1
Tomatoes	1 medium	1.4
Zucchini (cooked)	1 cup	2.5

Dietary fiber values for vegetables are from:

- USDA Nutrient Data Base for Standard Reference, Release #18.
  http://www.nal.usda.gov/fnic/foodcomp/Data/SR18/sr18.html
  http://www.nal.usda.gov/fnic/foodcomp/search/

Dietary Fiber Content of Specialty Foods

Products	Serving Size	Fiber (grams)
Nutrition Kitchen Golden Soybean Pasta	2 oz (56 g) dry	11.0
Leda Nutrition Leda Apricot Bar (made with gluten-free flour mix [chickpea, corn, tapioca, rice], dried apricots, sultanas, dates, brown rice syrup, fruit concentrate, inulin, coconut, fructose, sodium bicarbonate, flavor)	1 bar (85 g)	8.5
Altiplano Gold Instant Hot Quinoa Cereal (Regular Flavor)	1 packet (48 g)	7.0
Ener-G Foods Seattle Brown Bread (made with Hi-Maize cornstarch, rice flour, yellow corn flour, Montina™ flour and potato flours)	1 slice (52 g)	6.0
Mona's Gluten-Free Golden Goddess Bread Mix (made with organic brown rice, tapioca starch, organic flax meal and sorghum flour)	1/4 cup (40 g) 1 slice	5.1
Heartland's Finest Linguine (made with navy bean and yellow corn flours)	2 oz (56 g) dry	5.0
Larabar Snack Bars Ginger Snap (made with dates, almonds, pecans)	1 bar (51 g)	5.0
Bumble Bar Original with Cashew (made with organic sesame seeds, cashews, flax seeds)	1 bar (45 g)	4.0
Perfect 10 Natural Energy Bar Apricot (made with apricots, dates, figs, hazelnuts, pecans, almonds, flax seeds, poppy seeds, sunflower seeds, pumpkin seeds)	1 bar (50 g)	4.0
Bob's Red Mill GF Mighty Tasty Hot Cereal (made with brown rice, corn, sorghum and buckwheat)	1/4 cup (42 g)	4.0
Bob's Red Mill Organic Creamy Buckwheat Hot Cereal	1/4 cup (41 g)	3.0
Mary's Gone Crackers Original Flavor (made with organic brown rice, quinoa, flax seeds, sesame seeds)	15 crackers (30 g)	3.0
Ancient Harvest Quinoa Flakes	1/3 cup (34 g) dry	2.6
Sylvan Border Farm Classic Dark Bread Mix (made with brown rice, garbanzo bean, amaranth, white rice and potato starch flours)	1 slice (56 g)	2.0
Authentic Foods Pancake & Baking Mix (made with brown rice flour and Garfava™ flour)	1/4 cup (35 g)	2.0
Breads from Anna Yeast-Free Bread Mix (made with tapioca flour, arrowroot flour, chickpea flour, navy bean flour, potato starch, millet, Montina™ flour)	43 grams	2.0

Dietary fiber values for gluten-free specialty foods are from package labels and/or company websites.

Nutritious Gluten-Free Alternatives

In many countries around the world, gluten-containing grains, especially wheat, are major staples in the diet. Having to completely eliminate wheat, barley and rye from the diet is definitely challenging – but the good news is that there are many healthy gluten-free alternatives available. These include amaranth, buckwheat, corn, Indian ricegrass (Montina™), flax, legumes (dried beans, peas and lentils), mesquite, millet, nuts, quinoa, rice, sorghum, teff and wild rice. These may be sold whole, milled into flour, flakes or grits, puffed, and/or incorporated into pasta, cereals, crackers and other gluten-free specialty products. Some of the more unique gluten-free alternatives are highlighted below. For additional information on how to use these alternatives see the gluten-free meal planning and cooking sections on pages 141-153.

AMARANTH

Amaranth is a broad-leafed plant which produces florets containing thousands of tiny grain-like, tan-colored seeds. Although it is used as a grain, it is not an actual grain but a member of the *Amaranthaceae* family, which is a relative of pigweed. This healthy seed has been used as a staple by many ancient civilizations around the world. Amaranth seeds can be used in a wide variety of ways.

Whole-Grain Amaranth

- ✦ It has a robust nutty flavor.
- ✦ In a heavy-bottomed saucepan with a tight-fitting lid, bring 1 cup of amaranth and 2 cups of liquid (e.g., water, gluten-free soup broth or fruit juice) to a boil and simmer for about 20 -25 minutes, or until all the liquid is absorbed. Turn off the heat and let stand, covered, for 5 minutes. Makes about 2 cups. Serve as a side dish to replace potatoes or rice.
- ✦ Can be: mixed with beans for a main dish; added to rice and cooked together for a unique flavor; used to thicken soup or stew.
- ✦ For a hot cereal, cook in fruit juice or water and add chopped dried fruits and nuts.

Amaranth Flour

- ✦ Best combined with other gluten-free flours to make pancakes, flat breads and other baked goods. To enhance the nutritional quality of baked-product recipes, replace 1/4 - 1/3 of gluten-free flours with amaranth flour.

Toasted Amaranth Bran Flour

- ✦ It has a mild, toasty nutty flavor that is very good in quick breads and cookies.
- ✦ Replacement quantities similar to amaranth flour.

Amaranth Starch

- ✦ Can be used as a thickener for puddings, soups and sauces.

Amaranth Bread Crumbs

- ✦ Made from amaranth and tapioca starch.

Puffed Amaranth

- ✦ Can be used as a hot cereal for infants or adults. Mix desired amount of warm liquid with puffed amaranth and stir.

- Add to baked products (e.g., cookies, granola bars); combine with spices for a stuffing or side dish; use as a breading for meat, fish or poultry.
- Also available as "Side Serves" which are savory flavored puffed amaranth that can be cooked and used as a substitute for rice pilaf.

Amaranth Cold Cereals

- Plain or flavored "Snaps" and "O's" cold cereals.

Amaranth Snack and Crackers

- Available in a variety of flavors.

Amaranth Pre-Gel Powder

- Used as a nutrition supplement in pancakes, puddings, soups, sauces and beverages such as smoothies.

Nutritional Information

- Amaranth is very high in protein, fiber, iron, magnesium, phosphorus, potassium, zinc and calcium. It is also a source of B vitamins. See pages 126-128 for nutrient composition.

Amaranth Recipes

- See pages 159-160, 175, 177,181.

References:

- Background information from Nu-World Amaranth publications. www.nuworldfoods.com

BUCKWHEAT

Buckwheat is thought to have originated in China. The largest producers of buckwheat today are China, Japan, Russia and North America, although it is also grown in Europe, India, Australia and South America. Buckwheat is botanically classified as a fruit, not a cereal grain, and is of the *Polygonaceae* family, which is closely related to rhubarb. Buckwheat is triangular in shape and has a black shell. The outer shell is removed (hulled) and the kernel inside is known as a groat. These groats are available in several different forms.

Roasted Groats

- Roasting gives the buckwheat kernels a distinctive, nutty flavor.
- Roasted groats are called "kasha" and are packaged in four granulations (whole, coarse, medium and fine).
- Can be steamed, boiled or baked and served "as is" with seasoning; added to soups and stews for thickening and flavor; used as a stuffing.
- In a heavy-bottomed saucepan with a tight-fitting lid, bring 1 cup of groats and 2 cups of liquid (e.g., water, gluten-free soup broth or fruit juice) to a boil and simmer for about 10-12 minutes, or until all the liquid is absorbed. Turn off the heat and let stand, covered, for 5 minutes. Makes about 2 cups.

Unroasted Groats

Whole – cooked and used as a side dish to replace potatoes or rice; as a stuffing for poultry; mixed with fruit and milk as a breakfast cereal. Cook according to roasted groat directions on page 112.

Ground – into grits and often labeled as "cream of buckwheat." Can be cooked and eaten as a hot cereal.

Ground – into flour:

- Dark flour has a stronger, distinctive flavor as it contains a higher percentage of finely milled particles of buckwheat hulls and is higher in fiber and nutrients
- Light flour has a mild, mellow flavor as it contains fewer buckwheat hulls.
- These flours can be added to pancakes, breads and muffins. Use nuts and spices to enhance the flavor of baked goods containing buckwheat flour.
- The flour is also used to make Japanese "Soba" noodles. They can be made from 100% pure buckwheat flour which is gluten-free. However, Soba noodles are often made with a combination of pure buckwheat flour and wheat flour and are not gluten-free.
- Be aware that some companies sell a buckwheat flour or pancake mix that is a combination of pure buckwheat flour and wheat flour, so be sure to look for 100% pure buckwheat flour.

Buckwheat Bran (Farinetta™)

- Is from the outer layer of the buckwheat groat and is high in fiber, protein, iron, riboflavin, niacin and numerous beneficial phytochemicals. Farinetta™ is licensed and trademarked by Minn-Dak Growers, Ltd.
- Can be used in pancake and muffin recipes or added to chili or casseroles.

Nutritional Information

- Buckwheat provides a good source of high-quality protein in the plant kingdom. It is high in magnesium, zinc, phosphorus, potassium, niacin, riboflavin, vitamin B_6 and fiber. It is also a source of iron. See pages 126-128 for nutrient composition.

Buckwheat Recipes

- See pages 160, 184, 192, 197.

References:

- Background information from the following company publications and websites:
  1. The Birkett Mills
     www.thebirkettmills.com
  2. Minn-Dak Growers Ltd.
     www.minndak.com
  3. Canadian Special Crops Association
     www.buckwheatforhealth.com

FLAX

Flax is a member of the *Linaceae* family and is widely grown across the Canadian prairies and northern USA. This flat, oval seed has a pointed tip and is about the size of a sesame seed. Some varieties of flax are grown for human food consumption while other varieties are used to produce fiber for industrial purposes (e.g., linoleum flooring, linen clothing). The brown and yellow flax seeds grown for human consumption are very similar in their nutritional composition. Flax is available as an oil, whole seed or ground flax seed (also known as milled flax seed). Grinding ensures that all seeds are broken up, enabling the nutrients present to be absorbed by the body. Ground flax seed can be purchased in vacuum-sealed packages on store shelves or in plastic bags found in the refrigeration section. Whole flax seed can also be ground in a coffee grinder, food processor or blender to the consistency of finely ground coffee.

Storage and Handling

- Whole flax seed can be stored at room temperature for up to one year.
- Ground flax seed should be stored in a sealed opaque container in the refrigerator or freezer. For optimum freshness, it is best to grind flax seed as you need it, since the natural fats in flax seed go rancid quickly if left exposed to heat or air.
- Flax oil is very perishable and should be kept refrigerated in an opaque container.

Using Flax

- Flax oil is best used in cold foods such as fruit smoothies and salad dressings. It is not recommended for frying as it breaks down when exposed to high temperatures. The oil can also be drizzled over cooked gluten-free pasta.
- Whole flax seed and ground flax seed have a light, nutty flavor which becomes more robust when the flax is roasted. Whole and ground flax seed can be used in a wide variety of foods such as muffins, breads, pancakes, waffles, cookies, fruit cobblers, hot cereals, casseroles, meat loaf, burgers, stew, spaghetti sauce, rice dishes and salads. Mix ground flax in fruit smoothies, pudding, cottage cheese, ice cream, yogurt and frozen yogurt.
- Substitute ¼ cup of ground flax in recipes containing rice bran. It will give a better texture and is less heavy.
- When adding ground flax to a recipe extra liquid must be added (e.g., for every 3 tbsp. of flax add 1 tbsp. liquid).
- Baked goods containing ground flax have a chewier texture and tend to brown more rapidly so the temperature may need to be reduced.
- **Flax can be used as an egg replacer.** To replace 1 egg, soak 1 tsp. of ground flax in ¼ cup boiling water for 5 minutes. Cool before using. Works best in cookie and snack bar recipes.

Nutritional Information

- Flax has been consumed throughout history for its nutritional and health benefits. It is rich in alpha-linolenic acid (an essential omega-3 fatty acid), fiber (soluble and insoluble) and plant lignans. These components play a role in the maintenance and improvement of general health. Flax helps promote bowel regularity due to its very high fiber content. It may also help protect against coronary heart disease, as well as breast and colon cancer. In addition, autoimmune diseases, like many other chronic diseases, are a disease of inflammation, and flax is being studied for its positive role in immune and inflammatory reactions.

- Flax oil is high in omega-3 fatty acids but does not contain any fiber and lignans (a type of phytochemical). Note: some flax oils add lignans back after the oil is extracted from the seed.
- Whole flax seeds are an excellent source of fiber. In order to gain all the benefits of flax seed, including the omega-3 fatty acids, lignans, protein, vitamins and minerals, it is important to grind the whole flax seed. This improves the bioavailability of the these components.
- Flax is very high in iron, magnesium, zinc, calcium, phosphorus, potassium, thiamin, niacin, vitamin B_6 and protein. It is a source of other B vitamins and other nutrients. See pages 126-128 for nutrient composition.

Recipes

- See pages 173-174, 177, 182, 198, 199.

References

- Background information and excerpts taken from the following company publications and websites:
    1. Flax Council of Canada – www.flaxcouncil.ca
    2. Saskatchewan Flax Development Commission – www.saskflax.com
- There are many research articles on the beneficial effects of flax that can be found at the Flax Council of Canada site.

MESQUITE

Mesquite is the North American name for a woody leguminous plant of the genus *Prosopis*. There are over 45 species native to arid and semi-arid regions of North and South America, Africa and southern Asia, ranging from eight-foot shrubs to sixty-foot tall trees. The wood chips of the tree are dried and used to impart the unique mesquite flavor to grilled foods.

These trees contain bean pods that come in different sizes, depending on the specific variety of mesquite tree, and are harvested for a variety of purposes. In some countries, the pods are processed into a syrup, jelly, tea or coffee. The entire pod can also be ground into a coarse, mealy flour that has a cinnamon-mocha aroma and sweet, chocolate, molasses-like flavor with a hint of caramel. Alternatively, a combination of milling and sieving techniques using only the pulp of the bean pod can be used to produce a finer flour (80-100 mesh) that has a sweeter and more concentrated aroma and flavor than the flour from the whole bean pod. The light tan-colored mesquite flour has been a dietary staple for indigenous people for centuries. Mesquite flour has recently been introduced to the North American market and can be used as a baking ingredient or flavoring agent in many foods. It can be combined with other gluten-free flours to make pancakes and baked products such as breads, muffins, cakes, cookies, pie crusts and brownies or it can also be added to hot cereal (e.g., cream of brown or white rice), meat dishes, soups and gravies.

Nutrition Information

- The nutritional composition of the mesquite flour varies considerably depending on the variety of mesquite plant, the soil type in which it is grown, and whether the whole pod or the pulp of the pod is used.
- The whole-pod flour is higher in protein and calcium than the flour made only from the pulp. However, both types of flours are very high in fiber and are also a source of iron, magnesium, calcium, thiamin, niacin and vitamin B_6. See pages 126-128 for nutrient composition.

Recipes

- See pages 172, 183.

References

- Background information from:
  1. Felker P. Mesquite Flour: New Life for an Ancient Staple. Gastronomica. 2005; 5 (2): 85-89.
     www.ucpress.edu
  2. Email and telephone correspondence with Peter Felker. Contact: peter_felker@hotmail.com
  3. Email and telephone correspondence with Kathryn Ehrhorn, San Pedro Mesquite Company.
     www.spmesquite.com
  4. Email and telephone correspondence Jim Byrd, Cocina deVega, Inc..
     www.cocinadevega.com
  5. Casa deFruta Company
     www.casadefruta.com
  6. See page 131 for additional research articles on mesquite.

MILLET

The term millet refers to various grasses that grow in semi-arid regions of the world. The six species of major importance are proso, finger, foxtail, barnyard, browntop and pearl. Most millet species are used for animal or bird seed, however, pearl and finger millets are used for human food consumption. Millet is closely related to corn and belongs to the *Gramineae* family. It is primarily used as a food crop in Africa, Asia and India. Millet seed is very small, round in shape and can be yellow, white, gray or red. The most common variety found in North America is the light yellow millet that has a slight corn-like, sweet nutty flavor. Millet is hulled and the inner seed is available as whole seed, coarsely ground into grits or finely ground into flour.

Whole-Grain Millet

- Can be cooked in water or broth and eaten alone as a cereal, as a side-dish such as pilaf, or used for poultry stuffing or as a salad.
- Rinse the millet seed in cold water and drain. In a heavy-bottomed saucepan with a tight fitting lid, bring 1 cup of millet and 2½ cups of liquid to a boil and simmer for about 20 minutes, or until all the liquid is absorbed. Turn off the heat and let stand, covered, for 5 minutes. Makes about 3½ cups.

Puffed Millet

- Use as a cold cereal or crush it for a breading.

Millet Flour

- Similar in texture to rice flour and produces a delicate, dry crumb with a pale yellow color in baked products.
- Best combined with other gluten-free flours.
- Can become rancid easily, therefore, purchase in small amounts or grind millet in a grain mill and use as needed. Store in a tightly covered container in the refrigerator or freezer.

Nutritional Information

- Millet is a good source of easily digestible protein. It is also a source of thiamin, riboflavin, niacin, vitamin B_6, folate, fiber, iron, magnesium and zinc. See pages 126-128 for nutrient composition.

Millet Recipes

- See pages 159, 186, 191.

References:

- Background information from:
    1. http://www.hort.purdue.edu/newcrop/afcm/millet.html
    2. http://www.cgiar.org/impact/research/millet.html
    3. http://www.nap.edu/books/0309049903/html/39.html

MONTINA™ (Indian Ricegrass)

Indian ricegrass (IRG), is a perennial, native bunch grass from the family *Achnatherum hymenoides*, but is not related to rice. It acquired the Indian portion of its name from the fact that the Native Americans had used the small black seeds of the grass as a staple that was ground into flour for a flat bread. It grows wild from southern Manitoba, Canada to higher elevations in southern California. In the early 1990s, Montana State University (MSU) conducted extensive research on IRG and determined that this fairly drought-resistant, hardy plant was very nutritious and also gluten-free. Amazing Grains Grower Cooperative was formed as a result of collaboration between MSU, government and others to grow and market IRG and registered the trade name Montina™ for IRG products. Amazing Grains has 56 producer/members in six states that have over 4,000 acres planted to IRG. It is milled, processed and packaged in a dedicated gluten-free facility. All Montina™ products and their ingredients are tested for gluten using the ELISA test before entering the production facility.

Montina™ is sold in two forms.

Montina™ Pure Baking Supplement (100%Montina™ Flour)

- A light brown-gray-colored flour that has a sweet, nutty, almost "wheat-like" flavor.
- Best combined with other gluten-free flours. Can substitute 25% Montina™ for one of the primary flours in baked products.

Montina™ All Purpose Baking Flour Blend

- This is a blend of white rice flour, tapioca flour and Montina™ flour.
- In most cases can be used cup for cup to exchange for any flour. This is not a complete mix and will require xanthan gum and other ingredients in baked recipes. Can be used in breads, muffins, pancakes and waffles, as well as a thickener in stews and gravies.

Nutritional Information

- Montina™ is very high in protein, fiber and iron. It is also a source of calcium. Its complete nutritional composition profile is unknown as it has not been analyzed for other nutrients. See pages 126-128 for nutrient composition.

Montina™ Recipes

- See pages 162, 167, 172, 200.

References:

- Background information and excerpts taken from Amazing Grains Grower Cooperative publications.
  www.amazinggrains.com

QUINOA

Quinoa (pronounced "keen-wah") has been consumed for thousands of years in South America and was a staple of the Incas, who called it "the mother grain." It is not actually a grain but the seed of a broad-leafed plant from the *Chenopodiaceae* family which is a close relative of the weed, lamb's quarters. There are hundreds of varieties of quinoa, ranging in color from white to red and purple to black. Many varieties are now grown in North America. The plant stalks grow three to six feet high, containing clusters of seeds near the top of the stalk. The seed looks like a cross between sesame seed and millet. Quinoa seeds are naturally covered with saponin, an extremely bitter resin-like substance which protects it from birds and insects. To be edible the saponin must be removed. Some companies specially process the quinoa to remove this bitter coating, making it pan-ready and fast cooking. Quinoa is sold in several forms.

Quinoa Seed

- Can be used as a side dish instead of potatoes or rice or in salads, pilafs, stuffings, casseroles and puddings, as well as a thickener for soups, chili and stews.
- Rinse the quinoa in cold water and drain. In a heavy-bottomed saucepan with a tight-fitting lid, bring 1 cup of quinoa and 2 cups of liquid to a boil and simmer for about 15 minutes, or until all the liquid is absorbed. Turn off the heat and let stand, covered, for 5 minutes. Makes about 3 cups.
- Can also be cooked in the microwave using a round 2-quart microwave-safe casserole or bowl. Combine 1 cup quinoa and 2 cups water, cover loosely with plastic wrap and microwave on high for about 10-12 minutes, or until most of the water is absorbed. Remove from microwave, stir once and let stand, covered, for 5 minutes before serving.

Quinoa Flakes

- Can be eaten as an instant hot breakfast cereal. Add ⅓ cup of flakes to 1 cup of boiling water and boil for 1½-2 minutes, stirring frequently. Remove from heat and allow to cool. Add chopped nuts and dried fruits and sprinkle with brown sugar. Can also be cooked in the microwave. Combine flakes and water in a medium-to-large microwave-safe bowl and microwave on high for 2-2½ minutes. Stir before serving.
- Available in plain and various flavors (contains flaked quinoa, dried fruits, nuts or seeds, sugar and spices).
- Substitute quinoa flakes for up to ⅓ of the gluten-free flour in a cookie, muffin or bread recipe.
- Can also be added to pancakes and waffles.

Quinoa Flour

- A tan-colored flour with a slightly nutty, strong flavor so best combined with other gluten-free flours.
- Can be used in a variety of baked items, especially in highly spiced or flavored products.

Quinoa Pasta

- Quinoa is combined with corn or rice and is available in a variety of shapes.
- Cooks in 5-9 minutes.

Nutritional Information

- Quinoa contains more high-quality protein than any other grain or cereal. The quality of this protein compares very closely to that of dried skimmed milk. Quinoa is high in iron, magnesium, phosphorus and zinc. It is also a source of calcium, B vitamins and dietary fiber. See pages 126-128 for nutrient composition.

Quinoa Recipes

- See pages 160, 180, 186-187, 190.

References:

- Background information from:
  1. Northern Quinoa Corporation
     www.quinoa.com
  2. Quinoa Corporation
     www.quinoa.net
  3. Altiplano Gold, Inc
     www.altiplanogold.com

SORGHUM

Sorghum, also referred to as milo, is a member of the *Gramineae* family. This major cereal grain grows in hot, semi-arid tropical and dry temperate areas of the world, including the USA, Mexico, Africa, India and China. The round red or white seeds are slightly smaller than peppercorns. New food-grade varieties of sorghum have been developed in the USA. These sorghums have a hard white grain that is free of any bitter flavors or dark colors often associated with non-food grade sorghums. As a result of these characteristics, whole or decorticated kernels of white or tan sorghums can be flaked, puffed and micronized, and used in a wide range of food products such as cereals, granola bars, snack foods, baked products and beverages, including beer. Sorghum is available as a whole grain or can be milled into flour and grits.

Whole-Grain Sorghum

- Soak the grain overnight in water. Drain and combine 1 cup sorghum with about 2½-3 cups of water in a heavy-bottomed saucepan with a tight-fitting lid. Bring to a boil, reduce heat and simmer, covered, for about 30-45 minutes. Turn off heat and let stand 5-10 minutes. Drain any excess water. Combine with herbs and/or spices and use as a side dish such as pilaf or in casseroles, stuffings, salad, as well as a thickener for soups and chili.
- Can be used as an alternative for rice in puddings.

Sorghum Grits

- Can be prepared as a hot cereal served with dried fruits, nuts, sweetener and a dash of cinnamon and/or vanilla.

Sorghum Flour

- This light tan-colored flour has a slightly nutty, earthy flavor.
- A combination of sorghum flour and other gluten-free flours, especially bean flour or amaranth flour works well as sorghum's bland flavor and light color does not alter the taste of baked products.

Nutritional Information

- Sorghum is high in phosphorus and potassium. It is also a source of fiber, protein, thiamin, niacin, vitamin B_6 and iron. See pages 126-128 for nutrient composition.

Sorghum Recipes

- See pages 158-159, 166, 169, 177, 179, 200.

References:

- Background information from:
  1. Email correspondence with Dr. Lloyd Rooney, Cereal Quality Laboratory, Soil and Crop Science Department, Texas A & M University, College Station, TX.
  2. Email and telephone correspondence with Dr. Jeff Dahlberg, PhD, Research Director, National Sorghum Producers, Lubbock, TX. www.sorghumgrowers.com
  3. Email and telephone correspondence with Dr. Scott Bean, Research Chemist, United States Department of Agriculture-Agriculture Research Service, Manhattan, KS.
  4. See page 131 for additional research article on sorghum.

TEFF

Teff, or tef, a grass native to Ethiopia, belongs to the *Poaceae* family. It is also grown in India, Australia and Northwestern USA. Teff is the smallest of all grains in the world (about 100-150 teff grains equal the size of 1 wheat kernel). The teff grains range from milky white to almost black. In Ethiopia, white, red and brown are the most common types while the USA grows brown and ivory types. Teff has a unique nutty, mild molasses-like flavor and is sold both as a whole grain and as a flour. This major cereal crop in Ethiopia is ground into flour and fermented 1-3 days to make "Injera," a sour-dough-type flat bread that is moist and chewy. Authentic Injera is usually made from pure teff flour, however, many North American restaurants use a combination of teff flour and wheat flour which is not gluten-free. Injera is traditionally consumed with "wot," a spicy sauce or stew made of meat or ground legumes.

Whole-Grain Teff

- Add ½-1 tbsp. teff grain to a serving of gluten-free hot cereal (e.g., cream of brown or white rice cereal) while cooking.
- In a heavy-bottomed saucepan with a tight-fitting lid, bring 2 cups of lightly salted water to a boil and then add ½ cup teff grain. Cover and simmer 15-20 minutes, or until water is absorbed, stirring occasionally. Use as a side dish instead of potato or rice. For a breakfast cereal, add honey or brown sugar, raisins, nuts, chopped fruit and/or cinnamon for flavor.
- Cook teff with other gluten-free grains such as brown rice, buckwheat groats (kasha) or millet. Use 3 parts water or gluten-free broth to 1 part grains. Simmer for about 20 minutes, or until all the water is absorbed.
- Mix cooked teff with seeds, beans or tofu and garlic, herbs and onions to make a vegetarian burger.
- Use as a thickener for soups, stews and gravies. For stews or soups, add uncooked teff grain to the pot 30 minutes before serving or add cooked teff to the pot 10 minutes before serving.

Teff Flour

- Combine with other gluten-free flours in baked products, especially dark breads and cakes such as brownies, chocolate cake and gingerbread, as well as in muffin and cookie recipes. Can use 25-50% teff flour in the total flour blend. For pancakes, use 100% teff flour or a combination of teff and other gluten-free flours.

Nutritional Information

- Teff seeds are more nutritious than the major cereal grains (e.g., wheat, barley and corn) for several reasons: (1) the small seed size means the germ and bran (the outer portions where nutrients are concentrated) account for a higher proportion of the seed compared to other grains, and (2) the entire whole-grain teff seed is used. Teff is high in calcium, iron, magnesium, thiamin and zinc. It is also a good source of fiber, protein and B vitamins. See pages 126-128 for nutrient composition.

Teff Recipes

- See pages 160, 164, 171, 189.

References:

- Background information from:
    1. The Teff Company
       www.teffco.com
    2. www.hort.purdue.edu/newcrop/proceedings1993/V2-231.html
    3. http://www.nap.edu/books/0309049903/html/215.html
    4. See page 131 for an additional research article on teff.

WILD RICE

Wild rice, an aquatic grass indigenous to North America, grows extensively in shallow lakes and streams. Despite its name, it is not a member of the rice family but is from the *Zizania* family. Most wild rice grown in northern Saskatchewan and Manitoba, Canada, is "OCIA" certified organic. Wild rice has a distinct, nut-like, roasted flavor that is enjoyable by itself or combined with other ingredients. It is sold plain, mixed with other rices, as a flour or made into pasta.

Handling and Preparation

- Wash wild rice in a wire strainer and run cold water over it.
- In a heavy-bottomed saucepan, with a tight-fitting lid, combine 4 cups of water with 1 cup of wild rice. Bring to a boil and then simmer approximately 40-60 minutes, until the rice kernels have burst their shells and fluffed out. The volume of rice increases up to 4 times (i.e., 1 cup raw rice = 4 cups cooked rice).
- Cooked rice can be used in casseroles, salads or side dishes. It can also be combined with white or brown rice. Leftover cooked rice can be kept in the refrigerator for 1 week or frozen (it remains in excellent condition upon thawing). Cool rice before freezing.

Nutritional Information

- Wild rice is a source of fiber, protein, niacin, magnesium, phosphorus, potassium and zinc. See pages 126-128 for nutrient composition.

Wild Rice Recipes

- See pages 185, 190, 193.

References:

- Background information from Riese's Canadian Lake Wild Rice publications. www.wildlakerice.com

Gluten-Free Dietary Guidelines for Healthy Eating

The United States Department of Agriculture (USDA) new MyPyramid food guidance system and Canada's Food Guide to Healthy Eating (currently under review with new guidelines to be released spring 2006) are practical tools to help individuals make wise food choices. These tools differ somewhat with regard to the types of foods that are in specific groups, their serving size and recommended number of servings per day for each food group. However, the total amount per day for each group is based on factors such as age, body size, activity level and sex. For specific information about these tools and how to apply them to your individual needs see these links:

USA : www.mypyramid.gov
CANADA: http://www.hc-sc.gc.ca/fn-an/food-guide-aliment/index_e.html

The following chart has incorporated many of the key components of the American and Canadian tools with adaptations for the gluten-free diet. The symbol GF denotes gluten-free.

Food Group	Examples	Healthy Tips & Nutrition Facts
Grain Products	GF grain alternatives (e.g., amaranth, buckwheat, cornmeal, millet, oats [pure: see pages 19, 209, 275], quinoa, rice [brown, white or wild], sorghum, teff)	1. Choose GF whole grains* more often (e.g.,amaranth, buckwheat, brown rice, cornmeal {whole grain – not degermed}, millet, oats, quinoa, sorghum, teff, wild rice).
	GF bread, rolls, bagels, muffins	2. Choose enriched GF products more often. Not all GF breads, flours, cereals and pastas are enriched with iron and B vitamins and are often lower in fiber as many are made from refined flours and starches.
	GF ready-to-eat cold cereals	
	GF hot cereals (e.g., amaranth; cornmeal; cream of buckwheat or brown rice or white rice; quinoa, hominy or sorghum or soy grits; quinoa; rice flakes; soy flakes)	3. Choose breads, rolls, bagels, muffins, cereals and pasta from flours and starches that are higher in fiber, protein and vitamins and minerals (e.g., amaranth, brown rice, buckwheat, flax, legumes, mesquite, millet, Montina™, quinoa, sorghum, teff and wild rice).
	GF pasta (e.g., bean, 100% buckwheat, corn, pea, potato, quinoa/corn, quinoa/rice, soy, rice [brown, white, wild])	
	GF corn or rice tortillas	
	GF pancake or waffles	
	Popcorn	

* Whole grains contain the entire grain seed (usually called the kernel) and consist of three parts – the bran, germ and endosperm. Refined grains have most of the bran and some of the germ removed which results in the loss of dietary fiber, vitamins/minerals and other nutritional components.

Food Group	Examples	Healthy Tips & Nutrition Facts
Fruits	Fresh, frozen or canned fruits and fruit juices Dried fruits	1. To get more fiber, choose fruit instead of juice. 2. Choose unsweetened frozen fruit or canned fruit in 100% fruit juice or water. 3. Choose orange-colored fruits (e.g., apricot, cantaloupe, orange, mango, nectarine, peach, red or pink grapefruit) more often as they are high in vitamins, minerals and phytochemicals (naturally occurring healthy compounds). 4. Choose 100% fruit juice rather than fruit beverages which contain less juice and more added sugar. 5. Some juices (e.g., orange) are enriched with calcium and/or vitamin D. (Vitamin D can be added to juice in the U.S. but not Canada).
Vegetables	Fresh, frozen or canned vegetables and vegetable juices Dry bean, peas and lentils*	1. Choose dark green and yellow/orange vegetables (e.g., broccoli, carrot, pumpkin, romaine lettuce, squash, sweet potato) more often as they are higher in vitamins, minerals and phytochemicals.
Milk Products	Milk (fluid and dried powdered) Milk (lactose-free, lactose-reduced) Cheese Yogurt and yogurt-based beverages Milk-based desserts (e.g., puddings made with milk, ice cream, frozen yogurt, ice milk)	1. Choose lower-fat milk products more often. 2. Milk and some yogurt products are enriched with vitamin D which is a key nutrient that aids in the absorption of calcium. Cheese, ice cream, commercial pudding cups and some yogurts are not enriched with vitamin D. 3. Many brands of non-dairy beverages (e.g., nut, potato, rice, soy) and some orange/other fruit juices may be enriched with calcium and/or vitamin D but may not provide the other nutrients found in milk products. 4. For individuals with lactose intolerance see pages 101-102.

* In MyPyramid these can be counted either as vegetables or in the meat and alternatives group.

Food Group	Examples	Healthy Tips & Nutrition Facts
Meats, Beans and Alternatives	Meats, poultry, fish, shellfish, eggs	1. Choose leaner meats and poultry as well as legumes more often.
	Legumes (dried beans, peas & lentils)	2. Flax seeds and walnuts, along with some fish (e.g., herring, salmon, trout) are high in omega-3 fatty acids which play a positive role in heart health.
	Nuts and seeds	
	GF tofu, GF tempeh, GF texturized vegetable protein, GF veggie burgers	3. Some seeds and nuts (almonds, hazelnuts, sunflower) are good sources of vitamin E.
Oils*	Oils (e.g., canola, coconut, corn, cottonseed, olive, palm kernel, peanut, safflower, sesame seed, walnut)	1. All oils and fats are a mixture of unsaturated fatty acids and saturated fatty acids.
	Food naturally high in oils (e.g., avocado, flax, nuts, olives, some fish)	2. Most oils (except coconut and palm kernel) contain more monounsaturated and polyunsaturated fatty acids.
	Solid fats (butter, beef fat [tallow, suet], chicken fat, pork fat [lard], stick margarine, shortening)	3. Solid fats and coconut and palm kernel oils contain more saturated fatty acids and/or trans fats than unsaturated oils.
	Foods high in solid fats (e.g., many cheeses, cream, well-marbled cuts of meat, regular ground beef, bacon, poultry skin)	4. Limit solid fats and coconut and palm kernel oils as saturated fats and trans fats raise LDL (bad) cholesterol levels in the blood which are a factor in coronary heart disease.

* This group is in MyPyramid. Canada's Food Guide does not specifically include this group.

Nutrient Composition of Gluten-Free Grains, Flours, Starches, Gums, Legumes, Nuts & Seeds

FOOD ITEM	Weight in Grams (1 cup)	VITAMINS B₁ Thiamin mg	B₂ Riboflavin mg	B₃ Niacin mg	B₆ Pyridoxine mg	Folate mcg	MINERALS Calcium mg	Iron mg	Magnesium mg	Zinc mg	PROTEIN grams	CARBO-HYDRATES grams	DIETARY FIBER grams
GRAINS, FLOURS & STARCHES													
Almond Flour (Almond Meal)	112	0.17	0.70	3.5	0.12	42	289	4.3	338	3.7	23.6	21	14.7
Amaranth Seed	195	0.16	0.41	2.5	0.44	96	298	14.8	519	6.2	28.2	129	18.1
Amaranth Flour	135	0.11	0.28	1.7	0.30	66	207	10.3	359	413	19.5	89	12.6
Arrowroot Starch (Arrowroot Starch Flour)	128	0.00	0.00	0.0	0.01	9	51	0.4	4	0.1	0.4	113	4.4
Buckwheat Bran (Farinetta™)	137	0.14	0.58	9.6	0.29	41	104	13.6	878	12.2	49	71	22.7
Buckwheat Groats (roasted, dry)	164	0.37	0.44	8.4	0.58	69	28	4.1	362	4.0	19.2	123	16.9
Buckwheat Groats (roasted, cooked)	168	0.07	0.07	1.6	0.13	24	12	1.3	86	1.0	5.7	34	4.5
Buckwheat Flour (whole groat)	120	0.50	0.23	7.4	0.70	65	49	4.9	301	3.7	15.1	85	12
Chestnut Flour	100	0.35	0.05	0.9	0.67	110	64	2.4	74	0.4	5.0	78	NA
Corn Bran (crude)	76	0.01	0.08	2.1	0.12	3	32	2.1	49	1.2	6.4	65	60
Corn Flour – Yellow (whole grain)	117	0.29	0.09	2.2	0.43	29	8	2.8	109	2.0	8.1	90	15.7
Corn Flour – Yellow (Masa, enriched)	114	1.63	0.86	11.2	0.42	266	161	8.2	125	2.0	10.7	87	NA
Corn Flour – Yellow (degermed, unenriched)	126	0.09	0.07	3.4	0.12	60	3	1.2	23	0.5	7.0	104	2.4
Cornmeal – Yellow (degermed, enriched)	138	0.99	0.56	6.9	0.36	322	7	5.7	55	1.0	11.7	107	10.2
Cornmeal – Yellow (degermed, unenriched)	138	0.19	0.07	1.4	0.36	66	7	1.5	55	1.0	11.7	107	10.2
Cornmeal – Yellow (whole-grain)	122	0.47	0.25	4.4	0.37	30	7	4.2	155	2.2	9.9	94	8.9
Cornstarch	128	0.00	0.00	0.0	0.00	0	3	0.6	4	0.1	0.3	117	1.2
Flax Seed	168	2.76	0.27	5.2	0.80	146	428	9.6	659	7.3	30.7	49	45.9
Flax Seed Meal (Ground Flax)	130	2.14	0.21	4.0	0.62	113	332	7.5	510	5.6	23.8	38	35.5
Garbanzo Bean (Chickpea) Flour	120	0.58	0.25	1.8	0.64	668	126	7.5	138	4.1	23.2	73	20.9
Garfava™ Flour	157	NA	NA	NA	NA	NA	104	7.9	NA	NA	34.9	92	12
Hazelnut Flour	112	0.72	0.12	20.2	0.63	127	128	5.3	183	2.7	16.7	19	10.9
Mesquite Flour	146	0.28	0.09	4.5	0.34	26	196	5.1	125	3.1	11.8	122	46.1
Millet (raw)	200	0.84	0.58	9.4	0.77	170	16	6.0	228	3.4	22.0	146	17
Millet (cooked)	174	0.18	0.14	2.3	0.19	33	5	1.1	77	1.6	6.1	41	2.3
Millet Flour	120	0.76	0.48	2.8	NA	NA	NA	9.2	NA	NA	13.7	89	10.3

NA = Not available

FOOD ITEM	Weight in Grams (1 cup)	VITAMINS B₁ Thiamin mg	B₂ Riboflavin mg	B₃ Niacin mg	B₆ Pyridoxine mg	Folate mcg	MINERALS Calcium mg	Iron mg	Magnesium mg	Zinc mg	PROTEIN grams	CARBO-HYDRATES grams	DIETARY FIBER grams
Montina™ Flour	150	NA	NA	NA	NA	NA	83	10.8	NA	NA	25.5	105	36
Pea Flour – Golden	116						59	7.3	139	7.1	30.4	76	11.6
Potato Flour	160	0.37	0.08	5.6	1.23	40	104	2.2	104	0.9	11.0	133	9.4
Potato Starch	192	0.00	0.00	0.00	NA	NA	19	2.9	NA	NA	0.2	158	0.0
Quinoa Grain (raw)	170	0.34	0.67	5.0	0.38	83	102	15.7	357	5.6	22.3	117	10.0
Quinoa Flour	112	0.22	0.44	3.3	0.25	55	67	10.4	235	3.7	14.7	77	6.6
Rice Bran	134	3.60	0.38	62.8	4.25	36	54	10.3	974	7.4	19.4	68	39
Rice Polish	112	1.50	0.14	20	NA	NA	NA	9.0	NA	NA	12	76	12
Rice, Brown – raw (long grain)	185	0.74	0.17	9.4	0.94	37	43	2.7	265	3.7	14.7	143	6.5
Rice, Brown – cooked (long grain)	195	0.19	0.05	3.0	0.28	8	20	0.8	84	1.2	5.0	45	3.5
Rice Flour – Brown	158	0.70	0.13	10.0	1.2	25	17	3.1	177	3.9	11.4	121	7.3
Rice Flour – Sweet	120	NA	NA	NA	NA	NA	20	0.0	NA	NA	10.1	95	1.2
Rice Flour – White	158	0.22	0.03	4.1	0.69	6	16	0.6	55	1.3	9.4	127	3.8
Rice, White – raw (long grain, parboiled, enr.)	187	1.3	0.08	9.6	0.85	481	103	9.8	50	1.9	15.2	150	4.1
Rice, White – ckd. (long grain, parboiled, enr.)	158	0.34	0.03	3.6	0.25	128	30	2.9	14	0.6	4.6	41	1.4
Rice, Wild – raw	160	0.18	0.42	10.8	0.63	152	34	3.1	283	9.5	23.6	120	9.9
Rice, Wild – cooked	164	0.09	0.14	2.1	0.22	43	5	1.0	53	2.2	6.5	35	3.0
Sorghum Grain	192	0.46	0.27	5.6	1.13	38	54	8.5	365	3.0	21.7	143	12.1
Sorghum Flour	136	0.32	0.20	4.0	NA	NA	38	6.0	NA	NA	15.4	102	8.6
Soy Flour (full-fat)	84	0.49	0.97	3.6	0.39	290	173	5.4	360	3.3	29.0	30	8.0
Soy Flour (defatted)	100	0.70	0.25	2.6	0.57	305	241	9.2	290	2.5	47.0	38	17.5
Tapioca Starch (Tapioca Flour)	120	0.00	0.00	0	0.00	0	0	0	0	0	0.0	119	0.0
Teff Grain	180	0.70	0.20	2.7	NA	135	331	12.1	342	8.8	21.8	130	11.2
Teff Flour	130	0.51	0.14	1.9	NA	97	239	8.7	247	12.2	15.7	94	8.7
GLUTEN-CONTAINING FLOURS													
Wheat Bran	58	0.30	0.34	7.9	0.76	46	42	6.1	354	4.2	9.0	37	24.8
Whole-Wheat Flour	120	0.54	0.26	7.6	0.41	53	41	4.7	166	3.5	16.4	87	14.6
White Flour, All-Purpose (enriched)	125	0.98	0.62	7.4	0.06	229	19	5.8	28	0.9	12.9	95	3.4

NA = Not available ckd. = cooked enr. = enriched

Food Item	Weight in Grams (1 cup)	Vitamins					Minerals				Protein	Carbo-hydrates	Dietary Fiber
		B_1 Thiamin mg	B_2 Riboflavin mg	B_3 Niacin mg	B_6 Pyridoxine mg	Folate mcg	Calcium mg	Iron mg	Magnesium mg	Zinc mg	grams	grams	grams
Gums													
Guar Gum (1 tbsp.)	7	0.00	0.00	0.0	0.00	0	3	0.1	NA	NA	0.2	6	6.1
Xanthan Gum (1 tbsp.)	9	NA	NA	NA	NA	NA	3	0.1	NA	NA	0.5	7	6.8
Beans, Lentils & Peas (cooked)													
Black Beans	172	0.42	0.10	0.9	0.12	256	46	3.6	120	1.9	15.2	41	15.0
Cranberry (Romano Bean)	177	0.37	0.12	0.9	0.14	366	88	3.7	88	2.0	16.5	43	17.7
Fava (Broad Bean)	170	0.17	0.15	1.2	0.12	177	61	2.6	73	1.7	12.9	33	9.2
Garbanzo (Chickpea)	164	0.19	0.10	0.9	0.23	282	80	4.7	79	2.5	14.5	45	12.5
Kidney Beans – Red	177	0.29	0.10	1.0	0.2	230	50	5.2	80	1.9	15.4	40	13.1
Lentils	198	0.34	0.15	2.1	0.35	358	38	6.6	71	2.5	17.9	40	15.6
Navy Beans	182	0.43	0.12	1.2	0.25	255	126	4.3	96	1.9	15.0	47	19.1
Pinto Beans	171	0.33	0.11	0.5	0.39	294	79	3.6	86	1.7	15.4	45	14.7
Soybeans (mature)	172	0.27	0.49	0.7	0.4	93	175	8.8	148	2.0	28.6	17	10.3
Split Peas	196	0.37	0.11	1.7	0.1	127	27	2.5	71	2.0	16.4	41	16.3
White Beans	179	0.21	0.08	0.3	0.17	144	161	6.6	113	2.5	17.4	45	11.3
Nuts													
Almonds (whole, blanched)	145	0.29	0.81	5.3	0.17	44	313	5.4	399	4.5	31.8	29	15.1
Brazil Nuts (dried, unblanched)	140	0.86	0.05	0.4	0.14	31	224	3.4	526	5.7	20.1	17	10.5
Hazelnuts (Filberts)	135	0.87	0.15	2.4	0.76	153	154	6.3	220	3.3	20.2	23	13.1
Peanuts (dry roasted)	146	0.64	0.14	19.7	0.37	212	79	3.3	257	4.8	34.6	31	11.7
Pecans (halves)	99	0.65	0.13	1.2	0.21	22	69	2.5	120	4.5	9.1	14	9.5
Walnuts – English (shelled, halves)	100	0.34	0.15	1.1	0.54	98	98	2.9	158	3.1	15.2	14	6.7
Seeds													
Pumpkin Seeds (kernels, dried)	138	0.29	0.44	2.4	0.31	80	59	20.7	738	10.3	33.9	25	5.4
Sesame Seeds (kernels, dried, decorticated)	150	1.05	0.14	8.7	0.60	172	90	9.5	518	10.1	30.7	18	17.4
Sunflower seeds (hulled kernels, dry roasted)	128	0.14	0.32	9.0	1.0	303	90	4.9	165	6.8	24.7	31	14.2

Nutrient Composition Background Information

✦ Nutrient composition values can vary considerably depending on factors such as:
- the specific variety, growing conditions and processing of the grain, legume, nut or seed.
- the coarseness of the grind of the grain and sifting process used to produce the flour.
- individual laboratory analytical methods and testing equipment used for nutrient analysis.

✦ The weights in grams for 1 cup of the items in the chart on pages 126-128 are from the following sources:

1. **USDA Nutrient Data Base for Standard Reference, Release #18.**
   http://www.nal.usda.gov/fnic/foodcomp/Data/SR18/sr18.html
   http://www.nal.usda.gov/fnic/foodcomp/search/
   - Amaranth seed, arrowroot starch, buckwheat (flour and groats), corn bran, corn flours, cornmeals, cornstarch, flax seed, millet seed, potato flour, quinoa seed, rice (brown, white, wild), rice flours (brown and white), sorghum grain, soy flours and wheat (bran and flours).
2. **Bob's Red Mill**
   - Almond meal, garbanzo flour, guar gum, hazelnut flour, millet flour, potato starch, rice flour (sweet), sorghum flour, tapioca starch, teff grain, xanthan gum.
3. **Ener-G Foods**
   - Rice bran and rice polish.
4. **Amazing Grains**
   - Montina™ flour
5. **Authentic Foods**
   - Garfava™ flour
6. **Dowd and Rogers**
   - Chestnut flour
7. **Minn-Dak Growers, Ltd.**
   - Buckwheat bran (Farinetta™)
8. **Nu-World Amaranth**
   - Amaranth flour
9. **The Teff Company**
   - Teff (grain and flour)
10. **Saskatchewan Flax Development Commission**
    - Flax Seed Meal (Ground Flax)
11. **Mountain Meadows Food Processing Limited**
    - Pea flour (Golden)
12. **Peter Felker and Casa deFruta Company**
    - Mesquite flour

✦ Nutrient composition values for the grains, flours, starches, gums, beans, nuts and seeds are from:

1. **USDA Nutrient Data Base for Standard Reference, Release #18.**
   http://www.nal.usda.gov/fnic/foodcomp/Data/SR18/sr18.html
   http://www.nal.usda.gov/fnic/foodcomp/search/
   - Amaranth seed, amaranth flour (calculated based on 135 grams of amaranth seed), arrowroot starch, buckwheat (flour and groats), chestnut flour (calculated from 100 grams chestnuts), corn bran, corn flours, cornmeals, cornstarch, flax seed, flax seed meal (calculated based on 130 grams of flax seed), guar gum, millet, potato flour, quinoa seed, quinoa flour (calculated from 112 grams of quinoa seed), rice (brown, white and wild), rice flour (brown and white), sorghum flour (fiber value calculated from 136 grams of sorghum grain), sorghum grain (except folate, magnesium, zinc and vitamin B_6 – see reference on page 131), soy flours, wheat (bran and flours), xanthan gum.
   - Beans, nuts and seeds.
2. **Bob's Red Mill**
   - Almond meal, garbanzo flour, guar gum, hazelnut flour, millet flour, potato starch, rice flour (sweet), sorghum flour (except fiber value – see USDA reference above), tapioca starch, teff flour (calculated from 130 grams of teff grain: folate, iron, zinc, magnesium and fiber – see page 131), teff grain (except folate, iron, zinc, magnesium and fiber – see references on page 131), xanthan gum.
3. **Ener-G Foods**
   - Rice bran and rice polish.
4. **Amazing Grains**
   - Montina™ flour.
5. **Authentic Foods**
   - Garfava™ flour.
6. **Minn-Dak Growers, Ltd.**
   - Buckwheat bran (except fiber and protein – see references on page 131).

Additional References:

A) **Buckwheat Bran** (protein and fiber values)

Steadman KJ, Burgoon MS, Lewis BA, et al. Buckwheat seed milling fractions: Description, macronutrient composition and dietary fibre. *J of Cereal Sciences* 2001;33:271-278.

B) **Sorghum Grain** (folate, magnesium, zinc and vitamin B_6)

Waniska RD and Rooney LL. 2000. Structure and chemistry of the sorghum caryopsis. In CW Smith and RA Frederiksen (eds). *Sorghum: Origin, history, technology, and production*. John Wiley and Sons, Inc., New York, NY.

C) **Mesquite Flour** (nutritional composition values were derived by averaging data from the research articles below)

1. Becker R and Grosjean OK. A compositional study of pods of two varieties of mesquite (Prosopis glandulosa, P. velutina). *J Agric Food Chem* 1980;28:22-25.
2. Felker P, Grados N, Cruz G, et al. Economic assessment of production of flour from Prosopis alba and P. pallida pods for human food applications. *J Arid Environ* 2003; 53:517-528.
3. Saunders RM, Becker R, Meyer D, et al. Identification of commercial milling techniques to produce high sugar, high fiber, high protein and high galactomannan gum fractions from Prosopis pods. *Forest Ecology Management* 1986;16: 169-180.
4. Grados N and Cruz G. New approaches to industrialization of algarrobo (Prosopis pallida) pods in Peru. http://www.udep.edu.pe/upadi/prosopis/s3ctxt.pdf
5. Prokopuik D. 2005. Sucedáneo del café a partir de algarroba de Prosopis alba Griseb. (Coffee substitute from the pods of Prosopis alba Griseb). Tesis Doctoral (PhD Thesis). Registro N°2183. Universidad Politécnica deValencia, Espana.
6. Meyer D. 1984. Processing, utilization and economics of mesquite pods as a raw material for the food industry. Swiss Federal Institute of Technology, PhD Thesis Diss. ETH 7688.

D) **Teff Flour** and **Teff Grain** (folate, iron and fiber values)

Analzyed December 14, 2005 by Silliker Canada Co., 90 Gough Road, Unit 4, Markham, ON, Canada, L3R 5V5.

E) **Teff Flour** and **Teff Grain** (magnesium and zinc values)

Mengesha M. Chemical composition of teff compared with that of wheat, barley and grain sorghum. *Econ Bot* 1966.;20268-273.

Iron Content of Flours & Starches

(highest to lowest)

Flours & Starches (1 cup)	Iron (mg)
Buckwheat Bran (Farinetta™)	13.6
Montina™ Flour	10.8
Quinoa Flour	10.4
Amaranth Flour	10.3
Rice bran	10.3
Soy Flour (defatted)	9.2
Millet Flour	9.2
Rice Polish	9.0
Teff Flour	8.7
Garfava™ Flour	7.9
Flax Seed Meal (Ground Flax)	7.5
Garbanzo Bean (Chickpea) Flour	7.5
Pea Flour (Golden)	7.3
Sorghum Flour	6.0
Corn Flour (Yellow, degermed, enriched)	5.7
Cornmeal (Yellow, degermed, enriched)	5.7
Soy Flour (full fat)	5.4
Hazelnut Flour	5.3
Mesquite Flour	5.1
Buckwheat Flour (whole groat)	4.9
Almond Flour (Almond Meal)	4.3
Rice Flour (Brown)	3.1
Potato Starch	2.9
Corn Flour (Yellow, whole grain)	2.8
Chestnut Flour	2.4
Potato Flour	2.2
Corn Bran	2.1
Cornmeal (Yellow, degermed, unenriched)	1.5
Corn Flour (Yellow, degermed, unenriched)	1.2
Rice Flour (White)	0.6
Cornstarch	0.6
Arrowroot Starch (Arrowroot Starch Flour)	0.4
Rice Flour (Sweet)	0.0
Tapioca Starch (Tapioca Flour)	0.0

Iron Content of Seeds & Grains

(highest to lowest)

Seeds & Grains (raw) (1 cup)	Iron (mg)
Pumpkin Seeds (kernels, dried)	20.7
Quinoa	15.7
Amaranth	14.8
Teff	12.1
Rice (White, long grain, parboiled, enriched)	9.8
Flax Seed	9.6
Sesame Seeds (kernels, dried, decorticated)	9.5
Sorghum	8.5
Millet	6.0
Sunflower Seeds (hulled kernels, dry roasted)	4.9
Buckwheat Groats (roasted, dry)	4.1
Wild Rice	3.1
Rice (Brown, long grain)	2.7

Folate Content of Seeds & Grains

(highest to lowest)

Seeds & Grains (raw) (1 cup)	Folate (micrograms)
Rice (White, long grain, parboiled, enriched)	481
Sunflower Seeds (hulled kernels, dry roasted)	303
Sesame Seeds (kernels, dried, decorticated)	172
Millet	170
Wild Rice	152
Flax Seed	146
Teff	135
Amaranth	96
Quinoa	83
Pumpkin Seeds (kernels, dried)	80
Buckwheat Groats (roasted, dry)	69
Rice (Brown, long grain)	37

Folate Content of Flours & Starches

(highest to lowest)

Flours & Starches (1 cup)	Folate (micrograms)
Garbanzo Bean (Chickpea) Flour	668
Cornmeal (Yellow, degermed, unenriched)	322
Soy Flour (defatted)	305
Soy Flour (full fat)	290
Corn Flour (Masa, enriched)	266
Hazelnut Flour	127
Flax Seed Meal (Ground Flax)	113
Chestnut Flour	110
Teff Flour	97
Amaranth Flour	66
Cornmeal (Yellow, degermed, unenriched)	66
Corn Flour (Yellow, degermed, unenriched)	60
Quinoa Flour	55
Almond Flour (Almond Meal)	42
Buckwheat Bran (Farinetta™)	41
Potato Flour	40
Cornmeal (Yellow, whole grain)	30
Corn Flour (Yellow, whole grain)	29
Mesquite Flour	26
Rice Flour (Brown)	25
Rice Flour (White)	6
Corn Bran	3

Calcium Content of Flours & Starches

(highest to lowest)

Flours & Starches (1 cup)	Calcium (mg)
Flax Seed Meal (Ground Flax)	332
Almond Flour (Almond Meal)	289
Soy Flour (defatted)	241
Teff Flour	239
Amaranth Flour	207
Mesquite Flour	196
Soy Flour (full fat)	173
Corn Flour (Masa, enriched)	161
Hazelnut Flour	128
Garbanzo Bean (Chickpea) Flour	126
Garfava™ Flour	104
Buckwheat Bran (Farinetta™)	104
Potato Flour	104
Montina™ Flour	83
Quinoa Flour	67

Calcium Content of Seeds & Grains

(highest to lowest)

Seeds & Grains (raw) (1 cup)	Calcium (mg)
Flax Seed	428
Teff	331
Amaranth	298
Rice (White, long grain, parboiled, enriched)	103
Quinoa	102
Sesame Seeds	90
Sunflower Seeds	90
Pumpkin Seeds (kernels, dried)	59
Sorghum	54
Rice (Brown, long grain)	43
Wild Rice	34
Millet	16

* The bioavailability (ability of the body to absorb the nutrient) of calcium from many of these sources is unknown. Nevertheless, they also contain a variety of nutrients and dietary fiber that are important for good health.

Fiber Content of Flours & Starches

(highest to lowest)

Flours & Starches (1 cup)	Fiber (mg)
Corn Bran	60.0
Mesquite Flour	46.1
Rice Bran	39.0
Montina™ Flour	36.0
Flax Seed Meal (Ground Flax)	35.5
Buckwheat Bran (Farinetta™)	22.7
Garbanzo Bean (Chickpea) Flour	20.9
Soy Flour (defatted)	17.5
Corn Flour (Yellow, whole grain)	15.7
Almond Flour (Almond Meal)	14.7
Amaranth Flour	12.6
Buckwheat Flour (whole groat)	12.0
Garfava™ Flour	12.0
Rice Polish	12.0
Pea Flour (Golden)	11.6
Hazelnut Flour	10.9
Millet Flour	10.3
Cornmeal (Yellow, degermed, enriched)	10.2
Potato Flour	9.4
Sorghum Flour	8.6
Soy Flour (full fat)	8.1
Teff Flour	8.1
Rice Flour (Brown)	7.3
Quinoa Flour	6.6
Arrowroot Starch (Arrowroot Starch Flour)	4.4
Rice Flour (White)	3.8
Corn Flour (Yellow, degermed, enriched)	2.4
Rice Flour (Sweet)	1.2
Cornstarch	1.2
Potato Starch	0.0
Tapioca Starch (Tapioca Flour)	0.0

Fiber Content of Seeds & Grains

(highest to lowest)

Seeds & Grains (raw) (1 cup)	Fiber (mg)
Flax Seed	45.9
Amaranth	18.1
Sesame Seeds (kernels, dried, decorticated)	17.4
Millet	17.0
Buckwheat Groats (roasted, dry)	16.9
Sunflower Seeds (hulled kernels, dry roasted)	14.2
Sorghum	12.1
Teff	11.2
Quinoa	10.0
Wild Rice	9.9
Rice (Brown, long grain)	6.5
Pumpkin Seeds (kernels, dried)	5.4
Rice (White, long grain, parboiled, enriched)	4.1

Protein Content of Seeds & Grains

(highest to lowest)

Seeds & Grains (raw) (1 cup)	Protein (grams)
Flax Seed	30.7
Amaranth	28.2
Wild Rice	23.6
Quinoa	23.3
Millet	22.0
Teff	21.8
Sorghum	21.7
Buckwheat Groats (roasted, dry)	19.2
Sesame Seeds (kernels, dried, decorticated)	17.4
Rice (White, long grain, parboiled, enriched)	15.2
Rice (Brown, long grain)	14.7
Sunflower Seeds (hulled kernels, dry roasted)	14.2
Pumpkin Seeds (kernels, dried)	5.4

Protein Content of Flours & Starches

(highest to lowest)

Flours & Starches (1 cup)	Protein (grams)
Buckwheat Bran (Farinetta™)	49.0
Soy Flour (defatted)	47.0
Garfava™ Flour	34.9
Pea Flour (Golden)	30.4
Soy Flour (full fat)	29.0
Montina™ Flour	25.5
Flax Seed Meal (Ground Flax)	23.8
Almond Flour	23.6
Garbanzo Bean (Chickpea) Flour	23.2
Amaranth Flour (Almond Meal)	19.5
Rice Bran	19.4
Hazelnut Flour	16.7
Teff Flour	15.7
Sorghum Flour	15.4
Buckwheat Flour (whole groat)	15.1
Quinoa Flour	14.7
Millet Flour	13.7
Rice Polish	12.0
Mesquite Flour	11.8
Cornmeal (Yellow, degermed, enriched)	11.7
Rice Flour (Brown)	11.4
Potato Flour	11.0
Corn Flour (Yellow, whole grain)	10.7
Rice Flour (Sweet)	10.1
Cornmeal (Yellow, whole grain)	9.9
Rice Flour (White)	9.4
Corn Bran	6.4
Chestnut Flour	5.0
Arrowroot Starch (Arrowroot Starch Flour)	0.4
Cornstarch	0.3
Potato Starch	0.2
Tapioca Starch (Tapioca Flour)	0.0

Carbohydrate Content of Flours & Starches

(highest to lowest)

Flours & Starches (1 cup)	Carbohydrate (grams)
Potato Starch	158
Potato Flour	133
Rice Flour (White)	127
Mesquite Flour	122
Rice Flour (Brown)	121
Tapioca Starch (Tapioca Flour)	119
Cornstarch	117
Arrowroot Starch (Arrowroot Starch Flour)	113
Cornmeal (Yellow, degermed, enriched or unenriched)	107
Montina™ Flour	105
Corn Flour (Yellow, degermed, enriched)	104
Sorghum Flour	102
Rice Flour (Sweet)	95
Teff Flour	94
Garfava™ Flour	92
Corn Flour (Yellow, whole grain)	90
Millet Flour	89
Amaranth Flour	89
Buckwheat Flour (whole groat)	85
Chestnut Flour	78
Quinoa Flour	77
Rice Polish	76
Pea Flour (Golden)	76
Garbanzo Bean (Chickpea) Flour	73
Buckwheat Bran (Farinetta™)	71
Rice Bran	68
Corn Bran	65
Soy Flour (defatted)	38
Flax Seed Meal (Ground Flax)	38
Soy Flour (full fat)	30
Almond Flour	21
Hazelnut Flour	19

Carbohydrate Content of Seeds & Grains

(highest to lowest)

Seeds & Grains (raw) (1 cup)	**Carbohydrate** (grams)
Rice (White, long grain, parboiled, enriched)	150
Millet	146
Sorghum	143
Rice (Brown, long grain)	143
Teff	130
Amaranth	129
Buckwheat Groats (roasted, dry)	123
Wild Rice	120
Quinoa	117
Flax Seed	49
Sunflower Seeds (hulled kernels, dry roasted)	31
Pumpkin Seeds (kernels, dried)	25
Sesame Seeds (kernels, dried, decorticated)	18

GLUTEN-FREE MEAL PLANNING

Getting Started

Successful gluten-free meal planning requires a positive attitude, a little creativity and learning how to make substitutions for some ingredients and food items in favorite recipes and menu items. Fortunately, many foods are naturally gluten-free, including plain meats, fish, poultry, eggs, milk, cheese, yogurt, legumes (dried beans, lentils and peas), nuts, seeds, fruits, vegetables, and grain alternatives such as amaranth, buckwheat, corn, flax, millet, quinoa, rice, sorghum and teff. In addition, there are numerous gluten-free specialty products (e.g., pasta, breads and baked goods, cereals, sauces, soups) that can be substituted for traditional gluten-containing items (see pages 209-266).

Plan simple meals and snacks with plain foods in the beginning so you don't become overwhelmed with the new gluten-free lifestyle. Once you have mastered the basics gradually incorporate new items and try more complex dishes with multiple ingredients. To save time and energy, prepare gluten-free recipe and menu items that everyone can eat rather than having to "cook twice." Other family members can supplement their meal plan with gluten-containing bread or dessert items if desired.

Gluten-Free (GF) Meal-Planning Ideas

The following ideas for breakfast, lunch, dinner and snacks, including some of the recipes and gluten-free specialty products found in this book, can be used as a starting point to create your own favorite meals and snacks.

Breakfast

- GF cold cereal (see pages 209-211), sliced fresh fruit, milk*.
- GF Granola (see recipes on pages 174-175) and milk*.
- Hot cereal (white or yellow cornmeal, cream of white or brown rice, cream of buckwheat, quinoa or teff) with chopped dates, apricots or raisins, cinnamon, brown sugar and milk*.
- Shelley's High-Fiber Hot Cereal (see page 173), dried fruits, brown sugar and milk*.
- GF toast and yogurt with fruit**, chopped nuts, coconut or ground flax.
- GF toasted bread, bun, bagel or English muffin with cream cheese and fruit** or peanut butter and jam or honey, milk* or juice.
- GF muffin (see pages 168-170), fresh fruit** and yogurt.
- GF French toast (warm bread in microwave first to improve absorption of the egg mixture), fruit** and syrup.
- GF freezer waffles, fruit** and syrup and a glass of milk*.
- GF pancakes (use a GF mix or make your own, see pages 171-172), with fruit** and syrup.
- GF toasted bread and poached egg.
- Omelet (chopped green or red peppers, onion, shredded cheese) and leftover fried potatoes.
- Fruit smoothie (skim milk powder*, fresh or frozen fruit**, honey or sugar, ground flax, water, crushed ice).

* GF non-dairy substitutes (e.g., almond, potato, rice or soy beverages) can replace milk.

** Fruits (e.g., canned crushed pineapple or peach slices, fresh or frozen strawberries or blueberries, applesauce and a sprinkle of cinnamon, sliced bananas or kiwis).

Sandwich Tips

Gluten-Free breads can become dry and crumbly so here are a few tips:

- When you buy rice bread, slice (if not sliced) and freeze immediately, placing waxed paper between slices so you can remove one at a time. Seal in a plastic bag.
- Toasting bread improves flavor and keeps it from crumbling.
- Make a sandwich on lightly toasted bread and freeze it for lunch the next day.
- Consider buying a bread machine, as homemade gluten-free breads are much fresher and more economical than ready-made breads.
- Try open-face sandwiches and put them under a broiler. (e.g., tuna or pure crab meat with shredded cheese; toasted cheese, tomato and bacon).

Lunch

- Homemade soups (vegetable, chicken, corn chowder, salmon chowder, cream of potato, lentil, pea, etc.) and a GF muffin or bagel with melted cheese.
- GF soup (see pages 256-259) and GF bread sticks, brushed with melted butter and garlic powder and heated in the oven.
- Toasted GF cheese bread or GF grilled cheese sandwich with canned or homemade GF soup.
- Egg salad on toasted GF bagel and fresh fruit.
- GF bagel with turkey, lettuce, tomato, cucumbers, sprouts and avocado; baby carrots and fresh fruit.
- Fettuccini Alfredo (GF pasta, butter or margarine, garlic powder, Parmesan cheese, milk) and salad.
- GF pasta with homemade cheese sauce or GF Tomato Pasta Sauce (in jars or homemade) and salad.
- GF crackers, hummus (chickpeas, sesame seed oil, garlic), raw vegetables and fresh fruit.
- Wild Rice and Vegetable Casserole (see page 193).
- GF Pasta and Cheese Dinner, raw vegetables and dip (GF salad dressing).
- Quinoa salad (see page 187) and glass of juice.
- Canned GF baked beans, coleslaw and homemade corn bread or Montina™ Vegetable Skillet Bread (see page 167).
- Green salad with added meat, chicken, canned shrimp, tuna or salmon and GF bun.
- GF pasta salad with chicken, GF ham or canned shrimp, tuna or crab and fresh fruit.
- Spinach salad with sunflower seeds, chickpeas, feta cheese, strawberries and GF rice crackers.
- Stuffed baked potato (cheese and GF ham or broccoli and cheese) – make ahead, freeze and heat in microwave.
- Black Bean Chili (see page 194) served over a baked potato or toasted GF bun, top with grated cheese.

- Pizza (use GF crust mix [see pages 231-237, 239-241] or GF prebaked frozen crust, GF pizza sauce, grated cheese, chopped green peppers, mushrooms, onions, GF ham or salami). For recipe, see page 163.
- GF hot dog bun and GF wiener or sausage, raw vegetables.
- Rice cakes with peanut butter and banana; melted cheese; egg, salmon or tuna salad.
- Moroccan Salad (see page 186) and GF roll or bread.
- Eggs scrambled in the microwave or an omelet with GF toast.
- GF pancakes, waffles or French toast (see breakfast ideas) and GF sausages.
- Leftovers (casseroles, chili, stew, meat and potatoes, chicken and rice).
- Precooked rice (stored and frozen to heat later) with shredded cheese and leftover meat or chicken and vegetables.
- Soft corn tortillas made into "wraps," stuffed with: (A) cooked mung bean noodles or rice noodles, meat or shrimp with vegetables (e.g., sprouts, tomatoes, cucumber, green pepper) drizzled with a mixture of GF soy sauce, honey, ginger and garlic powder **OR** (B) kernel corn with cooked rice and pesto sauce, add cooked ground beef, fresh vegetables, and top with salsa and yogurt or shredded cheese.

Dinner

- Rice, hamburger and tomato casserole with grated cheese.
- GF lasagne and salad.
- Shish Kebobs served over rice.
- GF pasta (see pages 249-252) with homemade cheese sauce or GF pasta sauce (in jars or homemade) and salad.
- Moroccan Millet (see page 191) and salad.
- Creamed salmon or tuna with green peas served on GF toast.
- Cabbage rolls or Lentil Leaf Rolls (see page 195).
- Homemade beef stew (thickened with GF starch) and GF bread.
- Chili con Carne, GF cornbread or corn chips and raw vegetables.
- Steak, baked potato, vegetables and a salad.
- Baked chicken* or fish*, rice or GF pasta, cooked vegetables and/or salad.
  * Crunchy Coating: crushed potato or tortilla chips, crushed GF cereal, nuts, rice bread crumbs or cornmeal. Also, see page 199 for Cajun Flax Coating recipe.
- Lentil stew and GF toasted cheese bread.
- GF tacos or tortillas – ground beef, GF taco seasoning, grated cheese, chopped lettuce and tomatoes, GF salsa and sour cream in corn tortilla or served over tortilla chips.
- Stir-fry beef, pork, chicken or seafood and vegetables, (GF soy sauce, arrowroot or tapioca starch, garlic and ginger, mixed with water to make a sauce) served over rice with toasted almonds and/or sesame seeds.
- Barbecue chicken, pork chops or fish (GF barbecue sauce) with rice pilaf (white, brown or wild) or Quinoa and Wild Rice Pilaf (see page 190) and vegetables.

- Lentil Pizza Squares (see page 196) and tossed salad.
- GF pizza (see lunch) and salad.
- Roast chicken or turkey with dressing (GF bread crumbs), mashed potatoes, gravy (thickened with GF starch) and vegetables.
- Sweet and sour meatballs served over rice with stir-fried vegetables.
- Oven-Fried Chicken (see page 198), baked potato, cooked vegetables or salad.
- Turkey meatballs with Lemon Sauce (see page 197), rice or kasha and cooked vegetables.
- Roast pork, applesauce, mashed potatoes, gravy (thickened with GF starch) and vegetables.
- Meatloaf (GF rice cereal, GF instant mashed potatoes, GF bread crumbs or crushed corn chips or potato chips and egg, herbs or spices), baked potato and tossed salad.
- Beef or chicken kabobs and millet, quinoa or buckwheat pilaf with nuts and dried fruits, and steamed vegetables.
- Poached or broiled salmon, brown and/or wild rice and green beans with slivered almonds.
- Hamburger patty or grilled chicken breast, corn on the cob, coleslaw and watermelon.
- Hearty Vegetarian Kasha Casserole (see page 192) and GF roll.
- Savory Pot Pie (see page 200) and salad.

Snacks

- Fresh or canned fruit.
- Fruit juice.
- Dried fruit (e.g., raisins, apricots, cranberries, blueberries, mangoes, apples).
- Pumpkin or sunflower seeds (plain or GF flavored).
- Nuts (plain).
- Dried fruit and nut mixtures.
- Soy nuts (plain or GF flavored) or corn nuts (plain).
- GF Granola (see pages 174-175).
- Celery sticks with peanut butter and raisins OR cream cheese.
- Raw vegetables and dip (made with yogurt/herbs or GF salad dressing).
- Popcorn.
- GF pretzels (see page 229).
- Plain corn tortilla chips, salsa, grated cheese and sour cream.
- GF flavored mini or large rice cakes (see page 228).
- Banana Seed Bread (see page 166).
- Apple Date Bread (see page 165).
- GF rice crackers with hummus.
- GF rice cakes or GF bagel with cream cheese and apple slices.

- GF rice cakes with peanut butter and jelly, honey or sliced bananas.
- GF snack bars (see pages 225-226).
- Fig Bars (see page 176) or Carrot Apple Energy Bars (see page 177).
- GF muffins (see pages 168-170) and cheese cubes.
- String cheese or cheese slices on GF rice crackers.
- Hard-boiled egg.
- GF soup and/or GF crackers.
- GF crackers and cheese or cheese spread.
- Puddings (see page 184) or try any GF pudding.
- Yogurt.

Note: See pages 226-230 for GF snack products.

Healthy Meal Planning Tips

Here are some specific ideas how to incorporate more nutritious items into the gluten-free diet.

Breakfast Boosters		
If you eat this	**Add this**	**Or try this instead**
Cream of white rice cereal	Nuts, seeds, ground flax, dried fruits, or fresh fruit	Cream of brown rice, cream of buckwheat, quinoa flakes, amaranth or teff
Puffed rice or corn cereal	Fresh fruit	GF granola with nuts, seeds, ground flax, dried fruits
GF white rice bread or bagel	Nut butter, cheese, poached egg, or omelet with chopped vegetables	GF enriched bread or bagel; or make your own bread and substitute brown rice, ground flax, or bean flours for some of the white rice, cornstarch, tapioca starch or potato starch
Fruit beverage or fruit drink	Fresh or frozen fruit or fruit juice plus yogurt or skim milk powder and ground flax to make a fruit smoothie	Calcium-fortified juice or 100-percent fruit juice
GF waffle or pancakes with syrup	Cottage cheese or yogurt and fruit	Substitute brown rice, buckwheat, bean flour, or ground flax for some of the white rice flour; or try GF fiber-rich frozen waffles

If you eat this	Add this	Or try this instead
Crêpes made with white rice flour and topped with syrup	A filling made with blended ricotta cheese, lemon or orange zest, and small amount of sweetener; a topping of berries, peaches, or other fruit, and maple syrup	Substitute almond or bean flour for some of the white rice flour
Fried egg and bacon	Low-fat mozzarella or feta cheese, veggies, and GF smoked salmon, turkey, or ham to make an omelet	Omega-3 rich egg; use a non-stick pan; try Canadian bacon or low-fat GF turkey or chicken sausage

Power Lunches and Dinners		
If you eat this	**Add this**	**Or try this instead**
Chicken rice soup	Fresh or frozen vegetables	Soups made with lentils, dried beans or peas, vegetables (squash, pumpkin, tomato)
White rice pizza crust, salami and cheese	Vegetables such as peppers, onions, zucchini and tomatoes	Add some amaranth or brown rice flour to your dough; use low-fat cheese
White rice pasta with butter or margarine	Low-fat cheese and vegetables	Enriched gluten-free pasta, brown rice, or lentil pasta; use less butter or margarine
White rice bread sandwich, butter or margarine, mayonnaise and luncheon meat	Sprouts, lettuce, tomatoes, avocado, shredded carrots	GF enriched bread or bagel; low-fat mayonnaise, salsa, or mustard; salmon, tuna, low-fat GF deli meats such as chicken, turkey, pastrami or ham
White rice and meat, fish or chicken	Fresh or frozen vegetables	Brown rice or a combination of brown, wild, and white rice; quinoa or buckwheat
Baked or mashed potato with butter or margarine	Cheese and chopped veggies such as broccoli in the baked potato; milk and grated low-fat cheese in the mashed potato	Use yogurt or low-fat sour cream instead of butter or margarine; try a sweet potato for more vitamin A
Iceberg lettuce salad, GF croûtons, cucumbers, and celery with salad dressing	Tomatoes, peppers, cauliflower, broccoli, mushrooms, shredded carrots, chickpeas, sunflower seeds	Romaine or spinach with strawberries or mandarin oranges, toasted slivered almonds, and/or sesame seeds with a fruit dressing or low-fat salad dressing

Smart Snacks		
If you eat this	**Add this**	**Or try this instead**
GF pretzels	Unsalted nuts	Trail mix with GF granola, dried fruits, nuts and seeds
Rice cakes or rice crackers	Cheese (cubes or string), hummus, nut butter with banana or apple slices	GF snack bar made with seeds, dried fruits and healthy GF grains (amaranth, flax, quinoa)
Fried corn chips	Salsa and shredded cheese	Baked corn chips with low-fat cheese and sour cream; popcorn
Celery sticks	Peanut butter, cheese spread or low-fat cream cheese with raisins	Carrot or turnip sticks, peppers, cherry tomatoes, broccoli or cauliflower
GF cookie	Fresh fruit and a glass of milk or enriched GF dairy substitute	Add brown rice, flax or quinoa to the recipe; choose ready-made cookies that are lower in sugar and fat or made with non-hydrogenated oils
GF brownie	Mug of warm, steamed milk or enriched GF dairy substitute	GF crispy rice square (still not so nutritious, but often less fat)
GF muffin with white rice flour	Chopped nuts, mashed banana, dried fruits (raisins, cranberries, apricots, dates), ground flax	Pumpkin, pineapple, carrot or banana muffins made with some brown rice flour, almond flour or bean flour
Full-fat fruit-flavored yogurt	Fresh fruit and nuts	Plain low-fat yogurt with chopped fruits, nuts and small amount of sweetener

Reprinted with permission from: ***Rate Your Plate***, *Living Without* magazine, Fall 2003, pg. 26. www.livingwithout.com

Article by Julie Rothschild Levi and chart prepared by Shelley Case, RD.

Sample Seven-Day Gluten-Free Menu

Here is a sample menu to inspire you to eat safely, healthfully, and deliciously. Of course, different people have different tastes and nutritional needs, so adapt accordingly. Many of the meals and snacks work well when "on the go" (OTG). Stock up on these foods and cook extras for leftovers.

Monday:

Breakfast – Smoothie with fruit, yogurt and flax; gluten-free snack bar (OTG)

Lunch – Spinach salad with sunflower seeds, chickpeas, feta cheese, strawberries; gluten-free rice crackers

Hint: Make a homemade salad dressing to keep in the fridge at home and work.

Snack – Fresh pear and raw almonds (OTG)

Dinner – Gluten-free pasta with seafood or meat sauce and/or grated cheese, grilled veggies

Treat – Pudding* and gluten-free cookie

Tuesday:

Breakfast – Gluten-free bagel with nut butter, sliced bananas and yogurt (OTG)

Lunch – Baked white or sweet potato stuffed with broccoli and cheese and/or gluten-free deli meat; fresh fruit

Hint: Potato may be prepared the night before and reheated prior to eating. Cook extras for other dishes throughout the week.

Snack – Gluten-free granola with milk

Dinner – Turkey chili, gluten-free cornbread or corn chips, veggie sticks

Treat – Berries topped with real whipped cream (optional)

Wednesday:

Breakfast – Omelet with veggies and cheese, leftover fried potatoes, ½ grapefruit

Lunch – Tuna fish on mixed greens with seasonal fruit, gluten-free purēed vegetable soup (eg. carrot, squash, potato) with grated Parmesan cheese

Hint: Make soup monthly and freeze small batches for quick and healthy lunches.

Snack – Gluten-free snack bar and yogurt (OTG)

Dinner – Beef or chicken kabobs, millet or buckwheat pilaf with nuts and dried fruit, steamed asparagus

Treat – Piece of a dark chocolate bar

Thursday:

Breakfast – Gluten-free waffle with pure maple syrup, cottage cheese and peaches

Lunch – Gluten-free pasta salad with veggies and leftover chicken or beef, fresh fruit

Snack – Trail mix of gluten-free cereal, nuts and dried fruit; hot chocolate or decaf latte (OTG)

Dinner – Poached salmon, brown and/or wild rice, garlic green beans

Treat – Ice cream* or sorbet with fresh fruit

***Choose from dairy products or enriched, non-dairy, gluten-free substitutes (made from soy, rice or almond).**

Friday:

Breakfast – Plain yogurt with fruit and unsweetened coconut, gluten-free toast with nut butter, calcium-fortified orange juice

Lunch – Gluten-free bagel with turkey, lettuce, tomato (option: sprouts, avocado); baby carrots, fresh fruit (OTG)

Snack – String cheese* and gluten-free crackers (OTG)

Dinner – Lamb stew with lentils, mixed greens salad

Hint: Use gluten-free starch, potato flakes, or diced potatoes to thicken.

Treat – Baked apple

Saturday:

Breakfast – Gluten-free cereal with nuts and/or seeds and milk;* fresh fruit or leftover baked apple

Hint: For a hot and healthy start, try cooked amaranth or quinoa, cream of buckwheat or cream of brown rice.

Lunch – Gluten-free grilled cheese* sandwich, gluten-free soup, veggie sticks

Hint: Use homemade stock or use gluten-free bouillon cubes as a safe and tasty base.

Snack – Gluten-free rice cakes with hummus (OTG)

Dinner – Hamburger patty or grilled chicken breast, corn on the cob, gluten-free coleslaw, watermelon

Treat – Vanilla ice cream* with warmed gluten-free brownie or cookie

Sunday:

Breakfast – Gluten-free blueberry pancakes, gluten-free breakfast sausage, glass of milk* or calcium-fortified juice

Lunch – Stir-fry with meat, seafood or tofu, Chinese veggies and brown rice topped with sesame seeds

Hint: Use gluten-free soy sauce. If dining out, bring your own soy sauce and ask the chef to use that in the preparation.

Snack – celery with nut butter and raisins (OTG)

Dinner – Gluten-free pizza, veggies and dip

Hint: Leftover pizza makes a great grab-and-go snack – even when cold.

Treat – Popcorn (OTG)

Other ethnic alternatives:

Fish or vegetable sushi with gluten-free soy sauce
Meat or veggie fajitas (made with gluten-free corn tortillas)
Seafood paella
Wild mushroom risotto or polenta
Veggie, fish, or meat curry over basmati rice
Pad thai and fresh spring rolls made with rice paper

***Choose from dairy products or enriched, non-dairy, gluten-free substitutes (made from soy, rice, or almond).**

GLUTEN-FREE COOKING

Gluten-Free Baking

Gluten is the protein found in wheat flour that provides the structure for baked goods. In order to make tasty and satisfying gluten-free baked products it is essential to learn how to use different types and combinations of flours, starches and other ingredients, as well as specific baking techniques in order to compensate for the lack of gluten. This will take time and a lot of patience, perseverance and a sense of humor! But don't be discouraged, there are many excellent gluten-free cookbooks, newsletters and cooking classes/schools that provide detailed information about gluten-free baking and wonderful recipes (see pages 316-318). It is best to start with recipes that are easy to prepare such as pancakes, muffins and cookies. Once you master these, move on to more challenging recipes for breads, rolls, cakes and other items. But before you begin baking, read about the unique taste and texture properties of each flour and starch that are highlighted below. Also, a list of substitutions and general baking hints are found on pages 154-157.

Gluten-Free Flours and Starches

All flours and starches should be stored in airtight containers and labeled with their name and date. Some can be kept in a cool, dry, dark place, however, if you live in hot and/or humid climates, it is better to store them in the refrigerator or freezer. Also, regardless of the environment you live in, the following are best stored in the refrigerator or freezer for optimum freshness: amaranth flour, brown rice flour, corn bran, ground flax, millet flour, nut flours (almond, chestnut and hazelnut), potato flour, rice bran, rice polish and soy flour.

Almond Flour (Almond Meal) is made from blanched ground almonds which are high in fiber, protein and fat. Available in packages or grind your own in a small coffee grinder using blanched slivered almonds. Adds a rich texture and nutty flavor to baked products. Can also be used as a coating for chicken or fish.

Amaranth Flour is ground from the entire tiny, grain-like amaranth seed which is high in fiber, protein, calcium, iron and other nutrients. It has a nutty, slightly sweet toasted flavor and is best combined with other gluten-free flours. Very good in dark-colored baked products (e.g., chocolate cake, brownies, dark breads and muffins) and items with spices (e.g., pumpkin bread or muffins, spice cake). Also works well when combined with almond flour in light-colored, mild-flavored baked goods.

Amaranth Starch is made from part of the amaranth seed and can be used as a thickener in puddings, sauces, gravy and soups.

Arrowroot Starch (Arrowroot Starch Flour) is ground from the root of a tropical plant. A neutral-flavored, white-colored finely powdered starch, it can be blended with different flours to make baked products. Also an excellent thickener for fruit sauces and other sauces. Can be used for breading as it produces a golden brown crust. Arrowroot can be exchanged for cornstarch.

Bean Flours* can be made from various ground dried beans such as black, cranberry (romano), fava, garbanzo (chickpea), navy, pinto, soy and white. In order to reduce as much of the flatulent effects of the beans as possible, some companies specially treat (precook or micronize) the beans before milling. Bean flours are high in fiber, protein, calcium, iron and B vitamins, especially folate. By combining bean flours with other flours to totally or partially replace white rice flour, the nutritional quality and texture of baked products can be greatly improved. Works well when combined with sorghum flour in intensely flavored recipes such as gingerbread and chocolate cake. Introduce bean flours gradually into the diet and choose those that have been "treated" for better tolerance.

* Reference: Bette Hagman. *Alas! Not All Bean Flours Are The Same*. Gluten Intolerance Group Newsletter, April 2001

Buckwheat Flour is ground from unroasted buckwheat groats (hulled buckwheat kernels). The dark flour has a strong, distinctive flavor as it contains a higher percentage of finely milled particles of the black buckwheat hull and is higher in fiber and nutrients. The light flour has a milder, mellow flavor as it contains fewer or no buckwheat hulls and is consequently lower in fiber and some nutrients. Either flour is best used in small amounts to add flavor to bland flours in breads, muffins, and pancakes. Make sure to purchase 100% pure buckwheat flour as some companies sell a combination of buckwheat flour and wheat flour in one package.

Chestnut Flour is made from ground chestnuts which are higher in starch and lower in protein and fat compared to other nut flours. This light beige silky-textured flour adds a nutty flavor to baked products. Best combined with other flours.

Corn Bran is very high in insoluble fiber. Light in color, with a mild flavor, it can be added in small amounts to baked products such as muffins, breads and loaves.

Corn Flour, milled from finely ground dried corn kernels, is very light in texture and gives a mild. nutty flavor to baked goods. It is best used in combination with other flours.

Cornmeal is made from dried kernels of yellow, white or blue corn, however, it is not as finely ground as corn flour. It can be used as a breading or in corn bread, corn muffins and polenta.

Cornstarch is made from the endosperm of corn that is highly refined, resulting in little nutritive value. This heavy white, flavorless powder is blended with various flours and/or other starches and used to lighten baked goods. Also an excellent thickener.

Flax Seed Meal (Ground Flax) is produced from ground flaxseed which is high in fiber, omega-3 fatty acids, protein, B vitamins, calcium and other minerals. This dark brown meal adds a nutty flavor, crunchy texture and improves the nutritional profile of baked products. Due to its high fat content, baked products made with flax brown quickly so the temperature and baking time may need to be reduced. It can be purchased already ground in vacuum-sealed packages on store shelves or in plastic bags in the refrigerated section. The flax seeds can also be ground in a coffee grinder and used as needed.

Garbanzo Bean Flour is ground from garbanzo beans (also known as chickpea, besan, gram or channa). This popular tan-colored bean flour is best combined with other flours. See Bean Flours for more information.

Garfava™ Flour, developed by Authentic Foods, is the trademark name for a blend of garbanzo bean and fava bean flours that are specially processed. Creates baked goods with excellent volume and a good moisture content. See Bean Flours for more information.

Garbanzo and Fava Bean Flour is also available from other companies that may or may not be specially processed. See Bean Flours for more information.

Hazelnut Flour is made from ground hazelnuts (also known as filberts). High in protein, fiber and other nutrients which can improve the nutritional quality of baked goods, it adds a rich texture and nutty flavor.

Mesquite Flour comes from the ground bean pods of the mesquite tree. Available as a light tan coarse meal or fine flour that is very high in fiber. Has a cinnamon-mocha aroma and slightly sweet chocolate, molasses-like flavor with a hint of caramel. Best combined with other flours to make pancakes, muffins, breads, cakes and cookies.

Millet Flour, ground from the tiny millet seed, is light yellow in color and has a slightly sweet corn-like, nutty flavor. High in protein and B vitamins as well as a source of fiber and minerals, it is best combined with other flours, comprising no more than 20-25% of the total flour blend.

Montina™ Flour is ground from the seeds of Indian ricegrass that is very high in fiber, iron and protein. A light brown, gray-colored flour with a sweet, nutty, almost "wheat-like" flavor, it can replace up to 25% of one of the primary flours in baked products.

Nut Flours are made from ground almonds, chestnuts or hazelnuts. Keep refrigerated or frozen in airtight containers for optimum freshness. See individual nut flours for more information.

Potato Flour is not the same as potato starch and they cannot be substituted for one another. The flour is made from whole potatoes, including the skin, resulting in a heavier product with a light tan color and slight potato flavor. Due to its heavy texture, it is best used in small amounts and combined with other flours. Adds crispness and density to baked products.

Potato Starch is made only from the starch portion of the potato. This bland-flavored, fine white powder works well in many baked products when used at approximately 30-40% of the total flour mixture. Sift or whisk potato starch before measuring as it lumps easily.

Quinoa Flour is ground from the quinoa seed which is high in protein, iron and other nutrients and is also a source of fiber. This tan-colored flour has a slight nutty but strong flavor which can overpower baked goods, it is therefore best to limit to 25% of the total flour mixture. Works well in highly spiced or flavored baked products.

Rice Bran is the outer layer of the brown rice kernel and is high in fiber. It can be added in small amounts to baked goods to add a nutty flavor and improve the nutrient and fiber content.

Rice Cereal (Cream of Brown Rice or Brown Rice Cream) is made from whole-grain brown rice that is coarsely ground and can be cooked in 3-4 minutes as a hot cereal.

Rice Cereal (Cream of White Rice or White Rice Cream) is made from coarsely ground white rice and can be cooked in 3-4 minutes as a hot cereal.

Rice Flour (Brown) is made from whole-grain brown rice that is very finely ground. This slightly tan-colored flour is higher in fiber and other nutrients than white rice flour. If brown rice or white rice flour is used by itself in baked products, they tend to be gritty, crumbly and dry out quickly, therefore it is best combined with other flours and starches. Adds a nutty flavor to baked goods.

Rice Flour (Sweet), also known as sticky, sushi or glutinous rice flour, is different from white rice flour although they look alike. Made from ground sticky short-grain white rice that is higher in starch than brown or white rice, it makes an excellent thickener for sauces, gravy and puddings as it keeps liquids from separating when they are chilled or frozen. Can be used in small amounts in flour blends for baked products.

Rice Flour (White) is made from ground white rice (contains no bran or polish) thus is lower in fiber and nutrients than brown rice flour. This starchy white flour has a bland flavor and is best combined with other flours in baked products.

Rice Polish is made from part of the rice bran and rice germ (the layer underneath the rice bran). Lighter in color than pure rice bran, it is a good source of fiber and can be substituted for rice bran in other recipes.

Sorghum Flour is ground from new food-grade sorghum varieties (also known as milo). This light tan-colored flour has a slightly nutty, earthy flavor. Combine with other flours, especially bean flour, to produce a wide variety of excellent baked products.

Soy Flour, available as whole or defatted, is made from ground dried soybeans. This yellow, slightly nutty and "beany" tasting flour is best combined with other flours, especially rice, in baked products containing fruits, nuts, spices or chocolate. Very high in protein, fiber, B vitamins, iron and calcium.

Tapioca Flour (Tapioca Starch), also known as tapioca starch flour, is made from the root of the tropical cassava plant and is very low in nutrients. A pure white powder, it can be used to make up to 25-50% of the total flour blend. Used to lighten baked goods and create a chewy texture in breads. Also used as a thickener for soups, sauces, gravy and stir fries, and as a breading, as it browns quickly and produces a crispy coating.

Teff Flour is made from the ground whole grain tiny teff seeds from a grass native to Ethiopia. This nutty, molasses-like brown flour can comprise 25-50% of the total flour blend. It works well in dark baked breads, muffins, cakes and cookies (e.g., chocolate cake, brownies, pumpernickel bread, gingerbread) and can also be added to pancakes and puddings. This very nutritious flour is high in protein, fiber and minerals such as iron and calcium. Make sure to purchase 100% teff flour as teff flour may sometimes be combined with wheat flour.

Whole-Bean Flour, from ground cranberry (romano) beans, is high in fiber, protein, vitamins and minerals. It can be used in a variety of baked goods when combined with other flours as it is a dark, stronger-tasting flour. See Bean Flours for more information.

For more information and recipes using some of these flours and starches see pages 111-121, 158-201.

Substitutions for Wheat Flour in Baking

A combination of gluten-free flours and starches makes a better product than single flours. A variety of gluten-free all-purpose baking flour mixes can be substituted for wheat flour and are available from many gluten-free companies (see pages 231-243). Also, the following are examples of gluten-free flour mixes that can be made at home and used in many different recipes.

CAROL FENSTER'S GLUTEN-FREE SORGHUM FLOUR BLEND

1 1/2 cups sorghum flour
1 1/2 cups potato starch OR cornstarch
1 cup tapioca flour
1/2 cup almond flour OR bean flour OR chestnut flour OR corn flour

- Mix ingredients and store in plastic self-seal bags or containers in the refrigerator. Before using in a recipe, take out the amount needed and allow to warm to room temperature before using.
- Makes 4 1/2 cups.

Reprinted with permission from: ***Gluten-Free 101: Easy Basic Dishes without Wheat*** by **Carol Fenster, PhD**, Savory Palate, Inc., 2006. www.glutenfree101.com

GLUTEN-FREE FLOUR MIXTURE BY CONNIE SARROS

2 1/2 cups white rice flour
1 cup potato starch
1 cup tapioca flour
1/4 cup cornstarch
1/4 cup bean flour
2 tbsp. xanthan gum

- Sift all of the ingredients together and store in plastic self-seal bags or containers and refrigerate until ready to use. If not used within 1 week, freeze the mixture. Before using in a recipe, take out the amount needed and leave at room temperature for 15 minutes before using.
- Makes 5 cups.

Reprinted with permission from: ***Wheat-free Gluten-free Reduced Calorie Cookbook*** by **Connie Sarros**, McGraw-Hill, 2001. www.gfbooks.homestead.com

GENERIC GLUTEN-FREE FLOUR MIXTURE

4 cups white rice flour
1 1/3 cup potato starch
1 cup tapioca flour

- Sift ingredients together and store in plastic self-seal bags or containers. Refrigerate for longer storage periods.
- Makes 6 1/3 cups.

Substitutions for Wheat Flour as a Thickener

Gluten-free flours, starches and other ingredients can be used as thickening agents in sauces, soups, stews, gravy, puddings and other food items. Each has its own unique properties, therefore some are more suitable than others for thickening. Starches should be mixed in cold water before using, added during the last 5 minutes of cooking and not overcooked. Flours should also be mixed in cold liquid before using. Gelatin needs to be softened in cold water, heated until the liquid is clear and then added to the food item to be thickened. Cooked starches are more clear and shiny, whereas cooked flours are more cloudy and opaque in appearance.

Substitutions for 1 tbsp. Wheat Flour

Starches	
Amaranth Starch	1½ tsp.
Arrowroot Starch	1½ tsp.
Cornstarch	1½ tsp.
Flours	
Bean (e.g., garbanzo/chickpea)	1 tbsp.
Brown Rice Flour	1 tbsp.
Sweet Rice Flour	1 tbsp.
Tapioca Flour	1 tbsp.
White Rice Flour	1 tbsp.
Others	
Gelatin Powder (unflavored)	1½ tsp.
Quick-Cooking Tapioca	2 tsp.

Food Item	Suitable Thickeners
Cream Soups	Amaranth starch, bean flour, rice flour (brown, sweet, white), tapioca flour
Fruit Sauces	Arrowroot starch, cornstarch, sweet rice flour
Fruit Pies and Cobblers	Cornstarch, quick-cooking tapioca
Gravy	Rice flour (brown, sweet, white), tapioca flour
Puddings	Amaranth starch, cornstarch, gelatin, sweet rice flour
Savory Sauces	Amaranth starch, arrowroot starch, bean flour, cornstarch, sweet rice flour
Stews	Bean flour, rice flour (brown, sweet, white), tapioca flour
Stir-Fry Dishes	Arrowroot starch, cornstarch, tapioca flour

General Baking Hints

Baking Tips

Store gluten-free flours and starches in plastic airtight containers with wide and tightly fitting lids. For optimum freshness keep in the refrigerator or freezer. Allow the cold flour or starch to return to room temperature before using.

- Label containers with the name of the item and date purchased.
- Measure flours and starches carefully. Inaccurate measurements can greatly affect the quality of gluten-free recipes because each flour and starch has very unique properties.
- Loosely spoon the flour or starch into the measuring cup, leveling the top with the flat side of a knife. Never pack down the flour.
- Use shiny, light-colored metal pans (gray not black) as products bake and brown more evenly in them than in dark pans which can leave edges crisp and over-browned.
- When using glass baking pans and non-stick metal baking pans (gray not black), reduce oven temperature by 25°F.
- Most gluten-free breads are better when baked at lower temperatures for longer periods of time. After the first 10-15 minutes of baking, tent the bread with foil to prevent over-browning.
- Baking is also affected by temperature and altitude. Slightly reduce the amount of liquid in the recipe if baking at a higher altitude or on a very humid day. For baking at very low altitudes, slightly increase the amount of liquid.
- Gluten-free bread dough tends to be softer, stickier and more batter-like. If it is too heavy and dry, the bread tends to be too crumbly.
- When making a gluten-free chocolate cake or brownies, grease the pan and then "flour" the pan with cocoa.

Texture Tips

- A combination of gluten-free flours and starches makes a better product than single flours.
- Gluten-free baked products often require more leavening than products made with wheat flour due to the lack of gluten which is necessary to form an elastic dough and enables the product to rise.
- It is important to use xanthan gum or guar gum in baked products in order to prevent crumbling. Add the gum to the dry ingredients as it does not mix with water. For every cup of gluten-free flour, use 1 teaspoon of gum for breads and ½ - ¾ teaspoon for other baked goods.
- Unflavored powdered gelatin also works as a binding agent and can prevent crumbling. If substituting gelatin for xanthan or guar gum, use twice as much gelatin. Soften the gelatin in half the water called for in the recipe before adding.
- Substituting buttermilk for the milk or water in recipes results in a lighter, more finely textured product. Carbonated beverages (not diet soft drinks) in place of water or milk can also result in a lighter-textured product (e.g., pancakes, cakes).
- Let gluten-free dough sit at least 30 minutes at room temperature to soften. This results in a better-textured product.

Flavor Tips

- To improve the flavor of gluten-free baked products use more herbs, spices and flavorings (approximately 1/3 - 1/2 more than normal).
- Adding chocolate chips, nuts, fruits (e.g., applesauce, bananas) dried fruits (e.g., apricots, cranberries, raisins) can also improve the flavor.
- Honey or molasses can provide more flavor than white sugar. You need to reduce the amount of liquid in the recipe if making this substitution. If a recipe calls for 1 cup of sugar, use 3/4 cup honey or molasses.
- Most gluten-free breads taste better toasted or warm.

Storage Tips

- Baked products made with gluten-free flours have no preservatives, become stale quickly and are quite perishable. Wrap them tightly in plastic wrap and store in airtight plastic containers or self-seal plastic bags. If the product will not be eaten within one or two days, freeze to ensure minimum loss of moisture and flavor. For breads, it is best to thoroughly cool, slice and separate each slice with wax paper before bagging and freezing.
- Placing baked products such as muffins in plastic bags when still warm can preserve moisture.
- Thaw frozen baked goods at room temperature instead of microwaving at full power; microwaving causes them to become rubbery and tough.

Thanks to the following gluten-free culinary experts for some of the background information on gluten-free flours and starches, substitutions and many of the above baking tips:

Carol Fenster, PhD, President and Founder of Savory Palate, Inc., gluten-free publishing and consulting firm. Author of:
Gluten-Free 101: Easy Basic Dishes without Wheat
Wheat-Free Recipes and Menus: Delicious, Healthful Eating for People with Food Sensitivities
Cooking Free: 220 Flavorful Recipes for People with Food Allergies and Multiple Food Sensitivities
www.savorypalate.com

Connie Sarros, Author of gluten-free cookbooks and other resources:
Wheat-Free Gluten-Free Recipes for Special Diets
Wheat-Free Gluten-Free Cookbook for Kids and Busy Adults
Wheat-Free Gluten-Free Dessert Cookbook
Wheat-Free Gluten-Free Reduced Calorie Cookbook
Newly Diagnosed Survival Kit
All You Wanted to Know About Gluten-Free Cooking DVD
www.gfbooks.homestead.com

Donna Washburn, P.H.Ec. and **Heather Butt, P.H.Ec.**, partners in Quality Professional Services, specializing in recipe development and bread machine baking. Authors of:
125 Best Gluten-Free Recipes
The Best Gluten-Free Family Cookbook
www.bestbreadrecipes.com

SORGHUM BREAD

Yield: 1 Load/12 Slices

Bette Hagman, a.k.a. the "Gluten-Free Gourmet," is an expert in the area of gluten-free baking. She has been developing recipes combining the new food-grade sorghum varieties with other gluten-free flours.

1 cup	**sorghum flour**
2/3 cup	**tapioca flour**
2/3 cup	**cornstarch**
1 1/2 tsp.	**xanthan gum**
1/3 cup	**non-fat dry milk powder OR nondairy substitute***
1/2 tsp.	**salt**
1 tsp.	**unflavored gelatin**
1 tsp.	**GF baking powder**
3 tbsp.	**sugar**
2 1/4 tsp.	**dry yeast granules**
2	**eggs**
1/2 tsp.	**dough enhancer OR vinegar**
3 tbsp.	**vegetable oil**
1 cup	**lukewarm water (more or less)**

- ✦ Grease a 4 1/2 x 8 1/2-inch loaf pan and dust with rice flour.
- ✦ Combine the dry ingredients in a medium bowl.
- ✦ In the mixing bowl of a heavy-duty mixer, whisk together the eggs, dough enhancer and oil. Add most of the water, holding back about 3 tbsp. to add as needed. Turn the mixer to low and add the flour mixture a little at a time. The batter should be the consistency of cake batter. Add the remaining water a little at a time to achieve this texture. Turn the mixer to high and beat for 3 1/2 minutes. Spoon the batter into the prepared pan, cover and let rise in a warm place; about 35 minutes for rapid rising yeast; 60 or so minutes for regular yeast, or until dough reaches the top of the pan.
- ✦ Bake for 50-55 minutes in a preheated 400°F oven, covering after 10 minutes with aluminum foil.
- ✦ Turn out immediately to cool. For a softer crust rub immediately with butter or margarine. Cool before slicing.

* *Bette wrote, "I used the adult drink powder Ensure as my nondairy substitute and it turned out very well. The extra flavor and vanilla in the powder made the best-tasting bread."*

This recipe was developed by **Bette Hagman** for **Twin Valley Mills,** and is reprinted with their permission. Twin Valley Mills, LLC., RR #1, Box 45, Ruskin NE, USA 68974;
Phone 402-279-3965;
www.twinvalleymills.com

Nutritional Analysis

1 serving = 1 slice

Calories (kcal)	152
Carbohydrates (g)	26
Dietary Fiber (g)	1
Fat (g)	5
Protein (g)	4
Iron (mg)	0.8
Calcium (mg)	56
Sodium (mg)	170

BASIC RYE BREAD

Yield: 15 Slices (1/2" thick)

Caraway seeds add classic rye bread flavor to this versatile bread.

Note: This recipe provides options for both bread machine and mixer.

Reprinted with permission from: ***Delicious Gluten-Free Wheat-Free Breads: Easy to make breads everyone will love to eat for the bread machine or oven*** – by **LynnRae Ries** and **Bruce Gross**, What No Wheat Publishing, 2003, www.whatnowheat.com

3	**eggs**
1/4 cup	**vegetable oil**
2 tbsp.	**molasses**
1 tsp.	**vinegar**
1 cup	**water**
3/4 cup	**white rice flour**
3/4 cup	**brown rice flour**
1/4 cup	**sweet rice flour**
1/2 cup	**potato starch**
1/2 cup	**tapioca starch**
1/4 cup	**millet, amaranth OR sorghum flour**
OR	**use 3 cups of your favorite GF flour mix instead of the above flours**
1 tsp.	**salt**
1/4 cup	**light brown sugar**
1 tbsp.	**xanthan gum**
1/2 cup	**non-fat dry milk powder**
1 tsp.	**dough enhancer (optional)**
2 1/2 tsp.	**bread machine yeast**
2 tbsp.	**caraway seeds, if desired**

✦ **Bread Machine:**

– Place ingredients into the bread machine according to the manual. Program the machine to knead (mix) the ingredients, rise once, then change to bake for 60-70 minutes. Rising time should be 50 minutes, or until the dough doubles in size. When done, remove the bread from the machine and place on a wire rack to cool. Remember to remove the bread machine paddles if they are stuck in the bread.

✦ **Mixer:**

– In a medium-sized bowl, mix all the liquid ingredients together and set aside.

– Place all the dry ingredients into mixer bowl and blend flours together on slow speed.

– Slowly add the liquid ingredients to the dry while the mixer is on low.

– Beat on high for 3-4 minutes. Mixture should look silky. If the dough is too dry, add liquid 1 tablespoon at a time.

✦ Place the dough into a 9 x 5-inch loaf pan that has been greased and dusted with rice flour. Bake in a preheated 350°F oven for 60-70 minutes. Start checking for the bread being done at 55 minutes. When done, remove from bread pan and place on cooling rack. Do not cut or package until the bread cools, approximately 2-3 hours.

Nutritional Analysis

(amaranth flour)

1 serving = 1 slice (1/2" thick)

Calories (kcal)	182
Carbohydrates (g)	31
Dietary Fiber (g)	2
Fat (g)	5
Protein (g)	4
Iron (mg)	0.9
Calcium (mg)	53
Sodium (mg)	210

(millet flour)

1 serving = 1 slice (1/2" thick)

Calories	183
Carbohydrates (g)	31
Dietary Fiber (g)	1
Fat (g)	5
Protein (g)	4
Iron (mg)	0.9
Calcium (mg)	50
Sodium (mg)	210

BROWN RICE BREAD

with variations for using Teff, Amaranth, Quinoa and Buckwheat

Yield: 1 Loaf/12 Slices

So far, this is the best gluten-free bread we have tried. Recipe adapted from Barbara Emch's, a fellow celiac.

Notes: ✦ Humidity: If humidity is too high, reduce the amount of water in the recipe to avoid over-rising. Many gluten-free bakers experience the frustrating situation in which a beautiful loaf of bread deflates once removed from the oven. You will need to experiment a little to get just the right amount of water in your bread, depending on the humidity in the air. If in doubt, use less water than the recipe calls for.

✦ Rapid Rise Yeast: You may use rapid rise yeast or regular yeast. If using rapid rise yeast, eliminate the cold oven/pan of hot water rise method and instead follow yeast package directions for rise time.

3	**large eggs (egg-free: see substitution below*)**
1/4 cup	**vegetable oil**
1 tsp.	**lemon juice**
2 cups	**tapioca starch flour**
2 cups	**fine brown rice flour**
2/3 cup	**instant non-fat dry milk powder (for dairy-free: see substitution below **)**
2 tsp.	**xanthan gum**
1 tsp.	**salt**
1 1/2 tbsp.	**active dry yeast**
4 tbsp.	**sugar**
1 1/4 cups	**warm water (105°-115°F)**

- ✦ Bring all refrigerated ingredients to room temperature. Grease a 5 x 9-inch loaf pan.
- ✦ In the bowl of a stand mixer, combine eggs, oil and lemon juice.
- ✦ In a medium bowl, combine tapioca starch flour, brown rice flour, dry milk powder, xanthan gum, salt, yeast and sugar. Add about 1 cup of the water to the egg mixture, then slowly add dry ingredients a little at a time until completely incorporated. If mixture is too dry, add remaining water (see humidity note). Mix batter on high speed for 3 1/2 minutes, then pour into prepared pan.
- ✦ Cover bread with foil and place in a cold oven. Set a pan of hot water on a lower shelf underneath the bread. Leave for 10 minutes with oven door closed. (This will cause the bread to rise quickly.) Remove bread from oven (do not uncover) and place in a warm place in the kitchen. Preheat oven to 400°F. Bread will continue to rise as oven preheats.
- ✦ Uncover bread and bake for 10 minutes to brown the top. Cover bread with foil and continue to bake bread for 30 minutes. Turn bread out onto a cooling rack. When completely cooled, wrap tightly to maintain freshness for as long as possible.

* **Egg-Free Substitution, Flax Seed:** This seed has many health benefits such as high-quality protein, fiber, B and C vitamins, iron and zinc, anti-cancer properties, omega-3 fatty acids, and many other benefits. To use as an egg substitute: grind 3 tablespoons flaxseed and add 1/2 cup + 1 tablespoon boiling water, let sit for 15 minutes, then whisk with a fork – this mixture will replace 3 eggs in a recipe. A clean coffee grinder works well to grind the small flaxseed.

** **Dairy-Free Substitution, Ground Almonds:** Use 2/3 cup ground almonds to replace 2/3 cup dry milk powder.

BROWN RICE BREAD

(continued)

Variations:

Teff Bread, Quinoa Bread, Amaranth Bread, or Buckwheat Bread

Substitute the following combination of flours for the 2 cups brown rice flour and 2 cups tapioca flour in the original recipe.

1 1/2 cups tapioca starch flour
1 1/2 cups brown rice flour
1 cup teff flour, quinoa flour, amaranth flour, OR light buckwheat flour

Light buckwheat flour is preferred to dark buckwheat flour. The dark flour gives a purple cast to the bread.

Reprinted with permission from: ***Cooking Gluten-Free! A Food Lover's Collection of Chef and Family Recipes without Gluten or Wheat*** by **Karen Robertson**, Celiac Publishing, 2002. P.O. Box 99603, Seattle WA, USA 98139; Phone 206-282-4822; www.cookingglutenfree.com

Nutritional Analysis
1 serving = 1 slice

	Original	Amaranth	Buckwheat	Quinoa	Teff	Dairy-Free & Egg-Free	Dairy Free	Egg Free
Calories	253	255	242	248	252	263	267	248
Carbohydrates (g)	47	45	42	44	45	47	46	48
Dietary Fiber (g)	2	3	3	2	2	3	3	3
Fat (g)	7	7	7	7	7	9	9	7
Protein (g)	6	7	6	6	6	4	5	5
Iron (mg)	1.0	1.8	1.2	1.8	1.6	1.1	1.2	1.0
Calcium (mg)	66	83	66	71	86	24	24	67
Sodium (mg)	257	258	256	258	258	217	234	240

MONTINA BREAD

Yield: 1 Loaf/12 Slices

The sweet, nutty flavor of Montina™ flour gives this bread a traditional "wheat-like" flavor.

Tip: For best results ... thin slices work well and toasting brings out additional flavor!

Reprinted courtesy of: **Amazing Grains Grower Cooperative**, 405 Main St. S.W., Ronan MT, USA 59684; Phone 877-278-6585 or 406-676-3536; www.amazinggrains.com

Nutritional Analysis

1 serving = 1 slice

Calories (kcal)	232
Carbohydrates (g)	39
Dietary Fiber (g)	3
Fat (g)	6
Protein (g)	6
Iron (mg)	3.5
Calcium (mg)	63
Sodium (mg)	365

3 cups	**Montina™ All-Purpose Baking Flour Blend***
1/4 cup	**sugar**
3 1/2 tsp.	**xanthan gum**
1 1/2 tsp.	**salt**
2/3 cup	**non-fat dry milk powder**
1 cup	**water**
1/4 cup	**butter-flavored shortening**
2 tsp.	**sugar**
1/2 cup	**warm water (110°F)**
4 1/2 tsp.	**yeast granules**
1 tsp.	**apple cider vinegar** **
3	**eggs**

- ✦ Combine Montina™, 1/4 cup sugar, xanthan gum, salt, dry milk powder in the bowl of a heavy mixer.
- ✦ In small saucepan, combine 1 cup water and shortening. Warm just until shortening is melted.
- ✦ Dissolve 2 tsp. sugar in 1/2 cup warm water and mix in the yeast. Let proof until bubbly.
- ✦ Turn the mixer on low, allowing all the dry ingredients to blend.
- ✦ Slowly add the warm water, shortening and vinegar. Blend thoroughly and then add the eggs.
- ✦ Add the yeast mixture to the bowl and beat on highest speed for 2 minutes.
- ✦ Cover the mixing bowl with plastic wrap and a towel and put in a warm place. Let the dough rise until doubled, approximately 1-1 1/2 hours.
- ✦ Return the bowl to the mixer and beat on high for 3 minutes.
- ✦ Spoon the dough into a greased 5 x 9-inch loaf pan, level dough as best you can, cover with plastic wrap and let rise until slightly above the top of the pan.
- ✦ Bake in a preheated 400°F oven for 10 minutes. At this point, place foil over the bread and bake 50 minutes longer.
- ✦ When baking is finished, remove bread from pan and cool on a wire rack.

* **Montina™ All-Purpose Baking Flour Blend** is a mixture of Montina Pure (100% Indian ricegrass), white rice flour and tapioca starch and is available from Amazing Grains Grower Cooperative.

** **Author's Note:** Other vinegars can be substituted for apple cider vinegar, except malt vinegar (which is not gluten-free).

CAROL FENSTER'S PIZZA

Serves: 6 (1 slice each)

This flour mixture produces a super pizza crust. Add the zesty sauce, grated mozzarella and your favorite toppings for a great lunch, dinner or snack.

Reprinted with permission from: ***Gluten-Free 101: Easy Basic Dishes without Wheat*** by **Carol Fenster, PhD.**, Savory Palate Inc. 2006; www.glutenfree101.com

Nutritional Analysis

(Brown Rice Flour)

1 serving = 1 slice

Calories (kcal)	147
Carbohydrates (g)	31
Dietary Fiber (g)	3
Fat (g)	2
Protein (g)	4
Iron (mg)	1.3
Calcium (mg)	54
Sodium (mg)	697

(Garbanzo/Fava Bean Flour)

1 serving = 1 slice

Calories (kcal)	130
Carbohydrates (g)	26
Dietary Fiber (g)	5
Fat (g)	2
Protein (g)	6
Iron (mg)	1.7
Calcium (mg)	66
Sodium (mg)	729

Sauce:

1 can	**(8 oz.) tomato sauce**
½ tsp.	**dried oregano**
½ tsp.	**dried basil**
½ tsp.	**dried rosemary**
½ tsp.	**fennel seeds**
¼ tsp.	**garlic powder OR 1 minced garlic clove**
2 tsp.	**sugar**
½ tsp.	**salt**

Crust:

1 tbsp.	**dry yeast**
¾ cup	**warm milk (110°F) – cow, rice, OR soy milk**
½ tsp.	**sugar**
⅔ cup	**garbanzo/fava bean flour OR brown rice flour**
½ cup	**tapioca flour**
2 tsp.	**xanthan gum**
½ tsp.	**salt**
1 tsp.	**gelatin powder**
1 tsp.	**Italian seasoning**
1 tsp.	**olive oil**
1 tsp.	**cider vinegar**

Sauce:

✦ Combine all sauce ingredients in a small saucepan and simmer for 15 minutes. (Makes about 1 cup, enough for a 12-inch pizza.)

Crust:

✦ Dissolve yeast and sugar in warm milk for five minutes. In a food processor, blend all crust ingredients, including yeast mixture, until a ball forms. Dough will be soft.

✦ Place dough on a greased 12-inch non-stick pizza pan. Liberally sprinkle rice flour over dough; then press dough into pan with your hands, continuing to sprinkle dough with flour to prevent sticking. Make edges thicker to contain toppings.

✦ Bake pizza crust in a preheated 400°F oven for 10 minutes. Remove from oven.

✦ Add sauce and toppings to crust. Bake another 20-25 minutes, or until top is nicely browned.

INJERA (ETHIOPIAN FLAT BREAD)

Yield: 1 Loaf/24 Slices

This flat, thin porous bread is a traditional Ethiopian finger food. Injera is served with "wot," a sauce or stew made with chicken, beef or lamb or spicy ground lentils and peas.

Note: Authentic Injera is made from pure teff flour; however, many North American restaurants often use a combination of teff flour and wheat flour.

Recipe courtesy of **Girma and Ethiopia Sahlu**, Regina SK, Canada

2 tbsp.	**yeast (2 packages)**
6 1/2 cups	**warm water**
1 1/2 lbs.	**teff flour (about 4 1/2 cups)**

- ✦ Dissolve the yeast in 1/4 cup water.
- ✦ Combine the teff flour, yeast and 6 1/4 cups water in a large bowl. Mix well. Ensure that no clumps are left at the bottom or side of the bowl.
- ✦ Cover the dough with plastic wrap and let it ferment for 2 to 3 days at room temperature. (Those with sensitive stomachs, may consider making the Injera the same day rather than waiting for 2-3 days. It will have a slightly "sweet" taste but that is considered normal.)
- ✦ Drain off the water that has risen to the top of the dough.
- ✦ Gradually add fresh warm water to the dough, just enough to make a thin smooth batter (like pancake batter); mix well. Cover the batter and let it stand until it rises, approximately 10 to 25 minutes.
- ✦ Heat a 10-inch skillet or frying pan until a drop of water bounces on the pan's surface.
- ✦ Scoop about 1/3 cup of the batter and pour it into the pan quickly. Swirl the pan so that the entire bottom is evenly coated. Cover the pan quickly and let the Injera cook for 1-2 minutes. (Injera does not easily stick or burn.) Remove the cover and wait for a few seconds. It is cooked through when bubbles or "eyes" appear all over the top. If your first try is undercooked, cook the next one a little longer or use a smaller amount (1/4 cup) of batter. Do not turn the Injera over in the pan. Use a spatula to remove the cooked Injera and place it on a clean towel.
- ✦ Let the Injera cool and then stack them on a serving tray. Do not stack hot as they will stick together.
- ✦ Continue making the Injera until the batter is finished.
- ✦ Injera should be soft and pliable so that it can be rolled or folded like a crêpe or tortilla. Properly cooked, Injera will be thinner than a pancake but thicker than a crêpe.

Nutritional Analysis

1 serving = 1 slice

Calories (kcal)	105
Carbohydrates (g)	21
Dietary Fiber (g)	2
Fat (g)	1
Protein (g)	4
Iron (mg)	2
Calcium (mg)	54
Sodium (mg)	7

APPLE DATE BREAD

Yield: 15 Slices (1/2" thick)

Apple juice, applesauce and dates make this bread moist and flavorful.

Note: This recipe provides options for both bread machine and mixer.

Reprinted with permission from: ***Delicious Gluten-Free Wheat Free Breads: Easy to bake breads everyone will love to eat for the bread machine or oven*** by **LynnRae Ries** and **Bruce Gross**, What No Wheat Publishing, 2003; www.whatnowheat.com

Nutritional Analysis

1 serving = 1 slice (1/2" thick)

Calories (kcal)	187
Carbohydrates (g)	39
Dietary Fiber (g)	2
Fat (g)	2
Protein (g)	4
Iron (mg)	0.7
Calcium (mg)	51
Sodium (mg)	208

3	**eggs**
1/2 cup	**chunky apple sauce**
3/4 cup	**apple juice or water**
1 tsp.	**apple cider vinegar**
1 tsp.	**vanilla extract**
1 tbsp.	**vegetable oil**

2 cups	**white rice flour**
1/2 cup	**tapioca starch flour**
1/2 cup	**cornstarch**

OR use 3 cups of your own favorite GF flour mix instead of the above flours

1/2 cup	**non-fat dry milk**
1 tsp.	**salt**
1 tbsp.	**sugar**
2 tsp.	**cinnamon**
1 tbsp.	**xanthan gum**
2 1/4 tsp.	**yeast**

3/4 cup	**finely chopped GF pitted dates**
1 tsp.	**orange zest**

✦ **Bread Machine:**
- Place ingredients into the bread machine according to the manual directions.
- Program the machine to knead (mix) the ingredients, add the dates and orange zest at the "add in time," allow the bread to rise once, then change to bake for 60-70 minutes. Rising time should be 50 minutes, or until the dough doubles in size.
- When done, remove the bread from the machine and place on a wire rack to cool. Remember to remove the bread machine paddles if they are stuck in the bread.

✦ **Mixer:**
- In a medium-sized bowl, mix all the liquid ingredients together and set aside.
- Place all the dry ingredients, including the yeast, into the mixer bowl and blend flours together on slow speed.
- Slowly add the liquid ingredients to the dry while the mixer is on low.
- Beat on high for 3-4 minutes. Mixture should look silky. If the dough is too dry, add liquid 1 tablespoon at a time.

✦ Add the dates and orange zest after the dough has been thoroughly mixed.

✦ Place the dough into a 9 x 5-inch loaf pan that has been greased and dusted with rice flour. Bake in a preheated 350°F oven for 60-70 minutes. Start checking for the bread being done at 55 minutes. When done, remove bread from pan and place on cooling rack. Do not cut or package until the bread cools, approximately 2-3 hours.

BANANA SEED BREAD

Yield: 1 Loaf/12 Slices

The combination of sorghum and bean flour really enhances the banana flavor of this loaf. Serve it for dessert or with a slice of old Cheddar for lunch or a snack.

1 cup	**whole bean flour**
1 cup	**sorghum flour**
1/4 cup	**tapioca starch**
1/4 cup	**packed brown sugar**
2 1/2 tsp.	**xanthan gum**
1 tbsp.	**bread machine yeast OR instant yeast**
1 1/4 tsp.	**salt**
1/2 cup	**sunflower seeds***
3/4 cup	**water**
1 cup	**mashed banana**
1 tsp.	**vinegar**
1/4 cup	**vegetable oil**
2	**eggs**

- ✦ In a large bowl or plastic bag, combine whole bean flour, sorghum flour, tapioca starch, brown sugar, xanthan gum, yeast, salt and sunflower seeds. Mix well and set aside.
- ✦ Pour water, banana, vinegar and oil into the bread machine baking pan. Add eggs.
- ✦ Select the Rapid 2-Hour Basic Cycle. Allow the liquids to mix until combined. Gradually add the dry ingredients as the bread machine is mixing. Scrape with a rubber spatula while adding the dry ingredients. Try to incorporate all the dry ingredients within 1 to 2 minutes. When mixing and kneading are complete, leaving the bread pan in the bread machine, remove the kneading blade. Allow the bread machine to complete the cycle.

* Use raw, unroasted, unsalted sunflower seeds. For a nuttier flavor, toast the sunflower seeds.

Variation:

Pumpkin seeds or chopped pecans can replace the sunflower seeds.

Reprinted with permission from: ***125 Best Gluten-Free Recipes*** by **Donna Washburn** and **Heather Butt**, Robert Rose Inc. Publisher, 2003; www.bestbreadrecipes.com

Nutritional Analysis

1 serving = 1 slice

Calories (kcal)	222
Carbohydrates (g)	30
Dietary Fiber (g)	4
Fat (g)	10
Protein (g)	7
Iron (mg)	2.0
Calcium (mg)	29
Sodium (mg)	282

MONTINA VEGETABLE SKILLET BREAD

Serves: 8

This bread is a good accompaniment to almost any type of meal or as a wonderful savory snack.

1 ¼ cup	**Montina™ Pure Baking Supplement***
1 cup	**cornmeal, plain**
4 tsp.	**baking powder**
1 tsp.	**salt**
1	**medium onion, chopped**
1	**medium red pepper, chopped**
1	**medium green pepper, chopped**
2	**large ribs celery, chopped**
3	**small hot peppers, finely chopped (optional)**
4 tbsp.	**safflower oil**
2	**eggs, lightly beaten**
1 cup	**low-fat buttermilk**

✦ Mix dry ingredients in a large bowl.

✦ Sauté vegetables in a 10-inch ovenproof skillet in 2 tbsp. oil for 5 minutes or until just softened.

✦ Add to dry ingredients and stir to coat.

✦ Add 1-2 tbsp. oil to skillet and heat in a preheated 400°F oven for 5 minutes.

✦ Combine eggs and milk and add to flour vegetable mixture. Allow to sit for 5 minutes. If needed, add more milk to make a very moist batter.

✦ Pour the batter into the hot skillet.

✦ Reduce oven temperature to 350°F and bake bread for about 40 minutes, or until lightly browned and firm.

✦ Slice and serve warm.

* **Montina™ Pure Baking Supplement** is 100% Indian ricegrass and is available from Amazing Grains Grower Cooperative.

Note: A well-seasoned iron skillet or any heavy pan or baking dish will work. Salt can be eliminated. Any type of milk works well. Sauteéd vegetables can be prepared ahead and refrigerated or frozen. Other vegetable such as yellow squash, zucchini or apple may be substituted or added. Do not overfill the pan since bread rises during baking.

This recipe was developed by **Michael and Bev Callihan** of Bozeman, MT for ***Amazing Grains*** and is used here with permission from: **Amazing Grains Grower Cooperative**, 405 Main Street S.W., Ronan MT, USA 59864; Phone 877-278-6585 or 406-676-3536; www.amazinggrains.com

Nutritional Analysis
per serving

Calories (kcal)	254
Carbohydrates (g)	35
Dietary Fiber (g)	3
Fat (g)	10
Protein (g)	9
Iron (mg)	2.7
Calcium (mg)	194
Sodium (mg)	554

MIGHTY TASTY MUFFINS

Yield: **12 Muffins**

The special flours and cereals used in these muffins complement the flavors of the brown sugar and spice mixtures.

2 tbsp.	**Bob's Red Mill™ Mighty Tasty GF Hot Cereal** *
2/3 cup	**low-fat (1%) milk**
1 tbsp.	**apple cider vinegar** **
1	**large egg**
1/3 cup	**molasses**
1 tsp.	**vanilla**
3/4 cup	**Bob's Red Mill™ GF Garbanzo and Fava Flour**
1/2 cup	**potato starch**
1/4 cup	**tapioca flour**
1/3 cup	**brown sugar, packed**
1 tsp.	**GF baking powder**
1/2 tsp.	**baking soda**
1 tsp.	**xanthan gum**
1/4 tsp.	**nutmeg**
1/2 tsp.	**cinnamon**
1/4 tsp.	**ground ginger**
1/4 tsp.	**allspice**
1/2 tsp.	**salt**

- ✦ In a large bowl, combine the first 6 ingredients. Let sit for 15 minutes, while the cereal softens.
- ✦ In a separate bowl, combine the remaining ingredients.
- ✦ Add the dry ingredients to the liquid ingredients and stir until just moistened.
- ✦ Spoon the batter into greased muffin tins. Fill tins 2/3 full.
- ✦ Bake in a preheated 350°F oven for approximately 20 minutes, or until the tops of the muffins are firm.

* Brown rice, corn, "sweet" white sorghum, buckwheat

** **Author's Note:** Distilled white vinegar is also gluten-free and can be substituted for apple cider vinegar.

Reprinted with permission from: **Bob's Red Mill Natural Foods, Inc.**, 5209 S.E. International Way, Milwaukie OR, USA 97222; Phone 800-553-2258 or 503-654-3215; www.bobsredmill.com
Recipe adapted by **Carol Fenster, PhD**, author of gluten-free cookbooks and President of Savory Palate Inc. www.savorypalate.com

Nutritional Analysis

1 serving = 1 muffin

Calories (kcal)	123
Carbohydrates (g)	27
Dietary Fiber (g)	2
Fat (g)	1
Protein (g)	3
Iron (mg)	1.1
Calcium (mg)	72
Sodium (mg)	213

BLUEBERRY SORGHUM MUFFINS

Yield: **12 medium muffins**

Sorghum flour, cornstarch and soy flour make an interesting gluten-free combination for these muffins.

1 1/2 cups **sorghum/cornstarch mix***
1/4 cup **soy flour**
1/4 cup **sugar**
2 1/2 tsp. **GF baking powder**
3/4 tsp. **salt**
1 tsp. **xanthan gum**
2 **eggs**
1 cup **low fat (1%) milk OR soy milk**
1/3 cup **vegetable oil**
1 tsp. **vanilla extract**
1 cup **blueberries (rinsed and drained)**

✦ In a large bowl, combine the dry ingredients and whisk together.

✦ Beat eggs lightly; add milk, oil and vanilla; beat until well mixed.

✦ Add wet ingredients to dry ingredients and beat until smooth. You can beat as long as needed, dough will not get "tough" like muffins made with wheat flour.

✦ Add blueberries and fold in gently.

✦ Spoon the batter into paper-cup-lined muffin tins. Fill cups 2/3 full.

✦ Bake in a preheated 350°F oven for 19 minutes, or until a toothpick comes out clean.

* **Sorghum Cornstarch Mix:**

3 cups **sorghum flour**
1 cup **cornstarch**

Recipe courtesy of **Amy Perry** and **Meredith Wiking** of **Nebraska Grain Sorghum Board**, 301 Centennial Mall South, P. O. Box 94982, Lincoln NE, USA 68509; Phone 402-471-4276; www.sorghum.state.ne.us

Nutritional Analysis

1 serving = 1 muffin

Calories (kcal)	166
Carbohydrates (g)	21
Dietary Fiber (g)	2
Fat (g)	8
Protein (g)	4
Iron (mg)	0.9
Calcium (mg)	87
Sodium (mg)	262

CARROT PUMPKIN MUFFINS

Yield: **30 Muffins**

This recipe is moist and delicious. Using applesauce and pumpkin reduces the fat and sugar content as compared to traditional carrot muffins or cake.

Tip: Use muffin liners instead of greasing pans (also helps maintain moisture for storing muffins). Use parchment paper (available from kitchen stores and some grocery stores) as the lining on the bottom of cake pans to avoid greasing pans (remove as much fat as possible).

Recipe courtesy of **Laurel Hutton, Laurel's Sweet Treats, Inc.**, 16004 SW Tualatin – Sherwood Road, #123, Sherwood OR, USA 97140; Phone 866-225-3432 or 503-625-3432; www.glutenfreemixes.com

Nutritional Analysis

1 serving = 1 muffin

Calories (kcal)	148
Carbohydrates (g)	27
Dietary Fiber (g)	1
Fat (g)	5
Protein (g)	1
Iron (mg)	0.3
Calcium (mg)	26
Sodium (mg)	252

1 3/4 cups	**sugar**
3	**egg whites**
1	**whole egg**
1/2 cup	**vegetable oil**
1 cup	**unsweetened applesauce**
1 cup	**puréed pumpkin**
1 tbsp.	**vanilla**
1 1/3 cups	**cooked puréed carrots**
3 cups	**flour mix***
1 tsp.	**salt**
1 tbsp.	**baking soda**
2 tsp.	**GF baking powder**
2 tsp.	**xanthan gum**
1 tbsp.	**ground cinnamon**

- ✦ In a large bowl, combine sugar, eggs and oil, cream until light and fluffy. Add applesauce, pumpkin, vanilla and carrots.
- ✦ Sift dry ingredients together and slowly fold into batter.
- ✦ Spoon batter into paper-cup-lined small muffin tins, filling cups 2/3 full, or into cake pans (one, 9 x 13-inch or two, 9-inch round).
- ✦ Bake in a preheated 350°F oven for 15-20 minutes (muffins) or 25-40 minutes for cake, depending on the size of the cake pans.
- ✦ Cool for 10 minutes. Remove cake from the pan and peel off the paper.

* **Flour Mix:**

3 parts	**rice flour**
1 1/2 parts	**potato starch**
1 part	**tapioca starch**

Variation:

To make **Carrot Cake**, eliminate the pumpkin and use all applesauce (total of 2 cups applesauce).

TEFF BANANA PANCAKES

Yield: 25 small pancakes

This basic pancake recipe is easy to make and is delicious with a variety of sweeteners and juices. Feel free to substitute maple syrup for honey, and juice for soy milk. Ground flax seeds easily take the place of eggs in these delicious pancakes made with naturally sweet teff and bananas. The batter is light and looks like pudding.

2 tbsp.	**flax seeds**
2	**bananas, ripe**
1 ½ cups	**vanilla soy milk**
1 tbsp.	**vanilla**
1 tbsp.	**honey**
1 ½ tsp.	**vegetable oil**
1 ½ cups	**teff flour**
1 tbsp.	**baking powder**
¼ tsp.	**sea salt**
½ tsp.	**cinnamon**

- ✦ Grind flax seeds in a blender until powdery. Add banana, vanilla soy milk, vanilla, honey and ½ tsp. oil. Blend well.
- ✦ In a large mixing bowl, combine teff flour, baking powder, sea salt and cinnamon. Stir in banana soy milk mixture.
- ✦ Place the griddle or skillet over medium heat. After a minute or two, brush on 1 tsp. of oil. Using a tablespoon, scoop up the batter and pour it on the hot griddle, 1 heaping tablespoon for each pancake.
- ✦ Cook pancakes for 3-4 minutes on the first side, or until you see tiny holes on the top of the pancakes. Flip them over and cook for another minute or two.
- ✦ Serve pancakes plain or dipped into yogurt.

Reprinted with permission from: **The Teff Company**, P.O. Box A, Caldwell ID, USA 83606; www.teffco.com; Phone 888-822-2221 and **Leslie Cerier**, 58 Schoolhouse Road, Amherst MA, USA 01002; www.lesliecerier.com

Nutritional Analysis

1 serving = 1 pancake

Calories (kcal)	54
Carbohydrates (g)	9
Dietary Fiber (g)	1
Fat (g)	1
Protein (g)	2
Iron (mg)	0.7
Calcium (mg)	64
Sodium (mg)	79

HEARTY MESQUITE MONTINA PANCAKES

Yield: 8 - 4" Pancakes

High-fiber mesquite and Montina™ add texture; banana and cinnamon add rich flavor – these are great breakfast pancakes.

1/3 cup	**mesquite flour**
1/3 cup	**Montina™ Pure Baking Supplement***
1/4 cup	**GF Flour Blend ****
2 tsp.	**sugar**
2 tsp.	**baking powder**
1/2 tsp.	**baking soda**
1/4 tsp.	**cinnamon**
1/4 tsp.	**salt**
1	**large egg**
1	**medium ripe banana, mashed**
1 cup	**milk (cow, rice or soy)**
1 tbsp.	**canola oil**
	additional oil for frying

- ✦ Blend all ingredients in a blender or whisk vigorously in a bowl. For lighter pancakes, sift the dry ingredients before blending.
- ✦ Let batter sit while preheating skillet or griddle to medium-high.
- ✦ Lightly oil hot skillet or griddle.
- ✦ Cook 1 "test" pancake using a scant 1/4 cup of batter. Adjust batter if necessary by adding more milk, a tablespoon at a time, if necessary. Cook until tops are bubbly (3-5 minutes). Turn and cook until golden brown (2-3 minutes).

* **Montina™ Pure Baking Supplement** is 100% Indian ricegrass flour sold under the trade name Montina by Amazing Grains Grower Cooperative.

** A variety of flours and starches can be used to make a GF Flour Blend (see page 154) or use an All-Purpose GF Flour Mix from gluten-free companies (see pages 241-243).

Adapted from and reprinted with permission from: ***Gluten-Free 101: Easy Basic Dishes without Wheat*** by **Carol Fenster, PhD.**, Savory Palate Inc. 2006. www.glutenfree101.com

Nutritional Analysis
1 serving = 2 pancakes

Calories (kcal)	229
Carbohydrates (g)	38
Dietary Fiber (g)	5
Fat (g)	6
Protein (g)	8
Iron (mg)	1.9
Calcium (mg)	233
Sodium (mg)	569

SHELLEY CASE'S HIGH-FIBER HOT CEREAL

Yield: 1 Cup

This quick, heart-healthy breakfast is packed with fiber and omega-3 fatty acids. Add a spoonful of brown sugar, chopped nuts and/or dried apricots or raisins for more flavor and extra nutrients.

Tip: Mix dry flax and the hot cereal in self-seal plastic bags and take it when travelling. The cereal can be cooked in the microwave in your hotel room. Another option is to order juice and/or coffee/tea and/or an egg at the restaurant and ask the server to heat the cereal and water in a bowl in their microwave. Most restaurants are very accommodating if you order some items off the menu.

3 tbsp. Flax Seed Meal (Ground Flax)*
3 tbsp. Cream of Brown Rice Hot Cereal
1 ⅓ cup water
dash of vanilla

- ✦ Combine the first 3 ingredients in a medium to large glass bowl.
- ✦ Cook on high in a microwave for 3-4 minutes, or until thick and creamy.
- ✦ Stir in vanilla.
- ✦ Serve with brown sugar, nuts and/or dried fruits.

* As flax is very high in fiber, it is important to gradually introduce it in small portions until tolerated. Start with 5 tbsp. hot cereal and 1-3 tsp. of ground flax initially and then gradually work up to 3 tbsp. flax and 3 tbsp. hot cereal. See page 105 for fiber tips.

Variations:

Substitute Creamy Buckwheat Hot Cereal or Bob's Red Mill Mighty Tasty Gluten-Free Hot Cereal™ for the Brown Rice Hot Cereal.

Nutritional Analysis

1 serving = 1 cup

	Brown Rice	Buckwheat	Bob's Mighty Tasty
Calories (kcal)	225	217	225
Carbohydrates (g)	30	29	29
Dietary Fiber (g)	7	8	9
Fat (g)	10	10	10
Protein (g)	6	8	7
Iron (mg)	1.2	1.2	1.2
Calcium (mg)	60	60	60
Sodium (mg)	16	13	16

CRUNCHY GRANOLA

Yield: **11 Cups**

This high-fiber granola is loaded with nutrients. Great for breakfast, as a snack, or it can be used to make granola bars or as a topping for yogurt, ice cream or frozen yogurt, or a fruit crisp (apple, blueberry, peach). Various substitutions can be used for the nuts and dried fruits.

½ cup	**shredded coconut**
½ cup	**sunflower seeds**
¼ cup	**sesame seeds**
1 cup	**chopped nuts**
½ cup	**chopped GF dates**
½ cup	**chopped dried apricots**
½ cup	**raisins**
	hot water
4 cups	**GF corn flakes**
3 cups	**GF crisp rice cereal**
3 tbsp.	**flax seed meal (ground flax)**
¼ cup	**oil**
½ cup	**honey**
1 tbsp.	**apple juice**
1 tsp.	**vanilla**
½ tsp.	**nutmeg**
½ tsp.	**cinnamon**

- ✦ Combine the coconut, sunflower and sesame seeds and nuts in a shallow pan and toast under the broiler for a few minutes (watch carefully to prevent burning). Remove from the oven, stir and return to the oven to finish toasting. Remove from the oven and cool.
- ✦ Soak the dried fruit in hot water to clean and soften for 10 minutes. Drain. Chop the fruit into bite-sized pieces.
- ✦ Combine the cereals, flax, coconut, nuts and seeds.
- ✦ Mix the oil, honey, juice, vanilla, nutmeg and cinnamon together.
- ✦ Place the cereal/nut mixture in a large roasting or broiler pan; pour the oil/honey mixture over and mix well.
- ✦ Bake in a preheated 300°F oven for 1 hour, stirring every 10-15 minutes. Add the dried fruits and return to the oven for the last 15 minutes.
- ✦ Remove the granola from the oven and let it cool. Stir a few times as it cools.
- ✦ Store in an air-tight container in a cool place (refrigerator or freezer).

Recipe courtesy of **Laurel Hutton, Laurel's Sweet Treats, Inc.**, 16004 SW Tualatin – Sherwood Road, #123, Sherwood OR, USA 97140;
Phone 866-225-3432 or 503-625-3432
www.glutenfreemixes.com

Nutritional Analysis

1 serving = ½ cup

Calories (kcal)	190
Carbohydrates (g)	25
Dietary Fiber (g)	2
Fat (g)	10
Protein (g)	3
Iron (mg)	2.8
Calcium (mg)	35
Sodium (mg)	83

AMARANTH GRAIN-FREE GRANOLA

Yield: **7-8 cups**

Eat this chunky granola out of hand as a snack, top it with fruit juice or milk for a quick healthy breakfast or sprinkle it over yogurt or ice cream for dessert.

1 ½ cups	**amaranth flour**
1 cup	**chopped walnuts OR other nuts**
½ cup	**potato starch**
½ cup	**peanuts**
½ cup	**sunflower OR sesame seeds**
½ cup	**unsweetened coconut**
1 ½ tsp.	**cinnamon**
¾ cup	**mashed bananas OR puréed fruit**
¼ cup	**maple syrup OR honey**
1 tbsp.	**lemon juice**
¼ cup	**vegetable oil**
1 ½ tsp.	**pure vanilla extract**
⅔ cup	**raisins**

✦ Combine the flour, walnuts, potato starch, peanuts, sunflower seeds, coconut and cinnamon in a large bowl.

✦ Mix the bananas or fruit purée, maple syrup, lemon juice, oil and vanilla in a small bowl. If the honey is very thick, heat the mixture briefly to liquefy.

✦ Pour the liquid mixture over the dry mixture. Stir well to coat dry ingredients. If the mixture seems too dry, add a few tablespoons of water.

✦ Spread the granola on a lightly oiled jelly-roll pan. Bake in a preheated 300°F oven for 45-60 minutes, stirring every 15 minutes. Remove the granola from the oven and let it cool. Stir in the raisins.

Recipe courtesy of **Nu-World Amaranth**, **Nu-World Foods**, PO Box 2202, Naperville IL, USA 60567; Phone 630-369-6819; www.nuworldfoods.com

Nutritional Analysis

1 serving = ½ cup

Calories (kcal)	248
Carbohydrates (g)	27
Dietary Fiber (g)	4
Fat (g)	14
Protein (g)	6
Iron (mg)	2.0
Calcium (mg)	42
Sodium (mg)	6

FIG BARS

Yield: **16 Fig Bars**

A healthy high-fiber treat for snacks or in the lunch bag.

Reprinted with permission from: ***Incredible Edible Gluten-Free Foods For Kids*** by **Sheri L. Sanderson**, Woodbine House, 2002; www.woodbinehouse.com

Nutritional Analysis

1 serving = 1 bar

Calories (kcal)	245
Carbohydrates (g)	36
Dietary Fiber (g)	3
Fat (g)	12
Protein (g)	3
Iron (mg)	1.3
Calcium (mg)	77
Sodium (mg)	175

1 ½ cups	**(9 oz.) dried figs**
¼ cup	**(4 oz.) finely ground pecans OR other nuts**
1 cup	**brown rice flour**
1 cup	**packed brown sugar**
½ cup	**tapioca flour**
¼ cup	**rice bran**
2 tsp.	**baking powder**
1 ½ tsp.	**xanthan gum**
¼ tsp.	**salt**
½ cup	**margarine OR butter, softened**
1	**large egg**

- Place the figs in a saucepan. Add enough water to almost cover the figs, about 1 cup. Bring to a boil. Remove from heat. Allow figs to cool in the saucepan with water.
- Meanwhile, in a mixing bowl, combine pecans, brown rice flour, brown sugar, tapioca flour, rice bran, baking powder, xanthan gum and salt.
- With a mixer on low, cut the margarine into the flour; mix until crumbly. Add the egg and mix well. Add 2 tbsp. of the reserved fig juice and mix well. Set aside.
- Put cooled figs in a food processor or blender and chop until the consistency is like thick preserves. Add 1 tbsp. reserved fig juice at a time, as needed, to get to spreading consistency, but no more than 4 tbsp. Set aside.
- In a well-greased 8 x 8-inch square baking pan, spread one half of the dough evenly. Spread the fig paste, carefully, over the dough. Spread or pat the remaining dough carefully over the figs.
- Bake in a preheated 375°F oven for 45-50 minutes, or until a toothpick inserted near the center comes out clean and the top is lightly browned. Remove from the oven. Cool for at least 10 minutes before slicing.
- Slice into 2 x 2-inch bars. Remove from the pan and allow to cool completely.
- The bars will keep, refrigerated, for up to a week.

CARROT APPLE ENERGY BARS

Yield: **18 Bars**

For a quick, easy, on-the-move breakfast or snack, choose these moist, nutritious bars.

Tips: ✦ For the dried fruit mix, we used 1/4 cup dried cranberries, 1/4 cup raisins, 2 tbsp. chopped dried mangoes, 1 tbsp. dried blueberries and 1 tbsp. chopped dried apricots.

✦ For a lactose-free bar, omit the milk powder.

✦ Try substituting grated zucchini for all or half of the carrots.

✦ Substitute cardamom for the cinnamon.

Reprinted with permission from: ***The Best Gluten-Free Family Cookbook*** by **Donna Washburn** and **Heather Butt**, Robert Rose Inc. Publisher, 2005; www.bestbreadrecipes.com

Nutritional Analysis

1 serving = 1 bar (3"x2")

Calories (kcal)	144
Carbohydrates (g)	24
Dietary Fiber (g)	3
Fat (g)	4
Protein (g)	5
Iron (mg)	1.7
Calcium (mg)	99
Sodium (mg)	139

1 1/4 cups	**sorghum flour**
1/2 cup	**amaranth flour**
1/3 cup	**rice bran**
1/4 cup	**ground flaxseed**
1/2 cup	**non-fat (skim) milk powder**
1 1/2 tsp.	**xanthan gum**
1 tbsp.	**GF baking powder**
1/4 tsp.	**salt**
2 tsp.	**ground cinnamon**
2	**eggs**
1 cup	**unsweetened applesauce**
1/3 cup	**packed brown sugar**
1 1/2 cups	**grated carrots**
3/4 cup	**dried fruit mix (see tips, at left)**
1/2 cup	**chopped walnuts**

- ✦ Line a 13 x 9-inch baking pan with foil and grease lightly.
- ✦ In a large bowl or plastic bag, combine sorghum flour, amaranth flour, rice bran, ground flaxseed, milk powder, xanthan gum, baking powder, salt and cinnamon. Mix well and set aside.
- ✦ In a separate bowl, using an electric mixer, beat eggs, applesauce and brown sugar until combined.
- ✦ Add flour mixture and mix just until combined. Stir in carrots, dried fruit and nuts. Spoon the batter into the prepared pan; spread to edges with a moist rubber spatula and allow to stand for 30 minutes.
- ✦ Bake in a preheated 325°F oven for 30-35 minutes, or until a cake tester inserted in the center comes out clean.
- ✦ Let cool in pan on a cooling rack and cut into bars.
- ✦ Store in an airtight container at room temperature for up to 1 week or individually wrapped and frozen for up to 1 month.

ALMOND DELIGHTS

Yield: **24 Cookies**

Apricots and almonds are a luscious combination.

1 1/4 cups	**slivered, blanched almonds**
3/4 cup	**sugar**
3	**egg whites, unbeaten**
1/4 cup	**finely-chopped dried apricots**

- In a blender, grind almonds as fine as possible.
- Mix nuts, sugar and egg whites in a saucepan.
- Cook over medium heat, stirring constantly, for 8-10 minutes, or until a path stays clean when a spoon is drawn through.
- Remove the pan from the heat; stir in apricots.
- Drop the batter by heaping teaspoonfuls onto a greased cookie sheet.
- Let cookies "rest" for 1/2 hour, then bake in a preheated 300°F oven for 12-15 minutes, or till delicately golden on exterior but soft inside.
- Remove from cookie sheets immediately.

Reprinted with permission from: ***Wheat-Free, Gluten-Free Recipes for Special Diets*** by **Connie Sarros**, 2003; www.gfbooks.homestead.com

Nutritional Analysis

1 serving = 1 cookie

Calories (kcal)	73
Carbohydrates (g)	9
Dietary Fiber (g)	1
Fat (g)	4
Protein (g)	2
Iron (mg)	0.3
Calcium (mg)	19
Sodium (mg)	8

SORGHUM PEANUT BUTTER COOKIES

Yield: **72 Cookies**

Peanut butter and brown sugar are a dynamite flavor combo, and sorghum and garbanzo flours add interesting texture to a favorite cookie recipe.

1 ½ cups	**creamy peanut butter**
1 cup	**shortening OR margarine**
2 ⅓ cups	**firmly packed brown sugar**
6 tbsp.	**low-fat (1 %) milk**
2 tsp.	**vanilla**
2	**eggs**
3 cups	**sorghum flour**
½ cup	**garbanzo bean (chickpea) flour**
½ cup	**sweet rice flour**
4 tsp.	**xanthan gum**
1 tsp.	**salt**
1 ½ tsp.	**baking soda**

- ✦ Combine the peanut butter, shortening, brown sugar, milk and vanilla in a large bowl. With an electric mixer, beat on medium speed until well blended.
- ✦ Add the eggs. Beat just until blended.
- ✦ Combine the flours, salt and baking soda. Add to creamed mixture at low speed. Mix just until blended.
- ✦ Using a mini ice cream scoop, drop dough portions 2 inches apart on baking sheets lined with parchment paper. Flatten slightly in a crisscross pattern with the tines of a fork.
- ✦ Bake in a preheated 375°F oven for 8-10 minutes, or until set and just beginning to brown.
- ✦ Cool for 2 minutes on the baking sheets. Remove the cookies from the pan and cool completely.

Recipe courtesy of **Barbara Kliment, Executive Director** of **Nebraska Grain Sorghum Board**, 301 Centennial Mall South, P. O. Box 94982, Lincoln NE, USA 68509; Phone 402-471-4276; www.sorghum.state.ne.us

Nutritional Analysis

1 serving = 1 cookie

Calories (kcal)	113
Carbohydrates (g)	14
Dietary Fiber (g)	1
Fat (g)	6
Protein (g)	2
Iron (mg)	0.6
Calcium (mg)	11
Sodium (mg)	71

RUM AND QUINOA CRUNCH COOKIES

Yield: **50 Cookies**

Quinoa has more high-quality protein than any other grain. These crisp cookies can be flavored to suit your taste.

3/4 cup	**butter OR margarine**
1 cup	**sugar**
2	**eggs, beaten**
2 tsp.	**rum extract**
2 cups	**NorQuin quinoa flour**
1/4 cup	**white rice flour**
1 1/2 tsp.	**baking powder**
1/3 cup	**toasted quinoa grain**

- In a large bowl, cream butter; add sugar; cream together thoroughly.
- Add beaten eggs and rum extract.
- Mix dry ingredients together and add to wet ingredients. Mix well.
- Chill the dough for several hours or overnight.
- Roll out a small amount of dough at a time on a lightly floured surface (use rice flour). Cut the dough into desired shapes and place on greased cookie sheets OR shape the dough into balls OR drop by teaspoonfuls onto a cookie sheet. Flatten with a rice-floured glass to 1/4" thickness.
- Bake in a preheated 350°F oven for 10-15 minutes.

Variation:

2 tsp. lemon extract or 2 tsp. almond extract may be substituted for the rum extract.

Recipe is courtesy of: **El Peto Products Ltd.**, 65 Saltsman Dr, Cambridge ON, Canada N3H 4R7; Phone 800-387-4064 or 519-650-4614; www.elpeto.com and **Northern Quinoa Corporation**, Box 519, Kamsack SK, Canada S0A 1S0; Phone 866-368-9304 or 306-542-3949; www.quinoa.com

Nutritional Analysis

1 serving = 1 cookie

Calories (kcal)	67
Carbohydrates (g)	9
Dietary Fiber (g)	0.4
Fat (g)	3
Protein (g)	1
Iron (mg)	0.6
Calcium (mg)	13
Sodium (mg)	35

CRANBERRY PISTACHIO BISCOTTI

Yield: 64 Cookies

These have the appearance and texture of traditional twice-baked biscotti, but are much easier and faster to make. We like to dip them in a sweet Italian dessert wine or in coffee.

Tips: ✦ Biscotti will be medium-firm and crunchy; for softer biscotti, bake for only 10 minutes in Step 5; for very firm biscotti, bake for 20 minutes.

✦Store in an airtight container at room temperature for up to 3 weeks, or freeze for up to 2 months.

✦If you prefer, you can use a 13 x 9-inch baking pan instead of the two 8-inch pans.

✦Try orange-flavored cranberries and substitute orange zest for the lemon zest.

✦Substitute pecans or hazelnuts for the pistachios.

Reprinted with permission from: ***The Best Gluten-Free Family Cookbook*** by **Donna Washburn** and **Heather Butt**, Robert Rose Inc. 2005; www.bestbreadrecipes.com

Nutritional Analysis

1 serving = 1 cookie

Calories (kcal)	62
Carbohydrates (g)	10
Dietary Fiber (g)	1
Fat (g)	2
Protein (g)	2
Iron (mg)	0.5
Calcium (mg)	15
Sodium (mg)	17

1 ½ cups **amaranth flour**
½ cup **soy flour**
⅓ cup **potato starch**
¼ cup **tapioca starch**
1 ½ tsp. **xanthan gum**
1 tsp. **GF baking powder**
pinch **salt**
4 **eggs**
1 ¼ cups **sugar**
1 tbsp. **grated lemon zest**
1 tsp. **vanilla**
1 ½ cups **coarsely chopped pistachios**
1 cup **dried cranberries**

✦ Line two 8-inch square baking pans with foil and grease lightly. For the second baking, use ungreased baking sheets.

✦ In a large bowl or plastic bag, combine amaranth flour, soy flour, potato starch, tapioca starch, xanthan gum, baking powder and salt. Mix well and set aside.

✦ In a separate bowl, using an electric mixer, beat eggs, sugar, lemon zest and vanilla until combined.

✦ Slowly beat dry ingredients into the egg mixture and mix just until combined. Stir in pistachios and cranberries. Spoon into the prepared pans. Using a moistened rubber spatula, spread the batter to the edges and smooth the tops.

✦ Bake in a preheated 325°F oven for 30-35 minutes, or until firm or tops are just turning golden. Let cool in the pans for 5 minutes.

✦ Remove Biscotti from the pans, remove foil and let cool on a cutting board for 5 minutes.

✦ Cut Biscotti into quarters, then cut each quarter into 8 slices. Arrange slices upright (cut sides exposed) at least ½ inch apart on baking sheets. Bake for an additional 15 minutes, until dry and crisp. Transfer to a cooling rack immediately.

FLAX PUMPKIN SQUARES

Yield: 9 Servings

Cinnamon, nutmeg and cloves add the perfect flavor note to this pumpkin dessert.

Crust:

3/4 cup	**GF cornflakes (crushed)**
1/4 cup	**flaxseed (ground)**
1/4 cup	**butter, melted**
1 tbsp.	**sugar**
1/4 tsp.	**cinnamon**
1/4 tsp.	**nutmeg**

Filling:

8 oz.	**cream cheese (at room temperature)**
1/4 cup	**sugar**
1	**egg**
2/3 cup	**canned pumpkin**
1/4 tsp.	**cinnamon**
1/4 cup	**ground flaxseed**
1/4 tsp.	**ground cloves**
1/4 tsp.	**salt**

- In a small bowl, combine cornflakes, flaxseed, butter, sugar, cinnamon and nutmeg. Mix thoroughly and press into a foil-lined, 8-inch square pan.
- In a large mixing bowl, beat cream cheese until fluffy.
- Beat in sugar and then egg.
- Beat in pumpkin, cinnamon, flaxseed, cloves and salt.
- Spoon the batter over the prepared crust. Level out the top of the cake.
- Bake in a preheated 325°F oven for 40 minutes. Remove from the oven and cool on a wire rack for 1 hour.
- Refrigerate until completely cooled. Remove and cut into squares. Top with whipped cream if desired.

Reprinted with permission from: ***The Essential Flax*** by **Saskatchewan Flax Development Commission**, 2005, A5A 116 - 103rd St. East, Saskatoon SK, Canada S7N 1Y7; Phone 306-664-1901; www.saskflax.com

Nutritional Analysis

1 serving = 3"x3" piece

Calories (kcal)	272
Carbohydrates (g)	20
Dietary Fiber (g)	5
Fat (g)	20
Protein (g)	6
Iron (mg)	2.8
Calcium (mg)	63
Sodium (mg)	242

CHOCOLATE MESQUITE BROWNIES

Yield: **12**

Brown sugar brownies – irresistible!

½ cup	**mesquite meal (flour)**
½ cup	**unsweetened cocoa**
1 cup	**brown rice flour**
1 cup	**brown sugar**
2 tbsp.	**tapioca starch**
1 tsp.	**baking powder**
1 tsp.	**baking soda**
2 tsp.	**cornstarch**
½ tsp.	**sea salt**
1	**large egg**
1 cup	**water**
½ cup	**vegetable oil**
1 tsp.	**vanilla extract**

- ✦ In a large bowl, combine all of the dry ingredients.
- ✦ Add the wet ingredients and mix until smooth.
- ✦ Pour the batter evenly into a greased 9 x 12-inch baking pan.
- ✦ Bake in a preheated 350°F oven for 25-35 minutes, depending on the depth of the pan, altitude and your patience.

Tips: ✦ For a more chocolatey brownie, add ½ cup chocolate chips to batter.

✦ For mocha brownies, substitute strong coffee or espresso for the cup of water.

Recipe courtesy of: **San Pedro Mesquite Company**, P.O. Box 338, Bowie AZ, USA 85605; www.spmesquite.com

Nutritional Analysis

1 serving = 1 slice

Calories (kcal)	241
Carbohydrates (g)	37
Dietary Fiber (g)	4
Fat (g)	11
Protein (g)	3
Iron (mg)	1.4
Calcium (mg)	53
Sodium (mg)	258

CREAMY "I CAN'T BELIEVE IT'S NOT RICE!" PUDDING

Yield: 5 Servings

A traditional dessert favorite, this "rice pudding" version uses buckwheat groats instead of rice. Serve warm or cold, garnished with whipped cream and chopped nuts and/or fresh fruit. A splash of maple syrup is also a delicious option.

Note: Groats are hulled crushed kernels of grain that are often cooked as rice is cooked. Buckwheat groats (kasha) are the most common, but oat and barley groats are also available.

Recipe courtesy of: **The Birkett Mills**, 163 Main St, Penn Yan NY, USA 14527; Phone 315-536-3311; www.thebirkettmills.com

Nutritional Analysis
1 serving

Calories (kcal)	440
Carbohydrates (g)	82
Dietary Fiber (g)	8
Fat (g)	9
Protein (g)	13
Iron (mg)	2.4
Calcium (mg)	122
Sodium (mg)	195

4 cups	**water**
¼ tsp.	**salt**
2 tbsp.	**butter OR margarine (optional)**
2 cups	**whole white buckwheat groats (Wolff's or Pocono)**
2	**eggs**
1 cup	**low-fat (1%) milk**
⅓ cup	**honey (preferably clover OR other mild honey)**
1 tsp.	**vanilla extract**
½ tsp.	**ground cinnamon**
½ tsp.	**grated lemon peel**
dash	**fresh nutmeg**
1 tbsp.	**dark rum (optional)**
1 cup	**grated apple, cored but not peeled**
¼ cup	**raisins**
½ cup	**sour cream**
	whipped cream and chopped nuts OR fresh fruit, for garnish

✦ In a medium saucepan, heat water, salt and butter. Quickly stir in buckwheat groats. Reduce heat to low and cover pan tightly. Simmer for 15 minutes, until groats are tender and the liquid is absorbed.

✦ Beat together the eggs, milk and honey until well-blended. Add the vanilla, cinnamon, lemon peel, nutmeg and rum.

✦ In a large bowl, combine groats, apple, raisins and milk/egg mixture.

✦ Spread the pudding evenly in a buttered 8-inch square pan.

✦ Bake at 350°F for 25-30 minutes, stirring every 5 minutes.

✦ Remove the pudding from the oven. Let it cool for 15 minutes, then stir in the sour cream.

✦ Garnish individual servings as you prefer.

WILD RICE FRUIT DESSERT

Yield: 10 Servings

This version of the ever-popular "Ambrosia" has the added texture of wild rice. The whole family will love this one.

Recipe courtesy of: **Riese's Canadian Lake Wild Rice**,
La Ronge SK, Canada S0J 1L0;
Phone 306-425-2314;
www.wildlakerice.com

Nutritional Analysis
1 serving

Calories (kcal)	329
Carbohydrates (g)	50
Dietary Fiber (g)	2
Fat (g)	13
Protein (g)	6
Iron (mg)	0.9
Calcium (mg)	26
Sodium (mg)	64

1 cup	**wild rice (4 cups cooked)**
14 oz.	**can pineapple chunks, drained**
10 oz.	**can mandarin oranges, drained**
14 oz.	**can fruit cocktail, drained**
½ cup	**chopped walnuts**
3 cups	**miniature marshmallows**
3 oz.	**cherry gelatin powder**
1 cup	**whipping cream**

- Wash wild rice in a wire strainer and run cold water over it.
- Combine 4 cups of water and 1 cup of wild rice in a large heavy saucepan. Bring to a boil; cover and simmer over low heat for approximately 45 minutes, until the rice kernels have burst their shells and fluffed out. Drain off any excess water. Stir with a fork; cover and let stand for 15 minutes.
- Place the wild rice in a large bowl and let cool.
- Drain the juice from the canned fruits.
- Add the fruit, rice, nuts and marshmallows to the cooled, wild rice.
- Mix in the dry gelatin powder.
- Whip the cream until stiff and fold into the fruit mixture.
- Refrigerate for at least 1 hour.
- Garnish with fresh fruit before serving.

MOROCCAN SALAD

Serves: **10**

This salad has been a catering favorite of mine and my clients for many years. When I first started making it, I used rice. Now I use other grains like quinoa and millet, and I have even used a variety of rice. The blending of sweet and savory in this salad makes it exotic.

3 cups **cooked quinoa – can use rice, millet or a combination of millet and quinoa**
½ **EACH, red, yellow and orange pepper, ¼ inch diced**
1 **medium red onion, ¼ inch diced**
½ cup **chopped GF pitted dates**
½ cup **diced dried apricots**
½ cup **dried cherries OR cranberries**
grated zest and juice of 1 orange and 1 lemon
2-3 tbsp. **extra-virgin olive oil**
⅛ tsp. **turmeric**
salt and freshly ground black pepper to taste
⅓ cup **toasted, slivered almonds**
2 tbsp. **sunflower seeds**
2 tbsp. **chopped parsley OR cilantro**

- ✦ Wash the quinoa, changing the water at least 5 times. Rub the grains with your hands and then let the grains settle to the bottom of the bowl each time before pouring off the water and then adding more fresh cold water.
- ✦ Bring a pot of lightly salted water to a boil.
- ✦ Add the quinoa and cook for 10 minutes.
- ✦ Drain the quinoa into a sieve. Rinse under cold water.
- ✦ Set the sieve over a saucepan of boiling water. Do not allow the water to touch the quinoa. Cover with a kitchen towel and lid. Steam the quinoa until it is fluffy and dry, about 10 minutes. Check the water level in the pan, adding more if necessary.

To Make the Salad:

- ✦ Toss everything together, except the almonds, sunflower seeds and the parsley.
- ✦ Taste for seasoning.
- ✦ Just before serving, stir in the almonds, then sprinkle the sunflower seeds and the parsley over the salad. Serve.

Recipe courtesy of: **Rebecca Reilly**, Culinary Expert and Author of ***Gluten-Free Baking: More Than 125 Recipes for Delectable Sweet and Savory Baked Goods, Including Cakes, Pies, Quick Breads, Muffins, Cookies, and Other Delights.***

Nutritional Analysis
1 serving

Calories (kcal)	219
Carbohydrates (g)	32
Dietary Fiber (g)	5
Fat (g)	8
Protein (g)	6
Iron (mg)	0.9
Calcium (mg)	41
Sodium (mg)	123

QUINOA SALAD

Yield: 6 Servings

The delicate flavor of quinoa is similar to couscous. Cooked quinoa can be used as a pasta substitute in cold pasta salads.

Lemon Garlic Dressing:

4	**garlic cloves, minced**
1/4 cup	**red wine vinegar**
1/4 cup	**canola oil**
1/4 cup	**water**
1	**lemon, juiced**
	salt and pepper to taste

4 cups	**cooked NorQuin quinoa**
1 cup	**grated carrots**
1/2 cup	**sliced green onions**
1/2 cup	**chopped celery**
1/4 cup	**sunflower seeds**
1/4 cup	**slivered almonds**
3 tbsp.	**sesame seeds**
1/2 cup	**sliced mushrooms**

- In a small bowl, combine all of the dressing ingredients and let stand for at least 10 minutes.
- Prepare the salad ingredients and combine in a large bowl.
- Toss the salad with the dressing and serve.

Recipe courtesy of **Northern Quinoa Corporation**, Box 519, Kamsack SK, Canada S0A 1S0; Phone 866-368-9304 or 306-542-3949; www.quinoa.com

Nutritional Analysis

1 serving = 1 cup

Calories (kcal)	358
Carbohydrates (g)	30
Dietary Fiber (g)	8
Fat (g)	22
Protein (g)	12
Iron (mg)	1.6
Calcium (mg)	100
Sodium (mg)	220

THAI HOT-AND-SOUR SAUCE

Yield: 1⅓ Cups

This delectable, spicy sauce is fabulous on tossed green salads, sliced tomatoes, steamed cabbage wedges, stir-fried vegetables and rice, and rice noodles with steamed veggies. You're bound to think of many other uses as well.

Reprinted with permission from: ***Food Allergy Survival Guide – Surviving and Thriving with Food Allergies and Sensitivities*** by **Vesanto Melina, MS, RD, Jo Stepaniak, MSEd** and **Dina Aronson, MS, RD**, Healthy Living Publications, 2004

⅓ cup **sesame tahini, other seed butter OR almond butter**
⅓ cup **fresh lime juice**
3 tbsp. **water**
2 tbsp. **balsamic vinegar**
2 tbsp. **dark sesame oil OR extra-virgin olive oil**
2 tbsp. **sugar**
2 tsp. **dried basil**
1 tsp. **dried spearmint**
1 tsp. **ground ginger**
1 tsp. **crushed garlic**
¼ tsp. **crushed hot red pepper flakes**

✦ Combine all of the ingredients in a small bowl and whisk until thick and smooth.

Nutritional Analysis

1 serving = ⅓ cup

Calories (kcal)	218
Carbohydrates (g)	15
Dietary Fiber (g)	2
Fat (g)	18
Protein (g)	4
Iron (mg)	1.4
Calcium (mg)	52
Sodium (mg)	11

TEFF POLENTA

Serves: 4

Flavored with sweet juicy tomatoes, fresh basil, garlic, and decorated with bright green peppers, here is an irresistible summer repast. Serve garnished with grated Fontina, Parmesan, Manchego, or sliced rounds of chèvre.

Note: Like the traditional Italian polenta made with cornmeal, this polenta can be served as a first course or a side dish, or sliced and toasted or grilled.

2 cups	**water**
2 tbsp.	**extra-virgin olive oil**
8 cloves	**garlic, thickly sliced**
1 cup	**coarsely chopped onions**
1 cup	**coarsely chopped green pepper**
2/3 cup	**teff grain**
1/2 tsp.	**sea salt**
2 cups	**coarsely chopped plum tomatoes**
1 cup	**coarsely chopped fresh basil**

- Boil the water in a tea kettle.
- Place the oil in a 10-inch skillet and warm over medium heat. Add the garlic and onions and sauté, stirring occasionally, for 5 minutes, or until fragrant. Add peppers and sauté for 2 minutes, or until bright green. Stir in the teff.
- Turn off the heat to prevent splattering and add the boiling water and salt. Turn the heat on and let the polenta simmer for 2 minutes. Add the tomatoes and basil.
- Cover and simmer for 10-15 minutes, stirring occasionally, until the water is absorbed. There may be some extra liquid from the tomatoes, but as long as the teff is not crunchy, the polenta is done.
- Taste and adjust the seasonings, if desired.
- Transfer the polenta to an un-oiled 9-inch pie plate. Let it cool for about 30 minutes. Slice and serve.

Reprinted with permission from: **The Teff Company**, P.O. Box A, Caldwell ID, USA 83606; www.teffco.com; Phone 888-822-2221 and **Leslie Cerier**, 58 Schoolhouse Road, Amherst MA, USA 01002; www.lesliecerier.com

Nutritional Analysis

1 serving = 1 slice

Calories (kcal)	223
Carbohydrates (g)	33
Dietary Fiber (g)	5
Fat (g)	8
Protein (g)	6
Iron (mg)	2.9
Calcium (mg)	107
Sodium (mg)	306

QUINOA AND WILD RICE PILAF

Yield: 6½ Cups

Mushrooms and bacon give this pilaf a rich satisfying flavor.

1 cup	**wild rice**
1 cup	**quinoa seed**
⅓ cup	**chopped GF bacon**
1 tbsp.	**margarine OR vegetable oil**
½ cup	**celery**
1	**onion, chopped**
1 cup	**sliced mushrooms**

- Wash the wild rice in a wire strainer and run cold water over it.
- In a large heavy saucepan, cook the wild rice in 4 cups of boiling water. Bring to a boil, cover and simmer over low heat for about 1 hour, until all the water has been absorbed.
- During the last 15 minutes, add quinoa and, if the rice is almost dry, 1 additional cup of boiling water.
- While the rice is cooking, fry the bacon in a pan. When crisp, remove and drain.
- Melt the margarine in a skillet and add the celery, onion and mushrooms; sauté for about 5 minutes.
- In a casserole, combine the vegetables and bacon with the rice and quinoa mixture.
- Microwave on high for 10 minutes or bake in a preheated 350°F oven for 30 minutes.

Recipe courtesy of ***Northern Quinoa Corporation***, Box 519, Kamsack SK, Canada S0A 1S0; Phone 866-368-9304 or 306-542-3949; www.quinoa.com

Nutritional Analysis

1 serving = ½ cup

Calories (kcal)	121
Carbohydrates (g)	21
Dietary Fiber (g)	2
Fat (g)	2
Protein (g)	5
Iron (mg)	1.7
Calcium (mg)	14
Sodium (mg)	111

MOROCCAN MILLET

Yield: 6 Servings

This pilaf is great as a one-dish meal or served with a fresh green salad. Peppers, especially red peppers, are among our best sources of vitamin C and the protective group of phytochemicals known as carotenoids. Millet and chickpeas are good sources of the yellow vitamins riboflavin and folate.

Reprinted with permission from: ***Food Allergy Survival Guide – Surviving and Thriving with Food Allergies and Sensitivities*** by **Vesanto Melina, MS, RD, Jo Stepaniak, MSEd** and **Dina Aronson, MS, RD**, Healthy Living Publications, 2004.

Nutritional Analysis

1 serving

Calories (kcal)	369
Carbohydrates (g)	63
Dietary Fiber (g)	10
Fat (g)	8
Protein (g)	12
Iron (mg)	3.8
Calcium (mg)	57
Sodium (mg)	1763

2 tbsp.	**coconut OR olive oil OR organic canola OR safflower oil**
1	**EACH, large red and green bell pepper, sliced into strips**
1	**large onion, sliced into half-moons**
2 tbsp.	**crushed garlic**
2 tsp.	**paprika**
½ tsp.	**salt**
1 tsp.	**ground cumin**
½ tsp.	**ground cinnamon**
¼ tsp.	**ground turmeric**
¼ tsp.	**ground ginger**
⅛ tsp.	**ground cayenne**
1½ cups	**millet**
3 cups	**GF vegetable stock***
1¾ cups	**drained cooked chickpeas OR a 15 oz. can**
¼ cup	**raisins OR chopped GF dates**
¼ cup	**sunflower seeds, pumpkin seeds OR pine nuts (optional)**
	salt and pepper to taste

✦ Place 1 tbsp. of the oil in a large roasting pan. Add the peppers, onion, garlic, paprika and salt. Toss until everything is evenly coated with the oil and well combined.

✦ Place in a preheated 450°F oven to roast for 20 minutes, stirring 2 or 3 times during the cooking cycle.

✦ Remove the vegetables from the oven and allow them to cool until safe to handle; then chop them coarsely.

✦ Meanwhile, heat the remaining tablespoon of oil in a large saucepan. Add the cumin, cinnamon, turmeric, ginger and cayenne. Stir over medium-high heat until the spices are uniform in color and well combined, about 30 seconds.

✦ Add the millet and stir quickly to coat, about 1 minute.

✦ Immediately pour in the vegetable stock and bring to a boil. Reduce the heat, cover and cook the millet until all the liquid is absorbed, about 20 minutes.

✦ Place the millet in a large bowl and fluff with a fork.

✦ Add the roasted vegetables, chickpeas, raisins and optional seeds. Season with salt and pepper to taste. Toss gently and serve.

* **Author Note:** Choose a lower-sodium gluten-free vegetable stock or broth.

HEARTY VEGETARIAN KASHA CASSEROLE

Yield: **6 Servings**

Hearty legumes and kasha are complemented by succulent leeks and piquant cayenne in this savory and substantial casserole.

Note: Kasha is the Russian name for savory or sweet dishes of boiled, baked or roasted buckwheat groats or whole-grain buckwheat. It is sometimes used for cooked millet and oats.

Reprinted with permission from: ***Buckwheat Recipes*** by **Canadian Special Crops Association**, 1215 - 220 Portage Ave., Winnipeg MB, Canada R3C 0A5; Phone 204-925-3780; www.buckwheatforhealth.com www.specialcrops.mb.ca

28 oz. can	**tomatoes**
3 cups	**diced cabbage**
2	**leeks, thinly sliced**
1/3 cup	**dried peas OR small white beans**
1/2 cup	**coarse kasha**
5 cups	**vegetable broth OR water**
1/2 cup	**brown rice**
1/2 tsp.	**salt**
1/2 tsp.	**cayenne pepper**
1 tsp.	**dried basil or 1 tbsp. chopped fresh**
1/4 cup	**chopped fresh parsley**

- ✦ Combine the tomatoes, cabbage, leeks, peas, kasha and vegetable broth in a crock-pot or large Dutch oven.
- ✦ Simmer, covered, for an hour. Add the brown rice, salt, cayenne and basil. Add more liquid if needed.
- ✦ Cook for an additional 20-30 minutes. Add the parsley just before serving.

Nutritional Analysis

1 serving

Calories (kcal)	210
Carbohydrates (g)	43
Dietary Fiber (g)	8
Fat (g)	1
Protein (g)	10
Iron (mg)	3
Calcium (mg)	102
Sodium (mg)	3002

WILD RICE & VEGETABLE CASSEROLE

Yield: **8 Servings**

Creamy wild rice has a nutty flavor that is wonderful with the robust flavor of broccoli, and also with the more delicate flavors of cauliflower and asparagus.

½ cup	**wild rice (2 cups cooked)**
	pepper and sage to taste
10 oz.	**can GF cream soup**
1 bunch	**broccoli, cauliflower OR asparagus, cut into florets or bite-sized pieces**
1 cup	**grated Cheddar cheese**

- Wash the wild rice in a wire strainer and run cold water over it.
- Combine 2 cups of water and ½ cup of wild rice in a heavy saucepan. Bring to a boil, cover and simmer over low heat for approximately 45 minutes, until the rice kernels have burst their shells and fluffed out. Drain off excess water. Stir the rice with a fork; cover and let stand for 15 minutes.
- Put the cooked rice, seasoned with a little pepper and sage, into a greased 1½-2 quart casserole.
- Cover with the undiluted cream soup.
- Steam the vegetables for 5 minutes, then place over the soup.
- Sprinkle with the cheese.
- Bake in a preheated 350°F oven for about 20 minutes.

Recipe courtesy of **Riese's Canadian Lake Wild Rice**, La Ronge SK, Canada S0J 1L0; Phone 306-425-2314; www.wildlakerice.com

Nutritional Analysis
1 serving

Calories (kcal)	131
Carbohydrates (g)	14
Dietary Fiber (g)	3
Fat (g)	6
Protein (g)	8
Iron (mg)	1.1
Calcium (mg)	144
Sodium (mg)	155

BLACK BEAN CHILI

Yield: 6-8 Servings (8 cups)

The goodness of chili in a flash. The range of ingredients provides a powerful phyto-chemical mix. This vegetarian chili is packed with a rainbow of carotenoids and allium family members and their perks, topped off with a hit of both soluble and insoluble fiber.

2 tsp.	**extra-virgin olive oil**
1 cup	**chopped onions**
3	**large cloves garlic, finely chopped**
1	**green bell pepper, diced**
1 cup	**½ inch cubes zucchini (1 medium)**
1 tsp.	**finely chopped jalapeño pepper**
2x19 oz. cans	**black beans, rinsed and drained**
28 oz. can	**whole tomatoes, coarsely chopped, with juice**
1 cup	**frozen corn kernels**
1 tbsp.	**chili powder**
1 tsp.	**ground cumin**
1 tsp.	**dried oregano**
	salt to taste
3 tbsp.	**chopped fresh coriander, for garnish**
	shredded light Cheddar cheese, for garnish (optional)

- ✦ Heat the oil in a large, heavy pot over medium heat.
- ✦ Add the onions and garlic; sauté for 5 minutes.
- ✦ Add the green pepper, zucchini and jalapeño pepper; sauté another 3 minutes.
- ✦ Add the black beans, tomatoes with juice, corn, chili powder, cumin and oregano.
- ✦ Reduce heat to medium-low and simmer, uncovered and stirring occasionally, for 30 minutes.
- ✦ Season with salt to taste.
- ✦ Garnish with coriander and Cheddar, if using, before serving.

Author's Note:

For a hearty Turkey, Chicken or Beef Black Bean Chili, sauté 1 lb. of ground meat in a heavy skillet. Drain off all fat; place the cooked meat in a colander and rinse with very hot or boiling water. Add to sautéed onions and garlic.

Nutritional Analysis

1 serving = 1 cup

Calories (kcal)	143
Carbohydrates (g)	31
Dietary Fiber (g)	9
Fat (g)	2
Protein (g)	8
Iron (mg)	3.1
Calcium (mg)	92
Sodium (mg)	581

LENTIL LEAF ROLLS

Yield: 10 Servings

These rice and lentil-filled "cabbage rolls" are beautifully flavored with dill.

3/4 cup	**short-grain rice**
3/4 cup	**water**
1/2 tsp.	**salt**
1 tbsp.	**canola oil**
1/2 cup	**finely chopped onion**
2 tbsp.	**chopped fresh dill**
1 tsp.	**salt**
1/8 tsp.	**pepper**
1 1/2 cups	**lentils, cooked**
30	**lettuce, Swiss chard, beet, spinach OR cabbage leaves***
1	**GF vegetable bouillon cube**
1/2 cup	**boiling water**
1/2 cup	**cream milk (10% MF)**

- ✦ Combine the rice, water and salt in a small saucepan. Bring to a boil, stir once and reduce the heat to simmer. Cover; cook for 12 minutes, until the water is absorbed.
- ✦ In a small skillet, over medium heat, heat the oil and sauté the onions for 4 minutes, until they start to turn brown.
- ✦ Combine the onions with dill, salt, pepper, lentils and rice.
- ✦ Prepare the leaves by washing them and cutting larger leaves into smaller pieces (approximately 3-4" squares).
- ✦ Blanch the leaves by putting them into a large bowl; pour boiling water over leaves; blanch for 30 seconds*.
- ✦ Drain the leaves, rinse in cold water and drain again.
- ✦ At the base of each leaf, put 1 1/2 tbsp. rice and lentil filling.
- ✦ Roll up leaves while tucking in sides.
- ✦ Place the rolls, seam down, in a lightly oiled 2-quart casserole.
- ✦ Dissolve the bouillon cube in boiling water. Pour over the rolls.
- ✦ Pour cream milk over the rolls.
- ✦ Cover with a few remaining leaves.
- ✦ Cover with a lid or foil. Bake in a preheated 325°F oven for 1 1/2 hours.
- ✦ Check the rolls after 1 hour. If they need more liquid, add a little cream milk.

* Cabbage leaves may need to be steamed longer to make them more pliable.

Adapted from and reprinted with permission from: ***Saskatchewan Pulse Growers***, 104 - 411 Downey Road, Saskatoon SK, Canada S7N 4L8; Phone 306-668-5556; www.saskpulse.com

Nutritional Analysis
1 serving

Calories (kcal)	123
Carbohydrates (g)	20
Dietary Fiber (g)	4
Fat (g)	3
Protein (g)	5
Iron (mg)	1.9
Calcium (mg)	54
Sodium (mg)	454

LENTIL PIZZA SQUARES

Yield: 12 Servings

Serve these pizza squares with a green salad for a casual main course or as a substantial snack.

1/4 cup	**canola oil**
3/4 cup	**chopped onion**
1 cup	**sliced mushrooms**
1	**garlic clove, minced**
4	**eggs**
1 1/2 cups	**lentil purée***
1 1/2 cups	**low-fat sour cream**
7 1/2 oz.	**can tomato sauce**
3/4 cup	**cornmeal**
1 tsp.	**crumbled dried basil**
1 tsp.	**crumbled dried oregano**
1/2 tsp.	**salt**
1 1/2 cups	**grated low-fat Cheddar cheese**
1 1/2 cups	**grated low-fat mozzarella cheese**
1/2 cup	**sliced pepperoni OR salami ****
1/2 cup	**diced sweet green pepper**

- ✦ In a skillet, heat the oil and add the onion, mushrooms and garlic. Sauté until the onion is translucent. Remove from the heat and let cool.
- ✦ In a large mixing bowl, beat the eggs. Blend in lentil purée, sour cream, tomato sauce, cornmeal, basil, oregano, salt and the mushroom mixture. Stir in the cheeses.
- ✦ Spoon the batter into a 9 x 13-inch baking dish sprayed with nonstick vegetable spray.
- ✦ Garnish with the pepperoni and green peppers.
- ✦ Bake in a preheated 350°F oven for 40-45 minutes, or until firm to the touch. Let stand 10 minutes before cutting. Cut into 12 squares.

* **Lentil Purée:**

3/4 cup	**lentils**
2 cups	**water**

- ✦ To prepare Lentil Purée, rinse the lentils and drain.
- ✦ Cover with water and bring to a boil. Reduce heat and simmer for 45-50 minutes.
- ✦ Drain off any excess liquid and mash the lentils with a potato masher.
- ✦ Cool the purée before adding to recipe.

** Gluten-free brand required.

Adapted from and reprinted with permission from: ***Discover the Pulse Potential*** (1994), by the **Saskatchewan Pulse Growers**, 104 - 411 Downey Road, Saskatoon SK, Canada S7N 4L8; Phone 306-668-5556; www.saskpulse.com

Nutritional Analysis

1 serving = 1 square

Calories (kcal)	292
Carbohydrates (g)	20
Dietary Fiber (g)	4
Fat (g)	17
Protein (g)	16
Iron (mg)	2.2
Calcium (mg)	226
Sodium (mg)	542

TURKEY MEATBALLS WITH LEMON SAUCE

Yield: 4 Servings

Kasha (roasted buckwheat groats) adds a distinctive nutty flavor to these tasty meatballs. This serves four as an hors d'oeuvre or serves two as a main dish with a marinated vegetable or tossed green salad.

1 cup	**cooked kasha (any granulation)**
1	**egg, beaten**
1 tsp.	**grated lemon zest**
1 ½ lbs.	**99% fat-free ground raw turkey**
2 tbsp.	**vegetable oil**
1 cup	**GF chicken OR turkey broth**
¼ cup	**plain yogurt**
1 tbsp.	**cornstarch**
1 tbsp.	**lemon juice**
1	**small carrot, finely shredded**
1	**green onion, diced**

- ✦ Prepare the kasha according to package directions, using chicken broth (gluten-free).
- ✦ Combine the kasha, egg, lemon zest and turkey in a mixing bowl; blend well.
- ✦ Shape the mixture into 12 balls.
- ✦ In a large skillet, heat the oil and brown the turkey balls on all sides. Add the broth; cover and simmer for 20 minutes. Use a slotted spoon to transfer the meatballs to a serving dish.
- ✦ In a small bowl, combine the yogurt, cornstarch and lemon juice.
- ✦ In the skillet, combine the yogurt mixture with the pan juices and cook until the sauce is thickened and bubbly. Add the carrot and onion. Cook for a few minutes and pour the sauce over the meatballs.

Author Note: The original recipe had 1 tsp. Worcestershire sauce, however, some brands of Worcestershire sauce contain malt vinegar (which is not gluten-free) and/or soy sauce (which often contains wheat).

Recipe adapted and reprinted with permission from **The Birkett Mills**, 163 Main St, Penn Yan NY, USA 14527; Phone 315-536-3311; www.thebirkettmills.com

Nutritional Analysis

1 serving

Calories (kcal)	326
Carbohydrates (g)	13
Dietary Fiber (g)	2
Fat (g)	11
Protein (g)	46
Iron (mg)	2.8
Calcium (mg)	45
Sodium (mg)	369

OVEN-FRIED CHICKEN

Yield: **6 Servings**

Ground flax seed and GF crackers or corn flakes are used to add crunch to this crispy chicken dish.

1	**egg, beaten**
3 tbsp.	**non-fat (skim) milk**
½ cup	**ground flax seed (flax seed meal)**
½ cup	**GF crackers OR GF corn flakes (finely crushed)**
¼ tsp.	**black pepper**
1 tbsp.	**dried parsley flakes**
1 tsp.	**chili powder**
1 tsp.	**garlic powder**
1 tsp.	**salt**
2-3 lbs.	**chicken pieces**
2 tbsp.	**melted butter***

✦ In a small bowl, combine the egg and milk.

✦ In a shallow container, combine the ground flax, GF cracker or corn flake crumbs, pepper, parsley, chili powder, garlic and salt.

✦ Skin the chicken and rinse with warm water. Pat dry.

✦ Dip the chicken pieces into the egg mixture; coat with the crumb mixture.

✦ Place the chicken on a greased 10 x 15-inch baking pan so pieces do not touch.

✦ Drizzle the chicken pieces with melted butter.

✦ Bake in a preheated 350°F oven for 45 minutes, or until chicken is tender and no longer pink. Do not turn chicken pieces while baking.

* For a lower-fat version, omit the butter.

Adapted from and reprinted with permission from: ***Flax: Family Favorites – Recipes and Healthful Tips*** by **The Flax Council of Canada**, 465 – 167 Lombard Ave., Winnipeg MB, Canada R3B 0T6; Phone 204-982-2115; www.flaxcouncil.ca *and* **Saskatchewan Flax Development Commission**, A5A - 116 - 103rd St. E., Saskatoon SK, Canada S7N 1Y7; Phone 306-664-1901; www.saskflax.com

Nutritional Analysis

1 serving

Calories (kcal)	291
Carbohydrates (g)	10
Dietary Fiber (g)	3
Fat (g)	12
Protein (g)	34
Iron (mg)	3.1
Calcium (mg)	56
Sodium (mg)	564

CAJUN FLAX COATING

Yield: 12 tablespoons

Suggested foods for coating: chicken, veal, beef, pork, catfish, turkey, redfish, shrimp.

2 tbsp. **paprika**
½ cup **ground flaxseed**
1 tbsp. **black pepper**
½ tsp. **ground cumin**
½ tsp. **cayenne pepper**
½ tsp. **ground oregano**
½ tsp. **ground thyme**
½ tsp. **dried basil**
GF seasoning salt, to taste

✦ Combine all ingredients, adding seasoning salt to taste.

Note: Used as a seasoning, this coating doesn't require the use of seasoned flour or an egg wash.

Reprinted with permission from: ***The Amaxing Flax Cookbook*** by **Jane Reinhardt-Martin, RD, LD**, 2004; www.flaxrd.com

Nutritional Analysis

1 serving = 1 tbsp.

Calories (kcal)	32
Carbohydrates (g)	3
Dietary Fiber (g)	2
Fat (g)	2
Protein (g)	1
Iron (mg)	0.6
Calcium (mg)	20
Sodium (mg)	66

CAROL FENSTER'S SAVORY PIE CRUST

for your favorite pot pie

Yield: 1 Pie/6 Slices

This savory crust uses Montina™ Pure (Indian rice grass) to add fiber and a hearty texture. The crust is surprisingly easy to handle and the dough can be made ahead and frozen for later use.

3/4 cup	**gluten-free flour blend of your choice OR Carol's GF Sorghum Flour Blend***
3/4 cup	**tapioca flour**
1/2 cup	**sweet rice flour**
1/4 cup	**Montina™ Pure Baking Supplement ****
1 tbsp.	**sugar**
1 tsp.	**EACH, xanthan gum and guar gum**
1 tsp.	**dried thyme leaves**
1/2 tsp.	**salt**
1/2 cup	**shortening *****
2 tbsp.	**butter OR margarine (non-diet)**
1/4 cup	**milk (cow, rice or soy)**
1	**egg, beaten for egg wash (optional)**

- Place the dry ingredients, shortening and butter in a food processor. Mix well. Add milk and blend until dough forms a ball. If dough is too stiff, add water a tablespoon at a time until you can shape the dough into a ball.
- Flatten the dough to 1-inch disk, wrap tightly and refrigerate for 1 hour so the liquids are well-distributed throughout the dough.
- Massage the dough between your hands until warm and piable, making the crust easier to handle. Roll half of the dough (keep the remaining half wrapped tightly to avoid drying out) to a 10-inch circle between 2 pieces of heavy-duty plastic wrap dusted with rice flour. (Use damp paper towel between countertop and plastic wrap to anchor plastic wrap.) Be sure to move the rolling pin from the center of the dough to the outer edge, moving around the circle in a clockwise fashion to assure uniform thickness.
- Remove the top plastic wrap and invert the crust, centering it over the pie plate. Remove the remaining plastic wrap and press the crust into place. If the dough cracks or splits, simply press the edges together again.
- Pour your favorite pot pie filling into the crust (see Note on page 201).
- Roll the remaining dough to a 10-inch circle between floured plastic wrap. Invert and center on filled crust. Don't remove the top plastic wrap until the dough is centered. Shape a decorative ridge around the rim of the pie plate. Prick the crust several times with a fork to allow the steam to escape. Freeze for 15 minutes. Brush with beaten egg, if desired, for shinier crust. Place the pie on a non-stick baking sheet.
- Bake the pie in a preheated 375°F oven for 15 minutes on the lowest oven rack to brown the bottom crust. Move to the next highest oven rack and bake another 25-35 minutes OR until the crust is nicely browned. Cover loosely with foil if the edges brown too much.
- Cool for 10 minutes on a wire rack before serving.

Nutritional Analysis

1 serving = 1 slice

Calories (kcal)	359
Carbohydrates (g)	44
Dietary Fiber (g)	1
Fat (g)	22
Protein (g)	3
Iron (mg)	1.2
Calcium (mg)	28
Sodium (mg)	247

CAROL FENSTER'S SAVORY PIE CRUST

(continued)

* **Carol's Gluten-Free Sorghum Flour Blend**
(makes 4 1/2 cups)

1 1/2 cups	**sorghum flour**
1 1/2 cups	**potato starch OR cornstarch**
1 cup	**tapioca flour**
1/2 cup	**corn flour OR bean flour OR almond flour OR chestnut flour**

** **Montina™ Pure Baking Supplement** is 100% Indian ricegrass flour sold under the trade name Montina by Amazing Grains Grower Cooperative.

*** Non-hydrogenated shortenings, made by Spectrum® or Smart Balance®, are available at health food stores.

Note: ✦ Filling options could include your favorite chicken, turkey or beef stew, or a hearty vegetable stew.

✦ If you prefer to make a **single-crust pot pie**, put your favorite filling into a greased casserole dish. Roll half of the dough to the appropriate size and lay it over the filling, shaping a decorative edge around the rim of the dish. Prick the top with a fork a few times to let steam escape. Brush the crust with beaten egg. Bake at 375°F for 25-35 minutes, or until the filling is hot and bubbly and the crust is golden brown. Freeze the remaining dough for another use.

✦ For a **dessert pie crust**, omit thyme leaves, add pie filling and proceed as on the previous page.

EATING AWAY FROM HOME

Once you've mastered the basics of the gluten-free diet, it is possible to eat away from home, whether it be at a restaurant or in the home setting of a friend, acquaintance, or stranger. A positive attitude and a game plan are essential for a safe and successful experience. Some excellent resources on the subject of eating out and traveling, including books, dining cards in English and foreign languages, and gluten-free travel clubs, are found on pages 319-320. Here are some helpful tips for eating out.

Restaurants

1. Selecting a place to eat

Successful dining out depends on a variety of factors, including the type of restaurant chosen.

- Be careful in restaurants where language may be a communication barrier. Food service and wait staff may not easily understand gluten-free restrictions. Foreign language restaurant cards listing allowed and not allowed ingredients and foods can be helpful (see page 319 for specific resources).
- Allow extra time to discuss specific needs for a gluten-free meal.
  - Fast food and quick service restaurants may have little time to thoroughly check ingredients and food preparation methods. Fortunately, some chains have an ingredient listing of their menu items which can be helpful in making safe food choices.
  - Fine dining restaurants offer a less hurried atmosphere and usually have more time to accommodate special needs. Call the restaurant the day before or earlier the same day and ask to speak to the chef to discuss meal options. Chefs are generally aware of gluten and can often substitute other ingredients and/or create an alternative dish.

2. Timing of Meals

- Avoid peak meal times. Dining early or late will allow more time and easier access to staff who can answer questions and usually accommodate special needs.

3. Explain Dietary Restrictions Briefly

- The terms "celiac disease" and "gluten-free" may be unfamiliar to those in the food service industry. However, many understand the concept of "food allergy." Briefly indicate that you have a serious food sensitivity and must avoid foods containing wheat, barley and rye in order to prevent getting sick. Ask the server and/or chef if they could help you with selection of safe menu items.

4. Ask Specific Questions

- It is essential to inquire about cooking methods, specific ingredients that are in the item and how it is served. Unfortunately, many servers are from a generation with little knowledge of cooking, where food comes from and food preparation methods, therefore it may be advisable to have the server or manager ask the chef very specific questions.
- Here are examples of foods and the potential problems involved with them:

  a) Salads and salad dressings

  - May contain croûtons; wheat-based Asian noodles; won tons; pasta or taco shells; or salad dressings containing unsafe ingredients (e.g., wheat flour or wheat starch, hydrolyzed wheat protein, soy sauce).

- Emphasize that no croûtons or other bread products be used. If no safe salad dressings are available, ask for oil and a lemon wedge or balsamic vinegar to be served on the side.

b) Marinades

- Teriyaki or soy sauce (made with wheat) or beer may used to marinade meat, fish or poultry.

c) Soups and Sauces

- Soups and sauces are often made with commercial soup bases or soup cubes containing wheat flour, wheat starch or hydrolyzed wheat protein. Roux (pronounced 'roo') is a combination of butter and flour which is used to thicken sauces. Many restaurants also use commercial canned, frozen or dry sauce mixes that contain unsafe ingredients.

d) Meat, Fish and Poultry

- May be dusted (or 'dredged') with flour or bread crumbs before grilling or frying.
- Some hamburger patties may contain wheat flour, wheat starch or bread crumbs.
- Seasonings containing wheat flour or wheat starch may be added to meat, fish or poultry.
- If prime rib is too rare for the customer's taste, the chef may "cook" it in a pot of au jus until it reaches the desired doneness. Au jus may come from a can or mix containing unsafe ingredients.
- Self-basting turkeys and imitation bacon bits may contain hydrolyzed wheat protein.
- Imitation seafood may contain wheat starch.

e) Fried Foods

- The oil used to deep-fry foods may be used for both breaded and non-breaded items, in which case they should be avoided. In large restaurants and fast food establishments, French fries are often cooked in separate fryers where there is less chance of cross contamination.

f) Hash browns and Rice

- Some frozen hash brown potatoes may contain wheat starch. Ask for ingredient information and whether any other ingredients have been added while cooking them (e.g., seasonings which may contain wheat flour, wheat starch or hydrolyzed wheat protein).
- Rice pilafs may have seasonings or added ingredients that may need to be avoided. Also, many restaurants use commercially packaged rice that is seasoned with unsafe ingredients (e.g., broth, soup bases, seasonings that contain wheat flour, wheat starch, hydrolyzed wheat protein). It is best to choose plain steamed rice cooked in water.

g) Pasta

- Some restaurants have gluten-free pasta, or check to see if you can bring your own pasta. Ask that fresh water be used, not the water that has been used to cook wheat pasta.

h) Vegetables

- Avoid battered vegetables or those prepared in sauces which are usually thickened with flour. Some vegetables may be sautéed or stir-fried with seasonings or soy sauce that contain wheat.

5. Food Preparation Equipment

✦ Request that your food be prepared on a clean grill or in a clean pan. If this is a problem, suggest cooking it on clean aluminum foil.

✦ Cooking methods such as steaming, poaching or baking are often safer choices.

6. Confirm Your Order Before Eating

✦ Is this the "special" meal I ordered?

✦ Were your instructions followed?

7. Thank the Chef and Food Server

✦ Leave a generous tip for good service and patronize the establishment again.

Adapted from ***Restaurant Dining: Seven Tips for Staying Gluten-Free*** by the Gluten Intolerance Group, Seattle, WA. www.gluten.net

Social Events

1. Call the hostess or catering staff before the event.

✦ If your hostess is not aware of your food restrictions, explain that you are on a special diet.

✦ When attending a banquet, contact the catering department and/or chef several days ahead of time to explain your dietary restrictions.

✦ Briefly explain your dietary restrictions and the need for plain foods. It is often possible for the planned menu items to be prepared without marinades, sauces or other unsafe ingredients (e.g., plain steak, chicken, fish, salad, vegetables, fruits) or a safe substitute may be available. Most people are more than willing to accommodate this special request if they know in advance, rather than scrambling at the last minute to make changes to the menu or food preparation methods or, worse yet, feeling awkward about not having something safe for you to eat. For those individuals who know you well, they may change the preparation method for the items or the menu choices altogether so that it is suitable for everyone. Many people find preparing a gluten-free meal an interesting challenge, while others may feel uneasy. If the hostess is concerned about what to serve, offer to bring something that is safe for you to eat.

✦ When invited to an event where you are unable to determine ahead of time what's on the menu, you may want to eat something before you leave home or take something with you to be on the safe side.

2. Always say thank you.

✦ A thank-you note, telephone call or email to the host or catering department for accommodating your special dietary needs is always greatly appreciated.

GLUTEN-FREE SHOPPING

In the beginning, be prepared to spend a lot more time in the stores shopping for gluten-free foods. You need to read every label and begin to learn which ingredients are gluten-free and which contain gluten. Excellent resources to take with you are:

Canadian Celiac Association *Pocket Dictionary: Acceptability of Foods and Ingredients for the Gluten-Free Diet*

This pocket-sized book provides a brief description of each item along with an assessment of its acceptability for the gluten-free diet.

Clan Thompson *Celiac Pocket Guide to Foods*

This pocket-sized book includes many foods from major brands found in the USA that are gluten-free.

To order these resources see pages 314-315.

Caution

Manufacturers often change ingredients in their products. Always check ingredient labels for changes and the inclusion of suspect ingredients. If in doubt, phone the manufacturers. Be very explicit in your request for information:

- Is there any wheat, rye, triticale, spelt, kamut, barley or oats or their derivatives in the product?
- Are the components of a particular ingredient also free of the offending grains?
  - baking powder (may contain wheat starch).
  - seasonings (may contain wheat starch, wheat flour or hydrolyzed wheat protein).
  - modified food starches made from wheat.
  - hydrolyzed plant or vegetable protein from wheat.
  - soy sauce (often contains wheat).
  - worcestershire sauce (some contain malt vinegar).

HELPFUL HINTS

Set up files in a 3-ring binder to organize all the product information you collect. Divide it into two sections:

- Regular Supermarket Foods
- Foods from Gluten-Free Companies

Take notes, including the date, when you call the manufacturers. Keep product lists from gluten-free companies and indicate whether or not you liked the product.

GLUTEN-FREE SHOPPING LIST

The following is a sample list to get you started on your gluten-free diet.

BREAD PRODUCTS
__ GF bread, bagels, buns, pizza crusts
__ GF freezer waffles
__ GF muffins

CEREALS
__ Amaranth, buckwheat, corn, millet, quinoa, rice, soy
__ GF corn flakes, GF crisp rice
__ Cream of buckwheat or rice (brown or white), cornmeal

PASTA
__ Corn, legume, potato, quinoa, rice, soy

CRACKERS/RICE CAKES
__ GF rice crisp/crunch crackers
__ GF plain or flavored rice cakes

RICE
__ Brown, wild, white

GLUTEN-FREE FLOURS
__ Amaranth flour
__ Arrowroot or tapioca starch
__ Bean flours
__ Cornstarch
__ Cornmeal
__ Mesquite flour
__ Montina flour
__ Potato starch
__ Quinoa flour
__ Rice flour (white, brown)
__ Sorghum flour
__ Soy flour
__ Teff flour

GLUTEN-FREE INGREDIENTS & BAKING MIXES
__ GF bread mix
__ GF pancake/waffle mix
__ GF muffin mix
__ GF baking powder
__ Baking soda
__ Xanthan gum or Guar gum

LEGUMES (DRY OR READY TO EAT)
__ Beans (e.g., garbanzo, kidney, white)
__ GF canned baked beans
__ Lentils, Split Peas

GRAINS, OTHER
__ Amaranth
__ Buckwheat groats
__ Flax seed or flax seed meal
__ Millet
__ Quinoa
__ Teff

SPICES
__ Black pepper
__ Onion powder
__ Garlic powder, fresh garlic

MISCELLANEOUS
__ Honey, molasses, sugar (brown, white)
__ Jam, jelly, marmalade
__ GF puddings
__ Gelatin (flavored)
__ Vanilla
__ Vinegar (except malt vinegar)

SAUCES
__ Ketchup, plain mustard and relish
__ GF barbecue sauce
__ GF pizza and pasta sauces
__ GF salsa
__ GF soy sauce

GF SOUPS, (see pages 256-259)

NUTS & SEEDS
__ Almonds, peanuts, pecans, walnuts
__ Pumpkin, sesame & sunflower seeds
__ Nut butters (almond, cashew, peanut)

MEAT, FISH AND POULTRY
__ Fresh or frozen (plain)
__ GF deli meats

DAIRY
__ Milk (whole, 2%, 1%, or skim)
__ Milk powder
__ Yogurt
__ Cheese
__ Eggs

FRUITS
__ Fresh, canned or frozen (plain)
__ Dried fruits

VEGETABLES
__ Fresh, canned or frozen (plain)
__ Tomato paste
__ Tomatoes, canned

FATS AND OILS
__ Butter or margarine
__ Vegetable oil (e.g., canola, olive)
__ GF salad dressings

Cross Contamination

In addition to always checking about ingredients in gluten-free foods, you must also be aware of the possibility of cross contamination (a process by which a gluten-free product comes into contact with something that is not gluten-free).

Avoiding Cross Contamination at Home

✦ Store all **gluten-free** products in separate labeled containers. Some families buy bright stickers and put them on everything that is and/or should remain gluten-free. In addition, you may want to keep all **gluten-free** foods in a separate place in the cupboard and refrigerator.

✦ Buy separate containers of items like peanut butter, jam or mayonnaise that are used by other family members and therefore could become contaminated.

✦ Buy squeeze bottles of condiments such as ketchup, mustard, relish and mayonnaise.

✦ Have a separate butter dish and cutting board that are used for **gluten-free** foods only.

✦ Have your own toaster. If not, use a toaster oven, where the rack can be removed and washed if others have used it.

✦ Always make sure that the counter space you are using to prepare **gluten-free** foods is freshly washed to ensure it is free from crumbs or flour dust.

✦ Make sure pots, utensils, etc., that are also used for other foods are thoroughly scrubbed before using with **gluten-free** foods.

✦ Have your own set of utensils and other items for gluten-free baking, e.g., wooden spoons, sifter.

Cross Contamination Outside of the Home

✦ Avoid buying products from bulk bins as the products can become contaminated by scoops that have been used in another bin.

✦ Be aware that French fries may have been cooked in the same oil where battered gluten-containing foods (e.g., fish, chicken fingers) have been fried.

✦ Request that the cook: (1) use clean utensils, (2) clean the grill or pan before preparing your food, and (3) keep your meal away from meals that contain gluten.

✦ Be careful at buffets as spoons may have been used for more than one dish.

✦ Check with airlines to see if a gluten-free meal can be ordered. However, always put "extra" snacks such as dried fruits, nuts and seeds, fresh fruit and/or mini rice cakes in your carry-on bag as the meal may not be appropriate or suitable. Also, you may encounter flight delays and need gluten-free snacks.

GLUTEN-FREE PRODUCTS

Gluten-free products listed on pages 209-266 were exhaustively researched from sources believed to be reliable at the time of printing and recorded from April 2005 to February 2006. However, the author assumes no liability for any errors, omissions or inaccuracies in the product information section. Many of the products are made by companies who manufacture gluten-free products exclusively. There are other companies who produce gluten-free as well as gluten-containing products. Most manufacturers have quality-control procedures and take extra precautions to prevent cross-contamination. However, manufacturers of gluten-containing and gluten-free products cannot guarantee that the product is 100% gluten-free, due to the possibility of cross-contamination or human error. It should also be noted that manufacturers of regular commercial food products often change ingredients used in their products. Carefully reading the labels on a regular basis, and contacting the company (if in doubt), is of utmost importance to confirm that the products have remained gluten-free.

The following gluten-free product lists are not all-inclusive and the availability of some products will vary depending on where you live in Canada or the USA. Also, companies discontinue products, therefore some items may no longer be available. The tables on pages 209-266 were designed to assist you in purchasing gluten-free products. The package sizes of these products are listed in ounces with the equivalent size in grams. Gluten-free products can be purchased from several sources:

GLUTEN-FREE COMPANIES AND DISTRIBUTORS

- A very large selection of products can be purchased directly (see pages 267-310).

HEALTH FOOD STORES

- Often carry a good variety of products.
- Be aware of cross-contamination, especially for items in bulk bins or those bulk bagged in the store. Ask what procedures they use to reduce the risk of cross-contamination, e.g., cleaning the area and equipment used to portion and package bulk items; keeping gluten-free foods separate from gluten-containing foods.

GROCERY STORES

- Most large chains carry some gluten-free products throughout the store. Examples include: baking mixes, cereals (cornmeal, hominy grits, puffed corn, millet or rice), cookies, crackers, rice cakes, gluten-free flours (potato, rice, soy) and starches (corn, potato, rice, tapioca), and pasta (corn, legume, quinoa, rice, soy).

COMMERCIAL BAKERIES

- Some bakeries make gluten-free products in addition to regular gluten-containing bakery items.
- Be aware of the possibility of cross-contamination. Ask the bakery what procedures they use to reduce the risk of cross-contamination: e.g., cleaning of area and equipment, baking gluten-free products in a separate area and in separate pans and/or on specific days when no gluten-containing items are produced.

CEREALS

- Most regular cereals (rice, corn) are NOT gluten-free as they usually contain barley malt (extract or flavoring), e.g., **Kellogg's Corn Flakes, Rice Krispies**.
- Some cereals labeled "**wheat free**" are **NOT** gluten-free: e.g., **Erewhon Crispy Brown Rice Cereal (Original and No Salt Added)** – contains organic barley malt.
- Products containing spelt or kamut are **NOT** gluten-free.

Company	Cereals		Grams	Ounces
ALTI PLANO GOLD	**Instant Hot Quinoa Cereal**	Regular, Chai Almond, Oaxacan Chocolate, Orange Date, Spiced Apple Raisin	384	13.54
	Made with organic flaked quinoa.			
ANCIENT HARVEST	Organic Quinoa Flakes		340 g, 4.54 kg	12 oz., 10 lbs.
ARROWHEAD MILLS	Corn Flakes		312	11
	Corn Grits (white or yellow)		680	24
	Maple Buckwheat Flakes, Sweetened Rice Flakes		341	12
	Rice and Shine Hot Cereal		680	24
BARBARA'S BAKERY	Brown Rice Crisps		312	11
	Fruit Juice Sweetened Corn Flakes		255	9
	Puffins, Honey Rice		340	12
BARKAT	Porridge Flakes (rice and millet)*		500	17.6
	Breakfast Pops*, Corn Flakes*, Chocolate Corn Flakes*, Chocolate Crunchies*, Rice Crunchies*, Muesli*		250	8.8
	*Organic			
THE BIRKETT MILLS	Pocono Cream of Buckwheat Hot Cereal		369	13
BOB'S RED MILL	Brown Rice Farina Hot Cereal		737	26
	Creamy Buckwheat Hot Cereal		510	18
	Mighty Tasty GF Hot Cereal*		680	24
	Millet Grits/Meal		454	16
	*Whole grain brown rice, corn, "sweet" white sorghum, buckwheat.			
CREAM HILL ESTATES	Lara's Thick Rolled Oats (Pure uncontaminated oats)		500 g, 1 kg, bulk	1.1 and 2.2 lb., bulk
CREAM OF THE CROP	Organic Buckwheat Hot Cereal		400	14.1
DIXIE DINERS' CLUB	Nutlettes		454, 908 g, 4.54 kg	1, 2, 10 lbs.
	Organic Nutlettes		340, 908 g, 4.54 kg	12 oz., 2 lbs., 10 lbs.
	Nutlettes Plus	Regular, Raisin, Sugar Not!	908	2 lbs.
	High Protein Soy Cereals			
	Nutlettes To Go	Regular, Raisin, Sugar Not!	51	1.8
	Smaps Cereal		280, 454	10, 16
	High protein soy cereals.			

Company	Cereals		Grams	Ounces
El Peto	**Cream of Rice***	Apple Cinnamon, Brown, White	500 g, 1 kg, 2.5 kg	17.5 oz., 2.2 lbs., 5.5 lbs.
	Corn Balls, Cocoa Balls		250	8.8
	Corn Flakes	Sweetened, Unsweetened	250	8.8
	*Also available in bulk.			
Ener-G Foods	Toasted Granola and Trail Mix		454	16
	Rice Nuts		227	8
Enjoy Life Foods	**Crunch Granola**	Cinnamon, Cranapple, Very Berry	363	12.8
	Casein, Egg, Nut and Soy-Free. Enriched with thiamin, riboflavin, niacin, Vitamins A, B_6, B_{12} and E, folate, calcium and zinc.			
EnviroKidz	**Organic Cereals**	Amazon Frosted Flakes	400	14
		Gorilla Munch	30, 284	1, 10
		Koala Crisp	324	11.5
		Peanut Butter Panda Puffs	300	10.6
Erewhon	Aztec Crunchy Corn & Amaranth		284	10
	Brown Rice Cream (organic)		454	16
	Corn Flakes (organic)		312	11
	Crispy Brown Rice (gluten-free label)		284	10
	Crispy Brown Rice with Mixed Berries (gluten-free label)		284	10
	Rice Twice		284	10
Glutano	Corn Flakes, Muesli		250	8.8
Gluten-Free Pantry	Crispy Rice Cereal		284	10
Glutino	Buckwheat Flakes		750	26.5
	Cereal O's	Apple & Cinnamon, Honey Nut	285	10.1
	Puffed Buckwheat		300	10.6
Health Valley	Blue Corn Flakes (organic)		312	11
	Corn Crunch Ems		357	12.6
	Rice Crunch Ems		357	12.6
Heartland's Finest	**Cero's***	Original, Cinnamon, Raspberry	280	10
	*Made with pinto bean and rice flours.			
Kinnikinnick	KinniKrisp Rice Cereal		375	13
	Casein-free			
Liv-N-Well	Buckwheat Flakes (hot cereal)		454 g, 2.27 kg, 20 kg	16 oz., 5 lbs., 44 lbs.
	Cream of Rice	Brown, White		
	Puffed Buckwheat		300 g, 10 kg	10.6 oz., 22 lbs.
Lundberg	Hot Rice Cereal – Purely Organic		280 g, 11.35 kg	10 oz., 25 lbs.
Miss Roben's	Buckwheat Flakes		454	1 lb.
Natural Food Mill Bakery	Granola, Coconut Granola		300	10.6
Nature's Path	Organic Crispy Rice		284	10
	Organic Fruit Juice Sweetened Corn Flakes		300, 750	10.6, 26.4
	Organic Honey'd Corn Flakes		300, 750	10.6, 26.4
	Organic Mesa Sunrise Multigrain*		300, 750	10.6, 26.4
	*Cornmeal, buckwheat, flax, amaranth.			

Company	Cereals	Grams	Ounces
NEW MORNING	Cocoa Crispy Rice Cereal	284	10
NU-WORLD AMARANTH	Amaranth Cereal Snaps (Original)	340	12
	Amaranth Cereal Snaps (Cocoa, Cinnamon)	284	10
	Amaranth-O's (Original, Peach, Strawberry)	284	10
	Puffed Amaranth Cereal (Original)	198	7
	Puffed Amaranth Hot Cereal (Berry Delicious)	198	7
ORGRAN	Muesli (Fruit & Almond)*	500	17.6
	Rice Porridge with Apricot*	375	13.2
	*Dairy-Free.		
PERKY'S	Nutty Flax, Nutty Rice	340	12
SCHÄR	Müsli	375	13.2
SHILOH FARMS	Polenta (coarse cornmeal)	425	15
	Soy Flakes	454	16
	Soy Nuggets	280	10

BAKED PRODUCTS

- Most gluten-free bread products are found in supermarket freezer sections or at some local bakeries.
- Some breads are vacuum-packed for a shelf life of 4 months to 1 year from the date of manufacture, e.g., **Ener-G Foods**, **Kingsmill**.
- Ready-to-eat gluten-free bread products are convenient but are expensive. More economical options include:
  - Use gluten-free mixes and bake your own, see pages 231-243.
  - Make your own using various gluten-free flours, see page 154.
  - A variety of bread, cookie, muffin and pastry recipes are found in the recipe section on pages 158-201.
  - There are many gluten-free cookbooks available (see pages 316-318).

BREADS

Company	Breads		Grams	Ounces
BARKAT	**Rice Breads***	Brown, Cinnamon & Raisin, Flaxseed, Multigrain, White	500	17.6
	*Dairy-Free.			
CHOICES BEST RICE BAKERY	**Brown Rice Breads**	Plain, Raisin, Soda	500	17.6
		Multi-Seed	530	18.7
		Sourdough	540	19
CYBROS	Mock Rye, Tapioca Almond		680	24
	100% Rice, Rice n' Raisin		454	16
EL PETO	Brown Rice*, White Rice*		various sizes	various sizes
	Cheese		670	23.5
	Flax*, Gourmet, Italian Style, Millet*, Italian Style with Fibre, Multi Grain*, Potato*, Raisin*, Tapioca*		650	22.5
	*Dairy-Free. All breads are egg-free. Breads are vacuum-packed for orders shipped outside of Ontario. Not shelf-stable.			

Company	Breads	Grams	Ounces
ENER-G FOODS	Brown Rice*, Hi-Fiber Rice, Papa's Raisin (no egg)*, Tapioca*, White Rice*, White Rice Flax*	454	16
	Corn*, Light Brown Rice*, Light Tapioca* Light White Rice*	228	8
	Four Flour*	576	20.3
	Fruit (seasonal)	794	28
	Harvest, Seattle Brown*	600	21.2
	Raisin*	672	23.7
	Rice Starch (low protein)*	490	17.3
	Breads are in shelf-stable vacuum packages and are enriched with thiamin, riboflavin, niacin, iron and folic acid. *Also available in 2-slice travel packages.		
ENJOY LIFE FOODS	Original Sandwich, Rye-less "Rye"	680	24
	Breads are Casein, Egg, Nut and Soy-Free. Enriched with thiamin, riboflavin, niacin, B_6, calcium, folate, magnesium.		
FOOD FOR LIFE	Bhutanese Red Rice*, Brown Rice*, China Black Rice*, Raisin Pecan*, Rice Almond*, Rice Pecan*, White Rice	680	24
	Made with brown rice flour and rice bran. *All breads are Dairy-Free.		
GILLIAN'S FOODS	Cinnamon Raisin*, French*	350	12
	No Rye Rye*, Sandwich*, Sundried Tomato & Roasted Garlic*	510	18
	*Dairy-Free.		
GLUTAFIN	GFWF Fiber Loaf (sliced or unsliced)*	400	14.1
	GFWF White Loaf (sliced or unsliced)*	400	14.1
	*Enriched with iron, calcium, niacin and thiamin.		
GLUTANO	White Sliced	300	10.6
	Wholemeal Sliced	500	17.6
GLUTEN-FREE COOKIE JAR	Cinnamon Raisin*	695	24.4
	Crusty French*, Crusty Herb*, Marble Rye*, Pumpernickel*	525	18.6
	Primo White*	635	22.4
	Pita Bread* (4)	340	12.0
	*Dairy-Free.		
GLUTEN-FREE CREATIONS	Almond Flax, Challah (Dinner), Cheddar Cheese, Ciabatti, Cinnamon Raisin, Hi Power Multigrain, Panetonne, Party Pumpernickel, Round Rye, Sandwich, Swedish Limpa Rye	various sizes	various sizes
GLUTINO	**Corn Breads** Corn	580	20.5
	Cheese, Fibre, Raisin, Premium Corn*, Premium Fibre*, Premium Flax Seed*	600	21.2
	Premium Cinnamon Raisin	648	22.9
	Rice Breads White Rice**	700	24.7
	White Rice with Fibre**	750	26.5
	*Gluten-Free, Casein-Free, no hydrogenated oil or refined sugar. **Gluten-Free/Casein-Free. All corn and premium breads enriched with thiamin, riboflavin, niacin, iron, calcium and B_6.		

Company	Breads		Grams	Ounces
It's Ok! Baked Goods	Whole Grain Bread*		768	27
	*Dairy-Free. Made with potato starch, tapioca, sorghum, garbanzo, quinoa, Montina™ and amaranth flours.			
Kingsmill	**Rice Breads***	Brown, Flax Seed, Raisin & Cinnamon, White	500	17.6
	*Dairy-Free. Available as shelf-stable or frozen bread.			
Kinnikinnick	Brown Sandwich		585	21
	Cheese Tapioca Rice, Robin's Honey Brown Rice, Raisin Tapioca Rice, Sunflower Flax Rice		650	23
	Festive (seasonal), Italian White Tapioca Rice, Tapioca Rice		600	21.5
	Many Wonder Multigrain Rice		660	23.5
	True Fibre Multigrain Rice		560	20
	White Sandwich		565	20
	All products are Casein-Free except Cheese Tapioca Rice Bread. Breads are enriched with thiamin, riboflavin, niacin, folic acid and iron.			
Mr. Ritt's Bakery	**Challah**	Braided, Cinnamon, Cinnamon Raisin	NA	NA
		Lite n White*, Mock Rye*	NA	NA
	*Dairy-Free.			
Natural Food Mill Bakery	**Breads**	Golden Rice*, Sandwich*	750	26.5
	Flatbread (7")* - 2/package		155	5.5
	*Dairy-Free.			
Panne Rizo	Brown Rice, Cinnamon Raisin, Dairy-Free Brown Rice*, Sesame White Rice		610	21.5
	Cheddar Scallion		625	22
	Egg-Free		600	21.2
	Foccacia (Thyme Scallion)		450	15.9
	Herbed		620	21.9
	*Dairy-Free.			
Schär	Bon Matín (sweet bread)		200	7
	Ertha Brown		500	17.6
	Pain Campagnard		320	11.3
	Pan Carré Sliced, Rustico Multigrain		400	14.1
Sterk's Bakery	**Breads**	Italian Cinnamon, Italian, Italian Hi-Fiber, Italian Raisin, Italian Whole Brown, Sandwich*	600	21.2
	*Dairy-Free.			
	Dutch Breads*	Cinnamon, Hemp, Light Brown, Raisin, White, Whole Brown	600	21.2
	*Dairy and Egg-Free.			
Whole Foods GF Bakehouse	Cinnamon Raisin, Prairie, Sandwich, Sundried Tomato Garlic		794	28
	Corn		340	12

YEAST-FREE BREADS

Company	Yeast-Free Breads		Grams	Ounces
EL PETO	Cheese		670	23.5
	Flax Seed, Hi-Fibre Brown Rice, Millet, Multi Grain, Potato, Tapioca, White Rice		650	22.5
	Yeast-Free breads are all Dairy-Free except cheese.			
ENER-G FOODS	YF Brown Rice Loaf		540	19
	YF White Rice Loaf*		636	22.4
	YF Sweet Loaf*		480	16.9
	*Available in 2-slice travel packages.			
FOOD FOR LIFE	**YF Rice Breads***	Brown	800	28.2
		Fruit & Seed Medley, Multiseed, White	725	25.6
	*All breads are Dairy-Free.			
GLUTEN-FREE CREATIONS	Yeast Free Bread		454	16
KINNIKINNICK	Candadi Yeast Free Multigrain Rice Bread*		650	23
	YF Tapioca Rice Bread*		600	21.5
	*Casein-Free and enriched with thiamin, riboflavin, niacin, folic acid and iron.			
NATURAL FOOD MILL BAKERY	**Rice Breads***	Brown, Multi Seed	800	28.2
		Fruit & Seed Medley, Potato, White	725	25.6
	*Corn, Dairy and Soy-Free.			
PANNE RIZO	Soda Bread		540	19

BAGELS, BAGUETTES, BUNS, MUFFINS, PIZZA CRUSTS, ROLLS

Company	Bagels, Baguettes, etc.		Grams	Ozs.	Number
BARKAT	**Pizza Crust***	Brown Rice, White Rice	150	5.3	1
	*Dairy-Free.				
CHEBE	**Frozen Dough**	Bread Sticks (Plain, Tomato Basil)*	340	12	12
		Rolls*, Sandwich Buns*	340	12	12
		"On-the-Go" Pizza Dough*	284	10	2
	*Yeast-Free.				
CHOICES BEST RICE BAKERY	**Buns**	Brown Rice Hamburger, WF Brown Rice, Multiseed	400	14.1	4
	Brown Rice Pizza Crust		280	9.9	2
	Rice Muffins	Banana, Blueberry, Bran, Cranberry	260	9.2	3
CYBROS	Mock Rye Rolls		340	12	10-12
	100% Rice Nuggets		340	12	24-26
	100% Rice Rolls		340	12	9-11
DIETARY SPECIALTIES	**English Muffins**	Plain, Cinnamon, Raisin	400	14.1	4
	Homestyle Rolls		340	12	4

Company	Bagels, Baguettes, etc.		Grams	Ozs.	Number
EL PETO	**Hamburger Buns**	Brown*, Brown (no corn)*, Italian with Sesame, Millet*, Multi-Grain*, Potato*, Tapioca*, White*	500	17.5	8
	Hot Dog Buns	Italian with Sesame, Millet*, Potato*, White*	500	17.5	8
	Dinner Rolls	Brown*, Italian, Gourmet, Multi Grain*, White*	500	17.5	8
	Gourmet Mini Sub Buns		480	16.9	4
	Rolls	Cheese, Fruit*, Raisin*	500	17.5	8
	Pizza Crusts*	Basil, Millet, Plain (pre-baked)	420	14.8	2
	Muffins**	Apple Spice, Banana, Blueberry, Carrot, Chocolate Chip, Cranberry, Raisin Rice Bran, Tropical Delight	460	16.2	6
	Waffles	Belgian (Regular; Corn/milk-free)*	300	10.5	2
	*Dairy-Free. **Also make Sugar-Free muffins sweetened with fruit juice.				
ENER-G FOODS	**Dinner Rolls**	Tapioca Dinner*	280	9.9	6
	Hamburger Buns	Brown Rice*	292	10.3	6
		Seattle Brown*	460	16.2	6
		Tapioca*	220	7.8	6
		White Rice*	292	10.3	6
	Hot Dog Buns	Tapioca*	220	7.8	6
		Seattle Brown*	440	16.2	6
	English Muffins	Brown (with sweet potato flour)*	488	17.2	4
		Plain (with tofu)	428	15	4
	Rice Pizza Shells (6") (low protein)*		252	8.9	3
	Rice Pizza Shells (10") (low protein)*		520	18.4	3
	Scones		400	14.1	6
	Products are in shelf-stable, vacuum packages. *Enriched with thiamin, riboflavin, niacin, iron and folic acid.				
ENJOY LIFE FOODS	**Bagels***	Classic Original, Old Fashioned Cinnamon Raisin, Toasty Onion, Very Blueberry	454	16	6
	*Casein, Egg, Nut and Soy-Free. Enriched with thiamin, riboflavin, niacin, B_{12}, iron, folate, calcium, magnesium and zinc.				
FOOD FOR LIFE	**Tortillas***	Brown Rice	340	12	6
		Sprouted Corn	283	10	6
	*Dairy-Free.				
FOODS BY GEORGE	**Muffins**	Blueberry, Corn	482	17	6
	English Muffins*	Cinnamon Currant, Plain, No-Rye Rye	397	14	4
	Pizza Crusts (6")*		255	9	3
	*Dairy-Free/Casein-Free.				
GILLIAN'S FOODS	**French Rolls***	Plain, Caramelized Onion, Cinnamon Raisin, Poppy Seed, Sesame Seed	624	22	6
	Pizza Crust*		454	16	2
	*Dairy-Free.				

Company	Bagels, Baguettes, etc.		Grams	Ozs.	Number
Glutafin	GFWF Pizza Base		220	7.8	2
	Rolls	GFWF Fibre*, GFWF White*	280	10	4
	*Enriched with iron, calcium, niacin and thiamin.				
Glutano	Par-Baked Baguette		200	7	1
	Par-Baked Rolls		200	7	2
Gluten-Free Cookie Jar	**Bagels**	Cinnamon Raisin*, Plain*, Poppyseed*, Pumpernickel*, Sesame*	560	19.6	6
	Rolls	Dinner*	390	13.6	6
		French*	665	23.4	4
		Portuguese Cheese	220	7.8	3
		Portuguese Cheese (mini)	280	9.8	12
	Scones	Blueberry, Irish Soda Bread	170	6.0	3
	Soft Pretzels*		560	19.6	6
	*Dairy-Free.				
Gluten-Free Creations	**Rolls**	Cinnamon, Pecan Caramel,	454	16	8
		Dinner, Rye,	340	12	4
		Hi Power Multigrain	397	14	4
Gluten-Free Pantry	White Rice Pizza Crust (shelf stable)		150	5.3	1
Glutino	**Bagels**	Cinnamon & Raisin	350	12.4	4
		Plain, Poppyseed, Sesame	300	10.6	4
		Premium – Plain, Sesame	650	22.9	4
	Baguettes	Premium Corn*	430	15.2	2
	English Muffins (corn)		325	11.5	4
	Hamburger Buns	Premium Corn*	560	19.8	6
	Hot Dog Buns	Corn	500	17.6	6
	Pizza Crusts	(pre-baked) Corn, Premium Corn*	375	13.2	4
	*Gluten-Free/Casein-Free, no hydrogenated oil or refined sugars. All corn and premium corn products are enriched with thiamin, riboflavin, niacin, iron, calcium and B_6.				
It's Ok! Baked Goods	Herb Crust Flatbread/Pizza Crust*		130	4.6	2
	Italian Sandwich Rolls*		340	12	4
	*Dairy-Free.				
Kingsmill	White Rice Pizza Crusts (pre-baked) (8")		150	5.3	1
	Available in shelf-stable or frozen packages.				
Kinnikinnick	Tapioca Rice English Muffins		375	13.5	4
	Tapioca Rice Hamburger Buns		400	14.5	4
	Tapioca Rice Hot Dog Buns		350	12.5	4
	Muffins	Blueberry, Carrot, Chocolate Chip, Cranberry,	300	12.5	6
	Pizza Crust (7")		540	19.5	3
	Pizza Crust (10")		660	23.5	3
	Tapioca Rice Bagels	Cinnamon Raisin, New York Style Plain, Sesame	400	13.5	4
	Tapioca Rice Multigrain Seed & Fibre Bun		400	14.5	4
	Tapioca Rice Tray Buns		350	12.5	6
	All products are Casein-Free and enriched with thiamin, riboflavin, niacin, folic acid and iron.				
Lifestream	Buckwheat Wild Berry Toaster Waffles*		312	11	8
	Mesa Sunrise Toaster Waffles*		312	11	8
	*Dairy-Free.				

Company	Bagels, Baguettes, etc.		Grams	Ozs.	Number
MR. RITT'S BAKERY	**Baguettes** (14")	French, Italian	NA	NA	1
	Rolls	Dinner	NA	NA	12
		Hamburger, Hot Dog	NA	NA	8
	Italian Herb Pizza Crust (8")		NA	NA	3
	Muffins*	Apple Crumb, Banana Chocolate Chip, Banana Walnut, Blueberry, Chocolate Chip, Lemon Poppy Seed, Lemon Raspberry, Orange Mock Corn			6
	*Dairy-Free.				
NATURAL FOOD MILL BAKERY	Golden Rice Buns		425	15	5
	Pizza Crusts (12")	Brown, White	400	14.1	1
NATURE'S HILIGHTS	Brown Rice Pizza Crust (frozen, fully cooked, ready to heat)		284	10	2
NU-WORLD AMARANTH	**Flatbread/Pizza Crust** (pre-baked) – 6"				
		Amaranth Buckwheat	113	4	2
		Amaranth Garbanzo	113	4	2
		Amaranth Sorghum	113	4	2
PANNE RIZO	Dinner Rolls (Brown)		460	16.2	4
	Hamburger Buns	Brown*, White	550	19.4	4
	Muffins	Banana Chocolate Chip*, Banana Pecan (sugar-free)*, Banana Strawberry*, Blueberry Lemon Poppy*, Carrot Walnut, Cranberry Orange*, Maple Pumpkin*, Raspberry White Chocolate	840	29.6	6
	Pizza Crusts (7")	Brown*, White	250	8.8	2
	*Dairy-Free.				
SCHÄR	Baguette		400	14.1	2
	Duo Lunch Rolls		150	5.3	2
	Panini White Bread Buns		200	7	2
	Pizza Base		300	10.6	2
	Sunna Wholemeal Bread Rolls		200	7	2
STERK'S BAKERY	**Bagels**	Plain*, Poppy Seed*, Sesame*	various weights		6
	Buns	Hamburger*, Hot Dog*, Italian, Italian Hi-Fiber	various weights		6
	Muffins	Apple Raisin*, Banana Blueberry*, Chocolate Blueberry*, Triple Berry*	various weights		6
	Pizza (12")	Italian, Yummy*	various weights		1
	*Dairy-Free.				
VAN'S	**Toaster Waffles**	Apple, Cinnamon, Original	255	9	6
		Blueberry, Flax	269	9.5	6
		Gourmet Buckwheat	269	9.5	6
	Toaster Mini Waffles (Wheat-Free)		213	7.5	32
	Wheat-Free products are Gluten-Free.				
WHOLE FOODS GF BAKEHOUSE	Cranberry Orange Scones		340	12	4
	Cream Biscuits		280	10	6
	Muffins	Blueberry, Cherry, Almond Streusel	454	16	6
	Pizza Crust		680	24	2

YEAST-FREE – BUNS AND ROLLS

Company	Buns and Rolls		Grams	Ozs.	Number
EL PETO	**YF Hamburger Buns**	Brown, Millet, Multi-Grain, Potato, Tapioca, White	650	22.9	8
	YF Hot Dog Buns	Millet, Potato, White	700	24.7	8
	YF Dinner Rolls	Brown, Multi Grain	480	16.9	8
	YF Pizza Crust	Plain, Millet	420	14.8	2
	All products are Dairy-Free.				
ENER-G FOODS	YF Rice Pizza Shells (6")		354	12.5	3
	YF Rice Pizza Shells (10")		900	31.7	3

CAKES, LOAVES, PIES, MISCELLANEOUS

Company	Cakes, Loaves, Pies, Miscellaneous		Grams	Ozs.	Number
BARKAT	Marble Cake		250	8.8	
CHOICES BEST RICE BAKERY	**Brown Rice Pudding Cakes**	Banana, Blueberry, Chocolate, Chocolate Vanilla, Marble, Lemon Poppy Seed	454	16	
	Rice Carrot Cake with Cream Cheese Icing		170, 510	6, 18	
	Honey Squares		200	7	3
	Rice Brownies		225	7.9	
	Rice Butter Tarts		120	4.2	6
DIETARY SPECIALTIES	Cheesecake		454	16	
	Classic Pound Cake		369	13	
	Pie Shells		400	14	2
EL PETO	**Pies** (8")	Apple*, Blueberry*, Cherry*, Peach Apricot*, Pumpkin*, Strawberry-Rhubarb*, Walnut	500	17.5	
	Pie Dough*		400	14	
	Tarts	Buttertart, Lemon*, Pecan, Raspberry*	NA	NA	6
	Tart Shells*	Sweetened, unsweetened	NA	NA	12
	*Dairy-Free.				
ENER-G FOODS	Brownies*		560	19.7	
	Cinnamon Rolls		672	23.7	8
	Donut Holes*		235	8.3	20
	Plain Donuts*		200	7	6
	Fruit Cake (seasonal item)*		567	20	
	Pound Cake*		249	8.8	
	*Enriched with thiamin, riboflavin, niacin, iron and folic acid.				
FOODS BY GEORGE	Brownies*		397	14	6x8" tray
	Crumb Cake		567	20	6x8" tray
	Pecan Tart		113	4	1
	Pound Cake		454	16	7" loaf
	*Dairy-Free.				

Company	Cakes, Loaves, Pies, Miscellaneous		Grams	Ozs.	Number
GLUTAFIN	**Cakes**	Banana	250	8.8	
		Date & Walnut	300	10.6	
		Lemon Madeira	280	9.9	
GLUTEN-FREE COOKIE JAR	Brownies*		340	12	4
	Bundt Cakes	Iced Chocolate*	515	18.4	3 small
		Iced Chocolate*	700	24.7	1 large
		Orange Chiffon*	275	9.8	3 small
		Orange Chiffon*	445	15.8	1 large
	*Dairy-Free.				
GLUTINO	Brownies		300	10.6	1
	Carrot Cake		325	11.5	1 tray
	Cup Cakes	Chocolate, Marble, Vanilla	200	7.1	6
	Date Squares		300	10.6	1 tray
	Queen Elizabeth Date Cake		325	11.5	
	Pie Crusts		175	6.2	3
IT'S OK! BAKED GOODS	Delicious Fudge Brownies*		80	2.8	2
	Delicious Fudgette Brownie*		60	2.1	1
	Delicious Cream Puffs (frozen)*		240	8.5	4
	*Dairy, Peanut and Tree Nut-Free.				
KINNIKINNICK	JB Brownie Squares		350	9	1
	Donuts	Chocolate Dipped, Cinnamon Sugar, Glazed Chocolate, Maple Dipped, Vanilla Dipped	480	17	6
	Fruit Cake (seasonal item)		500	18	1
	Tapioca Rice Cinnamon Buns		500	18	6
	All products are Casein-Free and enriched with thiamin, riboflavin, niacin, folic acid and iron.				
MR. RITT'S BAKERY	Angel Food (10")	various flavors*			1
	Brownies	Regular and Dairy-Free*			6
	Cheesecakes	Blueberry Crumb, Chocolate Chip, Crumb Top, Pineapple Crumb, Plain, Pumpkin, Raspberry Crumb			6 & 10 svg.
	Coffee Cakes	Almond*, Blueberry, Cocoa Orange*, Crumb Top			1
	Glazed Cakes	Boston Crème, Sacher Torte, Torte Chocolate, Torte Yellow			6 svg.
	Luncheon Cakes	Banana, Budapest Coffee, Dairy-Free Apple*, Jewish Apple, Lemon Pound, Plain Pound			6-8 svg.
	Tart	Linzertorte, Mixed Nut, Pecan, Sourcream Apple			6 svg.
	Tarts	Mixed Nut, Pecan			1 svg.
	*Dairy-Free. Note: Some items are only available in-store and cannot be shipped.				

Company	Cakes, Loaves, Pies, Miscellaneous		Grams	Ozs.	Number
NATURAL FEAST	**Pies** (Frozen)	Apple Cranberry, Apple Streusel, Blueberry Streusel	908	2 lbs.	8 svg.
		Chocolate Mousse, Pumpkin	817	1.8 lb.	
	Pie Shells		409	0.9 lb.	2
	Corn and Dairy-Free.				
NATURE'S HILIGHTS	Deluxe Double Chocolate Brownies (Frozen, ready to serve)		454	16	10
PANNE RIZO	Applesauce Spice Bars		400	14.1	6
	Apple Crostada, Berry Gallette		225	7.9	1
	Brownies (Macadamia Nut)		360	12.7	4
	Buttertarts		260	9.2	6
	Cinnamon Bun Swirls*		680	24	4
	Coconut Cherry Dream Bars		300	10.6	4
	Gramma's Cinnamon Dots		175	6.2	5
	Pecan Toffee Squares		420	14.8	4
	Pies (6")	Apple Cinnamon*	590	20.8	
		Cherry*, Pumpkin	470	16.6	
		Peach Blackberry*	550	19.4	
		Summer Berry*	475	16.8	
	*Dairy-Free.				
PATSYPIE	Double Chocolate Mint Brownies		300	10.5	
RED MILL FARMS	Banana Nut Cake, Dutch Chocolate Cake		340	12	
SCHÄR	Magdalenas (apricot-filled cupcakes)		150	5.3	
	Fantasia (sponge cake)		500	17.6	
	Meranetti (chocolate fudge cupcakes)		200	7	
STERK'S BAKERY	**Cakes**	Chocolate Sponge*, Vanilla Sponge*	various weights		
	*Dairy-Free.				
WHOLE FOODS GF BAKEHOUSE	Banana Bread		397	14	
	Carrot Cake		510	18	
	Pies	Apple, Cherry, Southern Pecan	454	16	

COOKIES

✦ **NOT** all **"wheat-free"** cookies are gluten-free. Some may contain **barley** or **regular oats**.

Company	Cookies		Grams	Ounces
ARICO NATURAL FOODS	**Cookie Bars**	Almond Cranberry, Chocolate Chip, Double Chocolate, Peanut Butter	40	1.4
	Cookie Bars (tub of 9)	Almond, Cranberry, Chocolate Chip, Double Chocolate, Lemon Ginger, Peanut Butter, Triple Berry	135	4.8
	Made with organic brown rice and teff flours. All bars are Corn and Dairy-Free.			

Company	Cookies		Grams	Ounces
AUNT CANDICE	Chocolate Chip, Sugar, Sweet Lemon		280	10
	10 cookies/box. Individually wrapped. Casein, Corn and Soy-Free.			
BARKAT	Caramel Qix Bar		28	1
	Cream Filled Wafers	Chocolate, Lemon, Vanilla	125	4.4
	Chocolate Hazelnut Bar		75	2.7
	Wafers		100	3.5
CHOICES BEST RICE BAKERY	**Rice Cookies**	Bird's Nest, Chocolate Chip, Ginger	200	7
		Brownie Chocolate Chunk, Shortbread	150	5.3
	Mediterranean Macaroons		260	9.2
CYBROS	Lemon Almond, Peanut Butter, Sugar		255	9
DIETARY SPECIALTIES	Chocolate Chip, Cinnamon, Coconut, Orange		125	4.4
EL PETO	Almond Shortbread*, Carob Chip*, Chocolate Chip*, Chocolate Coconut Macaroons*, Coconut Macaroons*, Chocolate Hazelnut, Cinnamon Hazelnut*, Gingersnaps*, Raspberry Hazelnut*		200	7
	*Dairy-Free.			
ENER-G FOODS	Almond Butter, Biscotti (Chocolate Chip)		208	7.3
	Biscotti (Plain)		280	9.9
	Chocolate Chip Potato*		272	9.6
	Chocolate Hazelnut		304	10.7
	Chocolate Sandwich		270	9.5
	Cinnamon		250	8.8
	Coconut Macaroons*		256	9
	French Almond		bulk only	bulk only
	Ginger*		224	7.9
	Lemon Sandwich		250	8.8
	Vanilla Chocolate Sandwich		280	9.9
	Vanilla Lemon Cream		260	9.2
	Vanilla, White Chocolate Chip Macademia Nut		288	10.2
	*Also available in bulk.			
ENJOY LIFE FOODS	Chewy Chocolate Chip, No-Oats "Oatmeal", Snickerdoodle		28*	1*
	Chewy Chocolate Chip, Double Chocolate Brownie, Gingerbread Spice, No-Oats "Oatmeal", Snickerdoodle		170**	6**
	Casein, Egg, Nut and Soy-Free. *2 cookies/pack. **12 cookies/box.			
ENVIROKIDZ	Vanilla Animal Cookies		255	9
FORTITUDE	Ginger & Spice, Lemon & Vanilla, Orange & Cinnamon		164	5.8
GLUTAFIN	Biscuits		200	7
	Bourbon Chocolate Cream Biscuits, Custard Creams		125	4.4
	Chocolate Chip Cookies, Milk Chocolate Biscuits, Milk Chocolate Digestives, Sweet Biscuits, Tea Biscuits		150	5.3
	Shortbread Biscuits		100	3.5

Company	Cookies		Grams	Ounces
GLUTANO	Apricot Biscuits, Chocolate Chip Biscuits, Custard Cream Biscuits, Double Chocolate Sandwich Cookies, Ginger Lemon Sandwich Cookies, Luxury Ginger		150	5.3
	Biscuits, CoCo Cookies, Ginger Cookies, Half Covered Chocolate Cookies, Hazelnut Cookies, Short Cake Ring Biscuits, Tarteletts, Wizard Biscuits		125	4.4
	Chocolate O's Sandwich Cookies		175	6.2
	Digestive Maize		200	7
	Half Covered Chocolate Digestive Biscuits		240	8.5
	Caramel Crunch Cookies, Wafers		100	3.5
	G-Man Cookies		130	4.6
	Break Bar		45	1.6
	Big Break Bar		50	1.8
	Break Bar (Orange) – 5 bars		135	4.8
GLUTEN-FREE COOKIE JAR	Brown Sugar Wafers, Chocolate Chip, Chocolate Chip Walnut, Cookie Jar Cut-outs, Decorated Cut-outs, Italian Ricotta Cheese, Orange, Peanut Butter, Pumpkin		340	12
	All are Dairy-Free except Italian Ricotta Cheese.			
GLUTENFREEDA FOODS	**Real Cookies™**	Chip Chip Hooray, Chocolate Minty Python, Peanut Envy, Peanut Paul and Mary	454	16
	Refrigerated cookie dough.			
GLUTINO	**Dream Cookies***	Chocolate, Vanilla, Zebra	125	4.4
		Shortcake	125	4.4
	Wafer Cookies	Chocolate, Vanilla	130	4.6
		Lemon	200	7.1
	*Dairy-Free.			
JENNIES	Almond Macaroons, Coconut Macaroons		227	8
	Coconut Macaroons	Carob Chip, Chocolate Chip, Coconut, Dutch Chocolate, Fruit Filled, Rum	57	2
	Unsweetened Macaroons	Carob, Chocolate, Coconut	127	4.5
KINGSMILL	Chocolate Chip		110	4
	Cinnamon, Coconut, Orange		125	4.4
KINNIKINNICK	Ginger Snap		190	7
	Kinni-Betik*	Chunky Chocolate	230	8.5
	Kinni-Kritters		250	8.8
	KinniTOOS Sandwich Cream Cookies	Chocolate, Vanilla	230	8
	Montana's Chocolate Chip		220	8
	Wolfesbrand	Almond, Double Chocolate Almond, Lemon Cranberry	220	8
	All products are Casein-Free, except Kinni-Betic Chunky Chocolate. *Kinni-Betic cookies are Sugar-Free.			

Company	Cookies		Grams	Ounces
MR. RITT'S BAKERY	Almond Macaroons*		NA	NA
	Biscotti (various flavors)*		NA	NA
	Chocolate Chip**, Double Chocolate**, Mock Oatmeal**		NA	NA
	Sugar Cookies		NA	NA
	*Dairy-Free. **Dairy and Egg-Free.			
NANA'S COOKIE COMPANY	**Nana's No Gluten Cookies**	Chocolate, Chocolate Crunch, Ginger, Lemon	100	3.5
	Nana's No Gluten Cookie Bars*	Berry Vanilla, Chocolate Munch, Nana Banana	175	6.1
	*Individually wrapped bars, 5/box.			
	Nana's Temptations**	Chocolate, Chocolate Nut Chunk	227	8
	**Baked confection, individually wrapped, 5/box.			
NATURAL FOOD MILL BAKERY	**Cookies** (6)	Ginger Snap	200	7.1
		Butterscotch Pecan, Double Chocolate Delite, Maple Nut, Chocolate Mint	220	7.8
		Almond	240	8.5
		Chocolate Chip	250	8.8
	Tropical Treats*	Regular, Lite	90 g, 2.8 kg	3.2 oz., 6.4 lbs.
	*Available in single serve individually wrapped and box of 32.			
ORGRAN	**Biscotti***	Amaretti, Choc Chip, Lemon Poppyseed	150	5.3
	Cookies*	Apricot & Coconut, Cinnamon & Sultana	200	7
	*Dairy-Free.			
PAMELA'S PRODUCTS	**Biscotti**	Almond Anise, Chocolate Walnut, Lemon Almond	113	4
	Cookies	Chocolate Chunk Pecan Shortbread, Dark Chocolate-Chocolate Chunk*, Espresso Chocolate Chunk, Peanut Butter Chocolate Chip*	33, 150	1.2, 5.3
		Spicy Ginger*	150	5.3
	Made with organic ingredients. 33 g/1.2 oz. package contains 2 cookies.			
	Cookies	Chocolate Chip Walnut, Coconut*, Peanut Butter*	150	5.3
	No sugar – sweetened with maltitol.			
	Cookies (Shortbread)	Butter, Lemon, Pecan, Swirl	206	7.25
	Cookies (Traditional)	Carob Hazelnut, Chunky Chocolate Chip*, Chocolate Chip Walnut*, Ginger*, Peanut Butter*	206	7.25
	*Dairy-Free.			

Company	Cookies		Grams	Ounces
PANNE RIZO	**Biscotti**	Almond, Cranberry Pistachio (low fat), Mocha Almond (low fat), Star Anise Almond, Triple Chocolate	220	7.8
		Chocolate Swirled	225	7.9
	Cookies	Chocolate Dipped Macaroons*	160	5.6
		Chocolate Walnut, Ginger Chocolate, Tollhouse Regular, Tollhouse Dairy-Free, Low Sugar*	275	9.7
		Frosted Raspberry Swirls	175	6.2
		Pecan Snowballs	230	8.1
	Shortbread	Buttery, Pecan	240	8.5
		Sugar	265	9.3
	*Dairy-Free.			
PATSYPIE	**Biscotti**	Almond, Almond & Raisin, Chocolate Chip, Cranberry Orange	275	9.7
		Southern Pecan	250	8.8
	Cookies	Chocolate Chip, Peanut Butter, Raisin, Snappy Ginger	275	9.7
SCHÄR	Biscotti with Chocolate (Cioccolato), Biscuits with Cocoa Creme Filling (Cioccolini), Lady Fingers (Savoiardi)		150	5.3
	Chocolate Chip Biscuits (Pepitas), Solena Biscuits, Tea Biscuits (Frollini)		200	7
	Croissant (Sweet)		250	8.8
	Butter Biscuits (Duetto)		170	6
	Chocolate Snack		105	3.7
	Quadritos		40	1.4
	Wafers	Cocoa, Hazelnut, Vanilla	100	3.5
	Wafle Bread (Cialde Wafer)		75	2.6
SPRING BAKEHOUSE	**GF Crispy Thumbprints**	Blackberry, Chocolate Raspberry, Cinnamon Apricot, Strawberry	30, 200	1, 7
	Available as individually wrapped single cookie and package of 8 cookies.			
	Nutballz Energy Cookies	Almond Sesame, Chocolate Chip, Cinnamon	43	1.5
STERK'S BAKERY	Cherry Shortbread, Chocolate Chip, Coconut Macaroons, Shortbread, Snowball		various weights	
WHOLE FOODS GF BAKEHOUSE	**Cookies**	Chocolate Chip, Molasses Ginger, Peanut Butter	340	12
	Walnut Brownies		454	16

SNACK BARS

Company	Snack Bars		Grams	Ounces
AUNT CANDICE	**Protein Bars***	Almond Berry Breakfast, Double Chocolate Almond, Double Chocolate Cherry, Double Chocolate Coconut, Double Chocolate Peanut Butter, Green Life Spirulina, Peanut Butter Chocolate Chip, Chocolate Java Chip, Mint Chocolate	56	2
	*Casein, Corn & Soy-Free.			
BUMBLE BAR	Original		45	1.6
	Original with	Almond, Cashew, Hazelnuts, Mixed Nuts	4.5	1.6
	Chai with Almonds, Chocolate Crisp, Lushus Lemon		4.5	1.6
	All bars are Dairy-Free.			
ENER-G FOODS	Granola Bar (10/package)*		354	12.5
	*Also available in bulk.			
ENJOY LIFE FOODS	**Snack Bars** (5/box)	Caramel, Apple, Coco Loco, Very Berry	140	5
	Casein, Egg, Nut and Soy-Free. Enriched with thiamin, riboflavin, niacin, Vitamins B_6, B_{12}, folate, calcium, iron, magnesium and zinc.			
ENVIROKIDZ	**Crispy Rice Bars** (6/box)	Berry, Chocolate, Peanut Butter	170	6
GLUTINO	**Breakfast Bars*** (5/box)	Apple, Blueberry, Chocolate	200	7.1
	*Dairy-Free.			
HEAVEN SCENT	**Crispy Rice & Marshmallow Bars**	Original, Chocolate Chip, Soy Protein	57	2
LÄRABAR	**Energy Bars**	Apple Pie, Pecan Pie	45	1.6
		Cashew Cookie, Cherry Pie	48	1.7
		Banana Cookie, Chocolate Coconut Chew, Cinnamon Roll, Coca Môle, Lemon	51	1.8
	Made with dried fruits, nuts, spices.			
LEDA NUTRITION	**Leda Bars**	Apple Cinnamon, Apricot, Banana, Chocolate-Soy, Mint Chocolate	85	3
	Lite Bars	Apple, Apricot, Blueberry, Choc-Orange	50	1.8
	Made with chickpea, corn, tapioca, rice and dried fruits.			
OMEGA SMART	**Nutritional Bars***	Apricot Almond, Banana Chocolate Chip, Carrot Cake, Chocolate Nut, Cinnamon Apple, Pumpkin Spice, Raisin Spice	67	2.35
	*Dairy-Free.			
	Holistic Health Bars**	Almond Coconut, Chocolate Walnut, Wild Blueberry	NA	NA
	**Made with flax, dried fruits and goat milk.			

Company	Snack Bars		Grams	Ounces
OMEGA SMART	**Youth in a Bar**	Almond Macaroon, Chocolate Heaven, Wild Blueberry w/orange Essence	65	2.3
	Made with flax, dried fruits and goat milk.			
ORGRAN	**Fruit Bars***	Banana, Fig, Fruit Medley	90	3.2
	Fruit Filled Bars*	Apricot, Blueberry, Choc Cherry,	50	1.8
		Choc Hazelnut	80	2.8
	*Dairy-Free.			
PERFECT 10	**Bliss Bars***	Apricot Chocolate, Cranberry Chocolate, Lemon Chocolate	50	1.8
	*Made with dried fruits, nuts, seeds and pure dark chocolate.			
	Natural Energy Bars**	Apple Cinnamon, Apricot, Cherry, Cranberry, Lemon	50	1.8
	**Made with dried fruits, nuts and seeds.			
SPRING BAKEHOUSE	**Sacha Active Meals***	Apple Cinnamon, Beans and Cheese, Chocolate Coconut, Cranberry Cardamon, Indian Spice, Sun Dried Tomato	85	3
	*Dairy-Free except Beans and Cheese.			
THINK ORGANIC	**Snack Bars***	Apricot Coconut, Cashew Pecan, Cherry Nut, Chocolate Coconut, Cranapple, Tropical Nut	50	1.76
	*Dairy and Soy-Free.			
WELLNESS FOODS	Fibar[2] (contains psyllium husk)		40	1.4
	The Simply Bar	Cinnamon Vanilla, Cocoa, Cocoa Raspberry, Ginger Flax	40	1.4
	Bars made with soy protein, tapioca starch and brown rice.			

CRACKERS AND RICE CAKES

- ✦ Most crackers contain wheat, rye, oats, and/or barley. Read labels carefully.
- ✦ The majority of large and mini rice cakes are gluten-free, however, some multigrain rice cakes may contain **barley** and/or **oats** and are **NOT** gluten-free.

CRACKERS

Company	Crackers		Grams	Ounces
BARKAT	Cracker Bread		375	13.2
	Crisp Bread		250	8.8
BLUE DIAMOND	**Nut Thins**	Almond, Cheddar Cheese, Country Ranch, Hazelnut, Pecan, Smokehouse	120	4.25
DIETARY SPECIALTIES	**Gourmet Cheese Crackers**	Aged Parmesan, Italian Herb, Sesame	85	3
EDEN FOODS	Brown Rice Crackers		75	2.6
	Brown Rice Chips		50	1.7

Company	Crackers		Grams	Ounces
EDWARD & SON'S TRADING CO.	**Brown Rice Snaps**	Black Sesame, Buckwheat Tamari, Cheddar, Onion Garlic, Salsa, Tamari Seaweed, Tamari Sesame, Toasted Onion, Unsalted Plain, Unsalted Sesame, Vegetable	100	3.5
ENER-G FOODS	Broken Melba Toast		454	16
	Cinnamon Crackers		168	5.9
	Garlic Crackers*, Sesame Crackers*		300	10.6
	Gourmet Crackers (low protein)		200	7
	Onion Crackers		210	7.4
	Seattle Crackers		125	4.4
	*Enriched with thiamin, riboflavin, niacin, iron and folic acid.			
FORTITUDE	**Casabe Rainforest Crackers**	Original, Roasted Garlic, Wild Onion	100	3.5
	Made with casava pulp.			
GLUTAFIN	**Crackers**	Plain, High Fiber	200	7
	Crisp Bread, Savoury Biscuits		250	8.8
	Savoury Shorts		280	9.9
GLUTANO	Crackers		150, 300	5.3, 10.6
	Cracker Bread		275	9.7
	Crisp Bread		125	4.4
	Sesame Cracker		50	1.8
	Swedish Crisp Rolls		200	7
GLUTINO	**Bread Sticks**	Sesame*, Pizza Flavored*	150	5.3
	Crackers ("Ritz" Style)		150	5.3
	Flax Crackers	Apple & Raisin*, Banana*, Original*, Tomato & Onion*	230	8.1
	Rusks		125	4.4
	*Dairy-Free.			
HOL•GRAIN	**Brown Rice Crackers**	Lightly Salted, Lightly Salted Onion & Garlic, Lightly Salted Sesame, Unsalted	127	4.5
	Organic Brown Rice Crackers	Sea Salt	127	4.5
MARY'S GONE CRACKERS	**Organic Crackers**	Original, Black Pepper, Caraway, Herb, Onion	184	6.5
ORGRAN	**Crispbreads***	Corn, Rice, Rice & Cracked Pepper, Rice & Garden Herb, Salsa Corn	200	7
	*Dairy-Free.			
PANNE RIZO	Crostini Toasts*		145	5.1
	*Dairy-Free.			
SAN-J	**Brown Rice Crackers**	Black Sesame, Sesame	100	3.5
		Tamari	80	2.8
SCHÄR	Bread Sticks (Grissini); Cracker Toast (Fette Croccanti); Pizzirilli Crackers		150	5.3
	Crackers		200	7
	Crispbread (Fette Biscottate)		250	8.8
	Salti Crackers		175	6.2

RICE CAKES – LARGE

Company	Rice Cakes - Large		Grams	Ounces
LUNDBERG	**Eco-Farmed Rice Cakes**	Apple Cinnamon, Buttery Caramel, Honey Nut	269	9.5
		Brown Rice, Brown Rice (Salt-Free), Wild Rice	241	8.5
		Sesame Tamari, Toasted Sesame	255	9.0
	Organic Brown Rice Cakes	Brown Rice, Brown Rice (Salt-Free), Mochi Sweet, Popcorn, Tamari Seaweed, Wild Rice	241	8.5
		Caramel Corn, Cinnamon Toast, Koku Sesame, Koku Seaweed	269	9.5
		Sesame Tamari	255	9.0
PLUM-M-GOOD	**Organic Rice Cakes**	Brown Rice (Salted), Brown Rice (Unsalted), Brown Rice Sesame (Salted), Brown Rice Sesame (Unsalted), Multigrain (Salted)* Multigrain (Unsalted)*	185	6.5
	Regular Rice Cakes		185	6.5
	*Made with brown rice, buckwheat, millet.			
QUAKER (CANADA)	Butter Popcorn, Cracker Jack, Original		127	4.5
	Caramel Corn		186	6.6
	Caramel Chocolate Chip		199	7
	Savory Tomato and Basil		173	6.1
	White Cheddar		140	4.9
QUAKER (USA)	Apple Cinnamon, Caramel Corn		185	6.5
	Butter Popcorn, Lightly Salted, Salt Free		127	4.5
	Chocolate Crunch		205	7.2
	Peanut Butter Chocolate Chip		207	7.3
	White Cheddar		140	4.9

RICE CAKES – MINI

Company	Rice Cakes - Mini		Grams	Ounces
HAIN	**Mini Munchies**	Apple Cinnamon, Plain, Ranch, Strawberry	113	4
QUAKER (CANADA)	**Crispy Mini Rice Chips**	BBQ, Caramel, Cheddar, Crunchy Dill, Ketchup, Salt & Vinegar, Sea Salt & Lime, Sour Cream & Chives	100	3.5
QUAKER (USA)	**Crispy Mini Quakes**	Apple Cinnamon, Cheddar Cheese, Caramel Corn, Chocolate, Creamy Ranch, Nacho, Sour Cream and Onion	various sizes	various sizes

Snacks

Candy, Chips, Nuts, Seeds, Pretzels

✦ Read labels carefully. **Many snack foods contain wheat, rye, oats or barley:** e.g., flavored tortilla chips, potato chips, soy nuts, snack bars.

Company	Snacks		Grams	Ounces
Barbara's Bakery	**Cheese Puffs**	Original (Natural)	30, 200	1, 7
		Original Bakes	155	5.5
		Jalapeño	200	7
		White Cheddar Bakes	155	5.5
Barkat	**Pretzels**	Plain, Sesame	75	2.7
	Pretzel Sticks		75	2.7
Candy Tree	**Licorice** (Black)	Bites, Rope, Vines	74	2.6
	Vines	Cherry, Strawberry	74	2.6
	Organic corn-based candy.			
Cheecha Krackles	**Puffed Chips**	Luscious Lime, Original, Sea Salt & Vinegar	70	2.5
	Unpuffed Chips (GF label only)		350	12.3
	Potato Pasta Chips. Note: Also make Puffed (Nacho Cheese) and Unpuffed (Regular Label) which contain wheat-flour and are **NOT** Gluten-Free.			
Dixie Diners' Club	**Soy Beanits™**	Lightly Salted, Unsalted	454	16
Ener-G Foods	Crisp Pretzels (low protein), Sesame Pretzel Rings		75	2.7
	Wylde Pretzels	Lightly Salted, Poppy Seed, Sesame	113, 227	4, 8
Glutino	Pretzels		75, 400	2.6, 14.1
Lundberg	**Rice Chips**	Fiesta Lime, Honey Dijon, Pico De Gallo, Santa Fe BBQ, Sea Salt, Sesame & Seaweed	170	6
Masuya	**Rice Sembei Snacks**	Original (Lightly Salted), Dijon Mustard*, Sun Dried Tomato, Tamari (Soy Sauce)*	28, 113	1, 4
	*Dairy-Free. Soy sauce is gluten-free.			
Mochi	**Bake & Serve Rice Puffs**	Original, Cashew-Date, Chocolate Brownie, Pizza, Raisin-Cinnamon, Sesame-Garlic, Super Seed	354	12.5
Nu-World Amaranth	**Amaranth Mini-Ridges**	Cheddar, Rosemary Basil, Sun-Dried Tomato Basil	142	5
	Amaranth Snackers	BBQ Hot & Spicy, BBQ Sweet & Sassy, Chili Lime, French Onion, Garden Burst	170	6

Company	Snacks		Grams	Ounces
PHILLY SWIRL	**Original Italian Ice Swirls*** (cups)	Banana Berry, Cotton Candy, Hurricane, Paradise Punch, Rainbow, Sunburst	118 mL	4
	Swirl Stix* (14/box)	Banana Split, Cotton Candy, Orange Dream, Paradise Punch, Rainbow, Razzle Dazzle	728 mL	24.5
	Sugar-Free Swirl Stix* (12/box)	Cotton Candy, Hurricane, Orange Dream, Paradise Punch	624 mL	21
	Swirl Popperz* (8/box)	Cotton Candy, Cherry Melon, Orange Dream, Rainbow	712 mL	24
	*Dairy-Free.			
	Fudge Swirl Stix (12/box)	Fudge & Caramel, Fudge & Chocolate, Fudge & Vanilla	624 mL	21
	Fruit & Cream Stix	Berry & Vanilla, Cherry & Vanilla, Orange & Vanilla, Strawberry & Vanilla	356 mL	12
RUNNING RABBIT	**Licorice**	Black, Black Cherry, Lemon Honey, Raspberry	142	5
ST. CLAIRE'S ORGANIC	**Organic Licorice Sweets*** *Black Licorice		43, 227, 765	1.5, 8, 21
TERRA	Terra Chips Original (taro, sweet potato, yucca batata, parsnip, oils and salt)		28, 213	1, 7.5
	Terra Stix (Original)		227	8
	Taro Chip (Original Taro)		43, 170	1.5, 6
	Sweet Potato Chips (Original No Salt)		34, 170	1.2, 6

MISCELLANEOUS SNACKS

Company	Miscellaneous Snacks	Grams	Ounces
BARKAT	Ice Cream Cones (24)	120	4.2
	Waffle Ice Cream Cones	120	4.2
ENER-G FOODS	Communion Wafers (40/box)	40	1.4
	Made with "Soyquick" and rice flour.		

BAKING MIXES

Company	Baking Mixes		Grams	Ounces
1-2-3 GLUTEN-FREE	Chocolate Cake Mix*		727	25.6
	Cookies	Chewy Chipless Scrumdelicious Cookie Mix*	680	24
		Lindsay's Lipsmakin' Roll-Out Sugar Cookies*	612	21.6
	Aaron's Favorite Rolls*		400	14.1
	Allie's Awesome Buckwheat Pancakes*		680	24
	Devilishly Decadent Brownies*		866	30.6
	Flour Mix*		680	24
	Meredith's Marvelous Muffin/Quickbread*		467	16.5
	Pouncakes	Delightfully Gratifying Pouncake*	1.1 kg	38.7
		Peri's Perfect Chocolate Pouncake*	1.1 kg	38.1
	Southern Glory Biscuits*		503	17.8
	Sweet Goodness Pan Bars*		581	20.5
	*Dairy-Free.			
AMAZING GRAINS	All-Purpose Baking Flour Blend		680, 1.8 kg	24, 64
ARROWHEAD MILLS	Gluten-Free Chocolate Chip Cookie Mix*		366	12.9
	Gluten-Free All-Purpose Baking Mix*		794	28
	Gluten-Free Brownie Mix*		496	17.5
	Gluten-Free Pancake and Baking Mix		794	28
	Gluten-Free Pancake and Waffle Mix (Wild Rice)		907	32
	Gluten-Free Pizza Crust Mix		514	18.2
	Gluten-Free Vanilla Cake Mix		592	20.9
	*Dairy-Free.			
AUNT CANDICE	Chunky Chocolate Brownie Mix		454	16
	Old Fashioned Pancake Mix		680	24
	Roll Out Sugar Cookie Mix		454	16
	Casein, Corn & Soy-Free.			
AUTHENTIC FOODS	Bette's Gourmet Featherlight Rice Flour Blend*		1.36 kg	3 lbs.
	Bette's Gourmet Four Flour Blend*		1.36 kg	3 lbs.
	Bread Mixes	Cinnamon*, White* Corn	567 NA	20 NA
	Cake Mixes	Chocolate*, Lemon*,	312	11
		Vanilla*	341	12
	Falafel Mix*		567	20
	Muffin Mixes	Blueberry*, Cranberry*	454	16
		Chocolate Chip*	482	17
	Multi Blend Gluten-Free Flour*		1.36 kg	3 lb.
	Pancake Mix*		567 g, 3.18 kg	20 oz., 7 lbs.
	Pie Crust Mix*		341	12
	Pizza Crust Mix*		567	20
	*Dairy-Free.			

Company	Baking Mixes		Grams	Ounces
BARKAT	Bread Mix*		500	17.6
	Rustic Bread Mix*		1 kg	35.3
	*Dairy-Free.			
BOB'S RED MILL	All-Purpose GF Baking Flour		624	22
	GF Brownie Mix		595	21
	GF Chocolate Cake Mix		624	22
	GF Chocolate Chip Cookie Mix		680	24
	GF Pancake Mix		623	22
	Homemade Wonderful GF Bread Mix		454	16
	Wheat Free Biscuit and Baking Mix (GF)		680	24
BREAD'S FROM ANNA	Bread Mix (Rice & Soy Free)		588	20.8
	Bread Mix (Corn, Dairy, Rice & Soy Free)		535	18.1
	Bread Mix (Corn, Dairy, Rice, Soy & Yeast Free)		535	18.1
	Banana Bread Mix (Corn, Dairy, Rice, Soy & Yeast Free)		397	14
	Pie Crust Mix (Corn, Dairy, Rice, Soy & Yeast Free)		265	9.4
	Pumpkin Bread Mix (Corn, Dairy, Rice, Soy, Yeast Free)		680	24
'CAUSE YOU'RE SPECIAL!	**Biscuit Mixes**	Large	510	18
		Economy	1.02 kg	36
	Bread Mixes	Traditional French	595	21
		Cinnamon Raisin	737	26
		Homestyle White	595	21
		Mock Rye	609	21.5
	Cake Mixes	Chocolate Pound	541	19.1
		Golden Pound	553	19.5
		Moist Lemon – Small	419	14.8
		Moist Lemon – Large	839	29.6
		Moist Yellow – Small	419	14.8
		Moist Yellow – Large	839	29.6
		Old Fashioned Spice Cake	425	15
		Rich Chocolate – Small	397	14
		Rich Chocolate – Large	794	28
	Cookie Mixes	Chocolate Fudge Brownie	519	18.3
		Chocolate Chip	428	15.1
		Classic Sugar	360	12.7
	Muffin Mixes	Classic Muffin and Quickbread	394	13.9
		Lemon Poppyseed	396	13.9
		Sweet Corn Muffin	425	15
	Scone Mixes	Large	638	22.5
		Economy	1.28 kg	45
	Pancake and Waffle Mixes	Regular	553	19.5
		Economy	1.11 kg	39
	Pie Crust Mix		221	7.8
	Pizza Crust Mix		368	13
	All products are Casein-Free.			

Company	Baking Mixes		Grams	Ounces
CELIMIX (NELSON DAVID OF CANADA)	Apple Cinnamon Cake and Muffin Mix*		415	14.6
	Batter Coating Mix		240	8.5
	Bread Mixes	Flax Bread*, Potato Bread*, Rice Bread*, White Bread*	2 kg	4.4 lbs.
	Cake Mixes	Dutch Chocolate Supreme*	350	12.3
		White*	415	14.6
	Carob Cake & Loaf Mix*		415	14.6
	Cookie Mixes	Regular	300	10.6
		Shortbread*	170	6
	Dinner Roll Mix*		190	6.7
	Dutch Chocolate Supreme Brownie Mix*		400	14.1
	Hamburger Bun Mix*		190	6.7
	Lemon Loaf & Cake Mix*		415	14.6
	Muffin Mix*		430	15.2
	Pancake Mix	Regular*, Brown Rice*	600	21.2
	Pastry Mix		900	1.98 lbs.
	Pizza Crust Mix		350	12.3
	Tea Biscuit Mix		420	14.8
	Yorkshire Pudding Mix		300	10.6
	*Dairy-Free.			
CHEBE	**Bread Mixes**	Original	213 g, 2.5 kg	7.5 oz., 5.5 lbs.
		All-Purpose Dairy-Free*	213	7.5
		Focaccia Italian Flatbread*	213	7.5
	Cinnamon Roll-Up Mix*		213	7.5
	Garlic Onion Bread Sticks Mix*		213	7.5
	Pizza Crust Mix*		213	7.5
	*Casein-Free.			
DIETARY SPECIALTIES	**Bread Mixes**	Apple, Banana	598	21.1
		White	500	17.6
	Brownie Mix		680	24
	Cake Mixes	Chocolate	740	26.1
		White	750	26.4
	Cornbread Mix		530	18.7
	Muffin Mixes	Blueberry	567	20
		Bran	480	16.9
	Pancake Mix		485	17.1
	All mixes are Casein-Free.			
DOWD & ROGERS	**Cake Mixes**	Dark Vanilla, Dutch Chocolate Golden Lemon	408	14
EL PETO	All-Purpose Flour Mix (Regular*, Corn/Soy Free*)		500g, 1 kg, 2.5, 10, 20 kg	17.5, 35 oz., 5.5, 22 & 44 lbs.
	Bread Maker Mixes	Brown Rice*, White Rice*	350, 700 g,	12, 24.5
		Italian, Potato*	2.45 kg	5.4 lbs.
	Brownie Mix*		500	17.5
	Cake Mixes	Chocolate*, Lemon*, White*	500 g, 1 kg	17.5 oz., 2.2 lbs.
		Marble*	500	17.5
	*Dairy-Free. Brownie, Cake, Muffin and Pancake Mixes also available in Corn-Free formulations.			

Company	Baking Mixes		Grams	Ounces
EL PETO	Old Fashioned Cookie Mix*		750	26.5
	Muffin Mix*		500 g 1, 2.5 & 10 kg	17.5 oz., 2.2, 5.5 & 22 lbs.
	Pancake Mix*		500 g 1, 2.5 & 10 kg	17.5 oz. 2.2, 5.5 & 22 lbs.
	Perfect Pie Dough Mix*		500	17.5
	*Dairy-Free. Muffin and Pancake Mixes also available in Corn-Free formulations.			
ENER-G FOODS	Corn Mix		454	16
	GF Gourmet Blend		451	15.9
	Potato Mix (low protein), Rice Mix		567	20
GIFTS OF NATURE	All-Purpose Flour Blend		680 g, 1.36 kg, 4.54 kg	24 & 48 oz., 10 lbs.
	Bread Mixes	Buttermilk Cornbread	595	21
		French Bread & Pizza Crust	595 g, 4.67 kg	21 oz., 10.5 lbs.
		Sandwich White Bread and Roll	624 g, 5 kg	22 oz., 11 lbs.
	Buttermilk Biscuit & Baking Mix		539 g, 1.11 kg	19, 39
	Buttermilk Pancake & Waffle Mix		624 g, 1.25 kg, 5 kg	22 & 44 oz., 11 lb.
	Cake Mixes	Chocolate, Yellow	765	27
	Cookie Mixes	Fancy	482	17
		Triple Treat	850	30
	Fudge Brownie Mix		595	21
	Muffin Mixes	Basic	510 g, 1.53 kg	18, 54
		Cinnamon Spice, Vanilla Poppyseed	595	21
GILLIAN'S FOODS	Cinnamon Bread/Roll Mix*		454	16
	French Roll Mix*		454	16
	Pizza Dough Mix*		454	16
	*Dairy-Free.			
GLUTAFIN	**GFWF Mixes**	Bread*, Fibre Bread*, Cake*, Fibre**, Pastry*, White All-Purpose**	500	17.6
	*Enriched with vitamins and minerals. **Enriched with calcium.			
GLUTANO	**Mixes**	Bread & Cake, High Fibre Bread	500	17.6
		Flour Mix (for bread & cake)	750	26.5
GLUTEN-FREE COOKIE JAR	**Bread Mixes**	Primo White*	400	14.0
	Bread/Muffin Mixes	Banana*	590	20.8
		Blueberry*	450	16.0
		Corn*	500	17.6
		Pumpkin*	550	19.4
		Strawberry*	495	17.6
	Bagel/Soft Pretzel Mix*		830	29.4
	Scone Mix		330	11.6
	*Dairy-Free.			

Company	Baking Mixes		Grams	Ounces
Gluten-Free Cookie Jar	Donut & Donut Hole Mix*		570	20.2
	Buttermilk Pancake Mix		575	20.4
	Brownie Mix*		720	25.2
	Cake Mixes	Chocolate*	780	27.6
		Orange*, White*	905	32.0
	Cookie Mixes	Chocolate Chip*	455	16.0
		Italian Ricotta Cheese	885	31.4
		Orange*	975	34.4
		Peanut Butter*	735	26.0
		Pumpkin*	975	34.4
		Brown Sugar Wafer*	735	26.0
		Cookie Jar Cut-Outs*	720	25.2
	*Dairy-Free.			
Gluten-Free Creations	**Bread Mixes**	Almond, Flax, Rye	454	16
		Hi Power Multigrain	595	21
	Muffin Mix	Blueberry	595	21
	Perfect Mix		539	19
Gluten-Free Pantry	**Bread Mixes**	Bagel, Breadstick & Pretzel*	454	16
		Country French Bread and Pizza*	624 g, 2.27, 11.35 kg	22 oz., 5, 25 lb.
		Dairy-Free Sandwich Bread*	539	19
		Delicious Slicing Bread	482	17
		Favorite Sandwich Bread	624 g, 2.27, 11.35 kg	22 oz., 5, 25 lb.
		Light Rye-Style Bread	624	22
		Multi-Grain Bread with Seeds*	638	22.5
		Tapioca Bread*	624	22
		Tom's Light Bread*	428 g, 11.35 kg	15.1 oz., 25 lb.
		Whole Grain Bread*	500	17.6
	Quick Bread, Scone & Pancake Mixes	Apple Spice Quick Bread*	397	14
		Banana Quick Bread*	397	14
		Blueberry Buckwheat Muffin & Pancake*	425	15
		Bran Muffin*	397	14
		Buttermilk Brown Rice Pancake	454	16
		Cranberry Orange Bread & Muffin*	510	18
		Harvest Pumpkin Bread*	397	14
		Lemon Poppyseed Quick Bread*	397	14
		Muffin, Scone & Quick Bread*	425 g, 2.27, 11.35 kg	15 oz., 5, 25 lb.
		Quick Mix*	454	16
		Yankee Cornbread & Muffin*	340	12
	Dessert Mixes	Almond Orange Biscotti*	425	15
		Angel Food Cake*	454 g, 11.35 kg	16 oz., 25 lb.
		Chocolate Chip Cookie & Square*	539 g, 2.27, 11.35 kg	19 oz., 5, 25 lb.
		*Dairy-Free.		

Company	Baking Mixes		Grams	Ounces
GLUTEN-FREE PANTRY	**Dessert Mixes**	Chocolate Truffle Brownie*	737 g, 2.27, 11.35 kg	26 oz., 5, 25 lb.
		Coffee Cake*	595	21
		Crisp & Crumble Topping*	340	12
		Danielle's Decadent Chocolate Cake*	425 g, 2.27, 11.35 kg	15 oz., 5, 25 lb.
		Old Fashioned Cake & Cookie*	425 g, 2.27, 11.35 kg	15 oz., 5, 25 lb.
		Perfect Pie Crust*	454	16
		Spice Cake & Gingerbread*	397 g, 11.35 kg	14 oz., 25 lb.
	*Dairy-Free.			
GLUTINO	All-Purpose Corn Mix		1 kg	35.3
	All-Purpose Rice Mix		1 kg	35.3
	Cake Mixes	Dutch Chocolate, White	375	13.2
	Muffin Mix		500	17.6
	Pancake Mix		575	20.3
	Pie Crust Mix		1 kg	35.3
GRAIN PROCESS ENTERPRISES	Gluten-Free Bean Flour Bread Mix		2.5, 10 kg	5.5, 22 lbs.
	Grain Pro Rice Loaf Mix		2.5, 10 kg	5.5, 22 lbs.
HEARTLAND'S FINEST	Gluten-Free Baking Blend		454 & 908 g, 2.27 kg	1, 2 & 5 lb.
HODGSON MILL	Apple Cinnamon Muffin Mix		216	7.6
	Multi Purpose Baking Mix		340	12
	Made with millet, brown rice and garbanzo bean flours.			
HOL•GRAIN	**Mixes**	Chocolate Brownie, Chocolate Chip Cookie, Pancake & Waffle	454	16
KAYBEE	Basic Bread Mix		520	18.3
	Basic Cookie Mix		370	13.1
	Basic Muffin Mix		375	13.2
	Chocolate Brownie Mix		360	12.7
	Corn Bread Mix		240	8.5
	Cottage Pudding		270	9.5
	Deluxe Pancake Mix		360	12.7
	No-Knead Bun Mix		320	11.3
	Pizza Crust Mix		245	8.6
	Pyrogy Dough Mix		230	8.1
	Super Easy Cake Mix		260	9.2
	Wild Rice Pancake Mix		370	13
KINGSMILL	Rice Bread and Baking Mix		800	28.2
	Rice Cake and Cookie Mix		600	21.2
	Mixes available in bulk.			
KINNIKINNICK	**Kinni-Kwik Mixes***			
	Bread & Buns	Plain, Sunflower & Flax	1000	35.5
	Regular Mixes Breads	Candadi Yeast Free Rice, Tapioca Rice, White Rice, Yeast Free Brown Rice	650	23
	All mixes are Casein-Free. *Kinnni-Kwik mixes require only the addition of water.			

Company	Baking Mixes		Grams	Ounces
KINNIKINNICK	**Cake Mixes**	Angel Food	450	16
		Chocolate, Lemon, Sponge, White	500	18
	Cookie Mixes		650	23
	Miscellaneous	All-Purpose Celiac Flour	1000	35.5
		All-Purpose Mix	650	23
		Easy White Fibre Mix	250	9
	Muffin Mix	Cornbread & Muffin, Regular	650	23
	Pancake Mix		650	23
	Pastry & Pie Crust Mix		650	23
	Pizza Crust Mix		650	23
	All mixes are Casein-Free.			
KOKIMO KITCHEN	Chocolate Cake Mix*		640	22.6
	*Dairy-Free.			
LAUREL'S SWEET TREATS	Baking Flour Mix		454 g, 2.2 kg	16 oz., 5 lb.
	Bread Mixes	Banzo Bread	454	16
		Good Ol' Corn Bread	425	15
	Cake Mixes	Cameron's Vanilla	425, 850	15. 30
		Cinnamon Spice	425, 850	15, 30
		Mom's Chocolate	354, 709	12.5, 25
	Chocolate Dream Brownie Mix		553	19.5
	Cookie Mixes	Chocolate Chip	850	30
		Double Chocolate Chip	850	30
		Roll 'Em Out Sugar	652	23
	Dinner Roll Mix		567	20
	Honey Grahamless Crackers		454	16
	Pancake Mix		539 g, 2.2 kg	19 oz., 5 lb.
	Pizza Dough Mix		340	12
	All mixes are Casein-Free.			
MANISCHEWITZ	Homestyle Potato Latke Mix		170	6
	Mini Potato Knish Mix		170	6
	Potato Kugel Mix		170	6
	Potato Pancake Mix		85, 170	3, 6
	Sweet Potato Pancake Mix		170	6
MARLENE'S MIXES	Bun Mix*		312	11
	Biscuit Mix*, Fluffy Biscuit Mix		198	7
	Bread Mixes	Corn Bread*	280	10
		No Corn Bread*	340	12
		Egg Bread*	280	10
		Multi Blend Bread*	581	20.5
		Tapioca Rice Bread*	510	18
	Brownie Mixes	Butterscotch*	624	22
		Chocolate*	326	11.5
	Cake Mixes	Funnel*	280	10
		Yellow*	326	11.5
	Cinnamon Struesel Breakfast Bars*		510	18
	Dressing/Stuffing Mix*		184	6.5
	Hushpuppies Mix*		312	11
	Pancake/Waffle Mix*		227	8
	Pie Crust Mix*		312	11
	*Dairy-Free.			

Company	Baking Mixes		Grams	Ounces
MARLENE'S MIXES	Pumpkin Roll Mix*		340	12
	Rice Muffin Mix*		340	12
	Snack Crackers Mix*		340	12
	Spice Mixes*	Meat Loaf, Swiss Steak, Vegetarian Chili	30	1
		Roast Chicken	35	1.25
	*Dairy-Free.			
MICAH'S FAVOURITE	Brownie Mix*		700	24.7
	Chocolate Cake Mix*		886	31.3
	General All-Purpose Mix**		908	32
	Soy-Free Specialty Mix*		700	24.7
	*Corn, Egg, Dairy, Nut & Soy-Free. **Corn, Egg, Dairy & Nut-Free.			
MISS ROBEN'S	Bagel Mix*		672	24
	Biscuit Mix*		364	13
	Bread Mixes	Andi Wunderbread*	588	21
		Dinner*, French*	392	14
		Homestyle*	386	14
		Noah's*	456	16.3
		Potato*	532	19
		Traditional Cornbread*	420	15
		White Sandwich*	588	21
	Cake-Like Doughnut Mix*		868	31
	Cake Mixes	One Step Angel Food*	336	12
		Carrot*	616	22
		Chocolate*, Gingerbread*	588	21
		Pound*	532	19
		White*	812	29
		Yellow*	672	24
	Chewy Brownie Mix*		423	14.9
	Cookie Mixes	Animal*	364	13
		Crunchy Chocolate Chip*	840	30
		Crunchy Chocolate Sugar*	476	17
		Crunchy Sugar*	476	17
		Crunchy Versatile*	700	25
		Mock Graham Cracker*	364	13
		Mock Oatmeal Raisin*	840	30
		Roll & Cut Gingerbread*	588	21
		Roll & Cut Sugar*	532	19
		Soy-Free Chocolate Chip*	840	30
	Frosting Mixes	Double Chocolate Fudge*	537	19.2
		Milk Chocolate Buttercream*	599	21.4
		Vanilla Buttercream*	621	22.2
	Ice Cream Mixes	Chocolate FreeZ*	448	16
		Versatile FreeZ*	305	10.9
	Mock Goldfish Cracker Mix*		538	19.2
	Muffin Mixes	Blueberry*	756	27
		English Muffin*	392	14
		Versatile*	784	28
	Pancake & Waffle Mix*		336	12
	Pie Crust Mix*		308	11
	*Dairy-Free.			

Company	Baking Mixes		Grams	Ounces
MISS ROBEN'S	**Pizza Crust Mixes**	Corn Free*	409	14.6
		Small (12")*	336	12
		Large (18")*	504	18
	Popover or Pastry Mix*		174	6.2
	Soft Pretzel Mix		364	13
	Tortilla Mix*		409	14.6
	*Dairy-Free.			
MONA'S GLUTEN-FREE	**Bread Mixes**	French Bread*	605	21.3
		Golden Goddess Bread*	650	22.9
		Milk and Honey Brown Bread	600	21.2
	Happy Day Cake Mix*		685	24.2
	Mona's Bread, Roll & Pastry Mix		600	21.2
	Multi Mix*		680	24
	Pancake & Waffle Mix*		385	13.6
	Sunny Bun & Pizza Mix*		410	14.5
	*Casein-Free. All mixes are Corn & Soy-Free. Mixes also available in 5 lbs. (2.27 kg) and 10 lbs. (4.54 kg).			
NAMASTE FOODS	Blondies Mix		907	32
	Bread Mix		454	16
	Cake Mixes	Chocolate	822	29
		Spice Carrot	737	26
		Vanilla	765	27
	Cookie Mix		624	22
	Fudge Brownie Mix		907	32
	Muffin Mix	Regular	454	16
		Sugar-Free	397	14
	Pizza Crust Mix		765	27
	Waffle/Pancake Mix		680	24
	All mixes are Dairy, Corn, Potato & Soy-Free. Also available in bulk.			
NATURAL FOOD MILL BAKERY	Baking Mix (All-Purpose)		900	31.7
ORGRAN	**Bread Mixes**	GF Bread, Gourmet Pesto	450	15.9
	Cake Mixes	Chocolate, Vanilla	375	13.2
	Chocolate Mousse Mix		120	4.2
	Custard Powder Mix		200	7
	Falafel Mix		200	7
	Flour Mixes	Plain All-Purpose, Self-Raising Flour	500	17.6
	Gluten-Free Gluten Substitute		120	4.2
	Muffin Mixes	Chocolate, Lemon, Poppyseed	375	13.2
	No Egg-Egg Replacer		200	7
	Pancake Mixes	Apple & Cinnamon, Buckwheat	375	13.2
		Sorghum	250	8.8
	Pasta Flour		375	13.2
	Pizza & Pastry Multi Mix		375	13.2
	All mixes are Dairy-Free.			
PAMELA'S PRODUCTS	Amazing Bread Mix*		539	19
	Incredible Chocolate Chunk Cookie Mix*		386	13.6
	Irresistible Chocolate Brownie Mix*		454	16
	*Dairy-Free.			

Company	Baking Mixes		Grams	Ounces
PAMELA'S PRODUCTS	Luscious Chocolate Cake Mix*		595	21
	Ultimate Baking & Pancake Mix		680 g, 1.81 kg	24 oz., 4 lb.
	*Dairy-Free.			
PANNE RIZO	Classic White Cake Mix*		600	21.2
	Gluten-Free Flour Mix*		908 g, 2.27 kg	2 lb., 5 lb.
	Pizza Crust Mix*		300	10.5
	*Dairy-Free.			
THE REALLY GREAT FOOD COMPANY	**Biscuit Mixes**	Old Time	425	15
		Spinach & Cheese	284	10
	Bread Mixes	Biscuit Loaf	496	17.5
		Brown Rice Bread	595	21
		Old Fashioned Cinnamon Bread	567	20
		Dark European Bread	595	21
		French Bread/Country Farm Bread	369	13
		Home-Style Cornbread	794	28
		Irish Soda Bread	709	25
		Original White Bread	567	20
		Rye-Style Bread	539	19
		Zesty Cornbread	794	28
	Muffin Mixes	Apple Spice, Cornbread	369	13
		English Muffin	397	14
		Maple Raisin, Sweet Muffin	369	13
		Vanilla	340	12
	Pancake Mixes	Brown Rice Flour, Classic	454 g, 1.28 kg	16, 45
	Pizza Crust Mix		454	16
	Flaky Pie Crust Mix		369	13
	Cake Mixes	Aunt Tootsie's Brownie	595	21
		Aunt Tootsie's Devil's Food Cake	650	23
		Banana Bread	539	19
		Chocolate	650	23
		Coffee Crumb Cake	567	20
		Colonial Spice	709	25
		Gingerbread	539	19
		Grandma's Pound	567	20
		Lemon Poppy, Orange, Yellow	650	23
		Pineapple	567	20
		Pumpkin Bread	539	19
		White	397	14
		Yellow	650	23
	Cookie Mixes	Anise Biscotti	425	15
		Butter	425	15
		Chocolate Crinkle	454	16
		Cinnamon	425	15
		Lemon	567	20
		Lemon Poppyseed Biscotti	425	15
		Versatile	425 g, 1.28 kg	15, 45
	All mixes are Dairy-Free.			

Company	Baking Mixes		Grams	Ounces
THE RUBY RANGE	All-Purpose Mix		454, 908	1, 5 lbs.
	Cake or	Double Chocolate Truffle	295	10.4
	Cupcakes	Spice	309	10.9
	Old Fashioned Cookies		360	12.7
	Southwestern Pancakes		261	9.2
SCHÄR	Bread Mix (Mix B)		1 kg	2.2 lbs.
	Cake Mix (Margherita) (Mix A)		500	17.6
	Pastry Mix (Mix C)		1 kg	2.2 lbs.
Shiloh Farms	Bread & Pizza Crust Mix		482	17
	Cake & Muffin Mix		567	20
	Pancake & Waffle Mix		425	15
STERK'S BAKERY	All-Purpose Flour Mix		908 g, 2.27, 4.54 kg	2, 5, 10 lbs.
	Brownie Mix		475	16.8
	Cake Mixes	Banana, Carrot	650	23
		Chocolate, Lemon	400	14.1
	Pancake Mix		1, 2 kg	2.2, 4.4 lb.
SYLVAN BORDER FARM	Bread Mix, Bread Mix (Non-Dairy)*, Classic Dark Bread Mix		454	16
	Chocolate Cake Mix		794	28
	General Purpose Flour*		908	2 lb.
	Pancake & Waffle Mix*		340	12
	Lemon Cake Mix*		757	26.7
	*Dairy-Free.			
TOM SAWYER	All-Purpose Gluten-Free Flour		680 g, 2.27 kg	24 oz., 5 lb.

FLOURS

- ✦ Some "wheat-free" flours (e.g., kamut and spelt) are **NOT** gluten-free.
- ✦ Some buckwheat mixes contain **wheat flour and buckwheat flour**.
- ✦ When purchasing bulk-bagged gluten-free flours be aware of the possibility of cross-contamination with other gluten-containing flours. Ask the store what procedures they use when bagging their various flours.
- ✦ A variety of gluten-free all-purpose flour mixes and flours are listed below and on the following pages. Each flour has unique properties, therefore follow recipes closely!

All-Purpose Flour Mixes

1-2-3 GLUTEN-FREE
- ✦ **Flour Mix**
  – white rice flour, tapioca flour, potato starch, xanthan gum

AMAZING GRAINS
- ✦ **Montina™ All-Purpose Baking Flour Blend**
  – white rice flour, tapioca starch flour and Montina™ Pure Flour

All-Purpose Flour Mixes CONT'D.

AUTHENTIC FOODS

- **Bette's Gourmet Featherlight Rice Flour Blend**
  – white rice flour, tapioca flour, cornstarch, potato flour
- **Bette's Gourmet Four Flour Blend**
  – garfava flour, sorghum flour, corn flour, cornstarch, tapioca flour
- **Multi Blend Gluten-Free Flour**
  – brown rice flour, sweet rice flour, tapioca flour, corn starch, xanthan gum

BOB'S RED MILL

- **GF All-Purpose Baking Flour**
  – garbanzo flour, potato starch, tapioca flour, sorghum flour, fava bean flour

EL PETO

- **All-Purpose Flour Mix**
  – cornstarch, white rice flour, xanthan and/or guar gum
- **All-Purpose Flour Mix (Corn-Free/Soy-Free)**
  – potato starch, white rice flour, xanthan and/or guar gum

ENER-G FOODS

- **Gluten-Free Gourmet Blend**
  – white rice flour, potato starch, tapioca starch

GIFTS OF NATURE

- **All-Purpose Flour Blend**
  – brown rice flour, potato starch flour, white rice flour, Montina™ pure, sweet rice flour, tapioca flour, xanthan gum

GLUTAFIN

- **Gluten-Free Wheat-Free All-Purpose Mix**
  – maize starch, potato starch, powdered cellulose, whey protein concentrate, modified maize starch, rice flour, modified tapioca starch, dried glucose syrup, soya flour, guar & xanthan gums, hydroxymethylcellulose, salt, tricalcium phosphate

GLUTANO

- **Flour Mix**
  – rice flour, pre-gelatinized rice flour, maize flour, mono and diglycerides, guar gum

GLUTEN-FREE PANTRY

- **All-Purpose Sugar-Free Baking Mix**
  – buckwheat flour, soy flour, potato starch, white rice flour, tapioca starch, guar gum, salt
- **Beth's All-Purpose Gluten-Free Baking Flour**
  – rice flour, potato starch, tapioca starch, guar gum, salt

HEARTLAND'S FINEST

- **Gluten-Free Baking Blend**
  – white rice flour, sweet rice flour, tapioca starch, navy bean flour

HODGSON MILL

- **Multi Purpose Baking Mix**
  – whole grain millet flour, whole grain garbanzo flour, whole grain brown rice flour, xanthan gum

KINNIKINNICK

- **All-Purpose Celiac Flour**
  – white rice flour, potato starch, tapioca starch, sodium carboxymethylcellulose, guar gum
- **All-Purpose Mix**
  – white rice flour, tapioca starch, sugar, fructooligosaccharide, gluco delta lactone, dextrose, whole egg powder, sodium bicarbonate, egg white powder, pea fiber, soy lecithin, sodium carboxymethylcellulose, pea protein, fructose

All-Purpose Flour Mixes CONT'D.

LAUREL'S SWEET TREATS

- **Gluten-Free Baking Flour Mix**
  – white rice flour, potato starch, tapioca flour

MICAH'S FAVOURITE

- **General All-Purpose Mix**
  – potato starch, whole grain rice flour, tapioca starch, low fat soy flour, garbanzo bean flour

---

MISS ROBEN'S

- **Bette Hagman's Original Flour Mix**
  – white rice flour, potato starch, tapioca starch

MONA'S GLUTEN-FREE

- **Multi Mix**
  – organic brown rice flour, white rice flour, potato starch, tapioca starch, sorghum flour, xanthan gum

---

NATURAL FOOD MILL BAKERY

- **Baking Mix (All-Purpose)**
  – flaked corn, soy flakes, organic millet meal, organic sunflower seeds, flax meal, garfava flour

---

ORGRAN

- **Plain All-Purpose Flour Mix**
  – maize starch, tapioca flour, rice flour, guar gum, methylcellulose
- **Self-Raising Flour**
  – maize starch, tapioca flour, rice flour, glucono delta lactone, sodium bicarbonate, guar gum
- **Gluten-Free Gluten Substitute**
  – superfine rice flour, pea extract, maize starch, potato starch, guar gum, methylcellulose, carboxmethylcellulose, monoglycerides

---

PANNE RIZO

- **Gluten-Free Flour**
  – white rice flour, potato starch, tapioca flour

THE REALLY GREAT FOOD COMPANY

- **All-Purpose Rice Flour Mix**
  – white rice flour, potato starch, cornstarch, xanthan gum

THE RUBY RANGE

- **All-Purpose Mix**
  – rice flour, mesquite meal, potato starch flour, teff flour, tapioca flour, baking powder, baking soda, salt

---

STERK'S BAKERY

- **All-Purpose Flour Mix**
  – brown rice flour, corn flour, guar gum

SYLVAN BORDER FARM

- **General Purpose Flour Mix**
  – potato starch, white rice flour, brown rice flour, amaranth flour, quinoa flour, white cornmeal, garbanzo bean flour, soy flour

---

TOM SAWYER

- **All-Purpose Gluten-Free Flour**
  – white rice, sweet rice and tapioca flours, xanthan gum and gelatin

---

Bean, Chickpea, Lentil and Pea Flours

BEANS 'R US BEAN FLOUR (navy beans, black-eyed peas, soybeans)
- Gluten-Free Pantry

BETTE'S GOURMET FOUR FLOUR BLEND (garfava flour, sorghum flour, cornstarch, tapioca starch)
- Authentic Foods
- Miss Roben's

BLACK BEAN FLOUR
- Bob's Red Mill

CHICKPEA FLOUR (garbanzo bean flour)
- Authentic Foods
- Bob's Red Mill
- Gluten-Free Pantry
- Glutino
- Grain Process Enterprises Ltd.
- Miss Roben's
- Northern Quinoa Corporation

EASY WHITE FIBRE MIX (pea fibre, inulin, cellulose)
- Kinnikinnick

GARBANZO BEAN FLOUR (see chickpea flour)

GARBANZO BEAN FLOUR AND FAVA BEAN FLOUR
- Authentic Foods (developed original mixture called "Garfava Flour")
- Bob's Red Mill
- El Peto
- Grain Process Enterprises Ltd.
- Miss Roben's ("Garfava")

GREEN LENTIL FLOUR
- Northern Quinoa Corporation

GREEN PEA FLOUR
- Bob's Red Mill
- Northern Quinoa Corporation

NAVY BEAN FLOUR
- Heartland's Finest

PEA HULL FIBRE
- Kinnikinnick

PINTO BEAN FLOUR
- Heartland's Finest

ROMANO BEAN FLOUR (cranberry bean or whole bean)
- El Peto
- Glutino
- Grain Process Enterprises Ltd.

WHITE BEAN FLOUR
- Bob's Red Mill

YELLOW PEA FLOUR
- Northern Quinoa Corporation

Flours

Almond Flour
- Authentic Foods
- Bob's Red Mill
- Gluten-Free Pantry
- Grain Process Enterprises Ltd.
- Miss Roben's
- Mona's Gluten-Free
- Shiloh Farms

Amaranth Flour
- Arrowhead Mills
- Bob's Red Mill
- El Peto
- Glutino
- Grain Process Enterprises Ltd.
- Miss Roben's
- Native Seeds
- Northern Quinoa Corporation
- Nu-World Amaranth/Nu-World Foods (also carry Toasted Amaranth Bran Flour, Puffed Amaranth, Amaranth Pre-Gel Powder)

Arrowroot Starch
- Authentic Foods
- Bob's Red Mill
- El Peto
- Glutino
- Grain Process Enterprises Ltd.
- Miss Roben's
- Nelson David

Buckwheat Bran
- Minn-Dak Growers Ltd. – "Farinetta"

Buckwheat Flour
- Aliment Trigone Inc. (Cream of the Crop)
- Arrowhead Mills
- The Birkett Mills
- Bob's Red Mill
- Glutino
- Grain Process Enterprises Ltd.
- Hodgson Mill
- Minn-Dak Growers Ltd.
- Miss Roben's
- Nelson David
- Shiloh Farms

Chestnut Flour
- Dowd & Rogers

Corn Bran
- Glutino
- Grain Process Enterprises Ltd.

Corn Flour
- Authentic Foods
- Bob's Red Mill
- El Peto
- Glutino
- Grain Process Enterprises Ltd.
- Kinnikinnick
- Nelson David
- Shiloh Farms

Cornmeal
- Arrowhead Mills
- El Peto
- Glutino
- Grain Process Enterprises Ltd.
- Hodgson Mill
- Kinnikinnick
- Native Seeds
- Shiloh Farms

Flax Seed Meal (Ground Flax)
- Bob's Red Mill
- CanMar Grain Products Ltd.
- El Peto
- Glutino
- Grain Process Enterprises Ltd.
- Hodgson Mill
- Miss Roben's
- Mona's Gluten-Free
- Nature's Path
- Nelson David
- Omega Nutrition ("Nutri-Flax")

Flours cont'd.

Hazelnut Flour

- Bob's Red Mill

Mesquite Flour

- Casa deFruta
- Cocina de Vega
- Native Seeds

Millet Flour

- Arrowhead Mills
- Bob's Red Mill
- El Peto
- Grain Process Enterprises Ltd.

Montina™ Flour

- Amazing Grains
- Miss Roben's

Potato Flour

- Authentic Foods
- Bob's Red Mill
- Club House
- El Peto
- Ener-G Foods
- Glutino
- Grain Process Enterprises Ltd.
- Miss Roben's
- Shiloh Farms

Potato Starch Flour

- Authentic Foods
- Bob's Red Mill
- 'Cause You're Special!
- El Peto
- Ener-G Foods
- Gluten-Free Cookie Jar
- Gluten-Free Pantry
- Glutino
- Grain Process Enterprises Ltd.
- Kinnikinnick
- Manischewitz
- Miss Roben's
- Mona's Gluten-Free
- Nelson David
- The Really Great Food Company

Quinoa Flour

- Ancient Harvest
- Bob's Red Mill
- El Peto
- Grain Process Enterprises Ltd.
- Miss Roben's
- Northern Quinoa Corporation – "NorQuin" brand
- Shiloh Farms

Rice Bran

- Bob's Red Mill
- El Peto
- Ener-G Foods
- Glutino
- Grain Process Enterprises Ltd.
- Kinnikinnick
- Shiloh Farms

Rice Flour (Brown)

- Arrowhead Mills
- Authentic Foods
- Bob's Red Mill
- El Peto
- Ener-G Foods
- Glutino
- Grain Process Enterprises Ltd.
- Hodgson Mill
- Kinnikinnick
- Lundberg Family Farms
- Miss Roben's
- Mona's Gluten-Free
- Nelson David
- The Really Great Food Company
- Shiloh Farms

Rice Flour (Sweet)

- Authentic Foods
- Bob's Red Mill
- El Peto
- Ener-G Foods
- Gluten-Free Pantry
- Grain Process Enterprises Ltd.

Flours cont'd.

Rice Flour (Sweet) cont'd.

- ✦ Kinnikinnick
- ✦ Miss Roben's
- ✦ Mona's Gluten-Free
- ✦ The Really Great Food Company

Rice Flour (White)

- ✦ Arrowhead Mills
- ✦ Authentic Foods
- ✦ Bob's Red Mill
- ✦ 'Cause You're Special!
- ✦ Club House
- ✦ Cybros
- ✦ El Peto
- ✦ Ener-G Foods
- ✦ Gluten-Free Cookie Jar
- ✦ Gluten-Free Pantry
- ✦ Glutino
- ✦ Grain Process Enterprises Ltd.
- ✦ Kinnikinnick
- ✦ Miss Roben's
- ✦ Mona's Gluten-Free
- ✦ Nelson David
- ✦ The Really Great Food Company

Rice Polish

- ✦ Ener-G Foods

Sorghum Flour

- ✦ Authentic Foods
- ✦ Bob's Red Mill
- ✦ El Peto
- ✦ Gluten-Free Pantry
- ✦ Grain Process Enterprises Ltd.
- ✦ Miss Roben's
- ✦ Mona's Gluten-Free
- ✦ Twin Valley Mills, LLC.

Soy Flour

- ✦ Arrowhead Mills
- ✦ Dixie Diners' Club
- ✦ Eden Foods
- ✦ El Peto
- ✦ Glutino
- ✦ Grain Process Enterprises Ltd.
- ✦ Hodgson Mill
- ✦ Kinnikinnick
- ✦ Miss Roben's
- ✦ Nelson David
- ✦ Shiloh Farms

Tapioca Starch Flour

- ✦ Authentic Foods
- ✦ Bob's Red Mill
- ✦ 'Cause You're Special!
- ✦ Cybros
- ✦ Edward & Son's Trading Co.
- ✦ El Peto
- ✦ Ener-G Foods
- ✦ Gluten-Free Cookie Jar
- ✦ Gluten-Free Pantry
- ✦ Glutino
- ✦ Grain Process Enterprises Ltd.
- ✦ Kinnikinnick
- ✦ Miss Roben's
- ✦ Mona's Gluten-Free
- ✦ Nelson David
- ✦ The Really Great Food Company
- ✦ Shiloh Farms

Teff Flour

- ✦ Bob's Red Mill
- ✦ Grain Process Enterprises Ltd.
- ✦ Shiloh Farms
- ✦ The Teff Company

Note: The following distributors and stores also carry many of the flours from the companies listed above:

- ✦ Gluten-Free Mall
- ✦ Gluten-Free Market
- ✦ Gluten-Free Trading Company
- ✦ Gluten Solutions
- ✦ Liv-N-Well Distributors
- ✦ Specialty Food Shop
- ✦ The Dietary Shoppe
- ✦ Various Health Food Stores – e.g., Choices Markets, Whole Foods Market, Wild Oats

GRAINS

AMARANTH

- Arrowhead Mills
- Bob's Red Mill
- El Peto
- Grain Process Enterprises Ltd.
- Inca Organics
- Native Seeds
- Northern Quinoa Corporation
- Nu-World Amaranth/Nu-World Foods
- Shiloh Farms

BUCKWHEAT (Whole Groats, Roasted Groats [Kasha], or Grits)

- Aliment Trigone Inc. (Cream of the Crop)
- Arrowhead Mills
- The Birkett Mills
- Bob's Red Mill
- Grain Process Enterprises Ltd.
- Minn-Dak Growers Ltd.
- Northern Quinoa Corporation
- Shiloh Farms

FLAX (Whole Seed or Ground, Milled Meal)

- Arrowhead Mills
- Bob's Red Mill
- CanMar Grain Products Ltd.
- Dixie Diners' Club
- El Peto
- Gluten-Free Pantry
- Grain Process Enterprises Ltd.
- Hodgson Mill
- Nature's Path
- Nelson David
- Northern Quinoa Corporation
- Omega Nutrition

MILLET

- Arrowhead Mills
- Bob's Red Mill
- El Peto
- Grain Process Enterprises Ltd.
- Northern Quinoa Corporation
- Shiloh Farms

QUINOA (Golden or Black Seed)

- Ancient Harvest
- Arrowhead Mills
- Bob's Red Mill
- Eden Foods
- El Peto
- Grain Process Enterprises Ltd.
- Inca Organics
- Northern Quinoa Corporation – "NorQuin" brand
- Shiloh Farms

SORGHUM (GRAIN)

- Authentic Foods
- El Peto
- Grain Process Enterprises Ltd.
- Shiloh Farms
- Twin Valley Mills, LLC.

TEFF (GRAIN)

- Bob's Red Mill
- Shiloh Farms
- The Teff Company

Pastas

- ✦ Some **"wheat-free"** pastas are made from **kamut** or **spelt** and are **NOT** gluten-free.
- ✦ Some buckwheat pastas contain buckwheat flour and **wheat flour** and are **NOT** gluten-free.
- ✦ Gluten-free pastas are made from corn, legumes, potato, quinoa, rice or soy. However, check ingredient labels to make sure that no **wheat**, **spelt** or **kamut** has been added to these gluten-free ingredients.

Company	Pasta		Grams	Ounces
Ancient Harvest	Elbows, Garden Pagodas, Linguine, Rotelle, Shells, Spaghetti, Veggie Curls		227 g, 4.5 kg	8 oz., 10 lbs.
	Quinoa and corn flour pasta.			
Annie Chun's	**Rice Noodles**	Original, Hunan, Thai Basil	227	8
	Pad Thai Rice Noodles	Original, Thai Basil	227	8
Annie's Homegrown	Gluten-Free Rice Pasta & Cheddar Macaroni & Cheese		170	6
	White rice pasta.			
Barkat	**Corn Pasta**	Penne, Spirals	250	8.8
Bionaturae	Elbows, Fusilli, Penne, Spaghetti		340	12
	Organic pasta made with rice, potato & soy.			
Cafe Bonjour	**Brown Rice**	Elbows, Spaghetti	908	2 lb.
		Fusilli, Lasagna, Penne	454	1 lb.
	White Rice	Elbows, Spaghetti	908	2 lb.
	Also available in bulk.			
Celimix (Nelson David of Canada)	Brown Rice Elbows, Shells, Spaghetti		350	12.3
De Boles	Corn Elbows		340	12
	Corn Spaghetti		227	8
	Rice – Angel Hair, Fettuccine, Penne, Spaghetti, Spirals		227	8
	Rice – Lasagna		284	10
	Rice – Macaroni & Cheese, Shells & Cheese		206	7.25
Dietary Specialties	Elbows, Porridge, Spaghetti, Spirals, Tri-Color Alphabets		500	17.6
	Herb and Garlic Ziti, Tri-Color Shells		250	8.8
	Lasagna		100	3.5
Eden Foods	Bifun (Rice Pasta)		100	3.5
	Harusame (Mung Bean Pasta)		70	2.4
	Kuzu Noodles		100	3.5
Ener-G Foods	**White Rice**	Lasagna, Macaroni, Small Shells	454	16
		Spaghetti	446	15.8
		Vermicelli	298	10.5
	Low Protein/G.F. (cornstarch/potato starch)	Lasagna, Macaroni, Small or Large Shells, Spaghetti	454	16
Food For Life	Rice Elbows (Brown Rice)		454	16
Glutafin	Macaroni (Penne), Shells, Spaghetti, Spirals		500	17.6
	Lasagna, Tagliatelle Nests		250	8.8

Company	Pasta		Grams	Ounces
GLUTANO	**Corn Pasta**	Animal Shapes, Spaghetti, Spirals, Tagliatelle, Tri-Colour Spirals	250	8.8
		Macaroni	500	17.6
	Brown Rice Pasta	Fettuccini, Lasagne, Macaroni	250	8.8
GLUTINO	**Brown Rice Pasta**	Fusilli, Macaroni, Penne, Spaghetti	284	10
HEARTLAND'S FINEST	All Natural Macaroni & Cheese (white cheddar)		255	9
	Macaroni & Cheese (yellow cheddar)		227	8
	Pasta*	Elbows, Rotini, Ziti	340	12
		Linguini, Spaghetti	227	8
	*Made with navy bean and corn flours.			
LUNDBERG	**Organic Brown Rice Pasta**	Penne	340	12
		Rotini, Spaghetti	284	10
MRS. LEEPER'S	**Brown Rice Pasta**	Alphabets, Elbows*, Penne*, Kids Shapes, Spaghetti*, Vegetable Twists	340	12
	Corn Pasta	Elbows*, Rotelli, Spaghetti, Vegetable Radiatore	340	12
	Pasta & Sauce Mixes**	Beef Lasagna (corn lasagna)	200	7
		Beef Stroganoff (rice pasta)	200	7
		Cheeseburger Mac (rice pasta)	200	7
		Chicken Alfredo (rice pasta)	200	7
		Creamy Tuna (corn lasagna)	200	7
	*Available in bulk. **Serve as a side dish or meal. Ready in 5 minutes.			
NAMASTE FOODS	Cheez (Dairy/Casein-Free)		255	9
	Italian		255	9
	Mexican		248	8.75
	Rice pasta and seasoning packet.			
NORTHERN QUINOA CORPORATION	Elbows, Fettucine, Spirals		340	12
	Spaghetti		454	16
	Organic brown rice & quinoa pasta sold as "Norquin".			
NUTRITION KITCHEN	**Angel Hair***	Black, Golden, Green	227	8
	*Organic whole soybean pasta. Available in bulk.			
ORGRAN	Buckwheat Spirals		250	8.8
	Corn Pasta	Corn Spirals, Corn & Spinach Rigati, Corn & Vegetable Shells, Tomato & Basil Corn Pasta	250	8.8
	Rice Pasta	Garlic & Parsley Rice Shells, Rice Spirals, Vegetable Rice Spirals	250	8.8
	Rice & Corn Pasta*	Herb & Spinach, Lasagne Mini Sheets, Macaroni, Penne, Spirals, Tortelli, Vege-Animal Shapes, Vegetable Corkscrew	250	8.8
	*Also produce some organic rice & corn pasta in curls, penne & spirals.			
	Rice & Millet Spirals		250	8.8
	Spaghetti in Tomato Sauce		220	7.8

Company	Pasta		Grams	Ounces
PAPADINI	**Pure Lentil Bean**	Conchigliette (shells), Linguine, Orzo (rice shaped), Penne, Rotini (twists), Spaghetti	200	7
PASTARISO	**Rice**	Angel Hair, Elbows (Mini), Shells, (Regular & Mini), Spirals	200	7
		Elbows (Regular), Fusilli, Penne, Spaghetti	284	10
		Fettucine, Lasagna, Vermicelli	227	8
	Fortified Rice	Spaghetti*	284	10
	Rice Spinach	Elbows, Penne, Spaghetti	284	10
		Fettucine	227	8
		Spirals	200	7
	Rice Vegetable	Penne	284	10
		Shells, Spirals	200	7
	Rice Tomato	Penne	284	10
		Spirals	200	7
	RICE PASTA & Cheese Dinners (white cheddar)	Mac & Cheese	190	6.8
		Rice Mini Shells & Cheese	190	6.8
		Rice Mini Spaghetti & Cheese	190	6.8
		Rice Spinach Pasta & Cheese	190	6.8
	RICE PASTA & Cheese Dinners (yellow cheddar)	Rice Fettuccini & Cheese	190	6.8
		Rice Mac & Cheese	190	6.8
		Rice Mini Shells & Cheese	190	6.8
		Rice Mini Spaghetti & Cheese	190	6.8
		Rice Spinach Pasta & Cheese	190	6.8
	Pasta made from organic brown rice. *Fortified pasta also contains quinoa flour, ground flax, psyllium husks, FOS, vitamins B_1, B_2, B_3, B_6, folic acid, pantothenic acid, iron & magnesium. Most products available in bulk.			
PASTATO	Elbows*, Penne*, Spaghetti*		284	10
	Shells		200	7
	Pasta and Cheese Dinners (White or Yellow Cheddar)	Mac & Cheese, Mini Shells Mini Spaghetti*	190	6.8
	Pasta made from potato and organic brown rice. *Contains quinoa flour, ground flax, psyllium, FOS, Vitamins B_1, B_2, B_3, B_6, folic acid, pantothenic acid, iron and magnesium.			
RIZOPIA	**Brown Rice**	Elbows*, Fettuccine*, Fusilli*, Penne*, Shells*, Spaghetti*, Spirals*	454	16
		Lasagne*	340	12
	Brown Rice (organic)	Fusilli, Penne, Spaghetti	454	16
	Spinach Brown Rice Spaghetti*		454	16
	Vegetable Brown Rice Fusilli		454	16
	Corn Rice (organic)	Fusilli, Radiatore, Spaghetti	454	16
	White Rice	Spaghetti*	454	16
	Wild Rice (organic)	Elbows, Fusilli, Penne, Radiatore, Shells, Spaghetti	454	16
	*Available in bulk.			

Company	Pasta		Grams	Ounces
SCHÄR	Anellini, Capelli (Angel Hair), Conchigliette (Small Shells), Lasagne, Tagliatelle		250	8.8
	Fusillli, Penne, Pipette, Rigati, Spaghetti		500	17.6
THAI KITCHEN	**Dry Rice Noodles**	Stir-Fry Rice	397	14
		Thin Rice, Wide Rice	200	7
	Rice Noodle Meal Kits*	Lemongrass & Chili	150	5.3
		Original Pad Thai	170	6.0
		Pad Thai with Chili	170	6.0
		Thai Peanut	156	5.5
	NOODLE CARTS	Pad Thai, Thai Peanut, Roasted Garlic	200	7
	*Stir-Fry Rice Noodles with Sauce.			
TINKYADA	Elbows*, Fusilli*, Penne*, Shells*, Spaghetti*, Spirals*		454	16
	Grand Shells*		227	8
	Lasagna* or Lasagna**		280	10
	Spinach Rice Spaghetti*, Vegetable Rice Spirals*		340	12
	Elbows**, Penne**, Spaghetti**, Spirals**		340	12
	Spaghetti***		454	16
	Fettuccini*, Little Dreams*		397	14
	*Brown rice with rice bran. **Organic brown rice. ***White rice. All pasta available in bulk 4.54 kg (10 lbs.).			

ENTRÉES AND SIDE DISHES

Company	Entrées & Side Dishes		Grams	Ozs.	Serves
ALPINEAIRE Foods	**Side Dishes**	Brown Rice (Instant)	57, 227	2, 8	2, 8
		Corn, Sweet (Freeze-Dried)	43, 227	1.5, 8	2, 11
		French Cut Green Beans Almondine	50	1.75	2
		Garden Vegetables	43, 227	1.5, 8	2, 11
		Mashed Potatoes (Instant)	50, 198	1.75, 7	2, 8
		Peas (Freeze-Dried)	43, 227	1.5, 8	2, 11
	Note: Also have many other products.				
AMY'S KITCHEN	**Asian Meals**	Asian Noodle Stiry-Fry*	284	10	
		Thai Stir-Fry*	269	9.5	
	Bowls	Brown Rice and Vegetables*, Brown Rice & Vegetable (light in sodium)*, Brown Rice with Black-Eyed Peas & Veggies*, Mexican Casserole, Santa Fe Enchilada, Teriyaki*	284	10	
		Baked Ziti Bowl*	269	9.5	
	Chilies	Medium*, Medium Black Bean*, Medium with Vegetables*, Spicy*	417	14.7	
	*Casein-Free.				

Company	Entrées & Side Dishes		Grams	Ozs.	Serves
AMY'S KITCHEN	**Enchiladas**	Black Bean Vegetable*, Black Bean Vegetable (light in sodium)*	269	9.5	
		Black Bean Whole Meal*	284	10	
		Cheese	255	9	
		Cheese Whole Meal	255	9	
	Indian Meals	Mattar Paneer	284	10	
		Mattar Tofu*	269	9.5	
		Palak Paneer	284	10	
		Vegetable Korma*	269	9.5	
	Miscellaneous	Garden Vegetable Lasagna	291	10.3	
		Mexican Tamale Pie*	227	8	
		Rice Crust Cheese Pizza	340	12.0	
		Rice Crust Spinach Pizza*	397	14	
		Rice Mac & Cheese	255	9	
		Shepherd's Pie*	227	8	
		Tofu Rancheros	255	9	
		Tofu Scramble*	255	9	
	*Casein-Free.				
BARKAT	**Pot Meals**	Mexican	79	2.8	1
		Potato & Onion	56	2	1
		Rice & Tomato	71	2.5	1
DIETARY SPECIALTIES	**Entrées**	Chicken Nuggets*	454	16	
		Fish Sticks*	227	8	
		Lasagna with Meat Sauce	340	12	
		Linguini with Meat Sauce	454	16	
		Macaroni and Cheese	340	12	
		Ravioletti Primavera	340	12	
		Spaghetti & Meatballs	454	16	
	Filled Pasta	Cheese Ravioli, Meat Ravioli*, Spinach & Cheese Ravioli, Stuffed Shells & Tomato Sauce	454	16	
	Pizza	Cheese (8")	340	12	3
	*Casein-Free.				
DIXIE DINERS' CLUB	**Beef Not!***	Beef Strip, Chunk Beef, Ground Beef	454 g, 4.54, 22.7 kg	1, 10, 50 lbs.	
	Chicken Not!*	Chicken Chunk, Chicken Strip	454 g, 4.54, 22.7 kg	1, 10, 50 lbs.	
	Turkey Not!*	Ground Turkey	454 g, 4.54, 22.7 kg	1, 10, 50 lbs.	
	*Meat substitutes.				
DR. PRAEGER'S	Potato Crusted Filet Fish Sticks		320	11.3	
	Potato Crusted Fish Filet		297	10.5	
	Potato Crusted Fishies		340	12	
	Gluten-Free Pancakes	Potato	382	13.5	
		Broccoli, Spinach	340	12	

Company	Entrées & Side Dishes		Grams	Ozs.	Serves
FOODS BY GEORGE	Lasagna		340	12	
	Manicotti	Cheese, Spinach & Cheese	397	14	
	Pizza	Cheese	255	9	1
GLUTEN-FREE PANTRY	**Skillet Meals**	Pasta Fagioli	199	7	
		Singapore Sweet & Sour	177	6.25	
		Szechwan Noodle	177	6.25	
		Tex Mex	142	5	
		Stroganoff	184	6.5	
	Add meat or other protein food to the skillet meal mix.				
GLUTINO	Mac & Cheese (3 cheese)		300	10.6	
	Pizza Duo Cheese		175	6.2	
	Tomato and Cheese Pizza		350	12.3	2
HEALTH VALLEY	**Chilies**	Vegetarian Mild (Regular and No Salt), Vegetarian Mild with Black Bean, Mild with 3 Beans, Vegetarian Spicy (Regular and No Salt), Black Bean	425	15	
IAN'S NATURAL FOODS	Alphatots		336	12	
	Gluten-Free Chicken Nuggets		224	8	
	Gluten-Free Fish Sticks		224	8	
	Gluten-Free Mini Popcorn Turkey Dogs		224	8	
	Kids Meals	Chicken Fingers, Turkey Dogs	224	8	
INSTANT GOURMET	**Meal in a Cup**	Hearty Mountain Chili	94	3.3	1
		N'Oleans Chicken Gumbo	78	2.75	1
		Santa Fe Chicken	118	4.2	1
		Stroganoff with Beef & Rice	107	3.8	1
		Texas BBQ Chicken	116	4.1	1
LUNDBERG	**Lundberg's RiceXpress™**	Chicken Herb, Santa Fe Grill	250	8.8	
		Classic Beef (product re-formulated without malt extract)	250	8.8	
	Microwave. Ready to eat in 90 seconds.				
	Rice Sensations	Ginger Miso	207	7.3	
		Moroccan Pilaf, Zesty Southwestern	176	6.2	
		Thai Coconut Ginger	181	6.4	
	Cooks in 30 minutes.				
	Risottos: Eco-Farmed	Butternut Squash	164	5.8	
		Cheddar Broccoli	167	5.9	
		Creamy Parmesan, Garlic Primavera, Italian Herb	156	5.5	
	Risottos: Organic	Alfredo	156	5.5	
		Florentine, Tuscan	163	5.75	
		Porcini Mushroom	167	5.9	
MANISCHEWITZ	Lentil Pilaf Mix, Spanish Pilaf Mix		191	6.75	4
MY OWN MEALS	Beef Stew, Chicken & Black Beans, Mediterranean Chicken, My Kind of Chicken, Old World Stew		280	10	1
	Casein-Free. Fully cooked meals – heat and serve.				
NATURE'S HILIGHTS	Rice Crust Pizza (Soy Cheese Style)		312	11	2
	Tostada (Soy Cheese & Vegetarian Beans)		369	13	2

Company	Entrées & Side Dishes		Grams	Ozs.	Serves
NU-WORLD AMARANTH	**Side Serves**	Garlic-Herb, Savory-Herb, Spanish Tomato	75	2.63	
PACIFIC FOODS	**Ready to Serve Rice Dishes***	Lemon & Herb, Roasted Chicken, Spanish Style, Wild Rice & Mushroom	250	8.8	
	*In shelf-stable packages. Microwave for 1 minute.				
PANNE RIZO	Macaroni and Cheese		390	13.8	1
	Mini Pizzola	Various flavors	200	7	1
	Panini	Tuna Melt	310	11	1
		Oven Roasted Turkey	225	8	1
	Pot Pies	Chicken, Tomato Vegetable	300	10.6	1
PRIVATE RECIPES	**Special Diet Frozen Entrées**	Apple Braised Pork	225	8	1
		Beef and Vegetable Casserole	275	10	1
		Country Chicken	255	9	1
		Lemon Herb Fish	261	9.2	
		Pot Roast with Rice & Peas	255	9	1
		Sweet and Sour Chicken	295	10.5	1
		Turkey Dinner	265	9.5	1
PURFOODS/ GLUTEN-FREE MEALS	**Breakfast**	Breakfast Pizza, Breakfast Skillet California Breakfast, Denver Omelet, Florentine Omelet, Garden Frittata, Pancakes, Potato Cheddar Frittata, Rice Bread French Toast, Sweet Corn Cakes, Spinach & Feta Cheese Omelet, Vegetable Omelet, Zucchini Frittata	various sizes		1
	Beef	Beef Steak, Feta Burger, London Broil, Steak & Eggs, Steak Fajita Wrap, Steak with Mushrooms, Steak Pizzaiola	various sizes		1
	Fish	Salmon, Asparagus & White Rice; Salmon & Cream Cheese Omelet; Shrimp Scampi, Tuna Salad	various sizes		1
	Miscellaneous	Chicken Caesar Salad, Chicken Salad with Raspberry Vinaigrette, Chicken Three Bean Salad, Oriental Mexican Casserole, Chicken Noodle Soup, Portabella Napolean, Potato Lasagna	various sizes		1
	Pork	Pork Marsala, Pork Mustard, Pork Ragout, Pork Rosemary, Roasted Pork Loin	various sizes		1
	Poultry	Berry Good Chicken Breast, BBQ Chicken, Chicken Cacciatore, Chicken Chardonnay, Chicken Marsala, Chicken Verdue, Chicken Vesuvio, Lemon Rosemary Chicken, Seared Chicken Breast, Turkey Bolognese, Turkey Burger, Turkey Cutlet, Turkey Ratatouille, White Chicken Ratatouille	various sizes		1

Company	Entrées & Side Dishes		Grams	Ozs.	Serves
RICE EXPRESSIONS	Precooked Frozen Rice	Brown Rice, Long Grain Rice, Thai Jasmine	852	30	
		Three packages per box			
		Brown Rice Pilaf, Tex Mex Rice	568	20	
		Two packages per box			
TAMARIND TREE	Vegetarian Side Dishes:	Creamy Vegetable Medley with Nuts, Garden Peas & Sautéed Mushrooms, Golden Lentils with Vegetables, Curried Garbanzos and Potatoes, Savory Spinach with Indian Cheese, Tender Spinach & Garbanzos, Spicy Garden Vegetables, Aromatic Lentil Chili	262	9.25	1
	Microwave trays with precooked long-grain brown rice. Ready to eat in 5 minutes. No preservatives or MSG. Shelf stable for 2 years.				
TASTE ADVENTURE	Quick Cuisine "Entrées"	Black Beans & Rice Santa Fe Fiesta	170	6	4
		Lentil & Rice Bombay Curry	170	6	4
		Louisiana Red Bean Jambalaya	170	6	4
	Quick Cooking Chilies	Black Bean, Five Bean, Lentil, Red Bean	156	5.5	2

SOUPS

- ✦ Most canned soups are **NOT** gluten-free as they contain **wheat flour**, **barley**, **noodles**, hydrolyzed plant or vegetable protein (**HPP** or **HVP**) made from **wheat**.
- ✦ Bouillon cubes and soup broths often contain **wheat flour** or **HPP** or **HVP** made from **wheat** and are **NOT** gluten-free.
- ✦ Soup stock can be made from meat or poultry bones and a variety of vegetables.

Company	Soups		Grams	Ounces
ALPINEAIRE FOODS	Cream of Broccoli		71	2.5
	Kernel's Corn Chowder		113	4
AMY'S KITCHEN	Organic Canned Soups	Black Bean Vegetable*	411	14.5
		Chunky Tomato Bisque	411	14.5
		Cream of Tomato (reg; light sodium)	411	14.5
		Lentil*	411	14.5
		Lentil Vegetable (reg; light sodium)*	411	14.5
		Split Pea*	400	14.1
	*Casein-Free.			
CELIFIBR	Soup Base	Vegetarian Beef, Vegetarian Chicken, French Onion, Vegetable Medley	454	1 lb.
	Soup Cubes*	Vegetarian Beef, Vegetarian Chicken, Vegetable Medley	60	2
	*6 cubes/box.			

Company	Soups		Grams	Ounces
COOK IN THE KITCHEN	**Dried Soup Mixes**	Harvest Garden Vegetable	156	5.5
		Mediterranean Lentil Soup	156	5.5
		Dilled Tomato	156	5.5
		Welsh Potato	156	5.5
DIXIE DINERS' CLUB	**Beef Not!, Chicken Not! (Dried Soup Mix)**			
		Official Broth Mix (light colored)	454	16
		Official Onion Flavor Broth Mix	454	16
		Dixie Choice	227, 454	8, 16
	8 oz. = 48 servings.	16 oz. = 96 servings.		
EDWARD & SON'S TRADING CO.	**Miso-Cup** (Organic Instant)	Organic Reduced Sodium	29	1.0
		Organic Traditional with Tofu	36	1.3
		Original Golden	70	2.5
		Savory Seaweed	70	2.5
EL PETO	**Soup Concentrates*** (Dry Mixes)	Beef Broth, Onion, Tomato, Tomato Vegetable	350	12.5
		Chicken Broth, Vegetable	280	9.9
	*Dairy-Free.			
ENER-G FOODS	Cream of Mushroom Soup (dry mix)		25	0.88
GLUTINO	**Soup Mixes**	Beef Flavoured, Onion,	120	4.2
		Chicken Flavoured	160	5.6
		Cream of Mushroom	150	5.3
HEALTH VALLEY	**Fat-Free Soups**	Black Bean & Vegetable, Five Bean Vegetable, 14 Garden Vegetable, Supper Broccoli	425	15
	Organic Soups (No Salt)	Black Bean, Lentil, Potato Leek, Split Pea, Tomato, Vegetable	425	15
	Organic Soups (Regular)	Black Bean, Lentil, Potato Leek Split Pea, Tomato, Vegetable	425	15
	Organic Cream Soups*	Celery*, Chicken*, Mushroom*	411	14.5
		Seafood New England Clam Chowder*	425	15
		Seafood Manhatten Clam Chowder*	425	15
		Butternut Squash Soup*, Creamy Tomato*, Roasted Pepper Tomato*	946 mL	32
		*Contains dairy		
	Organic Broths	Beef Flavored, Chicken, Vegetable	403	14.25
	Organic Broths	Beef Flavored, Chicken, Vegetable	946 mL	32
	Organic No-Salt Added Broth	Chicken, Fat-Free Beef	403	14.25
	Organic Fat-Free Broth	Chicken, Mushroom, Vegetable	403	14.25
	Organic Low-Fat Broth	Chicken	403	14.25

Company	Soups		Grams	Ounces
IMAGINE	**Garden Natural Creamy Soups***	Broccoli, Butternut Squash, Portobello Mushroom**, Potato Leek, Sweet Corn, Tomato, Tomato Basil	473, 946 mL	16, 32
		Sweet Potato	946 mL	32
	*All soups are Dairy-Free. **All soups are organic except Portobello Mushroom.			
	Seafood Bisques***	Crab, Lobster	946 mL	32
	***Contains Dairy.			
	Organic Asian Broths	California Miso, Free Range Chicken	946 mL	32
	Organic Cooking Stocks	Beef, Chicken, Vegetable	946 mL	32
	Organic Garden Natural Broths	Beef, Free Range Chicken, Vegetable	473, 946 mL	16, 32
		No Chicken	946 mL	32
INSTANT GOURMET	**Low Carb Soups**	Bay Shrimp Bisque, Beefy Vegetable, Broccoli Cheddar, Chicken Vegetable, Chicken with Asparagus, Mushrooms with Chicken & Garlic	29	1
LEGUMES PLUS	**Soup Mixes**	Cajun Brown Rice Lentil*, Gourmet Herb Lentil	319	11.25
		Green Split Pea*, Zesty Tomato Lentil*	305	10.75
		Olde World Lentil, Wild Rice & Herbs Lentil*	269	9.5
		Red Curry Lentil*	326	11.6
		Yellow Split Pea	361	12.75
	*Also available in smaller serving sizes.			
MANISCHEWITZ	**Borscht**	Clear, No Sodium, Reduced Sodium, Reduced Calorie, Shredded Beets	936	33
	Schav		936	33
NUTRIMAX	**Soup Bases**	Beef, Tomato	325	11.5
		Chicken, Onion	375	13.2
ORGRAN	Garden Vegetable Soup for Cup		24	0.8
	Sweet Corn Soup for Cup		36	1.3
	Tomato Soup for Cup		36	1.3
	Soups are Dairy-Free. 2 soup packets per box.			
PACIFIC FOODS	**Broths**	Beef, Free Range Chicken	946 mL	32
	Organic Broths	Free Range Chicken*, Low Sodium Chicken, Mushroom, Vegetable*, Low Sodium Vegetable	946 mL	32
	Soups	Creamy Roasted Carrot, Roasted Red Pepper & Tomato*	454, 946 mL	16, 32
	Organic Soups	Creamy Butternut Squash*, Creamy Tomato*	454, 946 mL	16, 32
	*Also available in 240 mL/8 oz. single serves.			

Company	Soups		Grams	Ounces
SIMPLY ASIA	**Rice Noodle Soup Bowls**	Garlic Sesame, Sesame Chicken, Spring Vegetable	70	2.5
TASTE ADVENTURE	**Dried Soups**	Black Bean	130	4.6
		Curry Lentil	170	6
		Golden Pea	142	5
		Navy Bean	156	5.5
		Split Pea	142	5
		Sweet Corn Chowder	142	5
THAI KITCHEN	**Heat & Serve Soups** (canned)	Coconut Ginger, Hot & Sour	397	14
	Instant Rice Noodle Soup Bowls	Lemon Grass & Chili, Mushroom, Roasted Garlic, Spring Onion, Thai Ginger	70	2.4
	Instant Rice Noodle Soups	Bangok Curry, Garlic & Vegetable, Lemon Grass & Chili, Spring Onion, Thai Ginger & Vegetable	45	1.6
WHOLE FOODS MARKET	**365 Organic Broths**	Chicken, Vegetable	946 mL	32

COATINGS AND CRUMBS

Company	Coatings & Crumbs		Grams	Ounces
AUNT CANDICE	Breading Mix*		454	16
	*Casein, Corn & Soy-Free.			
CHOICES BEST RICE BAKERY	**Brown Rice Bread Crumbs**	Multiseed, Plain	340	12
	Brown Rice Bread Croutons		100	3.5
DIETARY SPECIALTIES	Rice Crumbs		454	16
EL PETO	Gluten-Free Bread Crumbs*		500	17.5
	Gluten-Free Stuffing*		300	10.5
	*Dairy-Free.			
ENER-G FOODS	Bread Crumbs (Stuffing)		284	10
FORTITUDE	Homestyle Golden Coatings		120	4.25
GILLIAN'S FOODS	**Bread Crumbs***	Cajun Style, Italian	340	12
	*Dairy-Free.			
GLUTEN-FREE COOKIE JAR	**Bread Crumbs***	Plain, Fresh Herb	454	16
	*Dairy-Free.			
GLUTEN-FREE PANTRY	Croutons*		113	4
	Herb-Flavored Rice Crumb Coating*		454	16
	Stuffing*		397	14
	*Dairy-Free.			
HOL•GRAIN	Brown Rice Bread Crumbs		113	4
KINNIKINNICK	Crispy Chicken Coating Mix*		500	18
	General Coating Mix*		500	18
	Graham Style Cracker Crumbs*		200	7.5
	*Casein-Free.			

Company	Coatings & Crumbs	Grams	Ounces
LAUREL'S SWEET TREATS	Onion Ring Batter	326	11.5
MISS ROBEN'S	Breading Batter Coating Mix	170, 510	6, 18
NATURAL FOOD MILL BAKERY	Bread Crumbs	275	9.7
NU-WORLD AMARANTH	Amaranth Bread Crumbs	170	6
ORGRAN	All-Purpose Crumbs*	300	10.6
	Coating & Stuffing Mix*	120	4.2
	*Dairy-Free.		
PANNE RIZO	Plain Rice Crumbs	250	8.8
	Herb Croutons	160	5.6
SCHÄR	Gluten-Free Bread Crumbs (Pangrati)	250	8.8

GRAVY MIXES

Company	Gravy Mixes	Grams	Ounces
GLUTINO	Brown Gravy Mix	159	5.6
ORGRAN	Gravy Mix	200	7
	Dairy-Free.		

SAUCES

Company	Sauces		Grams	Ounces
GILLIAN'S FOODS	**Sauces**	Chinese Hot, Honey Mustard Dipping, Marinara	125 mL	4
GLUTINO	BBQ Sauce*		125	4.4
	All Natural Dressings and Marinades Classic Caesar, Fine Herbs & Basalmic*, Peppercorn Garlic*, Naturally Italian*		340	12
	*Dairy-Free.			
MR. SPICE	Garlic Steak Sauce, Ginger Stir Fry Sauce, Honey BBQ Sauce, Honey Mustard Sauce, Hot Wing! Sauce, Indian Curry Sauce, Sweet & Sour Sauce, Tangy Bang! Hot Sauce, Thai Peanut Sauce		298	10.5
NUTRIMAX	**Pasta Sauces**	Alfredo	245	8.6
		Curry	260	9.2
		Pesto	155	5.5
PREMIERE JAPAN	**Wheat Free Sauces**	Hoisin, Teriyaki	251 mL	8.5
RAINFOREST ORGANIC	**Wheat-Free Sauces** (Organic)	Papaya Pepper	147 mL	5
		Ginger, Ginger Curry, Mango, Peanut	295 mL	10

Company	Sauces		Grams	Ounces
THAI KITCHEN	Sauces	Fish, Lemon Grass Splash, Spicy Thai, Plum Spring Roll, Red Chili Dipping	200	7
		Original Pad Thai, Peanut Satay	227 mL	8
THE WIZARD'S	Wheat-Free Sauces	Hot Stuff	147 mL	5
		Worcestershire	251 mL	8.5

SOY SAUCES

Company	Soy Sauces	Grams	Ounces
KARI-OUT	Panda Soy Sauce (Low Sodium Gluten-Free)	small individual packets	
LIFESOY	**Wheat-Free/Gluten-Free Tamari Soy Sauce** Original, Oriental Ginger, Shitake Mushroom, Spicy Garlic	500	17.6
SAN J	Organic Wheat-Free Tamari Soy Sauce (Gold Label)	284, 567 mL	10, 20
	Organic Lite Tamari Soy Sauce (25% less salt)*	284, 567 mL	10, 20
	Note: San J regular tamari and lite tamari soy sauces contain wheat. *In USA called "Reduced Sodium Wheat-Free Tamari".		

SPREADS

Company	Spreads	Grams	Ounces
No Nuts	Golden Peabutter	510	18

DAIRY/NON-DAIRY BEVERAGES

✦ Some non-dairy beverages are **NOT** gluten-free as they contain **barley malt**, **barley malt extract**, **barley malt flavoring**, or **oats**.

e.g., **Imagine Foods "Rice Dream" Non-Dairy Beverage** is made from rice but the enzymatic process utilizes a barley enzyme. Even though this enzyme is discarded after use, the final beverage may contain a minute residual amount of barley protein (0.002%).

Eden Soy Beverages all contain gluten EXCEPT "Eden Blend" and "Eden Soy Unsweetened".

Pacific Foods Non-Dairy Multigrain Beverage and **Non-Dairy Oat Beverage** contains **oats**.

Lactose-Reduced Dairy Products

LACTAID MILK (CANADA)
- ✦ Shelf stable (1 litre) – 2%
- ✦ Refrigerated (1 litre) – 2%
- ✦ Refrigerated (2 litres) – skim

LACTAID MILK (USA)
- ✦ Refrigerated (half gallon) – Fat-Free, Low-Fat (1%), Reduced Fat (2%), Whole, Calcium Fortified (Fat-Free)

LACTEEZE MILK
- ✦ Refrigerated (1 litre) – Skim, 1% and 2%
  (2 litre) – 2%

Soy Beverages

EDEN FOODS "SOY UNSWEETENED"
- ✦ Shelf stable (33.8 oz.)

ENER-G FOODS "SOYQUIK"
- ✦ Powder (16 oz/454 g)

IMAGINE FOODS "SOY DREAM" NON-DAIRY BEVERAGES
- ✦ Shelf Stable (8 oz. and 32 oz./240 mL and 946 mL)
  - Soy Dream Regular – Original, Vanilla, Carob
  - Soy Dream Enriched – Original*, Vanilla*, Chocolate*
- ✦ Refrigerated (32 oz.)
  Soy Dream Enriched – Original*, Vanilla*, Chocolate*
- ✦ Refrigerated (64 oz.)
  - Soy Dream Enriched – Original*, Vanilla*

  * Enriched with Calcium and Vitamins A, D, E and B_{12} in USA
  * Enriched with Calcium and Vitamins A, D, B_2, B_{12} and Zinc in Canada

Soy Beverages CONT'D

PACIFIC FOODS "NON-DAIRY SOY BEVERAGES"

- ✦ Shelf Stable (8 oz./240 mL)
  - Enriched Soymilk – Plain*, Chocolate*, Vanilla*
    * Enriched with Calcium and Vitamins A and D.
- ✦ Shelf Stable (32 oz./946 mL)
  - Organic Original Soy – Unsweetened
  - Select Soy – Low-Fat Plain, Low-Fat Vanilla
  - Ultra Soy – Plain*, Vanilla*
    * Enriched with Calcium and Vitamins A, D, E, B_2, B_6 and B_{12}.
- ✦ Shelf Stable (32 oz./946 mL)
  - Soy Blenders* – Low-Fat Plain, Low-Fat Vanilla
    * For use in coffee, latte, and chai beverages formulated for the food service industry.

SOYA WORLD "SO GOOD FORTIFIED" (CANADA)*

- ✦ Shelf Stable (250 mL) – Chocolate, Strawberry, Vanilla
- ✦ Shelf Stable (1 litre) – Original, Chocolate, Fat-Free, Fat-Free Vanilla, Omega Original**, Omega Vanilla**, Vanilla
- ✦ Refrigerated (946 mL) – Original, Chocolate, Fat-Free Vanilla, Strawberry, Vanilla, Soyaccino
- ✦ Refrigerated (1.89 litres) – Original, Chocolate, Fat-Free, Fat-Free Vanilla, No Sugar Added Original, No Sugar Added Vanilla, Omega Original**, Omega Vanilla**, Vanilla
- ✦ Refrigerated (2.84 litres) – Original

  * Fortified with Calcium, Iron, Phosphorus, Potassium, Zinc and Vitamins A, C, D, B_1, B_2, B_3, B_6, B_{12}, Folacin and Pantothenate.

  ** Contains flax seed oil.

SOYA WORLD "SO NICE SOYGANIC" (CANADA AND USA)*

- ✦ Shelf Stable (946 mL/32 oz.) – Natural**, Original, Cappuccino, Chocolate, Vanilla
- ✦ Refrigerated (946 mL/32 oz.) – Natural**, Original, Chocolate, Mocha, Vanilla, Noel Nog
- ✦ Refrigerated (1.89 litres/64 oz.) – Original, Chocolate, Vanilla, Unsweetened Low Carb
- ✦ Refrigerated (2.84 litres) – Original

  * All flavors except natural fortified/enriched with Calcium, Magnesium, Zinc and Vitamins A, C, D, B_1, B_2, B_3, B_6, B_{12}, Folacin and Pantothenate.

  ** Natural is non-fortified/enriched.

SUNRISE SOYA BEVERAGE (CANADA)

- ✦ Refrigerated (1, 1.9 and 3.95 litres) – Sweetened*
- ✦ Refrigerated (1.9 and 3.95 litres) – Unsweetened*
- ✦ Refrigerated (1.89 litres) – Enriched Original**, Enriched Unsweetened**

  * Non-fortified

  ** Fortified with Calcium, Phosphorous, Iron, Zinc and Vitamins A, C, D, B_1, B_2, B_3, B_6, B_{12}, Folacin and Pantothenate.

WHITE WAVE SILK SOY BEVERAGES (CANADA)*

- ✦ Refrigerated (946 mL and 1.89 litres) – Plain, Vanilla, Chocolate

  * Fortified with Calcium, Zinc and Vitamins A, B_2, B_{12} and D.

Soy Beverages CONT'D

WHITE WAVE SILK SOY MILK (USA)

- ✦ Refrigerated (8 oz/240 mL) – Plain*, Chocolate*, Vanilla
- ✦ Refrigerated (11 oz/330 mL) Single Serve) – Plain*, Chocolate*, Coffee Soylatte****, Spice Soylatte*, Vanilla*
- ✦ Refrigerated (32 oz/946 mL) – Plain*, Unsweetened*, Chai****, Chocolate*, Coffee Soylatte****, Mocha****, Vanilla*
- ✦ Refrigerated (64 oz/1.89 litres) – Plain*, Unsweetened*, Chocolate*, Enhanced******, Light Plain*, Light Chocolate*, Light Vanilla*, Vanilla*, Very Vanilla*****
- ✦ Shelf Stable (8.25 oz/244 mL) – Chocolate*, Very Vanilla*
- ✦ Shelf Stable (6.5 oz/192 mL Kids Pack) – Chocolate***, Strawberry***, Vanilla***
- ✦ Shelf Stable (32 oz/946 mL) – Plain*, Unsweetened*, Vanilla*
- ✦ Refrigerated (10 oz/295 mL) Silk Live! Smoothie – Mango**, Peach**, Raspberry**, Strawberry**

* Enriched with Calcium and Vitamins A, B_2, B_{12} and D.
** Enriched with Calcium, Zinc, Biotin and Vitamins A, B_2, B_3, B_6, B_{12}, C, D and E.
*** Enriched with Calcium and Vitamins A, B_2, B_{12}, C, D and E.
**** Enriched with Calcium, Zinc and Vitamins A, B_2, B_{12} and D.
***** Enriched with Calcium, Zinc and Vitamins A, B_2, B_6, B_{12}, C, D and E.
****** Enriched with Calcium, Zinc, Flax Oil and Vitamins A, B_2, B_6, B_{12}, C, D and E.

SOY YOGURTS

SOYA WORLD "SO NICE" YOGURTS (CANADA)

- ✦ Refrigerated Carton (175 g) – Peach, Strawberry, Vanilla
- ✦ Refrigerated Carton (440 g) – Plain, Peach, Vanilla, Strawberry

WHITE WAVE SILK CULTURED YOGURTS*

- ✦ Refrigerated Carton (32 oz./908 g) – Plain, Vanilla
- ✦ Refrigerated Carton (6 oz./170 g) – Apricot-Mango, Banana-Strawberry, Black Cherry, Blueberry, Key Lime, Lemon, Peach, Raspberry, Strawberry and Vanilla

* Enriched with Calcium.

RICE BEVERAGES

AMAZAKE RICE SHAKES*

- ✦ Refrigerated (8 oz) – Almond Shake, Chocolate Almond, Go Hazelnuts, Vanilla, Pecan Pie
- ✦ Refrigerated (16 oz) – Oh So Original, Almond Shake, Amazing Mango, Banana Appeal, Chocolate Almond, Chocolate Chimp, Cool Coconut, Go Hazelnuts, Rice Nog, Tiger Chai**, Vanilla Gorilla**
- ✦ Refrigerated (32 oz) – Oh So Original, Almond Shake, Rice Nog

* All made with organic brown rice. Chocolate Chimp and Vanilla Gorilla also contain soy protein.
** Enriched with vitamins and minerals.

Rice Beverages cont'd

Lundberg "Drink Rice" Non-Dairy Beverage*
- ✦ Shelf Stable (32 oz.) – Original, Vanilla
  - * Enriched with Calcium, Vitamins A and D.

Pacific Foods Non-Dairy Rice Beverages*
- ✦ Shelf Stable (32 oz.)
  - • Low Fat Rice – Plain, Vanilla
    - * Enriched with Calcium and Vitamins A and D.

Other Beverages

Blue Diamond "Almond Breeze" Non-Dairy Beverage*
- ✦ Shelf Stable (32 oz/946 mL) – Chocolate**, Original**, Vanilla**
  - * Enriched with Vitamins A, D, and E and Calcium.
  - ** Available in regular and unsweetened.

Eden Foods "EdenBlend" Brown Rice & Soy Beverage
- ✦ Shelf Stable (8.45 and 33.8 oz./250 mL and 1 litre)

English Bay Dairy-Free Beverage (Potato Based)
- ✦ Refrigerated (32 oz/946 mL) – Original, Chocolate
- ✦ Dry Mix* (2.2 lb/1 kg) – Original, Chocolate
  - * Makes 384 oz (12 liters).

Pacific Foods "Almond Low-Fat Non-Dairy Beverage"*
- ✦ Shelf Stable (32 oz.) – Original, Vanilla
  - * Enriched with Calcium, Vitamins A, B_2 and D.

Pacific Foods Hazelnut Non-Dairy Beverage*
- ✦ Shelf Stable (32 oz.) – Original
  - * Enriched with Calcium, Vitamins A, B_2 and D.

Tayo Foods Non-Dairy Drink (Potato Based Substitute) *
- ✦ Refrigerated (2 litres) – Original, Chocolate, Vanilla
- ✦ Shelf Stable (225 and 946 mL) – available spring 2006
  - * Fortified with Calcium, Folic Acid, Zinc, Vitamins A, B_2, B_6, B_{12} and D.

Vances DariFree Non-Dairy Beverage (Potato Based Substitute) USA*
- ✦ Dry Mix Potato Based Milk Substitute – Original
  - • 21 oz. Carton yields 6 quarts
  - • 25 lb. Box yields 115 quarts
- ✦ Dry Mix Potato Based Milk Substitute – Chocolate
  - • 23.3 oz. Carton yields 5 quarts
  - • 25 lb. Box yields 86 quarts
    - * Enriched with Calcium, Folic Acid, Biotin, Pantothenic acid, Vitamins A, B_1, B_2, B_3, B_6, B_{12}, C, D, E and K.

BEER

- Regular beer, ale and lagers are **NOT** gluten-free, as they are made from barley.
- There are several gluten-free products on the market (see below).

Company	Beer	Grams	Ounces
BARD'S TALE	Dragon's Gold Gluten-Free Beer*	341 mL	12
	*Sorghum, buckwheat and honey		
LA MESSAGÈRE	Gluten-Free Beer*	341 mL	12
	*Rice and buckwheat		
RAMAPO VALLEY BREWERY	Gluten-Free Honey Lager*	340 mL	12
	*Molasses and honey		

GLUTEN-FREE COMPANIES/DISTRIBUTORS

✦ = Products can be ordered directly from company

1-2-3 Gluten-Free Inc., 5145 Penton Road, Pittsburgh, PA, USA 15213
✦ Phone: 412-683-2424 FAX: 412-683-2499
Email: info@123glutenfree.com www.123glutenfree.com

- Gluten-free specialty company; dedicated gluten-free facility.
- Produce "1-2-3 Gluten-Free" baking mixes (biscuits, brownies, cakes, cookies, muffins, pancakes, rolls).
- Available in retail stores.
- Order direct by phone, fax, mail or internet; shipping charges based on weight; ships via FedEx Ground or USPS.

AlpineAire Foods, TyRy Inc., P. O. Box 1799, Rocklin, CA, USA 95677
✦ Phone: 800-322-6325/866-322-6325/ 916-624-6050 FAX: 916-624-1604
Email: info@aa-foods.com www.aa-foods.com

- Gluten-free fully prepared meals, side dishes, vegetables, fruits, desserts, beverages, soups, rice and legumes that are freeze-dried and specially packaged for a long shelf life. No preservatives or MSG. These instant foods are in re-sealable, lightweight, foil pouches (stable for 1 year) and can be prepared in the pouch by adding hot water. Also available in cans (stable for 5-20 years).
- Many products are gluten-free.
- Available in retail stores.
- Order direct by phone, fax or internet; shipping charges based on weight; ships via UPS Ground.

AltiPlano Gold, Box 156678, 50 California St., Suite 2500, San Francisco, CA, USA 94115
✦ Phone: 415-928-9928 FAX: 415-358-5564
Email: info@altiplanogold.com www.altiplanogold.com

- Gluten-free specialty company; products are tested for gluten using the ELISA test.
- Produce instant hot cereals made from organic flaked quinoa (various flavors) that are high in protein and fiber.
- Available in retail stores.
- Order direct by internet; shipping charges based on amount purchased; ships via UPS.

Amazake, Grainaissance Inc., 1580 - 62nd St., Emeryville, CA, USA 94608
Phone: 800-472-4697/510-547-7256 FAX: 510-547-0526
Email: amazake@grainaissance.com www.grainaissance.com

- Produce dairy-free, low-fat shakes from organic brown rice. Contains no added sweeteners. Some flavors contain soy protein, nuts and/or are enriched with vitamins and minerals.
- Most flavors are gluten-free except Mocha Java and Gimme Green.
- Available in retail stores.

GLUTEN-FREE COMPANIES/DISTRIBUTORS CONT'D.

Amazing Grains Grower Cooperative, 405 Main St. SW, Ronan, MT, USA 59864
✦ Phone: 877-278-6585/406-676-3536 FAX: 406-676-3537
Email: customercare@amazinggrains.com www.montina.com
www.amazinggrains.com

- Specialize in Montina™ products made from Indian ricegrass that is grown by its members and milled, processed and packaged in a dedicated gluten-free facility. The ricegrass is tested for gluten before it enters the milling facility.
- Available as Montina™ Pure Baking Supplement (Montina flour) and Montina™ All Purpose Flour Blend (white rice flour, tapioca flour and Montina flour).
- Available in retail stores.
- Order direct by phone, fax, mail or internet; shipping charges based on weight; ships via UPS Ground.

Amy's Kitchen Inc., Box 449, Petaluma, CA, USA 94953
Phone: 707-578-7188 FAX: 707-578-7995
www.amyskitchen.com

- Organic, vegetarian, prepared natural meals (e.g., pot pies, entrées, pizzas, whole meals, Asian and Indian meals, skillet meals, burritos, pocket sandwiches, veggie burgers, snacks, toaster pops, soups, chilies, refried beans, pasta sauces and salsas).
- A variety of products (over 50) are gluten-free and some are also dairy-free.
- Available in retail stores.

Ancient Harvest Quinoa Corporation, Box 279, 222 E. Redondo Beach Blvd., Unit B, Gardena, CA, USA 90248
✦ Phone: 310-217-8125 FAX: 310-217-8140
Email: quinoacorp@aol.com www.quinoa.net

- Organic quinoa products include quinoa grain, flour, cereal flakes and pastas (quinoa flour and corn flour) which are gluten-free.
- Regular supergrain organic pasta (whole-wheat and quinoa flour) is **NOT** gluten-free.
- Available in retail stores.
- Order direct by internet; shipping charges based on weight; ships via UPS Ground.

Annie Chun's Inc., 54 Mark Dr., Suite 103, San Rafael, CA, USA 94903
✦ Phone: 415-479-8272 FAX: 415-479-8274
Email: info@anniechun.com www.anniechun.com

- Asian sauces, noodles (chow mein, rice, soba) and meal kits (noodles and sauces).
- Rice noodles (original and flavored) are gluten-free.
- Available in retail stores.
- Order direct by internet; shipping charges based on amount purchased; ships via UPS.

GLUTEN-FREE COMPANIES/DISTRIBUTORS CONT'D.

Annie's Homegrown Inc., 580 Gateway Drive, Napa, CA, USA 94559
✦ Phone: 800-288-1089
Email: bernie@annies.com www.annies.com

- Produce pasta, macaroni and cheese dinners, canned pasta meals, cheddar snacks and vegetarian Indian entrées.
- Some products are gluten-free including all the vegetarian Indian entrées (sold under the name "Tamarind Tree") and the "Gluten-Free Rice Pasta and Cheddar".
- Gluten-free pasta produced in a dedicated gluten-free facility.
- Available in retail stores.
- Order direct by phone, mail or internet; shipping charges based on amount purchased; ships via UPS Ground.

Arico Natural Foods Company, P.O. Box 7115, Beaverton, OR, USA 97007
✦ Phone: 503-259-0871 FAX: 503-214-8842
Email: info@aricofoods.com www.aricofoods.com

- Gluten-free specialty company.
- Produce gluten-free, dairy-free cookies made from organic brown rice and teff. Cookies are individually wrapped and available in various flavors.
- Available in retail stores.
- Order direct by phone, fax, mail or internet; shipping charges based on weight; ships via UPS Ground or USPS.

Arrowhead Mills, Hain-Celestial Group, Consumer Relations Department, 4600 Sleepytime Drive, Boulder, CO, USA 80301
✦ Phone: 800-434-4246 FAX: 303-581-1520
Email: consumerrelations@hain-celestial.com www.arrowheadmills.com

- Wide variety of products (cereals, flours, mixes, legumes, seeds, pastas).
- Many products are gluten-free and are tested for gluten.
- Available in retail stores.
- Order direct by internet; shipping charges based on weight; ships via UPS Ground.

Aunt Candice Foods, Box 1457, Wilsonville, OR, USA 97070-1457
✦ Phone: 503-682-8733 FAX: 503-582-1433
Email: info@auntcandicefoods.com www.auntcandicefoods.com

- Gluten-free specialty company; dedicated gluten-free facility.
- Produce "Aunt Candice" mixes (breading, brownie, cookie, pancake), cookies and protein snack bars. Products are also casein, soy and corn-free.
- Available in retail stores.
- Order direct by phone, fax, mail or internet; shipping charges based on weight; ships via UPS Ground.

GLUTEN-FREE COMPANIES/DISTRIBUTORS CONT'D.

Authentic Foods, 1850 W. 169th St., Suite B, Gardena, CA, USA 90247
✦ Phone: 800-806-4737/310-366-7612 FAX: 310-366-6938
Email: sales@authenticfoods.com www.authenticfoods.com
www.glutenfree-supermarket.com

- Gluten-free specialty company; a dedicated gluten-free facility.
- A variety of "Authentic Foods" wheat-free and gluten-free baking mixes, flours and baking supplies.
- Mixes contain Garfava™ flour (chickpeas and fava beans) developed by founder of this company.
- Also carry other companies' products (cereals, pasta, snacks) and books.
- Available in retail stores.
- Order direct by phone, fax or internet; shipping charges based on weight; ships via UPS Ground.

Barbara's Bakery, 3900 Cypress Dr, Petaluma, CA, USA 94954
Phone: 707-765-2273 FAX: 707-765-2927
Email: info@barbarasbakery.com www.barbarasbakery.com

- Produce a line of natural cereals and snacks (chips, crackers, cookies and snack bars).
- Several cereals and snack foods are gluten-free.
- Available in retail stores.

Bard's Tale Beer Company LLC, 211 NW Ward Road,
Lees Summit, MO, USA 64063
Phone: 816-272-2015 FAX: 816-222-0413
www.bardsbeer.com

- Produce a gluten-free beer made from sorghum, buckwheat and honey called "Bard's Tale Dragon's Gold" which is available in 12 oz. bottles.
- Both founders of the company have celiac disease.
- Rigid quality control procedures are utilized to prevent cross-contamination.
- Available from select distributors (see website for contacts).

Barkat (see Glutano)

Bionaturae, Euro-USA Trading Co. Inc., P.O. Box 98, 5 Tyler Drive,
North Franklin, CT, USA 06254
Phone: 860-642-6996 FAX: 860-642-6990
Email: info@bionaturae.com www.bionaturae.com

- Organic food company that produces olive oil, basalmic vinegar, fruit spreads, tomato products and two lines of pasta (one is gluten-free).
- The company is one of the select few in Italy authorized by the Italian Ministry of Health to produce gluten-free pasta. Product is tested for gluten during each production cycle and also tested in the USA by an independent lab.
- Available in retail stores.

GLUTEN-FREE COMPANIES/DISTRIBUTORS CONT'D.

The Birkett Mills, Box 440A, Penn Yan, NY, USA 14527
✦ Phone: 315-536-3311 FAX: 315-536-6740
Email: service@thebirkettmills.com www.thebirkettmills.com

- One of the world's largest millers of buckwheat products.
- Process all buckwheat products in a self-contained mill dedicated solely to buckwheat grain. No other items are processed in their buckwheat milling systems. After milling, buckwheat products are packaged on totally dedicated equipment.
- They also do random testing for gluten in their products using the enzyme immunoassay that tests at sensitivity levels of 20 ppm.
- Available in retail stores.
- Order direct by phone, fax, mail or internet; shipping charges based on weight; ships via UPS Ground.

Blue Diamond Growers, 1802 C Street, Sacramento, CA, USA 95814
✦ Phone: 800-987-2329/916-442-0771 FAX: 916-446-8461
www.bluediamond.com

- World's largest tree nut processing and marketing company specializing in a variety of almond products (nuts, nut thins and "Almond Breeze" non-dairy beverage).
- Most products are gluten-free.
- Available in retail stores.
- Order direct by internet; shipping charges based on weight; ships via UPS.

Bob's Red Mill Natural Foods Inc., 5209 SE International Way,
Milwaukie, OR, USA 97222
✦ Phone: 800-553-2258/503-654-3215 FAX: 503-653-1339
800-349-2173 (mail orders) www.bobsredmill.com

- Mill and manufacture a very extensive line of whole-grain natural foods using flint-hard quartz millstones.
- Produce a large variety of products (baking ingredients, cereals, dried fruits, flours, mixes, nuts, legumes, seeds, soup mixes, spices/herbs and sweeteners). Many of these products are gluten-free. They also sell baking equipment and books.
- Gluten-free specialty products and many grains are milled in a separate production facility and are batch-tested using the ELISA test for gluten in Bob's Red Mill laboratory.
- Available in retail stores and in the Bob's Red Mill retail store.
- Order direct by phone, fax, mail or internet; shipping charges based on weight; ships via UPS Ground.

GLUTEN-FREE COMPANIES/DISTRIBUTORS CONT'D.

Breads From Anna, Gluten Evolution LLC., 612 Highway 1 West,
Iowa City, IA, USA 52246
✦ Phone: 877-354-3886/319-354-3886 FAX: 319-358-9671
Email: glutenevolution@earthlink.net www.glutenevolution.com

- Gluten-free specialty company; dedicated gluten-free facility.
- Products created by the owner who has celiac disease and is a graduate of a culinary school.
- Variety of gluten-free mixes (breads and pie crust) made from bean flours, Montina™, millet, tapioca and arrowroot that are high in protein and fiber.
- Available in retail stores.
- Order direct by phone, fax or internet; shipping charges based on amount purchased; ships via UPS Ground.

BumbleBar Foods Inc., 3808 N. Sullivan Road, Building 12, Suite 3,
Spokane, WA, USA 99216
✦ Phone: 888-453-3369/509-924-2080 FAX: 509-931-5000
Email: info@bumblebar.com www.bumblebar.com

- Dedicated gluten-free facility.
- Produce organic snack bars made with sesame and flax seeds, and other ingredients. All bars are gluten and dairy-free.
- Available in retail stores.
- Order direct by phone, fax, mail or internet; shipping charges based on weight; ships via UPS Ground.

Café Bonjour, Maplegrove Food and Beverage Corp.,
8175 Winston Churchill Blvd., Norval, ON, Canada L0P 1K0
Phone: 905-451-7423 FAX: 905-453-8137
Email: info@maplegrovefoods.com www.maplegrovefoods.com

- Gluten-free specialty company; dedicated gluten-free facility.
- Produce brown rice pasta in a variety of shapes. Also available in bulk sizes.
- Available in retail stores.

CanBrands Specialty Foods **(see Kingsmill)**

Candy Tree, Health Flavors Ltd., 50 Sodom Road, Brewster, NY, USA 10509
✦ Phone: 877-380-3422/845-278-8164 FAX: 845-278-6277
Email: info@healthflavors.com www.healthflavors.com

- Produce a variety of organic corn-based candies (toffee, lollipops, licorice) including a line of wheat-free/gluten-free licorice.
- Gluten-free products are tested for gluten.
- Available in retail stores.
- Order direct by internet at www.kitch-n-kaffe.com.

GLUTEN-FREE COMPANIES/DISTRIBUTORS CONT'D.

CanMar Grain Products Ltd., 2480 Sandra Schmirler Way,
Regina, SK, Canada S4W 1B7
Phone: 866-855-5553/306-721-1375 FAX: 306-721-1378
www.canmargrain.com
www.roastedflax.com

- Mill and manufacture raw and roasted flax products (whole seed and milled, ground flax) in a dedicated gluten-free facility.
- Retail products sold under the name "Flax For Nutrition" available in family size and bulk.
- Available in retail stores.

Casa deFruta, 10021 Pacheco Pass Highway, Hollister, CA, USA 95023
✦ Phone: 800-543-1702/408-842-7282 FAX: 408-842-0248
Email: info@casadefruta.com www.casadefruta.com

- Specialty store with a variety of products including fresh and dried fruits, nuts, chocolates, meats, cheese, wine, sauces and mesquite flour.
- Available in the Casa deFruta retail store or order direct by phone or internet; shipping charges based on amount purchased; ships via UPS Ground.

'Cause You're Special!, P. O. Box 316, Phillips, WI, USA 54555
✦ Phone: 866-669-4328/715-339-6959 FAX: 603-754-0245
Email: info@causeyourespecial.com www.causeyourespecial.com
www.glutenfreegourmet.com

- Gluten-free specialty company; dedicated gluten-free facility.
- A variety of "Cause You're Special" gluten-free, casein-free baking mixes (breads, biscuits, cakes, cookies, muffins, pancakes, pie crusts, pizza crusts, scones), flours and other baking ingredients. Also carry snack bars, other products and books.
- Available in some retail stores.
- Order direct by phone, fax or internet; shipping charges based on amount purchased; ships via UPS (all available services) and USPS Priority Mail.

CelifibR, Maplegrove Food and Beverage Corp.,
8175 Winston Churchill Blvd., Norval, ON, Canada L0P 1K0
Phone: 905-451-7423 FAX: 905-453-8137
Email: info@maplegrovefoods.com www.maplegrovefoods.com

- Dedicated gluten-free facility.
- Gluten-free bouillon cubes and soup base mix. Made with organic vegetables and cold pressed sunflower oil. Does not contain MSG or sulphites.
- Available in retail stores.

Celimix (see Nelson David of Canada)

GLUTEN-FREE COMPANIES/DISTRIBUTORS CONT'D.

Chebe, Prima Provisions Co., P. O. Box 991, Newport, VT, USA 05855
✦ Phone: 800-217-9510/802-334-8272 FAX: 802-334-5343
Email: info@chebe.com www.chebe.com

- Dedicated gluten-free facility.
- Mixes (bread, bread sticks, cinnamon rolls, pizza dough) and frozen dough (bread sticks, pizza and sandwich buns) made from manioc flour and manioc starch (also known as tapioca, yucca or cassava).
- Available in some retail stores.
- Order direct by phone, mail or internet; flat rate shipping charge; ships via UPS Ground.

Cheecha Krackles, CadCan Marketing and Sales Inc., 3412 9th St. SE., Calgary, AB, Canada T2G 3C3
✦ Phone: 877-243-3242/403-287-6731 FAX: 403-287-6732
Email: cheecha@telus.net www.cheecha.ca

- Hot-air puffed potato and unpuffed potato pasta chips that are low in fat.
- Puffed (Luscious Lime, Original and Salt/Vinegar flavors) are gluten-free.
- Unpuffed chips (gluten-free label only).
- Available in retail stores.
- Order direct by phone, fax, mail or internet; shipping charges based on weight; ships via UPS Ground.

Choices Markets, 8188 River Way, Delta, BC, Canada V4G 1K5
Phone: 604-940-8891 FAX: 604-940-8845
Email: comments@choicesmarket.com www.choicesmarket.com

- Western Canada's largest retailer of natural and organic foods with 6 locations in Vancouver and lower mainland area. Corporate nutritionist on staff.
- Carry a large selection of products including many gluten-free items from a variety of companies.
- Also produce gluten-free baked products (brown rice breads, buns, cakes, brownies, cookies, muffins, pizza crusts and squares) in their dedicated gluten-free facility called "Choices Best Rice Bakery" located at 2595 W. 16th Ave. in Vancouver. (Phone 604-736-0301).

Club House, McCormick Canada, P. O. Box 5788, London, ON, Canada N6A 4Z2
Phone: 800-265-2600/519-432-1166 www.clubhouse-canada.com

- Large variety of products (baking ingredients, food extracts and colors, dry sauces and seasoning mixes, spices).
- Many products are gluten-free (e.g., spices, potato flour, rice flour).
- Contact company for a listing of gluten-free products.

GLUTEN-FREE COMPANIES/DISTRIBUTORS CONT'D.

Cocina de Vega Inc., 8014 Olson Memorial Highway, Golden Valley, MN, USA 55427-4712
✦ Phone: 763-591-9087 FAX: 763-208-5556
Email: jim@cocinadevega.com www.cocinadevega.com

- Distributor of mesquite meal (flour) and bean pods.
- Meal is derived from ground whole pods using a hammermill and water cool mill process. Available in various sizes including bulk quantities.
- Order direct by phone, fax, mail or internet; shipping charges based on amount purchased; ships via USPS Priority.

Cook in the Kitchen, P. O. Box 3, Post Mills, VT, USA 05058
✦ Phone: 800-474-5518/802-333-4141 FAX: 802-333-4624
Email: info@cookinthekitchen.com www.cookinthekitchen.com

- Produce a variety of products (e.g., soups and mixes). Soups (4 flavors) are gluten-free.
- Available in some retail stores.
- Order direct by phone, mail or internet; shipping charges based on amount purchased; ships via UPS Ground.

Cream Hill Estates Ltd., 9633 rue Clément, Lasalle, Quebec, Canada H8R 4B4
✦ Phone: 866-727-3628/514-363-2066 FAX: 514-363-1614
Email: info@creamhillestates.com www.creamhillestates.com

- New gluten-free specialty company that mill and manufacture pure, uncontaminated oat products in a dedicated gluten-free facility.
- Their seed quality meets established standards of purity as specified by the Canadian Seed Grower's Association and regulated under the Canada Seeds Act. The oats are planted in fields that have not grown any wheat-related cereal crops for at least the three previous years. The fields are monitored for purity by crop inspectors from the Canadian Food Inspection Agency. The equipment used in planting, harvesting, transporting, processing and packaging is dedicated and/or cleaned to guarantee pure-oat production with no cross-contamination.
- The harvested crop is analyzed for purity using certified seed labs and the highly sensitive R5-ELISA test.
- Oat products sold under the name Lara's (rolled oats, oat flour and whole oats) that are available in family-size and bulk quantities.
- Available in retail stores.
- Order direct by phone, fax or internet; shipping charges based on weight; ships via UPS (in the USA) and CanPar (in Canada).

GLUTEN-FREE COMPANIES/DISTRIBUTORS CONT'D.

Cream of The Crop, Aliments Trigone Inc., 93 Aqueduc,
St.Francois-de-la Riviere, QC, Canada G0R 3A0
Phone: 877-259-7491/418-259-7414 FAX: 418-259-2417
Email: bio@alimentstrigone.com www.alimentstrigone.com

- Producer of organic products (green and black buckwheat, hemp, kamut, spelt and fresh garlic).
- Buckwheat products (flour, grits [sold as "cream of buckwheat"] and groats) are processed in a separate production area and are laboratory tested for gluten.
- Available in retail stores.

Cybros Inc., P. O. Box 851, Waukesha, WI, USA 53187-0851
✦ Phone: 800-876-2253/262-547-1821 FAX: 262-547-8946
Email: sales@cybrosinc.com www.cybrosinc.com

- Produce a variety of breads, buns, rolls and cookies. Some products are gluten-free.
- Available in retail stores.
- Order direct by phone, fax or internet; shipping charges based on weight; ships via UPS (Ground or Air).

De Boles, Hain-Celestial Group, Consumer Relations Department,
4600 Sleepytime Drive, Boulder, CO, USA 80301
Phone: 800-434-4246 FAX: 303-581-1520
Email: consumerrelations@hain-celestial.com www.hain-celestial.com

- Produce a variety of pastas (wheat, rice and corn).
- Corn and rice pastas in a variety of shapes and the macaroni/cheese and shells/cheese rice pasta are gluten-free.
- Available in retail stores.

The Dietary Shoppe Inc., 4436 Ridge Aenue, Philadelphia, PA, USA 19129
✦ Phone: 215-242-5302
Email: dietaryshoppe@juno.com http://dietaryshoppe.com

- A special diet food shop that carries a large variety of products from many companies suitable for various conditions including celiac disease.
- Operated by a registered dietitian.
- Available in the "Dietary Shoppe" retail store or order direct by phone or internet; shipping charges based on amount purchased; ships via UPS Ground.

GLUTEN-FREE COMPANIES/DISTRIBUTORS CONT'D.

Dietary Specialties, 10 Leslie Court, Whippany, NJ, USA 07981
✦ Phone: 888-640-2800/973-884-4402 FAX: 973-884-5907
Email: info@dietspec.com www.dietspec.com

- Gluten-free specialty company; dedicated gluten-free facility.
- Produce "Dietary Specialties" baking mixes (breads, cakes, muffins, pancakes), breads and cookies, as well as ready-to-eat frozen products (e.g., chicken nuggets, desserts, fish sticks, pastas, pie shells and pizza).
- Also carry a variety of low protein products from Dietary Specialties and other companies (Bi Aglut, Aproten).
- Available in retail stores.
- Order direct by phone, fax, mail or internet; shipping charges based on amount purchased.
- Grocery items shipped via UPS ground service and frozen items shipped express with freezer packs within contiguous USA.

Dixie Diners' Club, Dixie USA Inc., P. O. Box 1969, Tomball, TX, USA 77377
✦ Phone: 800-233-3668/281-516-3535 FAX: 800-688-2507
Email: info@dixieusa.com www.dixieusa.com
www.dixiediner.com

- Very extensive variety of health food products, including a unique line of soy-based products. Dixie's exclusive products are produced in several plants throughout the USA.
- Also carry other companies' products. Many products are gluten-free.
- Order direct by phone, fax, mail or internet; shipping charges based on amount purchased; ships via FedEx Ground.

Dowd & Rogers Inc., 1641 - 49th Street, Sacramento, CA, USA 95819
Phone: 916-451-6480 FAX: 916-736-2349
Email: info@dowdandrogers.com www.dowdandrogers.com

- Gluten-free specialty company.
- Produce "Dowd & Rogers" gluten-free/soy-free cake mixes made from white rice, Italian chestnut and tapioca starch flours. Also sell Italian chestnut flour.
- Available in retail stores.

Dr. Praeger's Sensible Foods, 9 Boumar Place, Elmwood Park, NJ, USA 07407
✦ Phone: 877-772-3437/201-703-1300 FAX: 201-703-9333
www.drpraegers.com

- A variety of kosher products (breaded fish, gefilte fish, minced fish, prepared pancakes, pizza bagels, vegetables, veggie burgers, organic soy ice cream and frozen fruit pops) that are low in saturated fat, cholesterol and sugar. All foods are certified kosher.
- Produce a line of gluten-free products (fish sticks and pancakes).
- Available in retail stores.
- Order direct by phone, fax or internet; shipping charges based on flat fee; ships via Overnight Express; frozen products shipped in a container with dry ice.

GLUTEN-FREE COMPANIES/DISTRIBUTORS CONT'D.

Eden Foods Inc., 701 Tecumseh Rd, Clinton, MI, USA 49236
✦ Phone: 800-248-0320/517-456-7424 FAX: 517-456-7025
Email: info@edenfoods.com www.edenfoods.com

- Large variety of organic, natural health food products (e.g., beans, condiments, crackers, oils, vinegars, pasta, quinoa, tomatoes, soy beverages and soy/rice beverages). Some products are gluten-free.
- Available in retail stores.
- Order direct by phone, fax, mail or internet; shipping charges based on amount purchased; ships via FedEx or UPS Ground.

Edward & Son's Trading Co., Inc., Box 1326, Carpinteria, CA, USA 93104
✦ Phone: 805-684-8500 FAX: 805-684-8220
Email: edwardandsons@aol.com www.edwardandsons.com

- Organic vegetarian foods under brand names: Edward & Son's, Organic Country, Native Forest, Let's Do Organic, Premier Japan, The Wizards, Troys Rainforest Organics.
- Brown rice snaps, instant soups, bouillon cubes, some sauces and gummi candies are gluten-free.
- Available in retail stores.
- Order direct by phone, fax, mail or internet; flat rate shipping; ships via FedEx Ground.

El Peto Products Ltd., 65 Saltsman Dr., Cambridge, ON, Canada N3H 4R7
✦ Phone: 800-387-4064/519-650-4614 FAX: 519-650-5692
Email: sales@elpeto.com www.elpeto.com

- Gluten-free specialty company; dedicated gluten-free facility.
- Wide variety of "El Peto" baked products (breads, buns, cakes, cookies, muffins, pies, pizza crusts), cereals, mixes, flours, grains and soups.
- Also carry other companies' products (e.g., cookies, crackers, pasta) as well as books.
- Distributor of Glutano, Barkat, Pastariso, Pastato and Tinkyada Products.
- Available in retail stores and the El Peto retail store.
- Order direct by phone, fax, email or mail; shipping charges based on weight; ships via UPS Ground.

Ener-G Foods, Box 84487, Seattle, WA, USA 98124-5787
✦ Phone: 800-331-5222/206-767-6660 FAX: 206-764-3398
Email: customerservice@ener-g.com www.ener-g.com

- Gluten-free specialty company; dedicated gluten-free and dairy-free facility and Kosher certified facility.
- Very large variety of "Ener-G" shelf-stable gluten-free baked products (breads, rolls, buns, cakes, cookies, crackers), baking ingredients, cereals, flours, dairy substitutes, mixes, pastas and snacks.
- Available in retail stores.
- Order direct by phone, fax or internet; shipping charges based on amount purchased; ships via FedEx or UPS Ground or USPS.

GLUTEN-FREE COMPANIES/DISTRIBUTORS CONT'D.

English Bay Blending, 1066 Cliveden Avenue, Delta, BC, Canada V3M 5R5
Phone: 800-399-3113
Email: info@englishbaydairy-free.com www.englishbaydairy-free.com

- Produce cookies, mixes, syrups, dressings and beverages.
- Non-dairy beverage made from potatoes is gluten, soy, rice and casein-free.
- Available as a dry mix or a liquid in shelf-stable cartons (two flavors).
- Available in retail stores.

Enjoy Life, Enjoy Life Natural Brands, 3810 N. River Road, Schiller Park, IL, USA 60176-2307
✦ Phone: 888-503-6569/847-260-0300 FAX: 847-260-0306
www.enjoylifefoods.com

- Gluten-free specialty company; dedicated facility free of gluten, dairy, egg, soy, peanut, tree nut, corn and potato; Kosher certified facility.
- A variety of "Enjoy Life" products (bagels, breads, granola cereals, cookies, snack bars) and baking ingredients.
- Available in retail stores.
- Order direct by phone, fax or internet; shipping charges based on weight; ships via UPS Ground.

EnviroKidz, Nature's Path Foods Inc., 9100 Van Horne Way, Richmond, BC, Canada V6X 1W3
✦ Phone: 888-808-9505/604-248-8777 FAX: 604-248-8760
Email: consumer_services@naturespath.com www.naturespath.com

- Variety of organic cereals, snack bars, cookies and waffles.
- Many products are gluten-free. All products are casein-free (except the chocolate crispy rice bar).
- Specific manufacturing processes are utilized to prevent cross-contamination. All gluten-free products are regularly tested for gluten.
- Available in retail stores.
- Order direct by phone or internet; shipping charges based on amount purchased; ships via UPS Ground.

Erewhon, US Mills Inc., 200 Reservoir St., Needham, MA, USA 02494
Phone: 800-422-1125/781-444-0440 FAX: 781-444-3411
www.usmillsinc.com

- Produce a variety of cereals; some products are gluten-free.
- Available in retail stores.

GLUTEN-FREE COMPANIES/DISTRIBUTORS CONT'D.

FarmPure Foods™, 426 McDonald St., Regina, SK, Canada S4N 6E1
Phone: 306-791-3770 FAX: 306-791-3767
www.farmpure.com

- Owned by over 200 pedigreed seed growers across Western Canada.
- Specialize in producing varietally pure grains including oats. The entire system from grain production through to manufacturing is designed to ensure purity.
- Oats will be processed in a new dedicated gluten-free facility opening fall 2006. A variety of oat products will be available.

Food For Life Baking Company, Box 1434, Corona, CA, USA 92878
Phone: 800-797-5090/951-279-5090 FAX: 951-279-1784
Email: info@foodforlife.com www.foodforlife.com

- Wholesale bakery that produces a variety of "Food For Life" specialty breads, buns, tortillas and pasta. Some breads, tortillas and pasta are gluten-free.
- Available in retail stores.

Foods By George LLC, 3 King St., Mahwah, NJ, USA 07430
✦ Phone: 201-612-9700 FAX: 201-684-0334
Email: info@foodsbygeorge.com www.foodsbygeorge.com

- Gluten-free specialty company; dedicated gluten-free facility.
- A variety of "Foods By George" baked products (brownies, cakes, muffins, tarts), pizza, lasagna and manicotti.
- Available in retail stores.
- Order direct by internet; shipping charges based on amount purchased; ships via UPS Ground, 3 day select service or 2nd day air.

Fortitude Brands LLC, P.O. Box 431304, Miami, FL, USA 33243-1304
✦ Phone: 866-664-5883 FAX: 305-662-4977
Email: contact@fortitudebrands.com www.fortitudebrands.com

- Gluten-free specialty company; dedicated gluten-free facility.
- Produce gluten-free cookies, crackers and coatings. Crackers sold under the name "Casabe Rainforest" and are made with high fiber casava pulp.
- Available in retail stores.
- Order direct by internet; shipping charges based on a flat rate; ships via UPS Ground.

GardenSpot's Finest, 438 White Oak Rd.. New Holland, PA, USA 17557
✦ Phone: 800-829-5100/717-354-4936 FAX: 877-829-5100/717-354-4934
Email: cs@gardenspotsfinest.com www.gardenspotsfinest.com

- Natural, organic and specialty food distributor that carries a variety of products. Many are gluten-free.
- Gluten-free products from Shiloh Farms and Foods By George.
- Order direct by phone, fax or internet; shipping charges based on weight; ships via UPS Ground or Air.

GLUTEN-FREE COMPANIES/DISTRIBUTORS CONT'D.

Gifts of Nature Inc., 810 - 7th St. East, Unit #17, Polson, MT, USA 59860
✦ Phone: 888-275-0003/406-883-3730 FAX: 406-883-3731
Email: giftsofnature@centurytel.net www.giftsofnature.net

- Gluten-free specialty company; dedicated gluten-free facility.
- Produce a variety of "Gifts of Nature" mixes (biscuits, breads, brownies, cakes, cookies, muffins, pancakes, pizza), flours and baking ingredients.
- Available in some retail stores.
- Order direct by phone, mail or internet; shipping charges based on weight; ships via UPS.

Gillian's Foods, Inc., 82 Sanderson Ave., Lynn, MA, USA 01902
✦ Phone: 781-586-0086 FAX: 781-586-0087
Email: chefbob@gilliansfoods.com www.gilliansfoods.com

- Gluten-free specialty company; dedicated gluten-free facility.
- Variety of "Gillian's" baked products (breads, rolls, pies, pie crust, pizza dough and bread crumbs), baking mixes, flours and sauces.
- Available in retail stores.
- Order direct by phone, fax or internet; shipping charges based on weight; ships via UPS (Ground, Next or 2nd day air or 3rd day select).

Glutafin, Nutricia Dietary Care, Newmarket Ave., Trowbridge, Wiltshire BA14 OXQ, England
Phone: 44 1225 711801 FAX: 44 1225 711567
Email: glutenfree@nutricia.co.uk www.glutafin.co.uk

- Gluten-free specialty company.
- Nutricia Dietary Care produces "Glutafin" products (breads, rolls, cakes, biscuits, crackers, pasta and mixes).
- Many of the gluten-free products are made with gluten-free flours and starches labeled as "Gluten-Free/Wheat-Free". However, they also produce a line of gluten-free products with wheat starch, which are not allowed on a gluten-free diet in Canada, the USA and some other countries. None of the wheat starch-based gluten-free products are listed in this Guide.
- Available from select gluten-free specialty companies and distributors in North America.

GLUTEN-FREE COMPANIES/DISTRIBUTORS CONT'D.

Glutano, Gluten-Free Foods Ltd., Unit 270 Centennial Park, Centennial Ave, Elstree, Borehamwood, Herts WD6 3SS, England
Phone: 44 20 8953 4444 FAX: 44 20 8953 8285
Email: info@glutenfree-foods.co.uk www.glutano.com
www.glutenfree-foods.co.uk

- Gluten-free specialty company; dedicated gluten-free facility.
- A variety of "Glutano" products (breads, cookies, crackers, cereals, pastas, pretzels and mixes), as well as "Barkat" gluten-free products (breads, pizza crusts, bread mix, cereals, pot meals, ice cream cones).
- They also sell "Odlums Tritamyl" products from Ireland which contain wheat starch, which is not allowed on a gluten-free diet in Canada and the USA.
- Available from gluten-free distributors and specialty companies in North America; and from health food stores and pharmacies in the U.K. and Europe.

Gluten-Free Cookie Jar, RR3, Box 117 EE, Meshoppen, PA, USA 18630
✦ Phone: 888-458-8360/570-965-2767 FAX: 570-965-0929
Email: dsutter@glutenfreecookiejar.com www.glutenfreecookiejar.com

- Gluten-free specialty company; dedicated gluten-free facility.
- Produce "Gluten-Free Cookie Jar" gluten-free baked products (breads, bagels, soft pretzels, rolls, cakes, and cookies), baking mixes (breads, bagels, soft pretzels, cakes, cookies, muffins, scones) and flours.
- Order direct by phone, mail or internet; shipping charges based on amount purchased; ships via UPS Ground.

Gluten-Free Creations Bakery and Bistro, 2940 E. Thomas, Phoenix, AZ, USA 85016
✦ Phone: 602-522-0659 FAX: 602-485-4411
www.glutenfreecreations.com

- Gluten-free specialty company; dedicated gluten-free facility.
- Produce a variety of baked products (breads, cakes, cookies, pizza crust, rolls) that are in vacuum-sealed packages with a one month shelf life.
- Available in some retail stores.
- Order direct by phone, fax, mail or internet; shipping charges based on amount purchased; ships via UPS Ground.

Glutenfreeda Foods Inc., 181 Shooting Star Lane, Friday Harbor, WA, USA 98250
✦ Phone: 360-378-3675
Email: yvonne@glutenfreeda.com www.glutenfreeda.com

- Gluten-free specialty company; dedicated gluten-free facility.
- Produce "Real Cookies™" refrigerated cookie dough that is gluten and dairy-free.
- Available in some retail stores.
- Order direct by phone or internet; shipping charges based on weight; ships via FedEx (2 day) in special styrofoam containers with cold packs.

GLUTEN-FREE COMPANIES/DISTRIBUTORS CONT'D.

Gluten-Free Mall

✦ Email: info@glutenfreemall.com www.glutenfreemall.com

- Gluten-free internet shopping mall carrying hundreds of gluten-free products from dozens of companies from around the world, as well as gluten-free books and cookbooks.
- Ships all products from a central warehouse with one shipping charge based on weight; ships via UPS.
- Ships dry goods and frozen products separately. Frozen products shipped in special freezer pack containers.

Gluten-Free Market, 210 McHenry Road, Buffalo Grove, IL, USA 60089

Phone: 847-419-9610 FAX: 847-419-9615

✦ Email: info@glutenfreemarket.com www.glutenfreemarket.com

- Gluten-free specialty retail store operated by a family with celiac disease.
- Nutritionist (has celiac disease) on staff.
- Carry a very large variety of products (breads, cereals, condiments, cookies, desserts, entrées, flours, frozen foods, mixes, pastas, sauces, soups, snacks), as well as books and gift baskets.
- Shop in person or order direct by phone, fax or internet; shipping charges based on weight; ships via UPS.

Gluten-Free Pantry/Glutino USA, P. O. Box 840, Glastonbury, CT, USA 06033

Phone: 800-291-8386/860-633-3826 FAX: 860-633-6853

✦ Email: pantry@glutenfree.com www.glutenfreepantry.com

www.glutenfree.com

www.foodchoices.com

- Gluten-free specialty company; dedicated gluten-free facility.
- Produce "Gluten-Free Pantry" mixes (breads, cakes, cereals, cookies, muffins, pastry, pancakes and scones).
- Also carry a wide variety of other companies' gluten-free products (e.g., breads, cereals, cookies, condiments, crackers, flours, pasta, snacks, soups), as well as bread machines and books.
- Available in retail stores.
- Order direct by phone, fax or internet; shipping charges based on amount purchased; ships via UPS (Ground, next day, 2nd or 3rd day) or FedEx Ground.

Gluten-Free Supermarket, 1850 West 169th Street, Suite B,
Gardena, CA, USA 90247

Phone: 800-806-4737/310-366-7612 FAX: 310-366-6938

✦ Email: sales@authenticfoods.com www.glutenfree-supermarket.com

- Gluten-free specialty distributor.
- Carry a variety of gluten-free products (cereals, pasta, snacks), "Authentic Foods" mixes, flours and other baking supplies, as well as books.
- Order direct by phone, fax, mail or internet; shipping charges based on weight; ships via UPS Ground.

GLUTEN-FREE COMPANIES/DISTRIBUTORS CONT'D.

Gluten-Free Trading Company, 3116 South Chase Ave., Milwaukee, WI, USA 53207
✦ Phone: 888-993-9933/414-747-8700 FAX: 414-747-8747
Email: info@gluten-free.net www.gluten-free.net
www.food4celiacs.com

- Gluten-free specialty retail store.
- Sell over 1000 gluten-free items from around the world.
- Shop in person or order by phone, fax or internet; shipping charges based on weight; ships via FedEx Ground.

Gluten Solutions Inc., 8750 Concourse Court, San Diego, CA, USA 92123
✦ Phone: 888-845-8836/858-292-4564
Email: info@glutensolutions.com www.glutensolutions.com

- Gluten-free specialty internet grocery store that sells over 500 of the most popular gluten-free products and books from 35 vendors.
- Ships all products from a central warehouse with one shipping charge based on weight; ships via UPS (Ground, Next Day, 2nd Day) or USPS Priority.

Glutino (formerly De-Ro-Ma), 2055 Boulevard Dagenais Ouest,
Laval, QC, Canada H7L 5V1
✦ Phone: 800-363-3438/450-629-7689 FAX: 450-629-4781
Email: info@glutino.com www.glutino.com

- Gluten-free specialty company; dedicated gluten-free facility.
- Wide variety of "Glutino" baked products (bagels, breads, buns, cakes, cookies, muffins, pie crusts, pizza crusts), mixes, flours, grains, salad dressings, pasta, pretzels, sauces and soups.
- Distributor of Aproten, Bi-Aglut, Dr. Schar and Glutafin (breads, cereals, crackers, cookies, mixes and pasta) in Canada and the U.S.
- Available in retail stores and the Glutino retail store.
- Order direct by phone, fax or internet; shipping charges based on weight; ships via UPS Ground or UPS Air (in the USA) or Purolator Ground (in Canada).

Grain Process Enterprises Ltd., 115 Commander Blvd., Scarborough, ON,
Canada M1S 3M7
✦ Phone: 800-387-5292/416-291-4004 FAX: 800-437-4420/416-291-2159
Email: orderdesk@grainprocess.com www.grainprocess.com

- Wholesale food processing company with an extensive line of products (baking ingredients, cereals, confectionary items, flours, mixes, nuts, oils, pastas, sweeteners, spices and other products). A variety of products are gluten-free.
- Individual consumers can purchase items in their retail store or order direct by phone, fax or mail; shipping charges based on weight; ships via Canada Post.

GLUTEN-FREE COMPANIES/DISTRIBUTORS CONT'D.

Hain Pure Foods, Hain-Celestial Group, Consumer Relations Department,
4600 Sleepytime Drive, Boulder, CO, USA 80301
Phone: 800-434-4246 FAX: 303-581-1520
Email: consumerrelations@hain-celestial.com www.hainpurefoods.com

- A variety of natural food products (e.g., "kidz" food and snack products, expeller–pressed oils and crackers).
- "Mini Munchie" rice cakes (four flavors) are gluten-free.
- Available in retail stores.

Health Valley, Hain-Celestial Group, Consumer Relations Department,
4600 Sleepytime Drive, Boulder, CO, USA 80301
Phone: 800-434-4246 FAX: 303-581-1520
Email: consumerrelations@hain-celestial.com www.healthvalley.com

- A variety of natural health-food products (e.g., chilies, soups, broths, cereals, crackers, cookies, snack bars). Some cereals, crackers, broth and soups are gluten-free.
- Available in retail stores.

Heartland's Finest, Heartland Ingredients, P.O. Box 313, Ubly, MI USA 48475
✦ Phone: 888-658-8909/989-658-8909 FAX: 989-658-8949
Email: jim@heartlandsfinest.com www.heartlandsfinest.com

- Gluten-free specialty company; dedicated gluten-free facility.
- Mill pinto and navy bean flours.
- Produce pasta (from bean and corn flours) that cooks in 3-5 minutes, requires no rinsing and can be served hot or cold. Also make a cereal called "Cero's" (made with bean and rice flours) and gluten-free mixes and a baking blend.
- Available in retail stores.
- Order direct by phone, fax, mail or internet; shipping charges based on weight; ships via UPS Ground.

Heaven Scent Natural Foods, 2516 California Ave., Santa Monica, CA, USA 90403
Phone: 310-829-9050 FAX: 310-829-6745
Email: info@heavenscentnaturalfoods.com www.heavenscentnaturalfoods.com

- Natural food company that produces bread crumbs, cookies, croutons and crispy rice and marshmallows bars. The bars are gluten and dairy-free.
- Available in retail stores.

Herbalicious ... Everything Nutritious, 612 West Main Street,
Mount Pleasant, PA, USA 15666
✦ Phone: 724-542-9745 FAX: 724-542-9746
Email: mail@everythingnutritious.com www.everythingnutritious.com

- Gluten-free specialty retail store operated by a registered dietitian.
- Carry a wide variety of gluten-free products (frozen and shelf-stable baked products, cereals, cookies, crackers, mixes, pastas, soups).
- Also sells other food products, supplements, toiletries, gift baskets and books.
- Shop in person or order direct by phone, fax or internet; shipping charges based on weight; ships via UPS Ground.

GLUTEN-FREE COMPANIES/DISTRIBUTORS CONT'D.

Hodgson Mill, 1203 Niccum Avenue, Effingham, IL, USA 62401
✦ Phone: 800-525-0177 FAX: 217-347-0198
Email: customerservice@hodgsonmill.com www.hodgsonmill.com

- Whole grain milling company using a stone grind milling process.
- Sell a variety of flours, mixes, baking ingredients and pastas. Several mixes and flours are gluten-free.
- Specialized cleaning procedures are utilized before production of gluten-free mixes which are ELISA-tested for gluten.
- Available in retail stores.
- Order direct by phone, fax, mail or internet; shipping charges based on amount purchased; ships via UPS Ground.

Hol•Grain, Conrad Rice Mill Inc., P. O. Box 10640, New Iberia, LA, USA 70562
✦ Phone: 800-551-3245/337-364-7242 FAX: 337-365-5806
Email: info@conradricemill.com www.conradricemill.com

- Oldest rice mill in North America.
- A variety of rice mixes, sauces, seasonings, snacks, soups, spices and wheat-free/gluten-free products. Brown rice crackers, brown rice bread crumbs, brownie mix, chocolate chip cookie mix, pancake/waffle mix and plain rice are gluten-free.
- Available in retail stores.
- Order direct by phone or internet; shipping charges based on amount purchased; ships via UPS Ground.

Ian's Natural Foods, 439 South Union Street, Lawrence, MA, USA 01843
Phone: 978-989-0601 FAX: 978-989-0602
www.iansnaturalfoods.com

- Produce natural frozen food products (entrées, fries and pancakes) with no artificial flavors, colors or preservatives.
- Also have a variety of products that are free of wheat, gluten, dairy, egg, nut and soy (chicken nuggets, fish sticks, shepherd's pie, potato puffs).
- Available in retail stores.

Imagine Foods, Hain-Celestial Group, Consumer Relations Department,
4600 Sleepytime Drive, Boulder, CO, USA 80301
Phone: 800-434-4246 FAX: 303-581-1520
Email: consumerrelations@hain-celestial.com www.imaginefoods.com
www.tastethedream.com

- Natural food products include beverages ("Rice Dream", "Soy Dream", "Power Dream Soy Energy Drinks"), frozen desserts and novelties and "Imagine" products (broths, soups). Many products are gluten-free.
- Available in retail stores.

GLUTEN-FREE COMPANIES/DISTRIBUTORS CONT'D.

Inca Organics, P.O. Box 61-8154, Chicago, IL, USA 60661-8154
Phone: 866-328-4622/312-575-9880 FAX: 312-575-9881
Email: incaorganics@aol.com www.incaorganics.com

- Bulk wholesaler of certified South American organic quinoa and black amaranth.
- Sell to distributors and food manufacturers in bulk quantities.

Instant Gourmet, AlpineAire Foods, P. O. Box 1799, Rocklin, CA, USA 95677
✦ Phone: 800-322-6325/866-322-6325/ 916-624-6050 FAX: 916-624-1604
Email: info@aa-foods.com www.aa-foods.com

- Instant gluten-free meals in ready-to-serve disposable cups (entrées, soups).
- Available in retail stores.
- Order direct by phone, fax or internet; shipping charges based on product weight; ships via UPS Ground.

It's OK! Baked Goods, GLP Free Manufacturng, 2409 Whitehaven Road, Grant Island, NY, USA 14072
✦ Phone: 866-658-6328/716-773-7745 FAX: 716-773-6012
www.oktoeat.com
www.okbrownie.com

- Gluten-free specialty company; dedicated facility free of gluten, dairy, peanut and tree-nuts.
- Produce breads, brownies, cream puffs, pizza crusts and rolls.
- Available in retail stores.
- Order direct by internet; contact company for shipping information.

Jennies, Red Mill Farms Inc., 290 S. 5th St., Brooklyn, NY, USA 11211
Phone: 718-384-2150 FAX: 718-384-2988

- Produce gluten-free coconut macaroons and "low carb" coconut macaroons in various flavors.
- Available in retail stores.

Kari-Out Company, 399 Knollwood Road, Suite 309, White Plains, NY, USA 10603
Phone: 888-328-1688/914-580-3200 FAX: 914-580-3248
www.kariout.com

- Manufacturer of take-out packaging containers, cleaning supplies and food ingredients (sauces, spices, seasonings).
- Produce "Panda Brand" gluten-free, low-sodium soy sauce available in individual packets, sold in bulk (350 packets/case) to distributors.
- Available to restaurants and other food service facilities.

GLUTEN-FREE COMPANIES/DISTRIBUTORS CONT'D.

Kaybee, Box 629, Cudworth, SK, Canada S0K 1B0
✦ Phone: 306-256-3424 FAX: 306-256-3424
Email: kaybee@sasktel.net

- Gluten-free specialty company; dedicated gluten-free facility.
- Variety of "Kaybee" gluten-free mixes (bread, buns, cakes, cookies, muffins, pancakes, pizza crusts, puddings, and perogies).
- Available in retail stores.
- Order direct by phone or fax. Shipping is free for orders of 24 packages or more; shipping parcels under 24 packages is a flat rate of $6.00 in Canada and $10.00 (U.S. funds) in USA.

Kingsmill Foods, Canbrands Specialty Foods, PO Box 117,
Gormley, ON, Canada L0H 1G0
Phone: 905-888-5836 FAX: 905-888-5594
Email: info@canbrands.ca www.canbrands.ca

- Gluten-free specialty company; dedicated gluten-free facility.
- Produce "Kingsmill" gluten-free breads, cookies, pizza crusts and baking mixes.
- Available in retail stores and from select distributors.

Kinnikinnick Foods, 10940 - 120 Street, Edmonton, AB, Canada T5H 3P7
✦ Phone: 877-503-4466/780-424-2900 FAX: 780-421-0456
Email: info@kinnikinnick.com www.kinnikinnick.com

- Gluten-free specialty company; dedicated gluten-free facility.
- On-site quality control lab that tests for gluten using the highly sensitive ELISA test.
- Very large variety of "Kinnikinnick" baked products (bagels, breads, buns, cakes, cereal, cookies, donuts, muffins, pizza crust) and baking mixes, as well as flours. All products are dairy-free/casein-free except cheese bread.
- Carry a variety of products from other companies (cereals, crackers, pasta).
- Available in retail stores and the Kinnikinnick retail store.
- Order direct by phone, fax or internet; shipping charges are a $10 flat rate for Canadian orders and $10 (U.S. funds) for USA orders valued up to $200.

Kokimo Kitchen Ltd., 2771 County Road 25, Castleton, ON, Canada K0K 1M0
✦ Phone: 888-344-7977/905-344-7960 FAX: 905-344-7961
Email: amazing@kokimokitchen.com www.kokimokitchen.com

- Gluten-free specialty company; dedicated gluten-free facility.
- Produce "Kokimo" mixes (pancakes, waffles and eggless French toast) made from buckwheat, cornmeal, brown rice, millet and Asian bean flours. Mixes are also dairy and egg-free. Available in family size and bulk quantities.
- Available in some retail stores.
- Order direct by phone, fax, mail or internet; free shipping with minimum orders; ships via CanPar.

GLUTEN-FREE COMPANIES/DISTRIBUTORS CONT'D.

Lactaid, McNeil Consumer Health Care, Guelph, ON, Canada N1K 1A5
Phone: 800-522-8243 www.lactaid.com

- "Lactaid" (lactose-reduced milk) is available in shelf-stable and refrigerated forms.
- "Lactaid tablets" and "Lactaid caplets".
- All products are gluten-free.
- Available in retail stores.

Lactaid, McNeil Nutritionals, 7050 Camp Hill Rd., Ft. Washington, PA, USA 19034
Phone: 800-522-8243 FAX: 215-273-4070
www.lactaid.com

- "Lactaid" (lactose-reduced milk) is available in refrigerated forms.
- "Lactaid tablets" and "Lactaid caplets".
- All products are gluten-free.
- Available in retail stores.

Lacteeze, Kingsmill Foods, 1399 Kennedy Rd., Toronto, ON, Canada M1P 2L6
Phone: 416-755-1124 FAX: 416-755-4486
www.kingsmillfoods.com
www.lacteeze.com

- "Lacteeze" (lactose-reduced milk) is available in shelf stable and refrigerated forms.
- "Lacteeze" drops and tablets.
- All products are gluten-free.
- Available in retail stores.

La Messagère, Les Bieres de la Nouvelle-France, 3451 Chemin de la Nouvelle-France, Saint-Paulin, Quebec, Canada J0K 3G0
Phone: 800-789-5962/819-268-5500 FAX: 819-268-5502
Email: bnf@telmilot.net www.baluchon.com/bnf

- Microbrewery that produces a variety of beers including La Messagère, a gluten-free beer (blonde ale) derived from rice and buckwheat.
- Available in liquor stores across Canada and in some specialty stores in 341 mL bottles.

Lärabar, Humm Foods Inc., P.O. Box 18932, Denver, CO, USA 80218
✦ Phone: 877-527-2227/720-945-1155 FAX: 720-941-1158
www.larabar.com

- Dedicated gluten-free facility.
- Variety of nutrition energy bars made from dried fruits, nuts and spices that are free of gluten, dairy and soy.
- Available in retail stores.
- Order direct by phone, fax or internet; shipping charges based on flat rate; ships via FedEx Ground.

Lara's (see Cream Hill Estates)

GLUTEN-FREE COMPANIES/DISTRIBUTORS CONT'D.

Laurel's Sweet Treats Inc., 16004 SW Tualatin – Sherwood Road, #123, Sherwood, OR, USA 97140

✦ Phone: 866-225-3432/503-625-3432 FAX: 503-625-0918
Email: sales@glutenfreemixes.com www.glutenfreemixes.com

- Gluten-free specialty company; dedicated gluten-free facility.
- Variety of baking mixes (breads, brownies, cakes, crackers, cookies, pancakes, pizza dough, rolls), onion ring batter and cake decorating supplies. All baking mixes are dairy-free.
- Order direct by phone, fax, email or internet; shipping charges based on weight; ships via FedEx or UPS (Ground) and USPS.

Leda Nutrition, P.O. Box 2613, Burleigh, DC, QLD, Australia 4220

✦ Email: admin@ledanutrition.com www.ledanutrition.com

- Gluten-free specialty company; dedicated gluten-free facility.
- Produce gluten-free, dairy-free nutrition snack bars made from gluten-free flour mixture (chickpea, corn, tapioca, rice and soy [in some bars]) and dried fruits.
- Available in retail stores.
- Order direct by internet; contact company for shipping arrangements for international orders.

Legumes Plus, Dixie USA Inc., P. O. Box 1969, Tomball, TX, USA 77377

✦ Phone: 800-233-3668/281-516-3535 FAX: 800-688-2507
Email: info@dixieusa.com www.dixieusa.com

- Produce a variety of lentil-based products (chilies, entrées, salads and soups).
- Most lentil soups, salads and entrées are gluten-free.
- Order direct by phone, fax, mail or internet; shipping charges based on amount purchased; ships via FedEx Ground.

LifeSoy, LifeMax Natural Foods Distribution Inc., 1773 Bayly St., Pickering, ON, Canada L1W 2Y7

Phone: 905-831-5433 FAX: 905-831-4333
Email: info@lifemax.ca www.lifemax.ca

- Wheat-free, gluten-free tamari soy sauces.
- Available in retail stores.

Lifestream Natural Foods, Nature's Path Foods Inc., 9100 Van Horne Way, Richmond, BC, Canada V6X 1W3

✦ Phone: 888-808-9505/604-248-8777 FAX: 604-248-8760
Email: consumer_service@naturespath.com www.naturespath.com

- Pasta and waffles from whole grains with no preservatives or artificial flavors.
- Toaster waffles (two flavors) are gluten and dairy-free.
- Available in retail stores.
- Order direct by phone or internet; shipping charges based on amount purchased; ships via UPS.

GLUTEN-FREE COMPANIES/DISTRIBUTORS CONT'D.

Liv-N-Well Distributors, 7900 River Rd, Unit #1, Richmond, BC, Canada V6X 1X7
✦ Phone: 877-270-8479/604-270-8474 FAX: 604-270-8477
Email: info@liv-n-well.com www.liv-n-well.com

- Gluten-free specialty food distributor.
- Sell wheat-free/gluten-free, low-protein, PKU, and dysphagia products.
- Very large selection of gluten-free baked products, flours, grains, mixes, cakes, cookies, crackers, pastas, sauces/condiments, snacks and soups from various companies (e.g., Aproten, El Peto, Ener-G Foods, Glutafin, Hol•Grain, JJB Naturals, Kingsmill, Maple Grove Food and Beverages, SHS), as well as books.
- Order direct by phone, fax, internet or in the Liv-N-Well retail store; shipping charges based on weight; ships via Canada Post or Courier.

Lorenzo's Specialty Foods Ltd., 1060 St. Mary's Road, Winnipeg, MB, Canada R2M 3S9
✦ Phone: 866-639-1711/204-253-1300 FAX: 204-253-4049
Email: hello@lorenzosfoods.ca www.lorenzosfoods.ca

- Gluten-free specialty retail store and bakery; dedicated gluten-free facility operated by a family with celiac disease.
- Carry a variety of gluten-free products (bagels, breads, buns, cakes, cereals, cookies, crackers, flours, frozen entrées, mixes, muffins, pasta, pizza, sauces, sausages, soups) from many companies, as well as books.
- Also produce fresh baked goods (breads, cakes, cookies, pies and squares).
- Shop in person.

Lundberg Family Farms, P. O. Box 369, 5370 Church St., Richvale, CA, USA 95974
✦ Phone: 530-882-4551 FAX: 530-882-4265
Email: question@lundberg.com www.lundberg.com

- Family-owned farm that grows and produces brown rice, specialty rice varieties and brown rice products.
- A variety of products (rice cakes, rice milk, rice snacks, rice syrup, cereal, pasta, rice side dishes). Most of these products are also organic and gluten-free.
- Available in retail stores.
- Order direct by mail or internet; shipping charges based on weight; ships via UPS.

Manischewitz, 340 Marin Blvd., Jersey City, NY, USA 07302
✦ Phone: 201-333-3700 FAX: 201-333-9153
Email: info@manischewitz.com www.manischewitz.com

- Largest USA manufacturer of processed kosher foods (gefilte fish, pastas, soups and soup mixes, snack foods, tams and crackers, matzos, potato and other mixes).
- Also produce products especially for Passover.
- A variety of products are gluten-free.
- Available in retail stores.
- Order direct by internet; shipping charges based on weight; ships via FedEx.

GLUTEN-FREE COMPANIES/DISTRIBUTORS CONT'D.

Marlene's Mixes, P.O. Box 1821, Whitehouse, TX, USA 75791
✦ Phone: 903-839-3892 FAX: 903-839-3494
Email: sales@marlenesmixes.com www.marlenesmixes.com

- Gluten-free specialty company; dedicated gluten-free facility.
- A variety of gluten-free, potato-free mixes (breads, cakes, cookies, muffins, pancakes, rolls, pie crust), spice blends and extracts. Can also order mixes free of soy, corn and/or sugar by special request.
- Available in some retail stores.
- Order direct by phone, fax, mail or internet; shipping charges based on amount purchased; ships via UPS Ground.

Mary's Gone Crackers, P.O. Box 1688, Orinda, CA, USA 94563
✦ Phone: 888-258-1250/925-258-1200 FAX: 925-258-1201
Email: info@marysgonecrackers.com www.marysgonecrackers.com

- Dedicated gluten-free facility.
- Produce gluten-free, high fiber crackers made from organic brown rice, quinoa, flax, sesame seeds and gluten-free tamari sauce.
- Available in retail stores.
- Order direct by phone or internet; shipping charges based on weight; ships via FedEx Ground.

Masuya (USA) Inc., 3550 Watt Avenue, Suite 140, Sacramento, CA, USA 95821
Phone: 916-979-7872 FAX: 916-979-7873
Email: contactus@masuyanaturally.com www.masuyanaturally.com

- Crispy, baked rice snack food in various flavors that are gluten-free.
- Available in retail stores.

Med-Diet Laboratories Inc., 3600 Holly Lane N., Suite 80, Plymouth, MN, USA 55447
✦ Phone: 800-633-3438/763-550-2020 FAX: 763-550-2022
Email: meddiet@med-diet.com www.med-diet.com

- Distributor of a variety of products for special dietary needs (gluten-free, cardiac, critical care, diabetes, dysphagia, low protein).
- Gluten-free baking mixes, breads, cookies and pastas from Aproten, Kingsmill and Med-Diet.
- Order direct by phone, fax, or internet; shipping charges based on weight; ships via UPS or FedEx.

Micah's Favourite, 421 Sandford Street, Newmarket, ON, Canada L3Y 4S5
✦ Phone: 905-898-0739
Email: randy@micahsfavourite.com www.micahsfavourite.com

- Gluten-free specialty company; dedicated gluten-free facility.
- Produce "Micah's" mixes (brownies, cakes, general purpose) and egg replacer.
- All products are also free of dairy, corn, egg and nut.
- Available in retail stores.
- Order direct by phone, fax or internet; shipping charges based on weight; ships via Canada Post Expedited.

GLUTEN-FREE COMPANIES/DISTRIBUTORS CONT'D.

Minn-Dak Growers Ltd., 4034 - 40th Avenue N., P.O. Box 13276, Grand Forks, ND, USA 58208

✦ Phone: 701-746-7453 FAX: 701-780-9050
Email: info@minndak.com www.minndak.com

- A processor, contractor and marketer of buckwheat to the domestic and international food ingredients industry. Dedicated gluten-free facility.
- Has the newest and largest dedicated buckwheat milling facility in North America.
- Buckwheat products include flour, Farinetta™ (buckwheat bran), groats, grits and kasha.
- Also processes safflower, sunflower seeds and mustard seeds.
- Order direct by phone, fax, mail or internet; shipping charges based on weight; ships via UPS Ground.

Miss Roben's, 91 Western Maryland Parkway, Suite 7, Hagerstown, MD, USA 21740

✦ Phone: 800-891-0083/301-665-9580 FAX: 301-665-9584
Email: info@allergygrocer.com www.allergygrocer.com

- Gluten-free specialty company; dedicated facility free of gluten, dairy, peanuts, tree nuts, eggs, soy, sesame and latex.
- Gluten-free/wheat-free mail-order supplier of over 450 products including flours, cereals, cookies, crackers, pastas, sauces, snacks, soups, ready-to-eat dinners and side dishes.
- Also produce "Miss Roben's" gluten-free mixes (bagels, breads, brownies, cakes, cookies, crackers, frostings, muffins, pancakes, pie and pizza crusts, pretzels and tortillas).
- Order direct by phone, fax, or internet; shipping charges based on amount purchased; ships via UPS Ground.

Mochi, Grainaissance Inc., 1580 - 62nd Street, Emeryville, CA, USA 94608

Phone: 800-472-4697/510-547-7256 FAX: 510-547-0526
Email: amazake@grainaissance.com www.grainaissance.com

- Produce a bake and serve rice puff snack made from brown rice in a variety of flavors. All flavors are gluten-free (except "mugwort") and dairy-free.
- Available in retail stores in the refrigerated section.

Mona's Gluten-Free, Mona's US LLC., 13422 NE 177th Place, Woodinville, WA, USA 98072

✦ Phone: 866-486-0701/425-486-0701 FAX: 425-486-0734
Email: mona@madebymona.com www.madebymona.com

- Gluten-free specialty company; dedicated gluten-free facility.
- Produce a variety of "Mona's" mixes (breads, cakes, pancake/waffle, pastry, pizza, all purpose). Also carry flours, starches and xanthan gum.
- Products available in single units, case lots and bulk.
- Order direct by phone, fax or internet; shipping charges based on weight; ships via FedEx or USPS.

GLUTEN-FREE COMPANIES/DISTRIBUTORS CONT'D.

Mountain Meadows Food Processing (see No Nuts)

Mr. Ritt's Bakery, 709 East Passyunk Ave., Philadelphia, PA, USA 19147-3016
✦ Phone: 877-677-4887/215-627-3034
Other location: 2nd & Vine Street, Millville, NJ, USA 08332
Phone: 877-677-4887/856-825-8770
Email: info@mrritts.com www.mrritts.com

- Gluten-free specialty bakery located in Philadelphia and an expanded facility in New Jersey; dedicated gluten-free facilities.
- A large variety of "Mr. Ritt's" products (breads, cakes, cheesecakes, cookies, mixes, muffins, pizza crusts, rolls, tarts).
- Shop in person at both locations.
- Order direct by phone; shipping charges based on weight; ships via UPS Ground.

Mr. Spice, Lang Naturals, 20 Silva Lane, Newport, RI, USA 02842-5638
✦ Phone: 800-728-2348/401-848-7700 FAX: 401-848-7701
Email: customerservice@MrSpice.com www.mrspice.com

- Produce a variety of sauces that do not contain any gluten, dairy, preservatives, salt or sulfites.
- Available in retail stores.
- Order direct by phone, fax, email or internet; shipping charges based on weight; ships via UPS Ground.

Mrs. Leeper's Inc., 2814 Clark Drive, Corinth, TX, USA 76210
Phone: 817-629-6275 FAX: 816-584-5070
Email: mrsleepers@aipc.com www.mrsleeperspasta.com

- Mrs. Leeper's brown rice and corn pastas are gluten-free.
- Also produce other pasta products under the brand name "Eddies" that contains wheat.
- Available in retail stores.

My Own Meals Inc., P.O. Box 334, Deerfield, IL, USA 60015
✦ Phone: 847-948-1118 FAX: 847-948-0468
Email: myownmeals@worldnet.att.net www.myownmeals.com

- Produce fully cooked single serve meals (in individual trays) in vacuum-sealed packages that requires no refrigeration.
- All meals are kosher and are free of soy, fish, shellfish and MSG.
- Some products are also gluten and dairy-free.
- Available in retail stores and from some gluten-free companies.
- Contact company for ordering information.

Gluten-Free Companies/Distributors cont'd.

Namaste Foods, P.O. Box 3133, Coeur D'Alene, ID, USA 83854
✦ Phone: 866-258-9493/208-772-6325 FAX: 208-772-4318
Email: admin@namastefoods.com www.namastefoods.com

- Gluten-free specialty company; dedicated gluten-free facility.
- Produce a variety of mixes (breads, brownies, cakes, cookies, muffins, pancakes, pasta blends, pizza crust) that are also free of corn, soy, potato, dairy and nuts.
- Available in retail stores.
- Order direct by phone, fax, mail or internet; shipping charges based on amount purchased; ships via FedEx Ground.

Nana's Cookie Company, 4901 Morena Blvd., Suite 401, San Diego, CA, USA 92117
✦ Phone: 800-836-7534/858-273-5775 FAX: 858-273-3432
Email: nanas@healthycrowd.com www.healthycrowd.com

- Produce cookies and cookie bars that are egg and dairy-free and sweetened with fruit juice. The gluten-free cookies are produced on dedicated equipment.
- Available in retail stores.
- Order direct by phone, email or internet; shipping charges based on weight; ships via UPS.

Native Seeds/SEARCH, 526 N. 4th Avenue, Tuscon, AZ, USA 85705-8450
✦ Phone: 866-622-5561/520-622-5561 FAX: 520-622-5591
Email: info@nativeseeds.org www.nativeseeds.org

- Non-profit seed conservation organization.
- Sell products that are native to southwestern USA and northwestern Mexico (beans, seeds, chili powder, whole chilies, salsas, sauces, baking mixes, jelly, syrup, herbal teas, amaranth, cornmeal and mesquite). Many products are gluten-free.
- Shop in person or order direct by phone, fax, mail or internet; shipping charges based on amount purchased; ships via UPS or USPS.

Natural Feast, Naturally ME Inc., 150 Main Street, Suite 11, Richmond, ME, USA 04357
✦ Phone: 866-628-6346 FAX: 207-737-2210
Email: cbessermin@naturalfeast.com www.naturalfeast.com

- Gluten-free specialty company; dedicated gluten-free facility.
- Produce frozen pies and pie shells that are also free of dairy, soy and corn. Pies are sweetened with fruit juice.
- Available in retail stores.
- Order direct by phone, fax, mail or internet; shipping charges based on weight; ships via FedEx (2 day) in insulated containers with dry ice.

GLUTEN-FREE COMPANIES/DISTRIBUTORS CONT'D.

Natural Food Mill Bakery, 481 Wellham Road, Unit 7, Barrie, ON, Canada L4N 8Z6
Phone: 800-353-3178/705-721-0919 FAX: 705-721-3345
Email: info@naturalfoodmill.com www.naturalfoodmill.com

- Gluten-free specialty company; dedicated gluten-free facility.
- Produce breads, buns, flatbreads, cookies, pizza crusts, bread crumbs, granola and baking mixes.
- Available in retail stores.

Nature's Hilights Inc., P. O. Box 3526, Chico, CA, USA 95927
✦ Phone: 800-313-6454/530-342-6154 FAX: 530-342-3130
Email: cynthia64@msn.com www.natures-hilights.com

- Gluten-free specialty company; dedicated gluten-free facility.
- Produces "Nature's Hilights" gluten-free pizza crust, tostadas and frozen desserts.
- Available in retail stores.
- Order direct by phone, fax or email; shipping charges based on amount purchased; ships via FedEx Ground.

Nature's Path Foods Inc., 9100 Van Horne Way, Richmond, BC, Canada V6X 1W3
✦ Phone: 888-808-9505/604-248-8777 FAX: 604-248-8760
Email: consumer_services@naturespath.com www.naturespath.com

- Produce a variety of organic products generally made from whole grains (cereals, waffles, snack bars, cookies and baking mixes). Products sold under the name of Nature's Path Foods, Lifestream Natural Foods and EnviroKidz.
- Many products are gluten-free. Specific manufacturing processes are utilized to prevent cross-contamination. All gluten-free products are regularly tested for gluten.
- Available in retail stores.
- Order direct by phone or internet; shipping charges based on amount purchased; ships via FedEx or UPS.

Nelson David of Canada, 66 Higgins Ave, Winnipeg, MB, Canada R3B 0A5
✦ Phone: 866-989-0379/204-989-0379 FAX: 204-989-0384
Email: crennnie244@aol.com

- Gluten-free specialty company; dedicated gluten-free facility.
- Produce "Celimix" gluten-free mixes (breads, biscuits, buns, cakes, cookies, muffins, pancakes, pastry, pizza crusts, Yorkshire pudding), egg replacer and pasta.
- Available in retail stores.
- Order direct by phone or fax; shipping charges based on weight; ships via Canada Post.

New Morning, US Mills Inc., 200 Reservoir St., Needham, MA, USA 02494
Phone: 800-422-1125/781-444-0440 FAX: 781-444-3411
www.usmillsinc.com

- Produce a variety of cereals; one product is gluten-free.
- Available in retail stores.

GLUTEN-FREE COMPANIES/DISTRIBUTORS CONT'D.

No Nuts, Mountain Meadows Food Processing Ltd., Site 13, Box 45, RR #1, Legal, AB, Canada T0G 1L0
Phone: 800-961-2470/780-961-2470 FAX: 780-961-3995
Email: info@peabutter.ca www.peabutter.ca

- Nut-free alternative spread made from golden peas, canola oil and icing (confectioner's) sugar. Product is free of gluten and dairy.
- Made in a dedicated nut and gluten-free facility.
- Available in retail stores.

Northern Quinoa Corporation, Box 519, Kamsack, SK, Canada S0A 1S0
✦ Phone: 866-368-9304/306-542-3949 FAX: 306-542-3951
Email: quinoa@quinoa.com www.quinoa.com

- Process a variety of gluten-free products (quinoa, amaranth, buckwheat, flax, legumes, millet, spices and wild rice) in a dedicated gluten-free facility.
- Quinoa is available as whole grain, flakes, flour and pasta.
- Company has developed a process to remove the bitter-tasting saponin coating from quinoa, making it ready to use and fast cooking.
- Available in retail stores.
- Order direct by phone or internet; shipping charges based on weight; ships via Canada Post.

Nutrimax, LifeMax Natural Foods Distribution Inc., 1773 Bayly St., Pickering, ON, Canada L1W 2Y7
Phone: 905-831-5433 FAX: 905-831-4333
Email: info@lifemax.ca www.lifemax.ca

- Produce mayonnaise, molasses, pasta sauces and soup bases that are gluten-free.
- Available in retail stores.

Nutrition Kitchen Inc., P.O. Box 396, Concord, MA, USA 01742
✦ Phone: 877-225-5651 FAX: 978-287-4647
Email: nutritionkitchen@yahoo.com www.theperfectpasta.com
www.wheatfreepasta.com

- Dedicated gluten-free facility.
- Produce organic soybean pasta that is high in protein, fiber, iron and calcium.
- Available in retail stores.
- Order direct by internet; shipping charges based on amount purchased; ships via UPS or FedEx Ground.

GLUTEN-FREE COMPANIES/DISTRIBUTORS CONT'D.

Nu-World Amaranth, Nu-World Foods, P. O. Box 2202, Naperville, IL, USA 60567
✦ Phone: 877-692-8899/630-369-6819 FAX: 630-369-6851
Email: customerservice@nuworldfamily.com www.nuworldfamily.com
www.nuworldfoods.com

- Gluten-free specialty company; dedicated facility free of gluten, dairy, egg, soy and nuts.
- Produce a variety of amaranth and amaranth-based products (bread crumbs, cereals, flat breads, flour, pre-gel powder, side dishes, snacks, toasted bran flour).
- Available in retail stores.
- Order direct by phone, fax or internet; shipping charges based on amount purchased; ships via FedEx Ground.

Omega Nutrition, 1695 Franklin. St, Vancouver, BC, Canada V5L 1P5
6515 Aldrich Rd., Bellingham, WA, USA 98226
✦ Phone: 800-661-3529 FAX: 604-253-4228 (Canada)
604-253-4677 (Canada) 360-384-0700 (USA)
360-384-1238 (USA)
Email: info@omeganutrition.com www.omeganutrition.com

- Over 400 natural health products such as specialty oils (flax, borage, sesame, sunflower, hazelnut, olive, pistachio, pumpkin, safflower), flavorings, nutritional supplements, flax seed meal and seed butters.
- Available in retail stores.
- Order direct by phone, fax, mail or internet; shipping charges based on weight; ships via UPS.

Omega Smart Inc., 250 Commercial Street, Manchester, NH, USA 03101
✦ Phone: 603-624-5924 FAX: 603-232-3571
Email: info@omegasmartbar.com www.omegasmartbar.com

- Produce gluten-free, dairy-free whole food meal replacement bars made from organic dried fruits, nuts, ground flax seed, soy flour, soynuts and agave syrup.
- Available in retail stores.
- Order direct by phone, fax, mail or internet; shipping charges based on weight; ships via UPS Ground.

Orgran, Roma Food Products, 47-53 Aster Ave., Carrum Downs, Vic 3201, Australia
Phone: 03 9776 9044 (Australia) FAX: 03 9776 9055 (Australia)
877-380-3422/845-278-8164 (N.A) 845-278-6277 (N.A.)
Email: info@orgran.com www.orgran.com

- Roma Food Products is Australia's major manufacturer of alternative grain, pasta and health foods.
- Produce "Orgran" wheat-free, gluten-free products (cereals, cookies, crisp breads, crumbs, fruit bars, mixes, pasta and soups) in a dedicated gluten-free facility. Products are tested for gluten using the ELISA test.
- All Orgran products are also free of dairy, yeast and egg.
- Available in retail stores.

GLUTEN-FREE COMPANIES/DISTRIBUTORS CONT'D.

Pacific Foods, 19480 SW 97th Ave., Tualatin, OR, USA 97062
Phone: 503-692-9666 FAX: 503-692-9610
Email: info@pacificfoods.com www.pacificfoods.com

- Produce a variety of non-dairy beverages (almond, grain, hazelnut, rice and soy), broths, soups, entrées and side dishes. Many of their products are gluten-free.
- Available in retail stores.

Pamela's Products, 200 Clara Ave., Ukiah, CA, USA 95482
Phone: 707-462-6605 FAX: 707-462-6642
Email: info@pamelasproducts.com www.pamelasproducts.com

- A variety of "Pamela's" cookies, biscotti and baking mixes (bread, chocolate brownie and pancake/baking). All products are gluten-free, except oatmeal cookies.
- Gluten-free products made on 100% dedicated machinery.
- Available in retail stores and from select online specialty companies.

Panne Rizo, 1939 Cornwall Ave., Vancouver, BC, Canada V6J 1C8
✦ Phone: 604-736-0885 FAX: 866-340-3722/604-736-0825
Email: info@pannerizo.com www.pannerizo.com

- Gluten-Free specialty bakery, deli and cafe; dedicated gluten-free facility.
- Produce gluten-free breads, buns, special occasion cakes, cookies, crackers, mixes, muffins, pies, pastries, pizza crusts and ready-to-eat entrées.
- Also carry other companies' products (cereals, cookies, crackers, pasta, soup cubes).
- Available in the Panne Rizo store or in some retail stores in western Canada.
- Order direct by phone, fax, email, mail or internet; shipping charges based on weight; ships via FedEx.

Papadini, Adrienne's Gourmet Foods, 849 Ward Dr., Santa Barbara, CA, USA 93111
Phone: 800-937-7010/805-964-6848 FAX: 805-964-8698
Email: info@adriennes.com www.adriennes.com

- Pure lentil bean pasta in a variety of shapes (high in protein and fiber).
- All products are gluten-free.
- Available in retail stores.

Paramed Inc., 995 Wellington, Suite 220, Montreal, Quebec, Canada H3C 1V3
✦ Phone: 888-606-6676/514-395-2458 FAX: 514-395-2396
Email: info@paramedinc.com www.paramedinc.com

- Gluten-free specialty food distributor. Carry products from Ener-G Foods, Kingsmill, Pastariso, Pastato and other companies.
- Order direct by phone, fax or internet; shipping charges based on weight; ships via Purolator.

GLUTEN-FREE COMPANIES/DISTRIBUTORS CONT'D.

Pastariso, Maple Grove Food and Beverage Corp.,
8175 Winston Churchill Blvd., Norval, ON, Canada L0P 1K0
Phone: 905-451-7423 FAX: 905-453-8137
Email: info@maplegrovefoods.com www.maplegrovefoods.com

- Gluten-free specialty company; dedicated gluten-free facility.
- Produce a large variety of "Pastariso" organic rice pastas (brown rice, rice spinach, rice vegetable, rice and cheese dinners) and potato/organic rice pasta called "Pastato" (variety of shapes, as well as pasta and cheese dinners). Some products also available in bulk.
- Some of the pastas are fortified with fiber from ground flax and psyllium husks as well as FOS, vitamins and minerals.
- Available in retail stores.

Pastato (see Pastariso)

PatsyPie Gluten-Free Bakery, 3060 rue Brabant-Marineau,
Ville St. Laurent, Quebec, Canada H4S 1K7
✦Phone: 877-287-9743/514-333-7253 FAX: 514-333-1916

- Gluten-free specialty company; dedicated gluten-free facility.
- Produce "PatsyPie" cookies, biscotti, brownies and other items. Contains no preservatives.
- Available in retail stores.
- Order direct by phone, fax or internet; shipping charges based on weight; ships via Canada Post.

Perfect 10 Natural Energy, Leed Products Inc., #2 - 68 Schooner St.,
Coquitlam, BC, Canada V3K 7B1
✦Phone: 604-540-1000 (Canada) FAX: 604-540-1030 (Canada)
866-800-9930/805-543-9930 (USA) 805-980-3475 (USA)
Email: info@perfect10bars.com www.perfect10bars.com

- Dedicated gluten-free facility.
- Produce snack bars made from dried fruits, nuts and seeds that are also dairy-free.
- Available in retail stores.
- Order direct by phone or internet; shipping charges based on weight; ships via USPS or DHL Ground.

Perky's Natural Foods, Enjoy Life Natural Brands, 3810 N. River Road, Schiller Park, IL, USA 60176-2307
✦Phone: 888-473-7597/847-260-0300 FAX: 847-260-0306
Email: info@perkysnaturalfoods.com www.perkysnaturalfoods.com

- Gluten-free specialty company that produces "Perky's" cereals which are gluten and nut-free.
- Available in retail stores.
- Order direct by phone, fax or internet; shipping charges based on weight; ships via UPS Ground.

GLUTEN-FREE COMPANIES/DISTRIBUTORS CONT'D.

Philly Swirl, 1102 N. 28th St., Tampa, FL, USA 33605
Phone: 877-379-4757/813-353-8645 FAX: 813-241-2591
www.phillyswirl.com

- Produce a variety of frozen dessert novelties (sorbets, ice cream bars) that are made in a dedicated peanut and tree nut-free facility.
- All products are gluten-free and many are dairy-free.
- Available in retail stores.

Plum-M-Good, Van Rice Products, #8 -1350 Valmont Way, Richmond, BC, Canada V6V 1Y4
Phone: 604-273-8038 FAX: 604-273-7324

- Variety of organic and regular rice cakes that are gluten-free.
- Available in retail stores.

Premier Japan, Edward & Son's Trading Co., Inc., P.O. Box 1326, Carpinteria, CA, USA 93014
✦ Phone: 805-684-8500 FAX: 805-684-8220
Email: info@edwardandsons.com www.edwardandsons.com

- Produce organic oriental sauces including "wheat-free" teriyaki and hoisin that are gluten-free.
- Available in retail stores.
- Order direct by phone, fax, mail or internet; flat rate shipping charge; ships via FedEx Ground.

Private Recipes, 12 Indell Lane, Brampton, ON, Canada L6T 3Y3
✦ Phone: 800-268-8199/905-799-1022 FAX: 800-561-9778/905-799-2666
Email: info@privaterecipes.com www.privaterecipes.com

- Manufacturer of a wide range of frozen food products in various textures for home use, hospitals, long term care facilities, day cares and schools.
- Products (cereals, soups, entrées, gravies, sauces, desserts) available in portioned formats and bulk.
- Produce a line of gluten-free frozen ready-to-eat entrées (also suitable for lactose-free and renal diets).
- Contact company for ordering information.

Purfoods/Gluten Free Meals, 718 S.E. Shurfine Drive, Ankeny, IA, USA 50021
✦ Phone: 866-942-7873/515-963-0641
Email: info@purfoods.com www.glutenfreemeals.com

- Produce ready to heat (microwave or oven) and eat gluten-free prepared fresh meals that are not frozen and do not contain preservatives. Special packaging permits refrigerated shelf-life of 2 weeks at delivery.
- A variety of entrées (beef, pork, poultry and fish), casseroles, salads and breakfast items (omelet, frittata, pizza, pancakes, French toast).
- Products are tested for gluten.
- Order direct by phone or internet; shipping charges based on amount purchased; ships via FedEx (2 day) in styrofoam packing with an ice gel.

GLUTEN-FREE COMPANIES/DISTRIBUTORS CONT'D.

Quaker Oats Canada, 14 Hunter St. East, Quaker Park, Peterborough, ON, Canada K9J 7B2
Phone: 800-267-6287 www.quakeroats.ca

- Extensive line of products. A variety of large and mini rice cakes are gluten-free.
- Available in retail stores.

Quaker Oats USA, P. O. Box 049003, Chicago, IL, USA 60604
Phone: 800-856-5781 www.quakeroats.com
www.quakeroatmeal.com

- Extensive line of products. A variety of large and mini rice cakes are gluten-free.
- Available in retail stores.

Rainforest Organic, Edward & Son's Trading Co. Inc., P.O. Box 1326, Carpinteria, CA, USA 93014
✦ Phone: 805-684-8500 FAX: 805-684-8220
Email: info@edwardandsons.com www.edwardandsons.com

- Organic wheat-free mango, ginger curry and papaya pepper sauces that are gluten-free.
- Available in retail stores.
- Order direct by phone, fax, mail or internet; flat rate shipping charge; ships via FedEx Ground.

Ramapo Valley Brewery, P.O. Box 1031, Hillburn, NY, USA 10931
✦ Phone: 845-369-7827 FAX: 845-369-7817
www.ramapovalleybrewery.com

- Produce a variety of beers, ales and lagers including a Gluten-Free Honey Lager made from hops, yeast, molasses and honey. Gluten-free beer done on separate equipment and is available in 12 oz. bottles.
- Available in some retail stores and restaurants.
- Order direct by phone, fax or mail; flat rate shipping charge; ships via FedEx Ground.

The Really Great Food Company, P. O. Box 2239, St. James, NY, USA 11780
✦ Phone: 800-593-5377/631-361-3553 FAX: 631-361-6920
Email: support@reallygreatfood.com www.reallygreatfood.com

- Gluten-free specialty company; dedicated gluten-free facility.
- Produce "Really Great Food Company" gluten-free mixes (biscuits, breads, cakes, cookies, muffins, pancake, pastry).
- Also carry other companies' products (cookies, flours, sauces, soups, vitamins and baking accessories).
- Available in some retail stores.
- Order direct by phone, fax or internet; shipping charges based on amount purchased; ships via UPS Ground.

GLUTEN-FREE COMPANIES/DISTRIBUTORS CONT'D.

Red Mill Farms Inc., 290 S. 5th St., Brooklyn, NY, USA 12111
Phone: 718-384-2150 FAX: 718-384-2988

- Produce gluten-free cakes and "Jennie's" coconut macaroons.
- Available in retail stores.

Rice Expressions, P.O. Box 1430, Pacific Palisades, CA, USA 90272
Phone: 310-820-4808 FAX: 310-820-2559
Email: info@riceexpressions.com www.riceexpressions.com

- Produce frozen pre-cooked, organic rice (brown, white, pilaf and tex-mex varieties) in plastic pouches that are heated in the microwave for 3 minutes.
- All products are gluten-free.
- Available in retail stores.

Rizopia Food Products Inc., 4490 Sheppard Ave. E., Unit #13, Toronto, ON, Canada M1S 4J9
✦ Phone: 416-609-8820 FAX: 416-609-8825
Email: info@rizopia.com www.rizopia.com

- Gluten-free specialty company; dedicated gluten-free facility.
- A large variety of rice pastas (white, brown, organic brown, organic corn and rice, organic wild). Also available in bulk sizes.
- Available in retail stores.
- Order direct by internet from online stores.

The Ruby Range LLC, 1231 Willow Lane, Estes Park, CO, USA 80517
✦ Phone: 970-577-0888 FAX: 303-279-5366
Email: ldcleene@msn.com www.therubyrange.com

- Gluten-free specialty company; dedicated gluten-free facility.
- A variety of "Ruby Range" mixes (all purpose, cookies, cupcakes, pancakes), as well as flours and baking ingredients. Mixes contain mesquite, teff and other gluten-free flours.
- Available in some retail stores.
- Order direct by phone, fax, mail or internet; shipping charges based on amount purchased; ships via UPS Ground.

Running Rabbit, Sonoma Specialty Kitchens, 1360 Industrial Ave., Suite G, Petaluma, CA, USA 94952
✦ Phone: 888-778-6399/707-778-6399 FAX: 707-778-6991
Email: sales@sonomaspecialtykitchens.com www.sonomaspecialtykitchens.com

- Gluten-free licorice (corn and tapioca starch-based) available in four flavors in the shape of a rabbit.
- Available in retail specialty stores.
- Order direct by internet; shipping charges based on amount purchased; ships via DHL.

Gluten-Free Companies/Distributors cont'd.

St. Claire's Organics, Eco Natural Solutions, 6235 Lookout Road, Suite A, Boulder, CO, USA 80301
✦ Phone: 877-684-5195/303-527-1554 FAX: 303-527-3885
Email: customerservice@econaturalsolutions.com www.econaturalsolutions.com

- A variety of organic candies (licorice, mints, tarts and aromatherapy pastilles) and hot cocoa mixes. All products are free of gluten, dairy, corn, soy and nuts. Contain no artificial colors, flavors or preservatives.
- Available in retail stores.
- Order direct by phone, fax, mail or internet; shipping charges based on weight; ships via UPS Ground.

San-J International, 2880 Sprouse Dr., Richmond, VA, USA 23231
Phone: 800-446-5500/804-226-8333 FAX: 804-226-8383
Email: sales@san-j.com www.san-j.com

- Produces tamari soy sauces (liquid, powder, low salt/lite), sauces (Asian, barbecue), instant miso soups and rice crackers.
- Wheat-free tamari soy sauces and rice crackers are gluten-free.
- Available in retail stores.

Schär, Dr.Schar GmbH, Winkelau 9, I-39014 Postal (BZ) Italy
Phone: 39 0473 293300 FAX: 39 0473 293399
Email: info@schaer.com www.schaer.com

- Gluten-free specialty company; dedicated gluten-free facility.
- Wide variety of "Schar" gluten-free mixes (all-purpose, bread, cake), baked products (breads, baguettes, biscuits, cakes, pizza crusts, rolls), cereal and pasta.
- Available from gluten-free specialty companies in Canada and USA; pharmacies and health food stores in U.K. and Europe.

Shalit Foods Inc., 94 Martin Ross Ave., Toronto, ON, Canada M3J 2L4
✦ Phone: 800-969-6991/416-650-9738 FAX: 416-650-5643
Email: info@shalitfoods.com www.shalitfoods.com

- Food service supplier of a very large variety of products for health care facilities, college/university dining services, airlines, hotels and restaurants in Canada and the U.S.
- Also offer a selection of complete meals and bulk entrées for health care facilities, including products that are suitable for gluten-free, lactose-free and renal diets. Complete meals are packed in three compartment trays which includes a protein, starch and vegetables.
- Contact company for ordering information.

Shiloh Farms (see Garden Spot's Finest)

- Large variety of products (breads, baking ingredients, flours, grains, legumes, dried fruits mixes, nuts, nut butters and snacks). Many products are gluten-free.
- Available in retail stores and from Garden Spot's Finest Distributors.

GLUTEN-FREE COMPANIES/DISTRIBUTORS CONT'D.

Simply Asia, Epicurean International Inc., 30315 Union City Blvd., Union City, CA, USA 94587
✦ Phone: 800-967-8424/510-675-9025 FAX: 510-675-9045
Email: information@simplyasia.net www.simplyasia.net

- A variety of Asian flavored noodles (rice or wheat) with sauces.
- Some rice noodle soup products are gluten-free.
- Available in retail stores.
- Order direct by internet; flat rate shipping charge; ships via DHL.

Soya World Inc., P. O. Box 3018, Vancouver, BC, Canada V6B 3X5
Phone: 888-401-0019/604-291-0910 FAX: 604-291-0981
Email: consumer@soyaworld.com www.soyaworld.com

- One of North America's largest producers of fresh and shelf-stable soy beverages ("So Good Fortified Soy", "So Nice Soyganic", "Sunrise Soy"), soy yogurt ("So Nice") and non-dairy frozen desserts and cones ("So Good").
- Beverages, frozen desserts (in tubs) and yogurts are gluten-free.
- Available in retail stores.

Specialty Food Shop, 555 University Ave., Toronto, ON, Canada M5G 1X8
✦ Phone: 800-737-7976/416-813-5294 FAX: 416-977-8394
Email: sfs@sickkids.ca www.specialtyfoodshop.com

- Specialty food retail store located in the Hospital for Sick Children.
- Carries over 1000 specialty products (gluten-free, low-protein, low-sodium, dysphagia, food allergies and intolerances, nutritional supplements, enteral feeding equipment, specialized infant feeding products/equipment and books).
- Large variety of gluten-free products from North American and European companies.
- Dietitians on staff for inquiries.
- Shop in person or order direct by phone or internet; shipping charges based on weight; ships via Purolator.

Spring Bakehouse, Spring Foods Inc., 4920 Pearl St. #D, Boulder, CO, USA 80301
✦ Phone: 720-227-0521 FAX: 720-227-0610
Email: customerservice@nutballz.com www.springfoodsinc.com

- Produce a variety of cookies and snack bars.
- Crispy Thumbprint Cookies, Nutballz Energy Cookies and Sacha Active Meal snack bars are gluten-free.
- Available in retail stores.
- Order direct by phone or internet; shipping charges based on weight; ships via UPS Ground.

GLUTEN-FREE COMPANIES/DISTRIBUTORS CONT'D.

Sterk's Bakery, 3866 - 23rd St., Vineland, ON, Canada L0R 2C0
✦ Phone: 800-608-4501/905-562-3086 FAX: 905-562-3847
Other location: 9 Industrial Drive, Thorold, ON, Canada L2V 1A1
Phone: 905-680-5054
Email: info@sterksbakery.com www.sterksbakery.com

- Gluten-free specialty company; dedicated gluten-free facilities.
- Owners have celiac disease.
- Produce a variety of bagels, breads, buns, cakes, cookies, mixes, muffins and pizza crusts.
- Also carry other companies' gluten-free products (cereals, crackers, flours, pasta, soup bases).
- Available in some retail stores and gluten-free specialty shops.
- Shop in person at Sterk's two locations.
- Order direct by phone, fax, email or internet; shipping charges based on amount purchased; ships via UPS Ground.

Sunrise Soya Foods, 729 Powell Street, Vancouver, BC, Canada V6A 1H5
Phone: 800-661-2326/604-253-2326 FAX: 604-251-1083
Email: consumer-info@sunrise-soya.com www.sunrise-soya.com

- Variety of tofu products and soy beverages. Many are gluten-free.
- Available in retail stores.

Sylvan Border Farm, Mendocino Gluten-Free Products Inc., P. O. Box 277,
Willits, CA, USA 95490-0277
✦ Phone: 800-297-5399/707-459-1854 FAX: 707-459-1834
Email: sylvanfarm@pacific.net www.sylvanborderfarm.com

- Gluten-Free specialty company; dedicated gluten-free facility; ELISA-test products for gluten.
- Produce "Sylvan Border Farm" gluten-free baking mixes packed in oxygen-free pouches with a shelf-life of 2 years.
- Available in retail stores.
- Order direct by phone, fax or internet; shipping charges based on product weight; ships via UPS Ground.

Tamarind Tree, Annie's Homegrown Naturals, 580 Gateway Drive,
Napa, CA, USA 94559
✦ Phone: 800-288-1089
Email: bernie@annies.com www.annies.com

- Shelf-stable, heat-and-serve vegetarian Indian cuisine entrées that are gluten-free.
- Some are low-fat and most are suitable for "vegan" diets.
- Available in retail stores.
- Order direct by internet; shipping charges based on amount purchased; ships via UPS Ground.

GLUTEN-FREE COMPANIES/DISTRIBUTORS CONT'D.

Taste Adventure, Will-Pak Foods Inc., Suite 200, 3350 Shelby St., Ontario, CA, USA 91764
✦ Phone: 800-874-0883/909-945-4554 FAX: 909-945-4545
Email: taste_adv@earthlink.net www.tasteadventure.com

- Low-fat soups, beans, quick cuisine entrées and chilies. Many products are gluten-free.
- Available in retail stores.
- Order direct by internet; shipping charges based on weight; ships via UPS Ground.

Tayo Foods (Canada) Inc., Food Steps International Inc., Box 48706, #1260 - 1500 West Georgia Street, Vancouver, BC, Canada V6G 2Z6
Phone: 866-327-4373/604-484-8363 FAX: 604-484-8389
Email: info@tayofoods.com www.tayofoods.com

- Gluten-free, potato-based, non-dairy substitute available in fresh (refrigerated) and shelf-stable packages in various flavors.
- Available in retail stores.

The Teff Company, P. O. Box A, Caldwell, ID, USA 83606
✦ Phone: 888-822-2221/208-455-0375
Email: teffco@earthlink.net www.teffco.com

- Grow and mill only teff grain (brown and ivory varieties); dedicated gluten-free facility.
- Grain and flour available in various sizes.
- Available in retail stores.
- Order direct by internet; shipping charges included in product price; ships via UPS Ground.

Terra, Hain-Celestial Group, Consumer Relations Department, 4600 Sleepytime Drive, Boulder, CO, USA 80301
Phone: 800-434-4246 FAX: 303-581-1520
Email: consumerrelations@hain-celestial.com www.terrachips.com

- Variety of chips made from exotic root vegetables (taro, sweet potato, yucca [cassava], batata and parsnip). Several products are gluten-free.
- Available in retail stores.

Thai Kitchen, Epicurean International Inc., 30315 Union City Blvd., Union City, CA, USA 94587
✦ Phone: 800-967-7424/510-675-9025 FAX: 510-675-9045
Email: info@thaikitchen.com www.thaikitchen.com

- Asian products include a variety of plain and flavored rice noodles, rice side dishes, sauces, soups and coconut milk. Many products are gluten-free.
- Available in retail stores.
- Order direct by mail, fax or internet; shipping charges are a flat rate; ships via UPS or DHL.

GLUTEN-FREE COMPANIES/DISTRIBUTORS CONT'D.

Think Organic!, Prime Health Dietary Supplements Inc., 2140 Eastman Ave., Suite 112, Ventura, CA, USA 93003

✦ Phone: 866-988-4465/805-644-4848 FAX: 805-644-6159
www.thinkproducts.com

- Snack bars made from fruits and nuts that are free of gluten, dairy and soy.
- Available in retail stores.
- Order direct by phone, fax, mail or internet; shipping charges based on weight; ships via UPS Ground.

Tinkyada, Food Directions Inc., 120 Melford Drive, Unit 8, Scarborough, ON, Canada M1B 2X5

Phone: 416-609-0016 FAX: 416-609-1316
Email: allen@tinkyada.com www.tinkyada.com
jojo@tinkyada.com www.ricepasta.com

- Gluten-free specialty company; dedicated gluten-free facility.
- Brown rice (with rice bran), organic brown rice and white rice pastas in a variety of shapes. Products also available in bulk.
- Available in retail stores.

Tom Sawyer Gluten-Free Products, 2155 W. Highway 89A, Suite 106, Sedona, AZ, USA 86336

Phone: 877-372-8800/928-282-6629 FAX: 928-282-5937
Email: tomsawyer@esedona.net www.glutenfreeflour.com

- Gluten-free specialty company.
- Produce gluten-free all purpose flour mix from white rice, sweet rice and tapioca flours, xanthan gum and gelatin.
- Available in some retail stores.

Troy's, Edward & Son's Trading Co., Inc., P.O. Box 1326, Carpinteria, CA, USA 93014

✦ Phone: 805-684-8500 FAX: 805-684-8220
Email: info@edwardandsons.com www.edwardandsons.com

- Organic wheat-free peanut and ginger sauces that are gluten-free.
- Available in retail stores.
- Order direct by phone, fax, mail or internet; flat rate shipping charge; ships via FedEx Ground.

Twin Valley Mills LLC., RR #1, Box 45, Ruskin, NE, USA 68974

✦ Phone: 402-279-3965
Email: sorghumflour@hotmail.com www.twinvalleymills.com

- Grow and mill only sorghum grain in a dedicated gluten-free facility.
- Sorghum flour available in 1.41 kg (2.5 lbs.) and 11.4 kg (25 lb.) containers.
- Order direct by phone, mail and email; shipping charges based on weight; ships via UPS Ground.

GLUTEN-FREE COMPANIES/DISTRIBUTORS CONT'D.

Vance's Foods, P. O. Box 627, Gilmer, TX, USA 75644
Phone: 800-497-4834 FAX: 800-497-4329
✦ Email: info@vancesfoods.com www.vancesfoods.com

- Produce dairy substitutes ("SNO*E Tofu", "Darifree").
- "Darifree" is a potato-based non-dairy substitute which is gluten and casein-free. Available as dry powder beverage mixes.
- Order direct by phone, mail or internet; shipping charges based on weight; ships via UPS Ground.

Van's International Foods, 20318 Gramercy Place, Torrance, CA, USA 90501
Phone: 310-320-8611 FAX: 310-320-8805
Email: customerservice@vansintl.com www.vansintl.com

- Produce frozen waffles (Belgian, organic, mini, regular and wheat-free).
- "Wheat-free" waffles (5 products) and "Gourmet Buckwheat" waffles are gluten-free.
- Available in retail stores.

Wellness Foods Inc., 337 Grace St., Toronto, ON, Canada M6G 3A8
Phone: 416-836-9926 FAX: 416-536-2832
✦ Email: info@wellnessfoods.ca www.wellnessfoods.ca

- Produce snack bars (high in fiber and protein) that are free of gluten, dairy and nuts.
- "Simply Bars" are made with soy and rice crisps. "Fibar 2" is made with soy and rice crisps, dried cranberries and psyllium fiber.
- Available in retail stores.
- Order direct by phone, fax or mail; flat rate shipping charge; ships via Canada Post.

White Wave Inc., 1990 N. 57th Court, Boulder, CO, USA 80301
Phone: 800-488-9283/303-443-3470 FAX: 303-443-3952
www.whitewave.com
www.silkissoy.com

- Produce an extensive line of soy products (milk, smoothies, yogurt, tofu, tempeh and other soy-based meat substitutes).
- Soy milks, smoothies, yogurt and plain tofu are gluten-free.
- Available in retail stores.

Whole Foods Market Inc., 550 Bowie St., Austin, TX, USA 78703-4677
Phone: 512-477-4455 FAX: 512-482-7000
www.wholefoodsmarket.com

- Largest retailer of natural and organic foods with over 180 stores in North America and the U.K.
- Carry an extensive line of products including many gluten-free items.
- Also produce gluten-free baked products (breads, cakes, cookies, muffins, pies and scones) in their dedicated gluten-free facility called Whole Foods Market "Gluten-Free Bakehouse" located in North Carolina. Products are frozen on the day they are baked and shipped to Whole Foods Stores in the USA.

GLUTEN-FREE COMPANIES/DISTRIBUTORS CONT'D.

Wild Oats Markets Inc., 3375 Mitchell Lane, Boulder, CO, USA 80301
Phone: 800-494-9453/303-440-5220 FAX: 303-928-0022
Email: info@wildoats.com www.wildoats.com

- Second largest natural food supermarket chain (over 110 stores) in the USA and Canada. Corporate nutritionists are on staff in most locations.
- Operate stores under a family of trade names including: Wild Oats Natural Marketplace, Capers Community Markets, Henry's Farmers Market and Sun Harvest.
- Carry a very large selection of products including many gluten-free items from a variety of companies.

The Wizard's, Edward & Son's Trading Co., Inc., P.O. Box 1326, Carpinteria, CA, USA 93014
✦ Phone: 805-684-8500 FAX: 805-684-8220
Email: info@edwardandsons.com www.edwardandsons.com

- Produce organic sauces including wheat-free "vegetarian worcestershire" and "hot stuff piquante" sauces that are gluten-free.
- Available in retail stores.
- Order direct by phone, fax, mail or internet; flat rate shipping charge; ships via FedEx Ground.

Gluten-Free Resources

Canadian Celiac Organizations

Canadian Celiac Association (CCA)
5170 Dixie Road, Suite 204
Mississauga, ON, Canada L4W 1E3
Phone: 800-363-7296/905-507-6208
FAX: 905-507-4673
www. celiac.ca
Email: info@celiac.ca

Fondation Québécoise de la Maladie Coeliaque
(Quebec Celiac Foundation)
4837 rue Boyer, Bureau 230
Montreal, Quebec, Canada, H2J 3E6
Phone: 514-529-8806
FAX: 514-529-2046
www.fqmc.org
Email: info@fqmc.org

American Celiac Organizations

American Celiac Disease Alliance (ACDA)
Formerly the American Celiac Task Force
www.americanceliac.org
Email: info@americanceliac.org

Celiac Disease Foundation (CDF)
13251 Ventura Blvd., Suite #1
Studio City, CA, USA 91604-1838
Phone: 818-990-2354
FAX: 818-990-2379
www.celiac.org
Email: cdf@celiac.org

Celiac Sprue Association/USA, Inc. (CSA)
P.O. Box 31700
Omaha, NE, USA 68131
Phone: 877-272-4272/402-558-0600
FAX: 402-558-1347
www.csaceliacs.org
Email: celiacs@csaceliacs.org

Children's Digestive Health and Nutrition Foundation: Celiac (CDHNF)
www.cdhnf.org
www.celiachealth.org

Gluten Intolerance Group (GIG)
31214 - 124th Ave. S.E.
Seattle, WA, USA 98092-3667
Phone: 206-246-6652
FAX: 206-246-6531
www.gluten.net
Email: info@gluten.net

National Foundation for Celiac Awareness (NFCA)
124 South Maple Street, Second Floor
Ambler, PA, USA 19002
Phone: 215-325-1306
FAX: 215-283-2335
www.celiacawareness.org
Email: info@celiacawareness.org

International Celiac Organizations

ARGENTINA: http://www.celiaco.org.ar

AUSTRALIA: http://www.coeliac.org.au

AUSTRIA: http://www.zoeliakie.or.at

BELGIUM: http://www.coeliakie.be
http://www.vcv.coeliakie.be

BRAZIL: http://www.acelbra.org.br

CHILE: www.coacel.cl

CZECH REPUBLIC: http://www.coeliac.cz

CROATIA: http://www.celiac.inet.hr

DENMARK: http://www.coeliaki.dk

FINLAND: http://www.keliakia.org

FRANCE: http://www.afdiag.org

GERMANY: http://www.dzg-online.de

HUNGARY: http://www.coeliac.hu

IRELAND: http://www.coeliac.ie

ISRAEL: http://www.celiac.org.il

ITALY: http://www.celiachia.it

LUXEMBURG: http://www.alig.lu

International Celiac Organizations CONT'D

MEXICO: http://www.celiacosdemexico.com

NETHERLANDS: http://www.coeliakievereniging.nl

NEW ZEALAND: http://www.coeliac.co.nz

NORWAY: http://www.ncf.no

PORTUGAL: http://www.celiacos.org.pt

RUSSIA: http://www.celiac.spb.ru

SPAIN: http://www.celiacos.org

SWEDEN: http://www.celiaki.se

SWITZERLAND: http://www.zoeliakie.ch
http://www.coeliakie.ch
http://www.celiachia.ch

UNITED KINGDOM: http://www.coeliac.co.uk

URUGUAY: http://www.acelu.org

Celiac Education, Research & Treatment Centers

Celiac Center at Beth Israel Deaconess Medical Center, Harvard Medical School
Boston, MA
Phone: 617-667-1272
www.bidmc.harvard.edu/celiaccenter

Celiac Disease Center at Columbia University
New York, NY
Phone: 212-305-5590
www.celiacdiseasecenter.columbia.edu

Celiac Disease Clinic at Mayo Clinic
Rochester, MN
Phone: 507-284-5255 (Patients)
507-284-2631 (Clinicians)
www.mayoclinic.org/celiac-disease

Celiac Disease Clinic, Department of Internal Medicine, University of Iowa Hospitals and Clinics
Iowa City, IA
Phone: 319-356-4060
www.uihealthcare.com

Celiac Group at University of Virginia Health System, Digestive Health Center of Excellence
Charlottesville, VA
Phone: 434-243-9309
www.healthsystem.virginia.edu/internet/digestive-health/patientcare.cfm

Stanford Celiac Sprue Management Clinic, Stanford University Medical Center
Stanford, CA
Phone: 650-723-6961
www.stanfordhospital.com/clinicsmedservices/clinics/gastroenterology/celiacsprue

University of Chicago Celiac Disease Program
Chicago, IL
Phone: 773-702-7593
www.celiacdisease.net
www.uchospitals.edu/specialties/celiac/index.php

University of Maryland Center for Celiac Research
Baltimore, MD
Phone: 800-492-5538 (Appointments)
410-328-6749
www.celiaccenter.org

William K. Warren Medical Research Center for Celiac Disease and the **Clinical Center for Celiac Disease at the University of California**
San Diego, CA
Phone: 858-534-4622 (Research Center)
http://celiaccenter.ucsd.edu

Celiac Disease & Gluten-Free Diet Resources

Celiac Disease: A Hidden Epidemic

- ✦ 352-page book by Dr. Peter H. R. Green, director of the Celiac Disease Center at Columbia University in New York, and science writer Rory Jones, who has celiac disease. Comprehensive information about celiac disease including symptoms, diagnostic tests, related conditions and complications, treatment, lifestyle issues and resources.
- ✦ Cost: $22.95 (U.S.); ISBN 0-06-0766693-X
  Harper Collins www.harpercollins.com

Wheat-Free, Worry-Free: The Art of Happy, Healthy Gluten-Free Living

- ✦ 393-page book by Danna Korn. Practical and inspirational guide to living a wheat-free, gluten-free lifestyle. Includes medical information, menu suggestions, shopping, recipes, nutritional aspects, traveling and eating-out tips, as well as positive strategies for emotional issues and psychological implications of coping with dietary restrictions.
- ✦ Cost: $14.95 (U.S.); ISBN 1-56170-991-3
  Hay House www.hayhouse.com www.glutenfreedom.net

Living with Celiac Disease: Abundance Beyond Wheat and Gluten (2nd Edition)

- ✦ 199-page book by Claudine Crangle, who has been living with celiac disease for over 30 years. Provides an overview of celiac disease and practical information on the gluten-free diet including foods and ingredients allowed and to avoid, shopping, food preparation tips, recipes, eating away from home, traveling, healthy lifestyle advice and resources.
- ✦ Cost: $24.95 (U.S.) and $28.95 (CDN); ISBN 1-55369-404X
  Your Health Press www.yourhealthpress.com

Living Gluten-Free for Dummies

- ✦ 384-page book in the easy-to-read "Dummies" format. Includes an overview of celiac disease and practical information about the gluten-free diet (foods and ingredients allowed and to avoid; meal planning; shopping; cooking tips; recipes; eating away from home and lifestyle issues).
- ✦ Cost: $19.99 (U.S.); ISBN 0-471-77383-2
  Published by For Dummies www.dummies.com www.glutenfreedom.net

---

American Dietetic Association's *Celiac Disease Nutrition Guide*

- ✦ 48-page booklet by dietitian Tricia Thompson. General overview of celiac disease and the gluten-free diet for people who are newly diagnosed. Includes information on grains, label reading, ingredients, nutritional concerns, menu suggestions, baking tips, eating away from home and resources.
- ✦ Cost: $10.00 ADA members, $13.00 non-members; ISBN 978-0-88091-364-5
  American Dietetic Association
  Phone: 800-877-1600 www.eatright.org

What? No Wheat? A Lighthearted Primer to Living the Gluten-Free, Wheat-Free Life

- ✦ 88-page illustrated book by LynnRae Ries. Provides information and inspiration in a cartoon-style format for both children and adults. Includes supporting medical information, as well as positive personal stories of those who are living the gluten-free life.
- ✦ Cost: $9.95 (U.S.); ISBN 0-9724154-0-8
  What No Wheat Publishing Enterprises, 4757 East Greenway Rd., Suite 107B, #91, Phoenix, AZ, USA 85032
  Phone: 602-485-8751 www.whatnowheat.com

Gluten-Free Living magazine

- Quarterly national publication covering all aspects of the gluten-free diet and celiac disease. Published and edited by journalists (one with celiac disease and one the parent of a celiac teen). Reviewed by a medical and dietetic advisory board who are well-known celiac disease experts.
- Subscriptions are $29 (1 year) or $49 (2 years). Orders outside USA (add $6 to 1 year and $12 to 2 year costs). Send check, money order, or Visa or MasterCard number/expiration date to:
  Gluten-Free Living, 19A Broadway, Hawthorne, NY, USA 10532
  Phone: 914-741-5420 www.glutenfreeliving.com

Living Without magazine

- Quarterly lifestyle magazine for people with food and chemical sensitivities including celiac disease, lactose intolerance, wheat intolerance, food allergies, anaphylaxis and multiple chemical sensitivities. Edited and published by Peggy Wagener, who has celiac disease, and reviewed by an advisory board (MDs, dietitians and directors of American celiac organizations).
- Subscriptions are $23 (1 year) or $40 (2 years) in U.S. funds. Send check or money order, or credit card number/expiration date to:
  Living Without, P.O. Box 2126, Northbrook, IL, USA 60065
  Phone: 847-480-8810 www.livingwithout.com

Canadian Celiac Association _Pocket Dictionary: Acceptability of Foods and Food Ingredients for the Gluten-Free Diet_

- 56-page pocket-size dictionary of more than 300 foods and food ingredients and over 300 food additives listed in alphabetical order for easy reference. Easy-to-understand description of each item and food ingredients classified by category (allowed, not allowed, or to check). Written by dietitians with expertise in celiac disease who did extensive research into ingredient-manufacturing practices and food-labeling regulations in the USA, Canada and Europe.
- Cost: $6.95 members, $9.95 non-members; ISBN 0-921026-21-8
  Canadian Celiac Association
  Phone: 800-363-7296/905-507-6208 www.celiac.ca

Celiac.com

- On-line resource since 1995 providing information and support for celiac disease and the gluten-free diet. Site provides a searchable database of over 1,000 articles on celiac disease, recipes, message board, celiac calendar and a bookstore. Managed by Scott Adams who has celiac disease.
- Quarterly newsletter ***Celiac.com's Guide to a Scott-Free Life Without Gluten*** available by subscription.
- www.celiac.com Email: info@celiac.com

Gluten-Free MD Resources

- Educational resources (audio CD and DVD) on celiac disease and gluten intolerance for health professionals, individuals with celiac disease and others featuring Dr. Michelle Pietzak, pediatric gastroenterologist and celiac expert.
- Cost: $25 (85 minute CD), $40 (2 hour DVD)
  New Era Productions
  Phone: 866-963-9372 www.glutenfreemd.com

Clan Thompson Celiac Resources

- ***Celiac Pocket Guide to Foods***
  62-page guide listing foods from major brands found in USA supermarkets, company phone numbers and gluten status of food additives.

- ***Celiac Pocket Guide to Restaurants***
  62-page guide contains gluten-free menus for 34 restaurants and space to add your own notes. URL's to each restaurant's online menu (when available) is also included, as well as tips for eating out.

- ***Celiac Pocket Guide to Over-the-Counter Drugs***
  44-page guide listing drugs from 54 different categories and phone directory of manufacturers in the USA.

- ***Celiac Pocket Guide to Prescription Drugs***
  44-page guide listing the most commonly used prescription drugs and toll-free directory of pharmaceutical companies in the USA.

- ***Celiac Pocket Guide to Everything Else***
  44-page guide listing cosmetics, personal care items, arts and craft items, etc.

> *Note:* Pocket guides are updated yearly and contain the gluten-free and vegetarian status for major brands found in USA supermarkets and drugstores, as well as contact information for manufacturers. Each Guide costs $4.95 plus shipping/handling.

- ***Celiac SmartList of Foods for Palm OS Handhelds, Windows or Macs***
  Includes over 4,300 items in 67 different categories of major brands of foods found in USA supermarkets. Can search by name of food, category or manufacturer.

- ***Celiac SmartList of Drugs for Palm OS Handhelds, Windows or Macs***
  Includes over 1,800 prescription and over-the-counter medications found in the USA. Can search by name of product, category or manufacturer.

- ***Celiac SmartList of Canadian Foods for Palm OS Handhelds, Windows or Macs***
  Includes over 2,400 items in 50 different categories of foods found in Canadian supermarkets. Can search by name of food, category, or manufacturer.

> *Note:* Information in SmartList software is verified directly with each manufacturer and updated regularly. SmartList software programs stand alone and don't require other programs to open them. Available for USA or Canadian products. Software can be searched by product name, category or manufacturer. Fully functional, free demo versions are available to download. Each program costs $14.95. One year subscription available for $49.95-$59.95.

- ***Celiac Newsletter***
  Free monthly email newsletter featuring news about celiac research, lists of gluten-free drugs and foods, recipes, and *Ask The Doctor* column.

> All resources available from:
> **Clan Thompson**, 42 Green St., Bridgton, ME, USA 04009
> www.clanthompson.com Email: celiac@clanthompson.com

Cooking Resources: Cookbooks

The Gluten-Free Gourmet Bakes Bread: More Than 200 Wheat-Free Recipes by Bette Hagman
✦ Cost: $18.00 ISBN 0-8050-6078-2 Owl Books

The Gluten-Free Gourmet Cooks Comfort Foods: Creating Old Favorites with the New Flours by Bette Hagman
✦ Cost: $27.50 ISBN 0-8050-7453-8 Henry Holt and Co.

The Gluten-Free Gourmet Cooks Fast and Healthy: Wheat-Free and Gluten-Free with Less Fuss and Less Fat by Bette Hagman
✦ Cost: $18.00 ISBN 0-8050-6525-3 Owl Books

More From the Gluten-Free Gourmet: Delicious Dining Without Wheat by Bette Hagman
✦ Cost: $18.00 ISBN 0-8050-6524-5 Owl Books

***The Gluten-Free Gourmet: Living Well Without Wheat* (Second Edition)** by Bette Hagman
✦ Cost: $18.00 ISBN 0-8050-6484-2 Owl Books

The Gluten-Free Gourmet Makes Dessert: More Than 200 Wheat-Free Recipes for Cakes, Cookies, Pies and Other Sweets by Bette Hagman
✦ Cost: $18.00 ISBN 0-8050-7276-4 Owl Books

Gluten-Free 101: Easy Basic Dishes Without Wheat by Carol Fenster
✦ Cost: $19.95 ISBN 1-889374-08-3 Savory Palate, Inc.

Cooking Free: 220 Flavorful Recipes for People with Food Allergies and Multiple Food Sensitivities by Carol Fenster
✦ Cost: $18.95 ISBN 1-58333-215-4 Avery

Wheat-Free Recipes & Menus: Delicious, Healthful Eating for People with Food Sensitivities by Carol Fenster
✦ Cost: $16.95 ISBN 1-58333-191-3 Avery

Books can be ordered direct from:
Savory Palate, Inc.
8174 S. Holly – PMB #404, Littleton, CO, USA 80122-4004
Phone: 800-741-5418 www.savorypalate.com

Wheat-Free Gluten-Free Cookbook for Kids and Busy Adults by Connie Sarros
✦ Cost: $15.95 ISBN 0-07-142374-5 McGraw Hill

Wheat-Free Gluten-Free Dessert Cookbook by Connie Sarros
✦ Cost: $15.95 ISBN 0-07-142372-9 McGraw Hill

Wheat-Free Gluten-Free Recipes for Special Diets by Connie Sarros
✦ Cost: $15.95 ISBN 0-9711346-2-6 Connie Sarros Publisher

Wheat-Free Gluten-Free Reduced Calorie Cookbook by Connie Sarros
✦ Cost: $15.95 ISBN 0-07-142375-3 McGraw Hill

Books can be ordered direct from:
Gluten-Free Cookbooks
3800 Rosemont Blvd., #103-D, Fairlawn, OH, USA 44333
Phone: 330-670-1356 www.gfbooks.homestead.com

125 Best Gluten-Free Recipes by Donna Washburn and Heather Butt
✦ Cost: $18.95 (U.S.), $19.95 (CDN) ISBN 0-7788-0111-X Robert Rose

The Best Gluten-Free Family Cookbook by Donna Washburn and Heather Butt
✦ Cost: $18.95 (U.S.), $19.95 (CDN) ISBN 0-7788-0065-2 Robert Rose

Books can be ordered direct from:
Quality Professional Services
1655 County Road 2, Mallorytown, ON, CANADA K0E 1R0
Phone: 613-923-2116 www.bestbreadrecipes.com

Cooking Gluten-Free! A Food Lovers Collection of Chef and Family Recipes Without Gluten or Wheat by Karen Robertson
✦ Cost: $24.95 ISBN 0-9708660-0-3 Celiac Publishing

Books can be ordered direct from:
Celiac Publishing
P.O. Box 99603, Seattle, WA, USA 98139
Phone: 206-282-4822 www.cookingglutenfree.com

Gluten-Free Baking: More Than 125 Recipes for Delectable Sweet and Savory Baked Goods Including Cakes, Pies, Quickbreads, Muffins, Cookies and Other Delights by Rebecca Reilly
✦ Cost: $27.50 ISBN 0-684-87252-8 Simon and Schuster

Delicious Gluten-Free Wheat-Free Breads by LynnRae Ries and Bruce Gross
✦ Cost: $16.95 ISBN 0-972415-1-6 What No Wheat Publishing

Book can be ordered direct from:
What No Wheat Publishing
4757 E. Greenway Rd., Suite 107B, #9, Phoenix, AZ, USA 85032-8510
Phone: 602-485-8751 www.whatnowheat.com

The Gluten-Free Kitchen: Over 135 Delicious Recipes for People with Gluten Intolerance or Wheat Allergy by Roben Ryberg
✦ Cost: $15.95 ISBN 0-7615227-2-7 Prima Publishing

Wheat-Free, Gluten-Free: 200 Delicious Dishes to Make Eating a Pleasure by Michelle Berriedale-Johnson
✦ Cost: $19.95 ISBN 1-572840455 Surrey Books

Together We're Better for Life: 25 Years & Growing **– Gluten-Free Recipes from the Canadian Celiac Association**
✦ Cost: $10.00 Canadian Celiac Association

Book can be ordered direct from:
Canadian Celiac Association
5170 Dixie Road, Suite 204, Mississauga, ON, Canada L4W 1E3
Phone: 800-363-7296 or 905-507-6208 www.celiac.ca

Sharing Our Best! **A Collection of Recipes by The West End Gluten Intolerance Group**
✦ Cost: $7.95

Book can be ordered direct from:
TWEGIC
10900 Brunson Way, Glen Allen, VA, USA 23060

Muffins From the Heart by Shirley Hartung
- Cost: $11.95

Book can be ordered direct from:

Edible Options
32 Layton Street, Kitchener, ON, CANADA N2B 1H2
Phone: 519-570-4912 www.edible-options.com

Cooking Resources: Miscellaneous

Glutenfreeda.com, Glutenfreeda Inc.
- On-line gluten-free cooking magazine. Over 50 photographed recipes each month, as well as articles and seasonal features, gluten-free product testing and menus. Recipe search capability by main ingredient, category or title. On-line cooking classes.
- Subscriptions are $30.00 (1 year) or $5.00 monthly in U.S. funds. www.glutenfreeda.com

---

Gluten-Free Baking and More **newsletter**
- Monthly ad-free print newsletter dedicated to gluten-free baking and cooking. Founded by Elizabeth Barbone, graduate of the Culinary Institute of America.
- Subscriptions are $48.00 (1 year) and $27.00 (6 months). Payment in U.S. funds.
Phone: 518-279-3884 www.glutenfreebaking.com

All You Wanted to Know About Gluten-Free Cooking
- DVD (72 minutes) featuring Connie Sarros, gluten-free cookbook author, that discusses all aspects of cooking gluten-free, including conversions about wheat recipes, recipe tips and trouble-shooting and healthy-eating guidelines.
- Cost: $30.00 plus shipping, available from **Gluten-Free Cookbooks** (see page 316).

Gluten-Free Customized Menus and Recipes
- Nine categories of menus (standard, shortcut, kosher, vegetarian, low-sodium, low-sugar/low-carb, low-fat, and a variety of allergy menus) that features approximately 41 recipes developed by Connie Sarros.
- Cost: $6.95; available from **Gluten-Free Cookbooks** (see page 316).

Carol Fenster's Downloadable PDF Booklets
- *Gluten-free Baking Tips and Techniques from My Kitchen to Yours*
- *Dairy-Free & Delicious: Tips for Using Non-Dairy Alternatives in Cooking*
- *Egg-Free and Excellent: Cracking the Case for Successful Baking Without Eggs*

Note: Each booklet is $6.95 and available from **Savory Palate, Inc.** (see page 316).

Incredible Edible Gluten-Free Foods for Kids (see page 321).

Nothing Beats Gluten-Free Cooking: A Children's Cookbook (see page 321).

Travel and Eating-Out Resources

Waiter ... is there Wheat in My Soup?
The Official Guide to Dining Out, Shopping and Traveling Gluten-Free and Allergy-Free.

- 365-page book by LynnRae Ries. Practical information on eating out, shopping and traveling for those with gluten intolerance or allergies to dairy, eggs, peanuts, tree nuts, wheat, fish, shellfish and soy. Includes an overview of gluten, casein and allergy-free diets, tips for dining out, menu items from international cuisines with descriptions about ingredients and preparation methods, directory of North American restaurants, specialty food companies, bed & breakfasts, camps, cruise lines, airlines, trains and parks that accommodate special diets.
- Cost: $21.95 (U.S.) and $26.95 (CDN); ISBN 0-9724154-2-4
- **What No Wheat Publishing**, 4757 Greenway Road, Suite 107B, #91, Phoenix, AZ, USA 85032-8510.
  Phone: 602-485-8751 www.whatnowheat.com

Let's Eat Out! Your Passport to Living Gluten and Allergy Free

- 496-page full-color book by Kim Koeller and Robert La France. Practical information on eating out in regular and ethnic restaurants for those with gluten intolerance or allergies to dairy, eggs, peanuts, tree nuts, wheat, soy, fish, shellfish and corn. Includes over 175 menu items from North American and international cuisines with descriptions, allergen-specific preparation requests, breakfast and snack ideas, sample menus, dining out and health phrases in four languages, travel resources and websites from over 45 different countries.
- Cost: $24.95 (U.S.); ISBN 0-9764845-0-1

***Multi-Lingual Phrase Passport:* Part of *Let's Eat Out!* Series**

- 132-page pocket-size guide provides over 1200 translations from English to French, German, Italian and Spanish. Relevant phrases (e.g., food allergy, ingredient and preparation techniques, dining, health and product) for eating out and traveling.
- Cost: $9.95 (U.S.); ISBN 0-9764845-4-4

***Pocket-Size Cuisine Passports*: Part of *Let's Eat Out!* Series**

- 104-page pocket size guides: 1) French and Italian Cuisine Passport, 2) Chinese, Indian and Thai Cuisine Passport, 3) American Steak, Seafood and Mexican Cuisine Passport. Each passport contains sample menus; menu items and descriptions; allergy reference guides.
- Cost: $6.95 (U.S.)
- **Gluten-Free Passport LLC**, 27 N. Wacker Dr., Suite 258, Chicago, IL, USA 60606-2800.
  Phone: 312-952-4900 www.glutenfreepassport.com

The Essential Gluten-Free Restaurant Guide

- 300-page book featuring over 3,900 restaurants across all 50 American states recommended by individuals with celiac disease, more than 80 gluten-free lists from national and regional chain restaurants and strategies for safely dining out.
- Cost: $20.95 (U.S.); ISBN 0-9776111-0-8

Triumph Dining Cards

- Laminated Dining Cards for 10 different cuisines (American, Chinese, French, Greek, Indian, Italian, Japanese, Mexican, Thai and Vietnamese). Each cuisine includes four statements: 1) foods I cannot eat, 2) foods that must be checked, 3) foods I can eat, and 4) a warning about cross-contamination. One side of each card is in English and the other is in the appropriate foreign language.
- Cost: $2.50/card or $9.95 (U.S.) for six cards.
- **Triumph Dining**, P.O. Box, Blawenburg, NJ, USA 08504.
  Phone: 609-564-0445 www.triumphdining.com

Bob & Ruth's Gluten-Free Dining & Travel Club

- ✦ A company specializing in assisting individuals on a gluten-free diet and/or their families with dining out and traveling.
- ✦ Quarterly newsletter featuring dining out and traveling tips, review of North American restaurant chain menus, recipes, member dining-out and travel experiences and upcoming travel opportunities.
- ✦ Going Out to Eat & Traveling Gluten-Free workshops
- ✦ Escorted "Gluten-Free Getaways" – mini (2-3 nights), destination resorts, cruises and tours of exotic places all over the world.
- ✦ Annual membership fee $40 (U.S.).
  Bob & Ruth's, 22 Breton Hill Rd., Ste 1B, Baltimore, MD, USA 21208.
  Phone: 410-486-0292. www.bobandruths.com

Children's Resources

Kids with Celiac Disease: A Family Guide to Raising Happy, Healthy, Gluten-Free Children

- ✦ 256-page book by Danna Korn. Provides parents with advice and specific strategies on how to deal with the diagnosis, cope with emotional challenges, and help their child develop a positive attitude. Practical information on menu planning, shopping, food preparation, recipes and eating outside the home (e.g., birthdays, restaurants, camps, vacations).
- ✦ Cost: $17.95 (U.S.); ISBN 1-89062-72-16
  Woodbine House, 6510 Bells Mill Rd., Bethesda, MD, USA 20817.
  Phone: 800-843-7323 www.woodbinehouse.com www.glutenfreedom.net

---

Gluten-Free Friends: An Activity Book for Kids

- ✦ 57-page illustrated book by registered dietitian Nancy Patin Falini. Designed for children age 4-11. The book features two friendly kids who explain what gluten is, describe how gluten makes them sick and which foods to avoid, and how to make healthy food choices. Easy-to-follow instructions for parents and caregivers to help them guide children through learning activities and explore their thoughts and feelings about living gluten-free.
- ✦ Cost: $18.95 (U.S.); ISBN 1-889374-09-1
  Savory Palate Inc., 8174 S. Holly – PMB #404, Littleton, CO, USA 80122-4004.
  Phone: 800-741-5418 www.savorypalate.com

Eating Gluten-Free with Emily: A Story for Children with Celiac Disease

- ✦ Illustrated book for young children by Bonnie J. Kruszka. A story about a 5-year-old girl who develops celiac disease and how she makes positive lifestyle changes to manage her disease.
- ✦ Cost: $14.95 (U.S.); ISBN 1-890627-62-3
  Woodbine House, 6510 Bells Mill Rd., Bethesda, MD, USA 20817.
  Phone: 800-843-7323 www.woodbinehouse.com

No More Cupcakes & Tummy Aches: A Story for Parents and Their Celiac Children to Share

- ✦ Illustrated book for children ages 3-8 by Jax Peters Lowell. A story of a little girl who learns about living gluten-free and being loved and feeling truly special.
- ✦ Cost: $22.99 (hard cover); ISBN 1-4134-6255-3
  $16.99 (soft cover); ISBN 1-4134-6254-5
  Xlibris Publisher. Phone: 888-795-4274 www.xlibris.com

The GF Kid: A Celiac Disease Survival Guide

- ✦ 64-page illustrated book for children ages 8-12 written by Melissa London. Light-hearted story that features information about celiac disease; the gluten-free diet; shopping tips; creative solutions for coping at school, parties and sleepovers; and several recipes.
- ✦ Cost: $14.95 (U.S.); ISBN 1-890627-69-0
  Woodbine House, 6510 Bells Mill Rd., Bethesda, MD, USA 20817.
  Phone: 800-843-7323 www.woodbinehouse.com

Incredible Edible Gluten-Free Foods for Kids

- ✦ Cookbook for Kids written by Sheri L. Sanderson. Includes 150 family-tested recipes, general food preparation tips, baking substitutes, as well as an overview of celiac disease and the gluten-free diet, tips for dealing with daycares and schools, and resources.
- ✦ Cost: $18.95 (U.S.); ISBN 1-890627-28-3
  Woodbine House, 6510 Bells Mill Rd., Bethesda, MD, USA 20817.
  Phone: 800-843-7323 www.woodbinehouse.com

Nothing Beats Gluten-Free Cooking: A Children's Cookbook

- ✦ 93-page cookbook featuring 65 recipes for breakfast, lunch, dinner, snacks, desserts and fruits and vegetables. Edited by Anne Lee, Laura Leon and Susan Cohen.
- ✦ Cost: $25 (includes shipping); ISBN 0-9742370-0-0
  www.celiacdiseasecenter.columbia.edu

R.O.C.K. (Raising Our Celiac Kids)

- ✦ Free support group for parents, families and friends of children on a gluten-free diet. Over 100 chapters in the USA and several in Canada. Founded by Danna Korn, mother of a child with celiac disease.
- ✦ www.celiackids.com Email: danna@celiackids.com

Allergy Resources

Food Allergy Survival Guide: Surviving and Thriving with Food Allergies and Sensitivities

- ✦ 384-page book by registered dietitians Vesanto Melina, Jo Stepaniak and Dina Aronson. Comprehensive resource on food sensitivities and other conditions (e.g., arthritis, asthma, ADHD, Candida, depression, dermatitis, digestive disorders including celiac disease, fatigue, headaches), diagnostic testing, nutritional concerns for various allergies, label reading and substitutions, meal planning, cooking tips, over 100 recipes (free of gluten, dairy, eggs, fish, shellfish, peanuts, tree nuts, soy, yeast and kiwi) with nutritional analysis and resources.
- ✦ Cost: $19.95 (U.S.), $29.95 (CDN); ISBN 1-57067-163-X
  Healthy Living Publications, Box 99, Summertown, TN, USA 38483
  Phone 888-260-8458

***Allergic Living* magazine**

- ✦ Quarterly magazine for people with food and environmental allergies and intolerances. Includes medical, nutritional and product information, as well as recipes. Editor has food allergies.
- ✦ Subscription rates: Canada $24.95 plus GST (1 year); $44.95 plus GST (2 years)
  USA $24.95 (U.S. funds) for 1 year (includes postage)
  Allergic Living, 2100 Bloor St. West, Suite 6-168, Toronto, ON, Canada M6S 5A5
  Phone: 888-771-7747 www.allergicliving.com

***Living Without* magazine** (see page 314)

Let's Eat Out! Your Passport to Living Gluten and Allergy Free (see page 319)

Waiter...Is there Wheat in my Soup? (see page 319)

Diabetes and Celiac Disease Resources

Managing Diabetes and Celiac Disease ... Together

- 50-page booklet that includes an overview of diabetes and celiac disease, meal planning, carbohydrate content of gluten-free flours and recipes with nutritional analysis.
- Published by the Canadian Celiac Association (CCA) and Canadian Diabetes Association (CDA).
- Cost: $11.95 (CDN) members; $13.95 (CDN) non-members
  Canadian Celiac Association, 5170 Dixie Road, Suite 204, Mississauga, ON, Canada L4W 1E3
  Phone: 800-363-7296 or 905-507-6208 www.celiac.ca

Diabetes, Celiac Disease and Me! An Introduction to Living with Both Diseases

- 37-page booklet that includes an overview of diabetes and celiac disease, sample menus, carbohydrate content of selected gluten-free foods and ingredients, and resources.
- Published by the Gluten Intolerance Group (GIG) and Houston Celiac Disease Support Group.
- Available in a free "pdf" that can be downloaded from www.gluten.net or www.houstonceliacs.org. Hard copy available for $10 from GIG (see page 311).

Pharmaceutical Resources

Clan Thompson Celiac SmartList of Drugs for Palm OS Handhelds, Windows or Macs (see page 315)

Clan Thompson Pocket Guide to Over-the-Counter Drugs (see page 315)

Clan Thompson Pocket Guide to Prescription Drugs (see page 315)

Glutenfreedrugs.com

- On-line resource containing information about over-the-counter and prescription medications listed by therapeutic category or alphabetical product name.
- Site developed and managed by Dr. Steve Plogsted, PharmD, Nutrition Support Services, Children's Hospital, Columbus, Ohio

INDEX

A

B

C

E

Entrée & Side Dish Recipes

F

O

P

Pancake Recipes

Pie & Pizza Recipes

ORDER FORM

GLUTEN-FREE DIET

A Comprehensive Resource Guide

Shelley Case, RD (Registered Dietitian)

Number of copies _____x $24.95 U.S. = $ ____________

Number of copies _____x $26.95 CDN = $ ____________

Shipping and handling (see below) = $ ____________

Subtotal = $ ____________

In Canada add GST (7%) = $ ____________
GST# 867639122

Total enclosed = $ ____________

Shipping & Handling
Add $5.00 for one book
$4.00 per book for 2-3 books
Contact Case Nutrition for larger orders or international orders

Please allow 3-4 weeks for delivery.

U.S. and international orders payable in U.S. funds.

NAME: ____________________

ORGANIZATION: ____________________

STREET: ____________________

CITY: ____________________ PROV./STATE: ____________

COUNTRY: ____________ POSTAL CODE/ZIP: ____________

TELEPHONE: ____________ FAX: ____________

Email: ____________________

We do not rent, lease or share our mailing list.

Please make check or money order payable to:

CASE NUTRITION CONSULTING
1940 Angley Court
Regina, Saskatchewan
Canada S4V 2V2
Phone/FAX: 306-751-1000
Web: www.glutenfreediet.ca
E-mail: info@glutenfreediet.ca

For fund raising or quantity discount rates, contact Case Nutrition Consulting.